The Moral Target

OXFORD ETHICS SERIES

SERIES EDITOR:
Derek Parfit, All Souls College, Oxford

C

The Moral Target

AIMING AT RIGHT CONDUCT IN WAR
AND OTHER CONFLICTS

F. M. Kamm

OXFORD
UNIVERSITY PRESS

OXFORD
UNIVERSITY PRESS

Oxford University Press is a department of the University of Oxford.
It furthers the University's objective of excellence in research,
scholarship, and education by publishing worldwide.

Oxford   New York
Auckland   Cape Town   Dar es Salaam   Hong Kong   Karachi
Kuala Lumpur   Madrid   Melbourne   Mexico City   Nairobi
New Delhi   Shanghai   Taipei   Toronto

With offices in
Argentina   Austria   Brazil   Chile   Czech Republic   France   Greece
Guatemala   Hungary   Italy   Japan   Poland   Portugal   Singapore
South Korea   Switzerland   Thailand   Turkey   Ukraine   Vietnam

Oxford is a registered trade mark of Oxford University Press in the UK and certain other countries.

Published in the United States of America by Oxford University Press
198 Madison Avenue, New York, NY 10016

Library of Congress Cataloging-in-Publication Data
Kamm, F. M. (Frances Myrna)
The moral target : aiming at right conduct in war and other conflicts / F.M. Kamm.
    p.   cm. — (Oxford ethics series)
ISBN 978-0-19-989752-0 (hardcover); 978-0-19-049063-8 (paperback)
1. War—Moral and ethical aspects. 2. Just war doctrine.
3. Military ethics. I. Title.
U22.K286   2012
172'.42—dc23   2011038688

In memory of my mother Mala, my father Solomon, and my aunt Sela, who helped each other through the Holocaust and thereafter.

CONTENTS

ACKNOWLEDGMENTS

Acknowledgments for help given to me on the essays in this book are, for the most part, found in the essays themselves. For help in bringing them together in this book, I am grateful to Jenn Valois and Margaret Collins for typing sections, to Margaret Collins for proofreading and respectful editing, and to Lynne Meyer Gay for excellent puzzle solving. I thank Ruth Klein for permission to use on the cover an image of a postcard (written by Mala Kamm requesting from an American relative affidavits to be able to leave a Nazi-controlled ghetto in Poland and go to the United States). I greatly appreciate the patience and professionalism of the staff at Oxford University Press and the care with which Micha Glaeser constructed the index. I am grateful to Maria Twarog, Agnes Mosejczuk, and Hubert Mosejczuk for their help in numerous ways that made possible my work on this book. Finally, I am most grateful to Derek Parfit, who welcomed me once again into the wonderful Oxford Ethics Series, which he edits.

INTRODUCTION

This book consists of independent essays written over the course of approximately fifteen years. With the exception of four, all the essays that compose the chapters have been published elsewhere. However, each has been revised for this volume. In revising, I have not usually attempted to make the content of earlier essays reflect my current views. Rather, I have sometimes changed language to clarify meaning and have noted where different views I subsequently came to hold may be found. I have not tried to eliminate some repetition between essays; a bit of this may even help with understanding.

The chapters are organized in two different ways: thematically by topic and chronologically within topics.

My interest in the topics usually derives from other work I have done in normative ethical theory.[1] That is, I have not usually started by being concerned with war or other conflicts per se, unlike some moral philosophers. Rather, having worked on a distinction or an issue in ethical theory, I noticed that it might have a practical implication and be used to improve on earlier discussions of a practical issue. Sometimes I was invited by others to consider the practical implications of more theoretical work I had done. Considering the practical role of elements of theory may not always lead to considering all the most interesting aspects of practical issues or to developing a unified theory of war or of other conflicts. Nevertheless, the focused results can be surprising and worthwhile.

My method in dealing with both ethical theory and practical issues makes heavy use of hypothetical cases and intuitive judgments about them. Such cases can be varied at will. One can thus test whether a factor is morally significant and accounts for one's judgment about the case by comparing the moral status of a case with the factor and a case without the factor, holding all other factors in the cases constant. While the cases may sometimes seem unrealistic, they are somewhat like artificial, controlled experiments in science, in which scientists change one variable at a time, holding everything else constant, in order to see if that variable is crucial to the explanation of a phenomenon. Just as artificially controlled conditions in a lab can lead to results that are applicable to real life, the result of hypothetical cases in philosophy can eventually yield results for real-life situations.

Using the method of hypothetical cases to explain one's own intuitive judgments about cases need not involve unaided introspective knowledge. It is more like inferring what drives one's responses by a process of testing and eliminating conjectures. Further, the fact that we may acquire knowledge about our judgments through inference suggests that we may also understand others' similar responses, even if they are not able to isolate a factor through consideration of many judgments about different cases.

Suppose a factor uncovered in this way has moral significance and provides a sufficient reason for responding differently to different cases. Then the factor justifies the differential responses. Furthermore, given that one's judgment about cases varies with the presence of a factor that is a sufficient reason, even though the intuitive judgment was originally not reached by consciously considering the factor, the judgment can be considered reasonable. It is not merely a feeling that one tries to "rationalize" (in the sense of providing a confabulation for it after the fact).[2]

The order of topics in the book moves (roughly) from beginning war to activities during war to problems after war. Chapters on conflicts other than war conclude the volume. The following are short summaries of each chapter.

Chapter 1, "Making War and Its Continuation Unjust," examines the connection between the idea of a just cause in just war theory and the idea of a state of affairs that, though it involves injustices, is still a justified peace. It also considers the relation between the state of affairs that should not be altered by war and the state of affairs that, if attained, must put an end to war. It is, in part, a discussion of and response to some work of Avishai Margalit.

Chapters 2–4 deal with the topic of the morality of conduct in war in chronological order. Chapter 2, "Justifications for Killing Noncombatants in War," considers some principles that are thought to help provide justifications—such as the Doctrine of Double Effect (DDE)—and problems with them. It then considers the implications of applying to war an alternative general moral theory of permissible harming of innocents, which I have discussed in other work. Chapter 3, "Failures of Just War Theory," is a more thorough examination of these issues, as well as of the morality of killing combatants in war. It begins by considering whether the DDE is a correct guide to conduct in war and argues that, contrary to the DDE, terror killing of combatants and sometimes even of noncombatants can be permissible. Then it considers whether the DDE, by contrast to other moral principles, does not rule out some harm that is impermissible. The chapter considers how any general moral principles applied to war may fail to distinguish among different types of innocent civilians whose inviolability may differ. It shows how this can affect judgments about whether harms are proportional to goods to be achieved in war. The relative violability of different noncombatants is also compared with the violability of different combatants relative to each other. Finally, possible grounds for group liability are investigated. Such grounds might make it permissible to harm citizens of an unjust state in ways not ordinarily permitted by general principles of permissible harm derived from considering nonwar cases. Chapter 4, "The Morality of Killing in War: Some Traditional and Nontraditional Views," is my most recent treatment of this topic. Its first section provides an overview of standard views on *jus in bello* (justice in carrying out a war). The next section considers some recent proposals by others for revising the standard theory. This section begins by examining revisionary proposals as to what combatants are permitted to do to other combatants. I examine Jeff McMahan's attack on the view that combatants on the just and unjust sides are morally equally permitted to engage in the same acts in war. I then consider whether terroristic and otherwise opportunistic use of combatants is permitted, what is proportional by contrast to unproportional harm to combatants, and what may be done to one's own combatants for the sake of one's own noncombatants. The next section deals with revisionary views about, and accounts ruling out, deliberate killing of noncombatants (as in, but not limited to, terror bombing). Finally, the chapter considers the permissibility of collateral harm to various kinds of noncombatants.

Chapter 5, "Collaboration with the Enemy: Harming Some to Save Others from the Nazis," may also be considered part of possible conduct in war. It deals with whether it is morally permissible to collaborate with the unjust side in a war, as some in the Jewish governing boards were said to have collaborated with Nazis, in order to reduce the harm that the unjust side will do. Recent discussions of collaboration and when it is permissible to redirect threats are used to examine this issue.

The next two chapters are concerned with a topic that has come to be called *jus post bellum* (justice after war). Chapter 6, "Moral Improvisation and New Obligations," examines the views of Barbara Herman about justice after the civil conflict in South Africa because her views also seem applicable to justice after war between states. Herman is concerned with whether and why truth and reconciliation commissions are a permissible substitute for punishment of offenders. I examine Herman's arguments and suggest a different one that may account for some of her conclusions. Chapter 7, "*Jus Post Bellum*, Proportionality, and Compensation," considers some requirements of justice after war suggested by Brian Orend, including his claim that being able to satisfy *jus post bellum* is a precondition for the justice of starting a war.

The next two chapters deal with violent conflict outside of standard war. Chapter 8, "Terrorism and Several Moral Distinctions," investigates different factors that might explain why terrorism, as standardly practiced, is morally wrong even if other forms of killing are sometimes permissible. It evaluates the possible moral significance of a nonstate agent being the one that attacks; of a noncombatant being the one who is harmed; of harm and terror being intended rather than occurring as side effects; and of harm and terror having a necessary role in producing a goal. Subsequent parts of the chapter consider whether the use of different types of terror for political rather than military use, independently of and in combination with physical harm, makes terrorism significantly wrong. Finally, cases where terrorism might be permissible are presented. Chapter 9, "Self-Defense, Resistance, and Suicide: The Taliban Women," concerns what may permissibly be done to resist oppression by those, such as the Taliban women, whose lives are radically restricted, sometimes on pain of death for opposition. From this we consider what third parties may do (and what they have done) to help and how this bears on a just cause for war.

The final chapter, "Nuclear Deterrence and Reliance on Harm," deals with an aspect of "cold war." In particular, it concerns issues raised by the opposing views of Michael Walzer and Paul Ramsey about whether it is permissible to rely on the possibility of harm to civilians in order to deter war. Nuclear weapons that would be used to strike military targets might cause side-effect harm to civilians. Some of this harm could be proportional to the use of the weapons and so morally allowed. However, keeping any nuclear weapons carries a risk of misuse, causing harm to civilians out of proportion to any military use of the weapons. The issue is whether it is consistent with not intending harm to civilians that we rely on the possibility of unproportional harm to them in order to deter war. Both Walzer and Ramsey support versions of the DDE, a priniciple that is commonly used to rule out intentional harm to civilians while not ruling out some side-effect harm. My discussion considers what is and is not consistent with the DDE, revisions of it, and (what I call) the Doctrine of Triple Effect (DTE).

The book does not include three other essays related to those described earlier. They are "Torture: During and after Action," in which I consider the nature of torture and the various occasions on which it could occur in order to determine whether it might be wrong to torture a wrongdoer held captive even if this were necessary to save his victims; "Terrorism and Intending Evil," in which I consider further some of the issues discussed in this book's Chapter 8; and "Reasons for Starting War: Goals, Conditions, and Proportionality," in which I first discuss whether having a right reason, in the sense of a right intention, for starting war is necessary in order for a war to be just and then examine ways in which the harms of war can be proportional to the achievement of the just cause and to other goods war can achieve. These essays were given as the 2008 Uehiro Lectures in Practical Ethics at Oxford University and published by Oxford University Press in 2011 as *Ethics for Enemies: Terror, Torture, and War*. They are more recent than most of the essays in the present collection but do not deal with many issues dealt with by the latter. *Ethics for Enemies* and *The Moral Target* may be treated as companion volumes.

Notes

1. For an overview of this work, see Chapter 1 in my *Intricate Ethics* (Oxford University Press, 2007).

2. I discuss the use of hypothetical cases further in "Understanding, justifying, and finding oneself," in *Annals of the New York Academy of Sciences*, volume 1234, pp. 168–172, as well as in the introductions to Kamm, *Creation and Abortion*, and *Morality, Mortality* vols. 1 and 2 (Oxford University Press, 1992, 1993, 1996).

The Moral Target

1

Making War and Its Continuation Unjust

I. Conceptual and Background Issues

A. *THE RELATION OF JUSTIFIED WAR AND JUSTIFIED PEACE*

Just war theory is concerned with when and in what ways it is *not unjust* to go to war. (Contrary to what it might be reasonable to think, just war theory is not necessarily concerned with when justice requires us to go to war.) Often, the attempt to defend human rights makes it not unjust to go to war. The protection of human rights also plays a part in deciding in what ways we may wage war. In this chapter, I shall examine, at a very general level, the thesis that we must tolerate some injustice and rights violations rather than make war to correct the injustice.

War is not limited to inter-nation conflict; there could be justified civil war. (We could also extend the discussion a bit beyond war to revolutions.) I shall take it that war involves physical force or other means (such as germ warfare, mind control, etc.) to control or destroy an opponent, offensively or defensively, on a large scale. (I shall refer to such physical force or other means as "force.") So just war theory is, in part, concerned with when mass force is not unjust. The ideas of being just (or not unjust) and being morally justified are distinguishable. For example, it might sometimes be morally justified to do what is unjust and morally unjustified to do what is just. However, it is not unreasonable to think that most just war theory is really about morally justifiable war. At least, that is what I shall assume here. For war to be justified requires that it at least be morally permissible though not necessarily obligatory.

If one is not justified in going to war, one is morally required to keep the peace in the sense of not engaging in force, offensively or defensively, on a large scale. So long as one is not justified in going to war, one is only justified in remaining at peace on the supposition that there is no condition in between war and peace.[1] To be in a *justified peace* for these reasons is to be in a condition that one could not justifiably alter by war. Call this Proposal 1, even though it is really no more than one conception of justified peace. However, since one might sometimes be justified in waiving one's right to engage in a justifiable war (e.g., if the war would be too costly), there could also be justified peace without this implying that *only* peace is justified (for it could also be permissible to supererogatorily pay the great cost). Those who agree to a truce might cease hostilities that could permissibly be re-continued. In this chapter, I shall use the sense of "justified peace" in which peace is justified because it is morally required, not because it is a permissible option. (Notice the following asymmetry, which results from this usage: Justified peace is required peace. Justified war is only permissible war.) Peace could also exist when one is wrongfully kept from going to war, and then it would not be a justified peace.

The theory of what it takes to have a morally justified peace—that is, a condition that one is morally obligated not to alter by war—seems to be the flipside of part of just war theory. This is because part of just war theory is about the conditions that one is *not* morally obligated not to alter by war. One can know when war is justified if one knows completely when it is not justified and hence when only peace is justified.

All this might seem to imply the following, barring special logistic problems in ending war: If one is about to go to war or has just started it, and one is offered terms that meet the requirements for a justified peace in the sense that there no longer will be a state of affairs whose correction justifies war, this is sufficient to make one morally required not to be at war. Call this Proposal 2. All this might also *seem* to imply that what must be done to end a justifiable, ongoing war in a morally appropriate way is to create, or offer to create, a condition one would not be justified in *beginning* a war to alter if it already existed. This implies that to continue an ongoing war rather than to have a certain condition (call it x) come about is not justifiable if going to war in order to alter condition x would be unjust. Call this Proposal 3, in which the conditions (states of affairs) that justifiably *prevent war* are the same as the conditions that justifiably *end war* that is already started.[2]

Proposal 1 deals with the relation between justifiable (or just) war and (one conception of) justifiable peace. Proposals 2 and 3 deal with the relation between beginning war and continuing war.

B. *PARTIAL JUSTICE AND WAR*

The next point is that war is not just merely because it aims to eliminate injustices even if the war could successfully eliminate injustices. This is because some injustices are not of the right type or significant enough to justify using large-scale force to correct them. The means must be suited and proportional to the nature of the injustice. The doctrines in just war theory of suitable aim and proportionality of means do not themselves commit one to any upper limits on what may be done if the cause is serious enough. Nor is proportionality a doctrine of tit for tat; a proportional response may involve more or less damage to an aggressor than the aggressor does or threatens to do. (Here is an example at the level of individuals: If two aggressors are about to cut off my leg, a proportionate response could include my killing each one of them if that is the only way to save myself from such a serious injury.) But the doctrines of suitable aim and proportionality do imply that not everything can be done to correct any injustice. Furthermore, they imply this not only when there are alternative means, appropriate and in proportion to an aim, that could be efficacious. Even if there are no alternative efficacious means, one may not use means not in accord with and out of proportion to an end. Here is an example: Suppose people had a moral right to have psychiatric services provided by national health care and it is unjust that psychiatric services are not covered by national health care. Still, it is not true that getting such services covered justifies a civil war.

If we combine Proposal 1—that peace is required because the peace involves no condition that can be justifiably altered by war—with the claim that eliminating rights violations does not always justify war, we can conclude that a justified peace could involve rights violations. Call this the Partial Justice Claim. I shall call the side that is harmed by injustices "Victim" and the side that causes the injustices and would be worsened if injustices were eliminated "Dominant." If there were no injustices whose elimination ever justified war—as some pacifists claim—then peace could be justified and in that sense be just even if the condition of justified peace were *completely* unjust in every other respect. I assume this is not true because some rights violations do make war just.

C. MARGALIT ON PEACE IN RELATION TO JUST WAR THEORY

In his unpublished paper, "A Just Peace or Just a Peace," Avishai Margalit defended something like the Partial Justice Claim without however associating it with a theory about just war as I have done.[3] There Margalit claimed that "just peace," which he discusses in the context of ending an ongoing war, is a peace that includes the *part of justice* which must be present for a *lasting peace* (rather than a mere truce) to be possible. (Margalit has a substantive view about what part of justice this is. But in this chapter, I am not concerned with the substantive issue.) Margalit denies that just peace designates a state in which peace exists *and* justice exists. Rather, he says, just peace need involve only the part of justice which is necessary to produce a lasting peace. In his view, the "just" truly modifies the peace in the sense that there is enough of justice achieved to make possible a lasting peace even if this means that some injustices continue. Margalit claims that in proposing his conception of just peace, he is *not* doing just war theory.[4] Let us consider this issue.

(i) One reason that could justify Margalit in making the claim that he is not doing just war theory is that his use of "make possible" or "necessary to produce" a lasting peace is a matter of descriptive sociology. That is, he might mean that certain conditions satisfying partial justice are either necessary to cause or actually do increase the probability of lasting peace. By contrast, just war theory deals with normative issues. However, Proposal 1 and the Partial Justice Claim can be the basis for at least a *partial normative* reading of "make possible" a lasting peace. That is, certain conditions satisfying partial justice make possible lasting peace *because* (a) Victim (or his agents) will be *morally* required to keep the peace *because* these are conditions that, according to the appropriate aim and proportionality thesis of just war doctrine, one is not justified in altering by means of war, and (b) there is an empirical assumption that people are more likely to keep and maintain peace when they are morally required to do so than when they are not. Conditions (a) and (b) form only a partially normative claim because (b) is an empirical assumption. (Lasting peace might also be possible because others may justifiably require that there be no war when there is such partial justice, and their being justified in requiring peace increases the probability that *they* will require it.)

A *fully normativized* version of a proposal for just peace would make no empirical claims about the increased likelihood of a lasting peace. It would claim only that certain conditions will make peace justified (just) *because* Victim (or his agents) will be morally required to keep the peace *because* war will not be morally justified to alter those conditions. The conditions will make war unjust. I am most interested in the fully normativized claim (which is my Proposal 1 combined with the Partial Justice Claim, minus the empirical assumption). However, I shall allow myself to assume the additional empirical claim that is part of the partially normativized claim.[5]

Hence, one might claim that describing the normative conditions for justified peace can be seen as the flipside of describing the *normative* conditions for just war (via consideration of when war *is not* just), and in that sense, it is part of just war theory. In the case where peace *already* exists, the peace is just if no war to alter it is a just war. In the case where war is ongoing, the peace offered is just if no continuation of war is just. If conditions (or offers of conditions) of partial justice make beginning or continuing war unjust, peace is justified (in the sense that it is required) with partial justice. On this view, we can take the crucial steps linking just peace theory as an empirical inquiry (into what makes peace likely) with normative just war theory; focusing on the part of justice necessary for peace provides a first step in a conceptual analysis that makes clear the connection between having a part of justice that justifies only peace and what makes war unjustified. Since just peace may entail only partial, rather than full, compliance with justice, it turns out that *just war* theory can be a part of a theory of partial compliance with justice in a way that is different from what is usually thought. That is, it is usually thought that war is part of partial compliance theory either because just war would not be necessary if there were no injustice or because war is itself an instance of a failure to completely comply with justice. The current point, by contrast, is that just war theory is part of partial compliance theory because once there is partial compliance with justice, it can be impermissible to be at war even if this is necessary to achieve perfect justice.

(ii) An alternative account of why Margalit might not be doing just war theory can be derived from his second Tanner Lecture. There he considers how war might become unjustified because one has promised to abide by an agreement that accepts a compromise over injustices.[6] Most importantly, he argues that one could be bound to keep the agreement not to go to war even if one has compromised on a matter that, without the agreement, would be a just cause for a war and could be corrected with proportionate harm. Just war theory does not standardly include "not violating a compromise to not pursue a just cause" on a checklist for permissible war. Hence, if Margalit is correct about the bindingness of such an agreement, it could explain why he is not really interested in just war theory.

In addition, he argues that if one is offered correction of the only condition that would justify war, but the correction is made contingent on foregoing the use of appropriate nonwar means to correct any remaining injustices, then it is morally permissible to refuse the offer and to go to war. This means that the refusal to give up the right to use appropriate nonwar means to correct another injustice can justifiably help determine that one goes to war even when correcting that other injustice could not itself justify going to war. Standard just war theory does not speak to this possibility. It may seem to deny what is claimed by Proposal 2, namely, that if one is offered what remedies a condition for which one may make war, one must not engage in war.

Does Margalit's view challenge the sufficiency of any first-order list of things for which one can and cannot be at war by suggesting that there is a metacondition on these, namely, whether the removal of a (first-order) condition that would justify war is made contingent on something else? (Call this the Anti-List Thesis.) Margalit does not provide a detailed explanation of how this Metacondition Requirement (as I shall call it) could be true. I shall consider a possible explanation later.[7] At this point, I wish to point out only that I believe the problem it raises for Proposal 2 needs to be avoided, and I shall try to show this in what follows.

In part II of this chapter, I shall consider in more detail what it means to be in or to be offered *unconditionally* a state of affairs that would not justify war. This is the minimal state of affairs which it would be unjustifiable to alter for the better by war. In that part of the chapter, I shall deliberately not distinguish discussion of states of affairs which should prevent justifiable war from beginning and states of affairs which justifiably end wars. In part III, I shall consider the implications for the achievement of complete justice of a justified peace that meets only the Partial Justice Claim. In part IV, I shall finally examine Proposal 3 more carefully, that is, whether there is no difference in the conditions that justifiably prevent and those that justifiably end war.[8] Throughout, my discussion focuses on conceptual analysis. As such, it is not my aim to argue for any substantive claims about what sorts of injustices actually make war justified or unjustified.

II. Proposal 2 and the Relative Injustice of War and the Absence of War

Consider a group, Victim, that seeks the elimination of injustices in its relation with a more powerful group, Dominant.[9] One way of understanding the issue we are discussing is to see it from the point of view of the unjustly treated group. If it asks itself the question, "How much of what we are owed are we morally required to forego trying to get in order to have peace?" they should answer, "Whatever would still leave us in a situation such that war is not justified to alter that situation for the better." Dominant is the group that would lose by the elimination of injustices because it perpetrates them and/or benefits from them. For Dominant, one question is, "How much must we give in order to be entitled to peace?" and a *morally* charged answer is, "The minimum necessary in order to put Victim in a situation where it is no longer morally justified in making war." If Dominant gives this much, at least unconditionally, he is morally justified in demanding peace. Notice that there is some asymmetry in the questions Dominant and Victim ask themselves. Victim is asking what he is morally required to do (forego). In one sense, Dominant is also asking a moral question of himself. However, he is not asking what he morally is required to do because the answer to that is, be perfectly just by giving up *all* unjust benefits. But doing this might be more than what would make Victim's war unjustified and more than one is obligated to do if one's obligation is merely to make Victim's war unjustified. Dominant is asking what he must give in order to put Victim in the moral wrong if Victim starts (or continues) to fight. If this is *all* Dominant asks, he is still interested in morality to the extent that he wants to be *morally* justified in demanding peace.

Suppose that it is the absence of x that would make Victim justified in going to war. Proposal 2 claims that once x is offered or is in existence, Victim has what he cannot have without losing the right to make war. According to this proposal, not only does Victim have no right to both condition x *and* to a warring posture, but Victim also has no right to choose between having condition x and maintaining a warring posture. If one can have condition x, it is wrong to forego or give it up in order to engage in war to get more of what is owed.

Does this amount to saying that if Dominant wants a justified peace (let alone be morally obligated to seek it), he should make Victim the minimal offer that (according to Proposal 2) Victim *has no right to refuse*? Not quite. To say Victim has no right to choose war over Dominant's offer does not preclude that Victim could make a different offer that is somewhat better for him and yet does not involve anything that Dominant has a right to be at war to avoid ceding. Suppose the offers Victim and Dominant make to each other are *each* such that both would have to accept either rather than fight. Then Victim may have as much right (maybe more) that his proposal be accepted by Dominant as Dominant has that his proposal be accepted by Victim. This implies that Dominant's offer is not one that Victim cannot permissibly refuse.[10] Yet each refusing the offer of the other cannot justifiably result in war when either proposal offers a condition that cannot permissibly be altered by war.

Why might Dominant want a justified peace if he does not care for perfect justice? Is Dominant obligated, for reasons other than that perfect justice should be done, to seek a peace that Victim is not justified in destroying even if Dominant does not want to? One possible answer to the latter question is that Dominant's warring resistance to Victim's justified war would be unjust, and this suggests that he morally must seek justified peace.[11] But why is *this* reason, which stems from justice, so important that Dominant has reason to heed it even if he does not heed the reason for pursuing perfect justice? Perhaps because here the consequence of his not rendering justice is permissible war and war is a state that may be assumed to be bad for Dominant as well as for others. However, this reason depends on the realistic possibility of actual war. If Victim lacked the capacity to fight, this reason would not exist. A reason independent of Victim's capacity to fight is that the absence of that part of justice that would eliminate grounds for justified war by Victim is a worse state for Victim than is the absence of perfect justice. Dominant has stronger moral reason to avoid doing the worst part of injustice, the injustice that justifies war.[12]

Does this also imply that Dominant's reason to give perfect justice is less strong than Victim's reason not to go to war for it? There seems to be a hierarchical relation between wrongs. In the cases we are discussing, if Victim's correcting injustices does not justify war, then Victim is wrong to wage war in order to correct Dominant's remaining *wrong* behavior. This implies that Victim's wrong must be avoided even though Dominant's wrong continues. If this is so, then it is not an open question which wrong is morally to be preferred—Victim's going to war for more than x (the condition whose presence makes war unjustifiable) or Dominant's keeping more than it should once it cedes x—if one of them must occur.

However, none of this guarantees that a war by Victim for more than x would produce a *worse* outcome than is present when Victim lacks more of what he is owed.[13] This is because the wrongness of doing something is not only a function of its bad consequences. It could also be wrong to correct an injustice even though correcting it would not produce a worse state of affairs than the continuation of the injustice. For example, it may be wrong to kill one person to save five from being killed even if five being killed is a worse state of affairs than one being killed. I think this case also supports the view that Dominant's wrong in not yielding everything that justice requires could be more serious than Victim's wrong in going to war for all these things. So Dominant could be responsible for a greater evil in not yielding the rest of perfect justice than Victim would be responsible for in making war to achieve perfect justice. Nevertheless, Victim would be wrong to do this.

III. Proposal 2 on Getting More of What One Is Owed

What about the part of what Victim is owed that goes beyond x and for which waging war is unjustifiable? This is the less crucial part of justice. (Call it y.) First, in what sense does getting y not alone justify going to war according to Proposal 2? In the sense that if x is already present or offered, we may not move to $x + y$ by war. Notice that this does not exclude the possibility that if x is *not* present or offered and Victim has a chance of getting y alone only by going to war, he may permissibly go to war. For in the latter case, the value of a less important part of justice can increase given that it is the only part that can be achieved. This is one ground for thinking that, contrary to standard just war theory, one cannot make a list of impermissible grounds for war that does not take into account whether one can successfully wage war for what is definitely a permissible ground (a recognized just cause). Hence, it is another way to argue for what I called the Anti-List Thesis (p. 7). For example, suppose that, although rebuffing aggression is a justified ground for war, one is not able to wage such a war. However, one could successfully wage a war against the current aggressor that harms it enough just to deter its future aggression without rebuffing the aggression that is already taking place. There is no nonwar means to produce this deterrence. Even if a war merely for deterrence is ordinarily impermissible, in the imagined circumstances might it not be permissible if it gives one some of what one should but cannot get from defeating current aggression? Perhaps the answer depends on how large collateral harm to civilians would be and whether this harm will be proportional to the good of deterrence as it might have been to defeating an actual attack. The harm that would be caused only to current aggressors to stop their future aggression seems quite permissible.

Still, suppose Victim physically could get (or retain) x and y together by war and such a war would be justified were it the *only way* to get x. This does not make war justified if x could be obtained in exchange for not going to war. According to Proposal 2, if achieving y does not justify war in the presence of x, it is not permissible to turn down the offer of x just because (and even if) *only* fighting would give both x and y.[14]

However, not using war to achieve y because doing so would not be justified need not involve any agreement not to pursue y by other means proportional to the achievement of y. It is just that there may be no actual means proportional to the achievement of y that Victim could use. For example, it may be that the only justifiable means of achieving y involves subtle politics and that mastery of such politics is beyond Victim's capacity. Then, unless Victim turns down the offer of x in order to achieve both x and y by war, he will never achieve y. According to the theory of just war being proposed here, Victim must still accept x rather than fight.[15]

Suppose y is something Dominant unjustly has that is transferable from him to Victim. Victim is not justified in going to war to get y, but Dominant is also not justified in going to war to keep it. This is at least because he has y unjustly. (It might also seem, given what I have said, that if Victim has x, his *keeping y* cannot morally justify a war. But I have so far spoken about Victim *getting* y, not about *keeping* it. The latter, as we shall see, may be a different matter.) This implies that if Victim could get y without war (e.g., take it without firing a shot when Dominant is asleep), then Dominant could not permissibly engage in war to stop Victim. However, this does not mean that Dominant could not permissibly resist by war any *warring* attempt by Victim to get y. Dominant could justifiably resist the use of unjustified means by Victim even if he could not permissibly resist Victim's transferring y by other means.[16, 17]

Suppose Victim is unjustified in waging war to get y if he has or will be given x. May he still permissibly *threaten war* to get both x and y, making the link between x and y nonnegotiable as part of this threat? Sometimes it may be permissible to threaten to do something that it is actually impermissible to do and that one would not do. (This would be like a permissible lie.) Such a threat might be permissible in Victim's case since he can then get both x and y, to which he has a right. One technique for increasing the effectiveness of a threat is creating a doomsday machine (i.e., a device that ensures that the threat gets carried out if Dominant does not concede x and y in the face of the threat). However, while it may affect the credibility of Victim's threat, it is not permissible for him to arrange for a doomsday machine which will impermissibly make war if only x and not y is offered. In this sense, x and y should not be irrevocably linked. This does not make the threat to veto any proposal containing just x worthless since Dominant may not be able to rely on Victim's doing the morally right thing (i.e., not carrying out the threat).

Proposal 2, for how to make war unjustified, can be extended to make other disfavored means for achieving ends unjustified. For example, suppose that the injustice Victim suffers is sufficient to justify employing deceit or betrayal (but not war) to correct it. This might lead Dominant to improve the condition of Victim just to the point where these techniques are no longer justified. This assumes that the use of these techniques is more threatening to Dominant than Victim's improved condition is and that Dominant's concern for justice is great enough that he would not want to prevent the use of these techniques in any way other than by eliminating the situation that justifies their use. But it does not assume that Dominant would eliminate the situation that justifies the use of these techniques *simply* because these techniques would be justified if their use were not actually realistically possible.

This position (like the one described on p. 9) might be attributed to a *conservative just* agent. She might be described as someone who is especially concerned about preventing the use of certain means of undoing injustices and therefore is very concerned about (a) getting rid of the situation that would make using these means permissible (b) when it is likely the means would be used. She would not be so concerned about eliminating other unjust situations since the use of these means is not justified in connection with them. Someone else might wish to eliminate the situation that justifies war simply because the justifiability of this most drastic means is a sign of how unjust the condition to be altered is. I am now imagining a more conservative agent than this, someone who fears that these drastic means will actually be used. However, she does not merely compromise from fear of war since she would fight to stop an unjustified war. Rather, she loses the will to defend herself against the war she fears will come, when war would be justified and defense against it unjustified.

My sense is that this conservative justice stance models the actual psychology of many people who make actual justice-motivated reforms. It helps explain why those who do not care for pure justice do nevertheless seek justifiable peace. It is a somewhat more self-interested explanation than that defense against a justified war would be unjustified since it takes into account the probability and dangers of such a justified war taking place.

IV. Possible Problem with Proposal 2

The positive aspect of Proposals 1 and 2 and the claim that unjust conditions sometimes justify wars is that if war is no longer just, when everything besides the condition of Victim is held constant, conditions must have improved for Victim. However, we should consider pernicious aspects of Proposal 2 and the Partial Justice Claim. One of these is that the solution of remaining grievances (y) can recede indefinitely into the future.[18]

Are the fully and partially normativized claims pernicious in the sense that they allow Victim to be cheated? If y were achievable in addition to x only by an *extra* war effort that y alone does not justify, then Victim was not being cheated in being required to settle for x without war. This is because he would not have been permitted in any case to do what would achieve y. However, if both x and y would have been achieved by the *same* war effort that the achievement of x alone justified, then if Victim settles for x and no war, he winds up with less than he could justifiably have achieved. After all, Dominant may see that if a just war is fought, he is threatened with Victim getting x and y. In order to avoid this large loss, he immediately offers a bargain that stops the just war: x alone with no war. But the fact that one does not get as much as one would have gotten does not mean one is cheated, especially when one also avoids war.

But now consider a hypothetical scenario suggested by Margalit in his second Tanner Lecture. Dominant offers Victim x but only *on condition* that Victim agrees to give up use of nonwar means that are appropriate to trying to achieve y. I originally claimed the following:[19] "Indeed, it may be morally wrong to give up pursuit of y by means proportional to its pursuit. Proposal 1 and the Partial Justice Claim do not endorse buying Victim's promise not to engage in behavior that remains justified. Buying out and being co-opted, with respect to such behavior, are not necessary corollaries of these positions." However, Proposal 2 does say that if x is given, war is no longer permissible, and this seems also to be true of the case in which x would be given, conditional on a promise to give up use of means appropriate for getting y.

Yet Margalit believes it is permissible both (i) for Dominant to make such an offer and (ii) for Victim to reject it.[20] This means that it would be permissible for Victim to go on fighting a war, seemingly contrary to what Proposal 2 implies. (One might be tempted to assume that Margalit thinks it is *permissible for Victim to reject the offer* only in cases where means appropriate to achieving y would be successful in achieving it. However, I think that he has in mind a different possibility as well, as we shall see in discussing [i].)

Let us first consider whether (ii) is true. One possibility is that even if achieving y does not justify war, getting or retaining the right to use means appropriate to achieving y does merit war even if one already has x. I think it is unlikely that this is true. In any case, let us suppose it is not true and consider whether there is another reason why (ii) might be true.

If war is justified in pursuit of x but not in pursuit of y, perhaps this implies that one must be willing to give up the pursuit of y, even by appropriate means, for the sake of achieving x. This would be the denial of (ii). We could symbolize this argument as follows, where "w" stands for "war" and ">" stands for "overrides."

$$x > -w$$
$$-w > y$$
therefore, $x > y$

If correct, this transitivity argument would imply that one should agree not to pursue y, even by appropriate means, if one is offered x. It would also support the characterization of someone who refused the agreement as continuing to fight in order to achieve y (or the right to pursue y).

I think the transitivity argument is wrong, for one might reason as follows: It is inappropriate to give up the pursuit of y for the sake of achieving x—that is a price one should not pay for x—at least when other ways that are appropriate to achieving x are available (e.g., war). This is so even though y is dominated by $-w$, which x dominates. The direct pairwise comparison between x and y introduces a factor that bears on the inappropriateness of trading one for the other. This inappropriateness is not present when $-w$ dominates y directly. Further, when one refuses to directly pay the price of y to achieve x, and this determines that one will continue to go to war for x, that does not mean that one is going to war to achieve y (and so acting contrary to $-w > y$), as well as to achieve x. This analysis shows that (ii) could be true. Victim could permissibly refuse to get x by giving up the right to pursue y by appropriate means even though it is not permissible to go to war to get y.[21]

Earlier (p. 7) I asked whether it was impossible to construct a list of just causes for war because refusing to accept the removal of a just cause when this is contingent on giving up some right meant that one would be permitted to go to war for the sake of that right. The answer is that this is not a reason why it is impossible to construct a list of just causes. If one refuses to accept the removal of the just cause because this is made contingent on giving up or not pursuing by any means some right, one is not claiming that one may go to war to retain or achieve that right. Hence, achieving the right does not become a new just cause. (We suggested another ground for the Anti-List Thesis on p. 10.)

The truth of (ii), however, should lead us to explicitly revise Proposal 2 so that it claims only that "If one is about to go to war or has just started a war and one is offered terms that meet the requirements for a justified peace, and they are not conditioned on the loss of appropriate rights, there will no longer be a state of affairs whose correction justifies war, and this is sufficient to make one morally required not to be at war." Call this Proposal 2R (i.e., revised). Proposal 2R speaks to having to desist from war only when eliminating the situation that justifies war is not made contingent on giving up on such things as rights even if one should not fight wars *for* them.

Now let us consider part (i) of Margalit's claim. He thinks that it is morally permissible for Dominant to try to make correction of the only situation that justifies war by Victim conditional on Victim's giving up the pursuit of y even by appropriate nonwar means. The reason he gives for this is that pursuit of y by appropriate means may deteriorate to using inappropriate means of war. Hence, he thinks, not agreeing to the condition for getting x creates (what he calls) a truce rather than a lasting peace.[22] But then it is the threat of war over y rather than the loss of y by other means that Dominant is trying to prevent. If this is so, it seems that instead of making the provision of x contingent on Victim's giving up y, Dominant should make the provision of x contingent on Victim's using only appropriate means to get y (even if he will not succeed) and also vigilantly work to see to it that only appropriate alternative means are employed. (Alternatively, of course, he could simply cede y.)

Margalit further claims that if Victim does agree to give up pursuing y in order to get x, he must keep this agreement even if it is a bad agreement. Margalit's reason for this is that it makes possible real (lasting) peace. But, of course, keeping the agreement is necessary for real peace only if Margalit is right in his assumption that use of appropriate means, or this plus the additional fact of a broken agreement, will deteriorate into the inappropriate means of war. Finally, it seems odd to argue for the impermissibility of breaking the agreement on the grounds that it is required for achieving real peace when Margalit also claims that it is permissible for Victim not to accept the offer of x tied to conditions that deny rights and for him to go on fighting for x instead. If peace is not important enough to require accepting the agreement tied to these conditions, why is it important enough to require not breaking the agreement? It would seem that some reason for not breaking the agreement would have to be provided simply by the fact that an agreement has been made rather than by the importance of lasting peace.

V. The Rejection of Proposal 3

A. CONTINUING WAR TO ACHIEVE WHAT IS NOT A JUST CAUSE FOR BEGINNING WAR

We have revised Proposal 2 to Proposal 2R, which makes the provision of x not contingent on giving up the right to use means appropriate to getting y. This implies that we should revise Proposal 3 to Proposal 3R so that it also requires ending war once condition x is offered only if it is offered in the same way. Let us assume this revision, henceforth.

Is Victim cheated in the following case? The war is *sufficiently in progress* so that part of the cost that it makes sense for Victim to expend in order to get both x

and y has already been paid, though without achieving x and y. Also, the cost expended is sufficient for Victim to *merit* x and y. Obviously, the sense of "merit" here is not merely that it is just that Victim gets x and y since it is being assumed that justice alone, without any investment in a war effort, would require that Victim get x and y. There is another sense of "merit x and y," namely, "earned x and y." In this sense, sadly, people often have to earn the condition to which they are entitled independently of effort.[23]

In our imagined case, an offer of only-x-with-no-further-war comes when Victim has already invested enough to have earned more. Once losses have already been suffered by Victim for x or for x and y, so that x and y have been earned, must a larger part of an ideally just state of affairs, not merely x alone, be offered to obligate Victim to stop fighting? Is what matters not only that the state of affairs offered be one that, if it existed already, could not be justly altered by starting war? Does it also matter what Victim has earned, given the size of the actual efforts he has already made when war has already been undertaken?

Suppose that before Victim is required to end a war, he is sometimes entitled to *more* than the state of affairs x that should prevent war. *This seems to be the denial of Proposal 3R (and 3)*, for Proposal 3R claims that the conditions which justifiably prevent war are the same as the conditions which justifiably end war. This rejection would mean that effort invested can sometimes make the pursuit of y at the cost of further war—in the strict sense of fighting *for y*—justified even when x is already ensured and even though beginning a war would not be justified in order to move from x to x and y.[24] Hence, this is a different position from one that says that in beginning war for a just cause one may also *aim* at achieving by war (i.e., fight for) things that are not contained in the just cause for war.[25]

Here is an example: Suppose war is permitted to end slavery but not just to get the right to free speech for those who are not slaves. To prevent war, Dominant may free slaves. If he does not and war ensues, the right to free speech may be earned in virtue of Victim's having waged war to end slavery. Dominant cannot be justified in requiring the war to end just because he will now end slavery when continuing war can get free speech. This means that things can now be justified to achieve free speech that could not have been justified before war started. We may permissibly pursue certain things *by war* that we could not *begin a war* to achieve.[26] The actual engagement in war has made Dominant liable to being attacked for the sake of y when he was not liable to this before. He has forfeited his right not to be harmed for the sake of y (or his right not to be harmed for the sake of y does not pertain to these circumstances).

An alternative way[27] of accounting for why Victim might continue fighting for something whose attainment would not have justified starting a war focuses on the possibility that in not conceding x before war, that is, in being recalcitrant, Dominant forfeits the right not to be subject to war on account of y. This can be true even if Victim has invested no large efforts and suffered no large losses yet. One virtue (it may be thought) of this alternative account is that whether or not

Victim has a right to continue the war to achieve y does not vary with how much he has already invested in the war. It is Dominant's recalcitrance in making Victim (permissibly) go to war for something for which he should not have had to go to war, not what Victim earns by great losses, that justifies the warring pursuit of y.[28]

I have been considering only a case where not having y is an injustice to Victim, who is pursuing war for x. However, it might be argued that all I have said in defense of Victim going after y could also be said in defense of some Vindicator of Victim stopping the injustice of Victim not having y. For example, it might be said, once one is at war with a certain country over genocide, a cause that justified beginning war, one might go all the way to establishing a democratic regime in that country if this is what Victim wants even if establishing such a regime would not have justified war to begin with. But if it were permissible to do this, the "earning" justification would have to go so far as to imply that the costs one had oneself borne gave one the right to pursue a good for others, unconnected with one's own status. On the other hand, if it were permissible to establish democracy only because nondemocratic countries tend to start unjust wars or produce other causes for just wars, Vindicator, in establishing democracy, would be acting in his own self-interest in trying to avoid a future war. Then the achievement of y would be "avoiding a future injustice or burden of war to Vindicator," and his investment in this war could explain his right to pursue the war in order to establish democracy in the country he was fighting.

B. *CONTINUING WAR TO DO MORE TO ACHIEVE A JUST CAUSE*

Suppose Proposal 3R is wrong. Could this also imply that if Victim does not achieve x despite much investment, he may permissibly do more to Dominant to *achieve x alone* than would have been permissible had he done it in *one fell swoop* at the beginning of a war? (In the case I am imagining, many losses were sustained because the offer of x was not forthcoming and pursuit of x justified the heavy investment already made.) I doubt it.

However, suppose that having actually undergone losses *would* justify Victim in doing more to achieve y or x itself. This would mean that it is not permissible to honestly threaten to do *in one fell swoop* at the beginning of a war all that one could honestly threaten to do based on losses already sustained and a longer recalcitrance on Dominant's part. This would defeat what seems to be a corollary of Proposal 3R, namely that there is symmetry in what can be done to achieve x in starting a war and in continuing it. However, one could, *at the beginning* of war, have foreseen that what one could threaten would permissibly increase based on investment. Victim's morally honest threat of justified war at the very beginning could have made reference to this.[29] That is, it could be part of the threat that the demands will rise (from x to also y) and (less likely) that the lengths to which one will go to achieve x will justifiably increase. Hence, what one could morally honestly threaten is not greater as war progresses than what one could threaten before war starts in at least one sense: What one is allowed to honestly threaten others with in the beginning of a war is to continue the war once started in light of what is earned by efforts invested and costs incurred and the added guilt of Dominant in being recalcitrant for a longer period of time. Suppose m is the upper limit on what Victim may do to others in war, including *all* this. Then he is not permitted to do m at one fell swoop in the beginning to get x and y when x alone is offered unconditionally in exchange for peace.

Rejecting the adequacy of Proposal 3R for war (and, by extension, its use as a guide to deciding about employing other means to achieve goals) diminishes the conservatism of the positions I have been describing. For Victim would be entitled to more, and to do more, before the continued use of disruptive and threatening mechanisms for change become morally illegitimate.

C. RETAINING BY WAR WHAT ONE MAY NOT ACQUIRE BY WAR?

There is at least one more reason that Proposal 3R may seem to cheat Victim. Suppose Dominant has begun a war of aggression against Victim, taking y from him but leaving him with x. Can Dominant put Victim in a position of being unjustified in continuing the war (that Dominant started) in order to regain y simply by noting that condition x is such that efforts to alter it for the better (e.g., gain y) would not justify starting a war? I do not think so. If Proposal 3R implies the opposite, it would be wrong.

But is this really an objection to Proposal 3R per se? For it would also be wrong to think that Victim could not *begin* a war to *prevent or undo y's being taken*, just as it would be wrong to think that he may not continue a war to undo y's being taken. This shows that war may be justified as a way of dealing with aggression per se and in order to *re*gain or retain things or rights threatened by aggression even if war is not justified to first get the thing or right in question. Does this view rest on a moral distinction between being harmed and not having one's condition improved? Not quite, for Dominant may have already been harming Victim by playing a significant causal role in Victim's not having some legal right y, but by nonwar (e.g., political) means, and this would not justify war. Furthermore, if there were no aggression, but y, to which one had a moral right, were taken away by an incorrect democratic majority vote, then Victim would be harmed, but it may be that war is still not permitted to regain y.

D. VICTORS IMPOSING INJUSTICES WHOSE REMOVAL IS NOT A JUST CAUSE

If Proposal 3R is wrong, does this affect Proposal 1? No. The relation between prevention and termination of war (the subject of Proposal 3R) does not affect the relation between justified war and justified peace (the subject of Proposal 1). Suppose one is justified in demanding more and doing more before one is required to end an ongoing war than one is justified in demanding or doing in one fell swoop to break a peace. Still, *whatever condition one is not justified in improving by continuing a war* is the condition that defines the justified peace that should end a war. This is all that Proposal 1 implies.

What if the war continues until victory for Victim, and he is now in a position of dominance? Can he dictate a peace that creates injustices toward former-Dominant so long as the injustices are not significant enough to make war by new-Dominant (or his Vindicator) justified? No, since what Victim is now justified in doing need not be the same as what others would not be justified in going to war to prevent him from doing. He may be doing something he should not be doing even if it is impermissible to correct it by war.[30]

But can former Victim at least call a condition with these injustices a justified peace in the sense that war to end it alone would be unjust?[31] If not, how could former-Dominant's peace offer, which refused to correct such injustices, have been called justified peace? How can the acceptability of former-Dominant's proposal be consistent with the unacceptability of new-Dominant's proposal? Can we treat new-Dominant's attempt to, for example, wrest from former-Dominant valid rights he already had in the same way we treat acts of aggression that take away rights? But we said that while aggression that *takes away* a lesser valid right can be a reason for war, if there is no aggression (but only a peace treaty) that takes away the rights, war may be impermissible and only peace justified.[32]

Conclusion

The requirements of just cause and proportionality in standard just war theory claim that altering affairs in the direction of greater justice often does not justify means such as war (or war carried on by certain means). One can be required to avoid starting or continuing war if the states of affairs (conditions) exist whose alteration for the better does not justify the use of warlike means. Then these are states of justified peace that make war unjust and hence set the limits of just war (Proposal 1). The Partial Justice Claim asserted that less than perfect justice can be involved in these states of justified peace.

One can be required to abstain from or end the use of certain warring means already justifiably undertaken by the provision of a state of justified peace not conditioned on loss of rights (part of Proposal 2R). Sometimes this is the same state that would have made beginning a war unjustified (limited Proposal 3R) and that contains less than perfect justice.

However, the state of affairs that should end a war is sometimes not the same as the one that should prevent one. This is the rejection of unlimited Proposal 3R, in particular, not when an unjustified delay in offering or providing this state of affairs results in investment of effort or suffering of losses by Victim that merits a better state of affairs than would have justified beginning war. (These conditions still need not be perfect justice.) Furthermore, what one is justified in threatening at t_1 to do in one fell swoop *at* t_1 to achieve a goal may be different from what one is justified in threatening at t_1 to do *ultimately* at t_2. One may threaten a response that will be sensitive to losses sustained in the pursuit, and delays in the receipt, of that whose absence originally made war justified.

Notes

This chapter is a revised version of "Making War (and Its Continuation) Unjust," *European Journal of Philosophy* (2001): 328–343. The original article was prompted by Avishai Margalit's "A Just Peace or Just a Peace," presented at the Colloquium on International Jurisprudence, organized by Prof. Lea Brilmayer, New York University Law School, February 1995. Subsequent to the publication of my article, Margalit discussed it and "fleshed out" (to use his term) the examples in it in his second Tanner Lecture on Human Values, 2005. I have taken account of his 2005 discussion in revising the original article. All references to Margalit are to the typescript of the final draft of the Tanner Lectures (subsequently published as *On Compromise and Rotten Compromises*, Princeton University Press, 2010). For comments, I am grateful to the audiences at the Columbia University Seminar on Human Rights (1996), the Ohio State Department of Philosophy (1996), the New York University Colloquium in Law, Philosophy, and Social Theory (1996), the New York chapter of the Society for Philosophy and Public Affairs (1996), the members of the Philamore Discussion Group (1996), and Ronald Dworkin, Jeff McMahan, and Thomas Nagel.

1. As we shall see, Avishai Margalit seems to deny this supposition by distinguishing between lasting peace and mere truce, both of which are alternatives to war.

2. Of course, when a war is ongoing, justifiably requiring that it end is not necessarily the same as requiring the end of a justified war since the war may not be justified to begin with. However, for the purposes of this chapter, I shall assume that we are trying to make unjustified the continuation of what has so far been a justified war. Even a war that is started justly could be fought by unjust means. (That is, it satisfies *jus ad bellum* but not *jus in bello*.) In this sense, there are conditions (i.e., use of unjust means) that could make it unjust to continue a war that are not among the conditions that make it unjust to start a war. Proposals 2 and 3 are not intended to imply otherwise. First, they are concerned with conditions that would come about if war stopped that could make continuing war unjust, not with conditions *in war*. Second, they only suggest that if a condition made starting war to alter it unjust, this condition coming about would make continuing war unjust; they do not claim that no other conditions could make it unjust to continue a war besides those that would make it unjust to start one.

3. This paper subsequently became part of his Tanner Lectures.

4. He said this in answer to a question I asked. In his second Tanner Lecture (p. 10), he also says that he is not doing just war theory. The reason he explicitly gives there is that just war theory is concerned with when war is permissible, not obligatory. However, he says, he is also concerned with when a country is not justified in remaining at peace but should go to war. I do not think this reason could be an adequate account of why he is not doing just war theory because it could still be true that the part of his discussion that deals with when it is impermissible to go to war deals with issues raised by just war theory.

5. We could also claim that just peace involves the partial conditions of justice that make possible lasting peace by using a normative theory other than that of just war. We

could use the normative theory of egoistic rationality. That is, we could argue that an agent *should* not go to war because it would be irrational for the agent to go to war once he is offered certain conditions, as it would be against his self-interest to do so. However, one of my concerns in this chapter is to make clearer that this "should" may amount to a moral "must," and hence going to war would be unjust and not merely imprudent.

6. See pp. 11–15, where he discusses cases based on ones that I discussed in the article on which this chapter is based and that I will discuss below.

7. See section IV.

8. Standard just war theory commonly distinguishes between the justice of going to war and justice in carrying out war. It claims that a war that it is unjust to begin might be carried out by just means and that a war that is justly begun might (incorrectly) be carried out by unjust means. It is possible that some conditions not only justify beginning a war to alter them but also justify the use of means in waging war that it would be unjust to use in war triggered by different conditions. Implicit in my discussion of the justice or injustice of beginning or continuing a war are considerations that also bear on the justice or injustice of using certain means to wage a war. That is, my discussion could be modified slightly so as to deal with the question of, for example, what conditions must be offered to make continuation of a war by *certain means* unjust even if continuation of the war by other *means* would not be unjust.

9. The following discussions include description of cases I had presented and that Margalit discusses and builds on in his second Tanner Lecture. He says that his "thought experiment is in a way a fleshing out of Frances Kamm's austere schematic account" (p. 11).

10. Thomas Nagel suggested this. It may bear on Jeff McMahan's argument against the permissibility of requiring unconditional surrender from an enemy in war. McMahan says that if it is impermissible to achieve by war some situation, such as Japan's not having an emperor, then one side may not demand that of the other side as a condition for peace. (See his "Just Cause for War," *Ethics & International Affairs* 19[3] [2005]: 1–21.) However, if this were true, it might also be impermissible for the other side to continue the war in order to resist that situation (e.g., to retain its emperor) as a condition on its agreeing to peace. However, as I note later, there may be a difference between fighting to achieve something and fighting to retain it, and also a difference between what one may demand rather than start a war and what one may demand to end a war.

11. However, if a defensive war against a justified war could itself be justified, this ground for Dominant being under an obligation to offer what would make peace justified will not succeed. (A justified defensive war against a justified offensive war seems unlikely if Dominant is perpetrating or benefiting from injustice. But what I have in mind is the possibility that one party could reasonably object to a change in a status quo and another party could reasonably object to the status quo. Then the second party could fight the first party, and the latter could justifiably defend itself.)

12. For more on such a set of reasons, see the discussion of a "conservative just agent" on p. 11.

13. I thank Liam Murphy for raising this point.

14. In his second Tanner Lecture, Margalit interprets me as saying that one should give up war as a way to achieve both x and y when one can still use other nonwarlike means to eventually achieve y (see pp. 10 and 13). But in the earlier published version of this text I specifically said (what the text here says) that the fact that there is no hope of appropriate means of achieving y is not a sufficient reason for continuing war when one is given x. It is possible, of course, that the only reason war is not thought proportional to achieving y once

x is available is that it is believed to be achievable by other means or believed to be achievable by other means within a certain time frame. This is really to move beyond a claim that y is not of the right type to be a just cause or that war is out of proportion to achieving it to a claim that war is not necessary or is not yet a last resort. Then if y were not achievable by other means or not achievable within a reasonable time, y might merit war even given x.

15. However, notice that if one must fight to get x, and the overall more costly strategy (in terms of harm) to all concerned gets one only x and the overall less costly strategy (for some reason) got one both x and y, then one should use the latter strategy.

16. I am grateful to Calvin Normore for the question which prompted this analysis.

17. Thomas Nagel pointed out that it would be paradoxical to claim that Dominant may permissibly resist an unjustified war by Victim on behalf of y if the reason the war is unjustified is that there would be disproportionate costs to achieve y *only because Dominant resists*. Then we could not, without circularity, justify Dominant's resisting the war on grounds that the war is unjustified. That is, we cannot say the war is unjustified because of the big losses that will occur and therefore Dominant's resistance to the war is justified if the big losses will not occur unless Dominant resists. Dominant cannot claim its resistance is justified because Victim's behavior is unjustified, if Victim's behavior would not be unjustified if Dominant were not resisting what he is doing.

One response to this argument is that Victim's original attack to get only y may be excessively costly. But there may also be some other ground besides high cost (or low probability of success, which also exists only because of Dominant's resistance) that makes Victim's use of war unjustified. This ground might be a violation of territorial sovereignty or the use of even low force to achieve a type of thing that force should not be used to achieve. (This might happen if one is in a democratic state or an international legal community committed to using only nonviolent means for certain ends.) Once we see that Dominant's resistance could be justified, we might then figure the expected costs of continuing war and argue that Victim's beginning a war for the sake of y is *also* unjustified because of the costs.

An alternative response to the threat of a circle is that Victim's war can be unjustified because of the large costs that will come from Dominant's expected though *unjustified* resistance. Indeed, this could be a particular corollary of the view that we may have to live with certain injustices rather than use war to eradicate them. Here the particular injustice is Dominant's expected and costly resistance to Victim's attack even though Dominant is not entitled to resist. For example, it might be said that we have to avoid using low-scale violence, which might be justified for y, to avoid the inevitable massive unjust resistance by Dominant. But, in this case, Dominant is not justified in resisting Victim's war; he will just resist anyway. This view is problematic, however, if it does not ever morally distinguish between disproportionate effects due to an intervening act by Dominant and disproportionate effects that are not due to an intervening act by Dominant.

The circle is connected to another important point. It might be suggested that there is always a way to make war unjustified besides providing Victim with what he cannot have without losing the right to make war. This other way is to raise the costs associated with fighting the war by raising the resistance triggered by any attack. But this is the wrong way to make Victim's attack unjustified. Just as it would be inappropriate to go to war for the sake of y, it is inappropriate to *make* the costs of getting x be out of proportion to what getting x merits by, for example, setting a nuclear weapon to go off if Victim attacks. Here is another example: If it is wrong for Victim to attack noncombatants to achieve x, then it is wrong for Dominant to place noncombatants on the front lines so that Victim can do nothing to achieve x except hit noncombatants. Moreover, it is wrong for Dominant to do this even if his doing it makes Victim's war unjustifiable. Hence, it may not always be morally correct to make war unjustifiable. (The possibility remains, of course, that Dominant's doing such impermissible acts, which raise the cost of any act of Victim's, fails to make Victim's acting impermissible; it only puts responsibility for injustices in the war on Dominant's shoulders.)

18. An additional concern, raised by Mary Ann Case, stems from the problem of equality. Suppose the achievement of y is not attainable by Victim 1 by any means short of war but is attainable by Victim 2 (or by Dominant) by means short of war (e.g., economic power). Then, some will have y when others do not have it, creating undeserved inequality.

19. In "Making War (and Its Continuation) Unjust," p. 333.

20. Second Tanner Lecture, p. 16.

21. I discuss other cases in which we go to war on account of certain factors but not to achieve them in my *Ethics for Enemies* (OUP, 2011), Chapter 3.

22. Margalit, p. 10. Margalit is here distinguishing between two alternatives to war: lasting peace and truce. I said (p. 1) that if one is not justified in going to war, one is justified only in remaining at peace. I take this to be lasting peace. A truce, by contrast, I take to be a nonwarlike state that is optional; it is permissible to end it by war.

23. Here is a possible analogy: One should be loved by one's parents, but if one is not, one may come to merit the love (even if one still does not get it) by good deeds and so on. But then, it might be said, one would not be getting what one is owed, that is, *unconditional* love, so the analogy is imperfect. Suppose your corporation owes you time off with pay just because every executive gets this. However, it refuses to abide by its obligations. You do some extra committee work that entitles you to time off with pay. You have now earned time off. Your claim to the time off is getting stronger and stronger. This is what I have in mind by speaking of earning that to which you are entitled. For help with the analogies, I thank Bonnie Kent and Susan Wolf.

24. Because the rejection of Proposal 3R might be based on the relevance of Victim's investment, it is fair to ask whether it is an example of the (supposed) fallacy of sunk cost, which leads people to throw good money after bad. (For example, suppose someone bought a movie ticket and now has lost interest in going. If this person goes anyway so as to save his investment, he loses even more utility by spending a miserable evening at the movies. The point is, cut your losses. This suggests that sometimes it is better that people die in vain [i.e., for no good result] than that they and more people die for the sake even of a good that is not worth the total cost.) But I have been discussing only cases where Victim might do more for x or pursue y when he has already done much for x, if doing more holds out the hope of actually getting x and/or x and y. Here the expectation is that one's overall utility will be greater at the end when one adds up what has already been invested, what will still be invested, and having x and y. The idea is that one earns a chance at this because one has already invested. I conclude this does not involve the fallacy of sunk cost.

25. The view that one may sometimes begin a war only because one has the aim of achieving things other than the primary just cause is defended by Thomas Hurka (and was at one time defended by McMahan), in his "Liability and Just Cause," *Ethics and International Affairs*, 21(2), 2007: 199–218.

26. (Even as aims conditional on having an independent just cause.) This is a view that was independently defended by Jeff McMahan in his and Robert McKim's "The Just War and the Gulf War," *Canadian Journal of Philosophy* 25 (December 1993): 501–541. He subsequently rejected the view. An alternative description (offered by Gopal Sreenivasan) of the

scenario I describe in the text is consistent with the correctness of Proposal 3R. It asks us to think of Victim as entitled to begin a new war in order to get y once he has invested in an earlier war. So he is entitled to continue warring to get y only because y is something he would now (at t_2) be entitled to begin a war to get even if it were not something he was entitled to begin a war to get before any war (at t_1). However, it seems odd to me to think of the continuation of the war as beginning a new war for y, and I do not see why having proceeded in the war for x (if that is all one was entitled to pursue in that war) should make it permissible to begin a new war that others may not. For example, if hostilities had ceased after x was achieved, is it clear that they may permissibly be restarted to get y? An alternative proposal of Sreenivasan's is that the right to demand y can be seen as belonging to a "right of just victory." But this implies that one may permissibly go on fighting for y only if one has already *won* the war for x. By contrast, I am suggesting that a sufficient investment in getting x, even if Victim has not already won it, may give a right to pursue y by war. Note that I have not revised the article on which this chapter is based to reflect my current view that, to a large extent, if a factor that would justify conduct is present, it may justify independently of an agent's aims.

27. Suggested by Jerome Schneewind.

28. Another possibility, suggested by Ronald Dworkin and Thomas Nagel, is that one may pursue y once a war is in progress because the cost of getting it has gone down and the probability of getting it has gone up given what one has already done to achieve x. But this account will not suffice if the cost is still too high and the probability of achievement still too small to have justified achieving y on its own initially.

29. I distinguish a morally honest threat from a bluffing threat even if the latter is permissible. In the former, one would permissibly do what one threatens to do. In the latter, what one may permissibly threaten at the very beginning of a war exceeds what one would and/or could permissibly do later (i.e., it exceeds what one could now honestly threaten to do later).

30. As Jeff McMahan emphasized.

31. I owe this question to Lewis Kornhauser.

32. I said in the beginning of this chapter that it was not my aim to argue for any substantive claims about what sort of abuses make war justified. It may be useful to now point out that because the four basic claims for which I have argued—Proposal 1 (a definition), the Partial Justice Claim, Proposal 2R, and the denial of Proposal 3R—are formal, they seem largely to be true regardless of whether a deontological, consequentialist, or virtue-based just war theory is used. This seems clear with respect to Proposal 1, as it is purely definitional. The Partial Justice Claim should be acceptable to consequentialists, given that they decide things by weighing costs and benefits, and the cost of some injustices will be outweighed by the cost of war, at least sometimes. There are obvious deontological reasons for thinking that not all steps may be taken in order to correct any injustice. Unless the only virtues are unlimited aggressiveness or the refusal at any cost to submit to disrespectful treatment, virtue theory will endorse the Partial Justice Claim as well. Finally, both deontological and consequentialist grounds have been suggested for rejecting Proposal 3R. The deontological ones are recalcitrance on Dominant's part plus investment on Victim's part. The consequentialist one is the possibility that the cost of achieving y goes down and the probability of achieving it goes up once we are at war over x. A virtue theory might provide grounds for the denial of symmetry in what one can do at the beginning of a war to achieve x or y and what one may do later in a war to achieve either, by emphasizing commitment to continued pursuit of a goal once one has started or debts to those who have suffered losses to see the fruition of their sacrifices.

2

Justifications for Killing Noncombatants in War

The Doctrine of Double Effect (DDE) says that we may not intend evil as a means to a greater good or as an end in itself, but it can be permissible to pursue a greater good as a final end by neutral or good means even if a lesser evil is a certain, foreseen side effect (if there is no other way to achieve the greater good).[1] The DDE has been used to distinguish morally between (1) terror bombing civilians in wartime and (2) bombing military targets, foreseeing with certainty that civilians will be killed as a side effect. The first is said to be impermissible; the second may be permissible. In this chapter I shall be concerned with how criticism and revisions of the DDE bear on these and related cases in the morality of war. I shall try to show how consideration of this issue can lead us to two new doctrines: the Doctrine of Triple Effect (DTE) and the Doctrine of Initial Justification (DIJ). They may do better at explaining permissible and impermissible conduct than the DDE.

1

It has been suggested that in many cases, such as terror bombing, where acting is impermissible, we need not be intending harm strictly speaking. For example, it might be that although we must intend the involvement and appearance of death of noncombatants in terror bombing in order to end a war, we need not intend their deaths. If they actually survive, that would not interfere with our ending the war. Of course, we know that the only thing we can do to involve them and make them appear dead will also cause their deaths, but this may only be foreseen and not intended.

 To deal with this problem, Warren Quinn[2] suggested that we focus on the wrongness of intending the involvement of a person without his consent in a way that we foresee will lead to significant harm to him (i.e., evil). This is instead of focusing on the wrongness of intending the harm to him (i.e., evil), as the DDE says. Let us say that Quinn's revision results in the DDE Revised (R). Henceforth, to mark my acceptance of this revision without adding words, I shall use "evil*" to mean "evil or involvement without consent that we foresee will lead to evil"[3] and say that the DDE(R) says that we must not intend evil*.

Now consider another problem with the DDE. Suppose a doctor is called and told that organs—innocently acquired—have arrived and must be transplanted quickly into his five patients. He drives to the hospital but on the road finds an immovable person in his path. If he takes a different route, he will be too late to do the transplants, and as he is the only one who can do them, the five will die. If he runs over the person on the road, he foresees but does not intend the death of the one. However, he knows (suppose) that if he gets to the hospital, he will save the five. (Call this Car Case I.) It seems impermissible for him to proceed. Yet the DDE does not seem to rule this out as the lesser evil is not intended.[4]

If it can be impermissible to do what causes death merely as a foreseen side effect even if a greater good will result (as in Car Case I), why is it not impermissible to engage in strategic bombing? That is, if Car Case I shows that the DDE is too liberal in permitting the killing of the one person, why does this objection not undermine the defense the DDE provides for strategic bombing? I suggest that it may, and we should provide another justification for the distinction between terror bombing and strategic bombing.

Some (e.g., Philippa Foot) have concluded on the basis of cases like Car Case I that the moral distinction between intending harm and foreseeing harm must be supplemented (or replaced) by the moral distinction between harming and not aiding: Doing foreseen harm to some in order to do greater good for others is impermissible, but allowing foreseen harm to occur to some by not aiding them in order to do greater good to others is permissible. But this conclusion banning harm is too strong: It matters, I believe, whether harm is the result of the greater good itself or instead the result of means that cause the greater good. For example, consider Car Case II. It is the same as Car Case I except that the doctor need not run over anyone to get to the hospital. However, he knows that if he saves the five (by perfectly innocent means), their being alive (rather than dead) and breathing normally will alter the causal events in the world so that germs hitherto safely closeted will kill one person who otherwise would not have been killed. It is still permissible to save the five, I believe. In Car Case I, the means to the greater good (driving to the hospital) causes the death of the one person; in Car Case II, the good achieved, not the mere means to it, causes the death of the one person.[5]

Can we use this point to explain the permissibility of strategic bombing? If so, we might have to determine whether the noncombatants were killed (a) as an effect of the means used to blow up the munitions factory or (b) as an effect of the munitions factory itself blowing up. Furthermore, we would have to be able to say that the blowing up of the factory was itself the greater good that could justify the death of bystanders. If we could say the latter, then even if the DDE(R) is incorrect, causing deaths by way of (b) could be permissible, although causing deaths by way of (a) would be impermissible.

But how can we say that the blowing up of a munitions factory is itself a greater good (comparable to saving more lives as in Car Case II)? It seems more like a means to a greater good; that is, if there are no munitions, more people will be alive (because not killed). Two suggestions might be made at this point. One suggestion is to distinguish between (1) a means to a good and (2) a component of that good. The second suggestion is to distinguish between (1′) means that cause a greater good, and (2′) means that have greater good as (what I call) a noncausal flip side. Consider the first suggestion. Components of a greater good are parts of it (for example, the saving of two of five people). They are not means to it. I believe it is sometimes true that components of a greater good may permissibly cause lesser evils that are ultimately justified only by the greater good, of which the components are parts.[6] However, if a munitions factory being blown up were in this way a component of a greater good, the greater good would have to be conceived as something like "the end of arms production." But is this not itself just a means to the real good of more people alive because not killed? On this view, therefore, the munitions factory being blown up is not a component of the greater good.

Now consider the second suggestion. It is not only the greater good itself (or its components) that it is permissible to create though we foresee it will cause a lesser evil. Means that have a noncausal relation to greater good may also cause a lesser evil. (The means that have only a causal relation to greater good may not be used if we foresee they will cause a lesser evil. This is what is true in Car Case I, where driving to the hospital causes the death of a bystander and also leads by a causal chain to saving five.) Consideration of cases may help us distinguish the causal from the noncausal relation I have in mind. In a version of the Trolley Case, a trolley is headed toward five people and will kill them, but a bystander can save them (only) by redirecting the trolley. However, once redirected, it will go off in a direction where one person will definitely be hit and killed by it. Typically, non-consequentialists think it is permissible (though not obligatory) to redirect even though this involves harming some in order to aid others.[7]

In the context where only the trolley threatens the five, the turning of the trolley threat away from them—by which I mean the moving of the trolley itself away—is the same event as their becoming free of threats, and this is the same event as their becoming saved. Hence, there is a noncausal relation between the turning away of the trolley and the five becoming saved. Furthermore, the state of affairs of their being saved is noncausally related to these events in that context.[8] Because this is true, I will say that the five being saved (the greater good) is the noncausal flip side of the turning of the trolley. Intuitively, I mean to distinguish this noncausal relation from a less "tight," ordinary causal relation that could connect the turning of the trolley and the saving of people, as in the following Van Case. A van is headed toward twenty people and will kill them. If we turn the trolley away from hitting five, the diverted trolley will gently push into those twenty and move them away from the van. Here the saving of the twenty is simply a causal consequence of the moving trolley. It contrasts with the relation between the five being saved and the moving of the trolley away from them. This is a contrast, as slim as it seems, that I think is crucial in a correct nonconsequentialist theory of permissible harm.[9]

Intuitively, it is also permissible to do acts (e.g., pushing a button that redirects the trolley) that cause the event (the turning of the trolley itself) that has greater good as a noncausal flip side and a lesser evil as an effect. We can explain this by noting that pushing the button—an event that per se does not have greater good as a noncausal flip side or aspect— also does not per se cause the death of the one. It causes the death of the one by causing the trolley to be diverted, and this diversion has the greater good as its noncausal flip side.

How does all this relate to the case of strategic bombing? Blowing up the munitions factory has as its noncausal flip side (not as a further causal consequence) the reduced ability to kill people, and in the context of war where munitions are necessary to kill people, this is the same as a greater number of people being alive. So the factory being blown up would itself be a means to the greater good that has greater good as its noncausal flip side. If the factory blowing up causes the lesser evil* and also has a noncausal relation to greater good, dropping the bombs is permissible. However, suppose the bombs themselves kill bystanders and also, as a causal consequence, blow up the factory. Then the means that would cause the lesser evil would have a purely causal relation to the greater good (i.e., the bombs cause the factory to blow up, and the blowing up has a noncausal relation to the greater good). This, according to the suggestion we are now examining, would not be permitted. In terror bombing, the evil* itself is a cause of greater good—neither the greater good nor means noncausally related to it cause a lesser evil*. Hence, terror bombing is impermissible according to the suggestion we are now examining. What if the munitions factory being blown up itself caused noncombatant deaths as a side effect but its blowing up had a purely causal relation to a greater good? For example, suppose there are no munitions being produced in the plant anymore, but blowing it up is necessary to create a diversion so that another military mission can succeed (or to cause fear in the population that will lead to their surrender). The suggestion we are now examining would not justify bombing the munitions factory in this case.

If some of these implications seem wrong, it may show that "war is special"— that is, principles that govern action in microinteractions between people in peacetime may not apply in wartime. This may be because enormous goods outweigh some acts otherwise impermissible or because an opponent's civilians ought not to be treated as ordinary bystanders.[10] Such a "war is special" justification might justify bombing the munitions plant as a diversion and using bombs in strategic bombing that themselves cause noncombatant deaths.

2

So far we have considered how one objection to the DDE(R) raised by Car Case I—that the DDE(R) permits too much—bears on the distinction between terror bombing and strategic bombing. We have also considered how some other proposed principles of permissible harm—that is, greater good itself may cause a lesser evil and means that have a noncausal relation to greater good may cause a lesser evil—might deal with terror and strategic bombing. (I have not yet said anything here about why these two principles are correct principles of permissible harm or what justifies them.) Now consider two more wartime cases that bear on both the correctness of the DDE(R) and the development of alternative principles of permissible harm.

Consider first the Enemy Massacre Case: A general wants to bomb through a wall so he can move to safety 100 people who are very important to the war effort. If the 100 are moved to the safe zone, however, this will lead the enemy to massacre 200 civilians. The deaths of the 200 would not be a direct effect of the bombing as it is the enemy's intervening acts that kill the 200. Nevertheless, we can imagine that the general would not act foreseeing this would happen. However, the collapse of the wall will stop a mudslide that was about to kill 500 other civilians. Saving these 500 is not the general's aim, as he is obligated to attend only to war-related goals. The general allows himself to act to save the 100 only because he believes that the greater good (500 saved plus 100 saved) will outbalance the lesser evil (200 dead in an enemy massacre). However, since he does not intend to stop the mudslide, he does not act with the ultimate aim of producing that greater good. (He does not even act intending to produce the greater good as a means to his acting on his aim of saving the 100. He need not do this, as the mudslide will stop without his intending that it do so, just if he acts. To say that he intends to stop the mudslide as a means to his acting to save the 100 suggests that if it did not occur as a side effect of his act, he would, as a rational agent, be committed to doing something in order to make the falling of the wall stop the mudslide. But as a rational agent, he need not be committed to doing this just because he wishes to take advantage of a connection that already exists between his acting to save the 100 and the greater good.)

It is permissible, I believe, for the general to act in the Enemy Massacre Case even though he does not aim at the greater good. But the DDE(R) says that it may be permissible to produce a lesser evil* as a side effect if we are pursuing a greater good as a final end (the suggestion being "only if").[11] Even intending the greater good as a means would not satisfy this condition. Acting because the greater good will occur is different from acting in order that it occur. In discussing the DDE, so much attention has been paid to the issue of whether or not we may intend a lesser evil* that none has been paid to whether or how we must intend the greater good.

But now notice that if we can distinguish conceptually between intending an effect and acting because we believe it will occur, a common test used to distinguish conceptually between intending and merely foreseeing an effect is shown to be inadequate. The Counterfactual Test says that to see whether someone acts while intending or alternatively merely foreseeing an effect, we should imagine (counterfactually) that the effect will not occur but everything else remains the same. If the person would not act because the effect would not occur, this shows, it is said, that he intended the effect. But in the Enemy Massacre Case, if the greater good (of 500 saved from a mudslide) did not occur and all else remained the same, the agent would not have acted. He acts only because he believes that this greater good will occur; he will not act unless he believes it will occur. His act is conditional on his belief that it will occur, but he is still not intending this greater good. So we see that the Counterfactual Test fails to distinguish between effects that are intended and effects where belief in their occurrence is a condition of action.

Now consider the Munitions Grief Case:[12] If we bomb a munitions factory and it is immediately rebuilt, it will be pointless to bomb it. It is only because civilians are killed as an (unavoidable) side effect of the factory blowing up that other citizens, consumed by grief, will be unable to rebuild. Hence, if we bomb, it would be because we believe the civilians would die. But this does not mean that we aim at their deaths. Though we take advantage of a side effect of our act to provide us with a reason for doing it, we need not be committed (as rational agents) to doing anything especially to make our act have that side effect. This is an indication that we do not intend the deaths. I believe bombing in the Munitions Grief Case can be permissible even if terror bombing is impermissible.

If we need not intend to hit the noncombatants if we act in the Munitions Grief Case, we need not violate the no-intending-evil* component of the DDE(R). But another component of the DDE(R) says that we may produce a lesser evil* foreseen as a side effect if we use neutral or good means with the aim of achieving a greater good. But the lesser evil* we produce in the Munitions Grief Case is not a mere foreseen side effect; we act because we believe it will occur. I claim that even if intending an evil* is impermissible, acting only because one believes it will occur may not be impermissible.

If we combine what I have said about the cases where action is permitted because of unintended greater good (Enemy Massacre Case) and unintended lesser evil* (Munitions Grief Case), we can revise the DDE(R) further. These cases show that one cannot only intend an effect or merely foresee it but also act because of it. On account of this third relation we can have to an effect, we could construct the Doctrine of Triple Effect Revised (DTE[R]): A greater good that we cause and whose expected existence is a condition of our action but which we do not necessarily intend may justify a lesser evil* that we must not intend but the expectation of which we may have as a condition of action.[13]

But now, in a variation on the Munitions Grief Case, suppose we had different sorts of ways of destroying the munitions plant. One of the ways would certainly involve the noncombatants and lead to their death, whereas each of the other ways has diminishing probabilities of this effect to the point of zero. If we choose a way that we foresee would involve bystanders because only then would the plant not be rebuilt, would we make this choice intending the bystanders' involvement? If so, it would be ruled out by the DDE(R) and the DTE(R). Suppose we adhere to these doctrines. Then as we acquire more precise ways to do strategic bombing, it may make no sense to bomb the plant. This is because the plant will be rebuilt, as the only permissible means of bombing will not involve harming any bystanders.[14]

I do not endorse the DTE(R). There are problems with it. A clear problem for the DTE(R) is that, like the DDE(R), it would permit the doctor to drive over the person in the Car Case since it allows a means to a greater good to have a lesser evil* as a side effect. So it does not avoid the earlier objection I discussed in section 1. Furthermore, both it and the DDE(R) are what I call state-of-mind principles. They make what is permissible dependent on the state of mind of the agent. But this seems wrong, quite generally. If an agent bombs a munitions plant and children die as a side effect, this can be permissible even if the agent intends the deaths, I believe. If the general in the Enemy Massacre Case would have impermissibly blown up the wall even had the act not rescued the 500, his act would still be permissible in the case where the 500 were, in fact, saved.

At this point, I am most interested in another problem for the DTE(R) since it will lead us to another principle of permissible harm that may account for the permissibility of acting in the Munitions Grief Case independently of the DTE(R).

3

The DTE(R) does not, I believe, properly distinguish between the permissibility of acting in the Munitions Grief Case and the impermissibility of acting in the following Two Factories Case: There are two munitions plants. So long as one of them is operating, there is no point in eliminating the other. We are able to bomb only one of the plants, but the foreseen side effect of this is that some noncombatants will be hit by the exploding plant and die. Only if this happens will the population be too consumed by grief to operate the second plant. Our previous analysis implies that if we proceed with the bombing, this does not mean we necessarily intend the involvement or deaths of the noncombatants; we may act only because we believe the involvement will take place. Hence, we need not violate the DDE(R) or DTE(R) in bombing in the Two Factories Case. Nevertheless, I suggest that bombing one plant in the Two Factories Case is not justified even if bombing in the Munitions Grief Case is.[15]

So far, in describing principles of permissible harm that differ from the DDE(R) and the DTE(R), I have discussed one that says that greater good may cause a lesser evil* and means that have a noncausal relation to greater good may cause a lesser evil*. Now, to deal with the Two Factories Case, we could add to that principle the claim that it is permissible for a lesser evil* that is an effect of greater good (or of means noncausally related to it) to (in a sense) *sustain* that greater good. This is so even if it is not permissible for evil* to *produce* that greater good. If a lesser evil* sustains a greater good, the greater good is not produced by it. I can try to show that in the Munitions Grief Case, the evil* sustains greater good, whereas in the Two Factories Case, evil* produces greater good.

Consider the Munitions Grief Case: The rebuilding of the factory is a second potential problem that comes about only as the causal consequence of our initially blowing up the factory. The blowing up leads to the potential rebuilding. Independent of this further causal consequence of the blowing up, the noncausal flip side of blowing up exists. The noncausal flip side is that people will be rid of the problem that existed at the time we acted (i.e., the threat of death from munitions as it existed before we did anything). This noncausal flip side would justify bad effects on civilians of blowing up the factory unless some new problem arose as a consequence of blowing up the factory and this new problem were not itself eliminated. So the noncausal flip side is a state that, when described independently of further causal consequences of it, would justify the lesser evil*. I shall call such a state the structural equivalent of the justifying good (structural equivalent, for short). This is because it has the structure of the ultimate good that justifies the death of the bystanders: more people alive rather than killed by munitions.[16] This structural equivalent provides us with a possible rationale for blowing up the factory, for we see that the structural equivalent of the justifying good involves something that could outweigh certain of the evils* that are effects of what we do, at least if the structural equivalent is sustained. Which evils*? The noncombatants killed by the blowing up of the factory.

The prospect of achieving the structural equivalent will not justify blowing up the factory (and killing bystanders) if we know that the factory will be rebuilt shortly anyway. So justification for blowing it up can depend on how the further causal consequences of blowing it up are likely to affect the existence of the munitions plant and its noncausal flip side as it is in the structural equivalent. It is a prerequisite of being justified in blowing up the factory that there be a prospect that a sufficient number of the people relieved of the munitions threat in the structural equivalent will remain unthreatened. In this way, the structural equivalent would become the greater good that, all things considered, justifies the lesser evil*.

One bad causal consequence of blowing up the factory is that this would lead to its being rebuilt. However, another side effect of the structural equivalent (dead bystanders) causes grief that stops the rebuilding. We could be justified in blowing up the factory if it were likely that the good that would ultimately justify the side-effect deaths would occur. When we are ultimately justified in acting in part because of the structural equivalent, I shall say that it provides an initial sufficient justification for blowing up the factory and for the side-effect killings. "Initial" refers to what exists if we blow up the factory independently of subsequent threats to this continuing created by further effects of what we have done. "Sufficient" refers to the good that is the flip side of the destruction of the factory being large enough, if it is sustained, to outweigh the death of bystanders.

Suppose that at least the initial sufficient justification for blowing up the factory is present. Then the hitting of the bystanders does not produce the structural equivalent of the good. Rather, it stands outside the structural equivalent and prevents threats to it (rebuilding) that arise from bringing about the structural equivalent. In that sense, the evil* (of dead bystanders) prevents the undoing of the good rather than bringing about or producing the good. We might instead say, more precisely, that in the Munitions Grief Case evil* produces the good by sustaining its structural equivalent rather than by producing its structural equivalent.

Consider by contrast the Two Factories Case. In it a second problem exists that is not just a causal consequence of what we do to get rid of another problem. That is, the second problem of another factory functioning exists independently of our blowing up one munitions factory. Given the existence of the two problems initially, we have no initial sufficient justification, as explicated earlier, for blowing up one factory. For when we blow up one factory and abstract from any new problem this causes (e.g., threat of rebuilding it), people are still subject to many fatal threats from the second munitions plant. That is, the structural equivalent of the justifying good does not yet exist as a flip side of blowing up one factory, and so it is not what causes the side-effect deaths. In the Two Factories Case, the structural equivalent is produced as a causal consequence of the bystanders being hit, as this causes the grief that stops the second factory from running. I believe this is what underlies the intuitive sense that bombing in the Two Factories Case is morally different from bombing in the Munitions Grief Case.[17] When some evil* is causally necessary for the existence of the structural equivalent that helps provide (at least) an initial sufficient justification of that evil*, the structural equivalent is produced by an evil* that is not already initially sufficiently justified (because the evil* is not produced by a structural equivalent). The evil* does not stand outside the structural equivalent of good and merely prevent its being undone by new threats caused by our successfully dealing with all the problems that originally prompted our action.

We can capture the idea behind this analysis as the Doctrine of Initial Justification (DIJ) (omitting "sufficient" for brevity's sake): It should be possible for lesser evils* to be caused by what at least initially sufficiently justifies them (which involves at least a structural equivalent that can become the good that ultimately justifies them) or by a means (or effects of means) that has at least the structural equivalent as its noncausal flip side or aspect. I believe that what motivates this doctrine is the concern (roughly) for the purity of causal chains. That is, it expresses a concern that the causal chain that leads to good G, where G justifies evil* E, need not involve evils* that are not at least initially sufficiently justified by what causes them. The DIJ is an attempt to get at the essence of the deep structure of nonconsequentialism with respect to harming innocents. Its motto is this: the possibility of initial sufficient justification all the way down. The DIJ could be used like the DDE(R) and the DTE(R) to test acts for permissibility and could supplant them for this purpose.[18]

Notes

The original version of this chapter was published in *Midwest Studies in Philosophy* 24 (2000), pp. 219–228.

1. I accept that there is a delicate distinction to be drawn between intending and aiming, such that all intendings involve aimings, but not the reverse. I also accept that those who are against intending an evil should be against aiming at it even when this does not involve intending it. (I owe these points to Michael Bratman.) Hence, I shall consider aiming at an evil to violate the DDE even when it does not amount to intending. Nothing I say in this chapter should depend on distinguishing intending from aiming.

2. In "Action, Intention, and Consequences: The Doctrine of Double Effect," reprinted in his *Morality and Action* (New York: Cambridge University Press, 1993, pp. 175–193).

3. The revision is not unproblematic, as it radically changes the apparent point of the DDE. Those defenders of the DDE (like Thomas Nagel) who focus on the wrongness of aiming at evil per se should be reluctant to accept it, I think.

4. This case is modeled on one described by Philippa Foot in "Killing and Letting Die," in *Abortion: Moral and Legal Perspectives*, ed. J. Garfield and P. Hennessy (Amherst: University of Massachusetts Press, 1984), pp. 178–185. It is also modeled on a case she used as an objection to the DDE (in "The Problem of Abortion and the Doctrine of Double Effect," *Oxford Review* 5 (1967), pp. 5–15): We must operate on five to save their lives, but doing so requires that we use a gas. It is harmless to the five, but it will unavoidably seep into a neighboring room, there killing an immovable patient. We may not operate, she concluded.

5. I first argued against Foot's conclusion in "Harming Some to Save Others," *Philosophical Studies* 57 (Fall 1989), pp. 227–260, and subsequently developed aspects of the larger theory I am discussing here (as well as some of its applications) in F. M. Kamm, *Morality, Mortality*, vol. 2, chapter 7, pp. 172–206 (New York: Oxford University Press, 1996) and in "Toward the Essence of Nonconsequentialism" (eventually published in *Fact and Value: Essays on Ethics and Metaphysics for Judith Jarvis Thomson*, ed. Alex Byrne, Robert C. Stalnaker, and Ralph Wedgwood, pp. 155–182 (Cambridge, MA: MIT Press, 2001). (Subsequent to the publication of the article version of this chapter, I expanded on and modified the theory in F. M. Kamm, *Intricate Ethics: Rights, Responsibilities, and Permissible Harm* [New York: Oxford University Press, 2007], chap. 5).

6. On this, see "Toward the Essence of Nonconsequentialism" and *Intricate Ethics*.

7. The one person is typically envisioned as on a side track, but this is not necessary. He could be in another part of the country and redirection of the trolley that leads to his being hit would still be permissible, I think.

8. I thank John Gibbons for his suggestion that there are two descriptions of the same event and that they are noncausally related to a state of affairs.

9. The analysis I have provided of the Trolley Case shows that diverting a trolley headed to the five is in some ways similar to deciding to turn a trolley at a crossroads to one rather than five, when the trolley must be turned somehow.

10. For such a suggestion about civilian status, see chapter 3, "Failures of Just War Theory."

11. This, I believe, is the standard way in which the DDE is presented. Different philosophers, without drawing attention to what they are doing, have described the DDE differently with respect to whether we are to intend the greater good. The traditional rendition requires aiming at a good greater than the evil side effect (not just any good). Here are three sample renditions: (1) "The agent acts with a good intention and seeks to realize a good end . . . the good end that the agent seeks to realize is not morally disproportionate to the bad consequence" (Nancy Davis, in "The Doctrine of Double Effect: Problems of Interpretation,"

reprinted in *Ethics: Problems and Principles*, ed. J. Fischer and M. Ravizza [Fort Worth: Harcourt Brace Jovanovich, 1992], p. 201); (2) "(a) the intended final end must be good . . . and (d) the good end must be proportionate to the bad upshot" (Warren Quinn, in "Actions, Intentions, and Consequences: The Doctrine of Double Effect," p. 175); and (3) "the good effect is the intended effect" (Baruch Brody, "Religion and Bioethics," in *A Companion to Bioethics*, ed. H. Kuhse and P. Singer [Oxford: Blackwell, 1998], p. 44). In (3), Brody is pointing to the fact that the foreseen/intended distinction in the DDE's account of permissibility is meant to distinguish the two effects—one good, which is intended, the other bad, which is foreseen. If this is the correct way of understanding the "double effect" point of the DDE, then the doctrine does not so much distinguish intending a bad effect from foreseeing a bad effect as it distinguishes intending a good effect from foreseeing a bad one. If this is so, and the good must be proportionate to the bad, this implies that we must intend a good greater than the evil. One account of the DDE that does not point to an intended greater good says that conditions to be met in order to permissibly produce a bad effect include "(1) one's action also had a good effect . . . and (4) the good effect was important enough to outweigh the bad" (*Cambridge Dictionary of Philosophy*, ed. R. Audi [Cambridge: Cambridge University Press, 1995]). (This entry also requires that one "did not produce the good effect through the bad" in addition to "not seeking the bad effect as an end or means." However, the DDE may not require that the good that justifies the bad not come about through the bad, only that we not intend that it do so. For an example, see the Track Trolley Case in note 18, this chapter.) This version of the DDE, which I think is unrepresentative, says only that a greater good should occur; it is not necessary that we intend it. This account also does not state that our act is permissible only if we act because we expected there to be a greater good. For it is quite possible that we would have been willing to act even if a greater good would not have occurred. Yet according to this version of the DDE, this would not make our act impermissible if a greater good would in fact occur. Even if a nonstandard version of the DDE required that we expect a good effect great enough to outweigh the bad, this state of mind is not the same as acting because of that expectation. For we might act expecting a greater good and our act be permissible even if we would have acted without the expectation and so did not act because of it. This nonstandard account of the DDE represents it as what I call a non-state-of-mind principle. This may be the correct way to represent a principle concerning harm, but I do not think it captures the point of the DDE. I also made these points in "The Doctrine of Triple Effect and Why a Rational Agent Need Not Intend the Means to His End," in *Proceedings of the Aristotelian Society*, 2000, Supplement (74): 21–39. A revised version of that article appears as chapter 4 in *Intricate Ethics*.

12. I first discussed this case in *Morality, Mortality*, vol. 2.

13. I first described the Doctrine of Triple Effect in "The Doctrine of Triple Effect and Why a Rational Agent Need Not Intend the Means to His End" and subsequently in *Intricate Ethics*.

14. For subsequent discussion of multiple possible ways of achieving a good, see *Intricate Ethics*, chaps. 4 and 5.

15. I discussed the Two Factories Case in *Morality, Mortality*, vol. 2, and in *Intricate Ethics*. (Sometimes it is called the Two Plants Case.)

16. Strictly speaking, the structure of the flip side need not be equivalent in all respects to the structure of the final good. For example, suppose the final good involves fewer or more people saved than would be the case in the flip side. This is all right so long as both flip

side and ultimate good share a component of good (e.g., a certain number of particular people) that is greater than the lesser evil*.

17. As it turns out, in the Two Factories Case, the ultimate justifying good (both factories out) is identical to the structural equivalent. This is because no further problems for the factories being out of commission are produced by what we do. But this fact, that our blowing up one factory can lead by a causal chain to the justifying good, does not mean that we have an initial sufficient justification for blowing up the first factory, for we lack even the structural equivalent without evil* (the deaths of bystanders) causing some further effect.

18. The DIJ is put in terms of the *possibility* of the initial sufficient justification to take account of cases where evil* is not actually initially sufficiently justified but it could have been. For example, consider the Track Trolley Case (owed to Keith DeRose). If we press a switch, it will turn a trolley away from five and toward one on a side track when the trolley gets to a cross-point. But pressing this switch also moves that side track with one person on it into the path of the trolley before the trolley gets to the cross-point. Hence, it is the person being hit that actually causes the trolley to stop. But it is not required that this happen in order to stop the trolley, as our pressing the switch would result in the trolley taking the other route later, and this other route satisfies the DIJ. I believe turning in Track Trolley is permissible. Here is a wartime case: We fire a flame missile toward a factory whose destruction would cause side-effect civilian deaths. We foresee, however, that civilians will notice and run in front of the missile, and their being set on fire is what will actually set the factory on fire (Civilians Aflame Case). The DIJ implies that it is permissible to fire the missile in this case because we do not require the civilians' being hit as a means of destroying the factory; if they did not run to the missile, it would destroy the factory. (Notice that it is not being said that it is permissible to fire the missile because "we do not act with the intention of using the civilians." The DIJ does not involve a state-of-mind principle. Suppose someone did fire the missile with the intention of using the civilians. The way in which their causal involvement comes about makes it as permissible for such an agent to act as for someone who did not intend the use of the civilians. For more on the DIJ and modifications to it, see *Intricate Ethics*.

3

Failures of Just War Theory

This chapter has three parts. In the first part, I shall try to provide an overview of issues related to both terror killing and nonterror killing inside and outside of standard war. It provides a framework within which we can locate some issues that will be explored in more detail in subsequent parts. The second part deals with the Doctrine of Double Effect (DDE) in standard just war theory. I criticize its prohibition on intending harm and consider cases where it is, for example, permissible to bomb combatants and noncombatants for purposes of terror. Through a different criticism of the DDE, as a way of helping to justify unintended noncombatant deaths, I am led in the third part to focus (a) on the relative degrees of inviolability of various types of people in intergroup conflict and (b) on a different justification for the permissibility of causing some types of foreseen noncombatant deaths.

I. Overview: Goals, Agents, and Means in Just War Theory

Standardly, discussion of terror and justice has occurred in connection with whether terror bombing is a just means by which to pursue a war, even one initiated in accordance with justice. That is, in standard just war theory, a distinction is drawn between *jus ad bellum* (whether the war is, in principle, justified) and *jus in bello* (whether the means used to carry it out are justified). Just war theory is deontological insofar as not every means is justified in the pursuit of just goals. Standardly, terror killing of noncombatants (TKN), which involves intentionally killing them in order to produce fear that will lead to surrender, is ruled out as a means in fighting a just war. Use of it will, it is said, make the war unjust even if it would be just when pursued by appropriate means.

However, suppose that those engaged in a just war of self-defense kill noncombatant, retired leaders of the enemy country, who previously unjustly started the war. This is done in order to frighten the enemy into surrendering.[1] Is such TKN permitted? I believe it is, and so it is a counterexample to the impermissibility of TKN.

Jus in bello theory further distinguishes how we may treat combatants from how we may treat noncombatants. This is referred to as the Principle of Discrimination. Hence, it remains possible that even standard *jus in bello* permits terror killing of combatants even though it rules out TKN. For example, would it have been permissible to drop an atomic bomb on Japanese soldiers in World War II to terrorize Japan?

Such issues are not what the topic of terror and justice is likely to call to mind since September 11, 2001, in part because the 9/11 terror did not occur during a standard, declared war between nation-states. Still, the focus in objecting to 9/11 remains the deliberate killing of noncombatants as a means to some end. Assuming this is an accurate characterization of what happened, we can also ask whether TKN on 9/11 would have been unjust as a means even if it had been used to pursue a just goal outside standard war.[2]

A short answer to this question is that a goal could be just and yet terror be an unjust means to achieve it simply because not all just goals are important enough or of the right type to justify killings, let alone terror killing. The *jus ad bellum* doctrine about standard war between nations deals in part with the issue of what injustices may be corrected by killing even carried out in ways typically permitted by *jus in bello*. And so, outside of standard war between nation-states, we must also consider whether an injustice is severe enough or of the correct type to merit being corrected by killing, whether terror killing or not, whether of noncombatants or of combatants.

For purposes of this discussion, let us suppose that even outside of standard war, the only injustices that could merit any sort of killing are the same as or analogous to those that would make standard war between nation-states permissible. In *jus ad bellum*, just cause for nation-states has gradually become limited to defense against an actual or imminent unjust attack on one's own nation or on another nation, with a possible further just cause being intervention to stop genocide perpetrated by a government against its own citizens.

Why cannot groups that form nations but lack a state satisfy the sufficient just cause criterion in the same way that nations that have states can? Furthermore, cannot groups that are not nations but are subject to genocide have the same just cause in defending themselves that others can have in defending them? And if a nation would have just cause in defending itself against the abrogation of many important rights by an aggressor who will use only powerful tranquilizers on them, why may not a group that is not a nation but is deprived of the same rights by an aggressor armed merely with such tranquilizers also have a just cause in defending itself by killing?[3]

Those who engage in killing outside of standard war between nation-states without a sufficient just cause fail a minimum standard analogous to a component of *jus ad bellum*. But meeting this minimum standard does not necessarily mean that members of the group may act as a state may act if it meets this standard. After all, those who fight on behalf of the group may officially represent no one but themselves. Why should they have the same rights to defend a population as states that have some claim to be the legitimate representative of people? Perhaps this failure to be a legitimate representative is sufficient to rule out the permissibility of killing in any way even for a sufficient just cause. Perhaps it is this failure to be a legitimate authority that makes the use of terror (which might be undertaken, rightly or wrongly, by a legitimate state) into the act of only a terrorist?

However, I find it hard to believe that members of a nonstate group could never legitimately represent and permissibly act for the sake of people who suffer sufficient injustice. For example, it is possible that some nonstates, such as the French underground in World War II, meet the requirements of being morally if not legally legitimate representative agents, and so it is possible that they could permissibly correct sufficient injustices by some form of killing. I also find it hard to believe that no *non*representative agent—a mere onlooker—could not sometimes have moral legitimacy in acting in a warlike manner. For example, suppose some sympathetic white individuals had begun killing slaveholders as a last resort had the North not fought the American Civil War. Their acts might have been permissible.

Standard just war theory typically assumes that means other than TKN are available with which to pursue a just war even if the war will then not be pursued as efficiently. Some states or nonstates that have a sufficient just cause to kill, however, may not have access to means of war aside from terror killing. Of course, they may have access to nonviolent protest.[4] But let us assume that this is not true or that the protest is sure to be ineffective. As an aid in considering whether nonstates—with a sufficient cause to kill and a valid claim to be (morally) legitimate agents—may resort to terror killing, we might consider whether a state that no longer had any other means of pursuing a sufficient just cause could permissibly resort to terror killing. It will also help to consider whether, if they lack the means to terror-kill combatants, they may then terror-kill noncombatants.

In considering these questions, we should keep in mind that if it were ever permissible to terror-kill,[5] it might be permissible for one side in a conflict to use terror but impermissible for the other side to use it. This could be because one side may have no other means by which to pursue a goal that would justify terror against combatants or noncombatants, while the other side either has alternative, morally preferable means or does not have a goal whose achievement justifies the use of terror.

But even when one side has other means by which to wage the war, it too might be permitted to use terror if there were a discount ratio between terror and nonterror deaths. For example, suppose there were a 1,000:1 ratio between combatant nonterror and combatant terror deaths. Then terror killings would not be prohibited but only have greater negative value relative to nonterror deaths. Hence, it might be permissible to avoid a thousand nonterror combatant deaths by terror killing one combatant (who would not otherwise have been killed). Furthermore, it would violate a certain sort of *requirement of proportionality* to kill 1,001 combatants without terror rather than terror-kill one other combatant.

So far, this overview of considerations gives rise to the following checklist (or decision tree, if used by the agent himself) in figure 3.1. This checklist is tentative and preliminary to further discussion. It assumes the necessity of using some harmful means, the likelihood of success of using the means, and the proportionality of collateral and noncollateral harm to achieving a goal.

Finally, I will assume throughout that the means employed would be necessary and useful in bringing about a just cause. This is because standard just war theory holds that a just cause is insufficient to justify the use of harmful means that are neither necessary nor useful to achieve the just cause. While I make the assumption of efficacy, I do not agree that it is required. For suppose a single guilty aggressor is attacking you and nothing you do will stop him and you know this. Is it not still permissible to resist what he is doing while he is attacking (so long as harm to him is proportional to his attack) even if this has no further good consequences for anyone? I believe so.[6]

II. War and General Moral Principles[7]

Now let us assume for purposes of argument that an agent has passed the sufficient just cause and morally legitimate agent points on the checklist in figure 3.1. He may use means other than TKN, and we must decide on the permissibility of his using TKN. In this section, I will consider an explanation common in standard just war theory for why TKN is impermissible in war and contrast it with types of killing in war that this theory has considered permissible. I will argue that the explanation fails, for it implies that (a) what is permissible is impermissible and (b) what is impermissible is permissible; hence, it cannot account for the distinction in the permissibility of different acts.[8]

The DDE is standardly appealed to in order to explain why TKN is impermissible even as a means to a greater good.[9] One traditional interpretation of the DDE says that it is absolutely impermissible to act or refrain from action intending an evil even as a means to a greater good.[10] It also says that it might be permissible to pursue a greater good by neutral or good means even if one will cause an evil as a certain and foreseen side effect as long as the evil is less than (or, more generally, proportional to) the good to be achieved and there is no better way to achieve the good.[11] (Note that one may foresee that one's act will lead another agent to do something that causes a harm greater than the good that one's act will produce. This is not considered harm that one has caused and so the DDE need not take it to always interfere with the permissibility of one's act. However, the DDE applies to omissions as well as to actions, and if one fails to act, intending to allow another agent to cause harm, it seems that his harm will count against one's omission. I shall be focusing on the cases in which one's act causes a bad effect without an intervening agent.)

Hence, according to the DDE, bombing a munitions plant to get rid of munitions (called "strategic bombing"), foreseeing that it will certainly kill some children as a side effect, may be permissible, but intentionally killing an even smaller

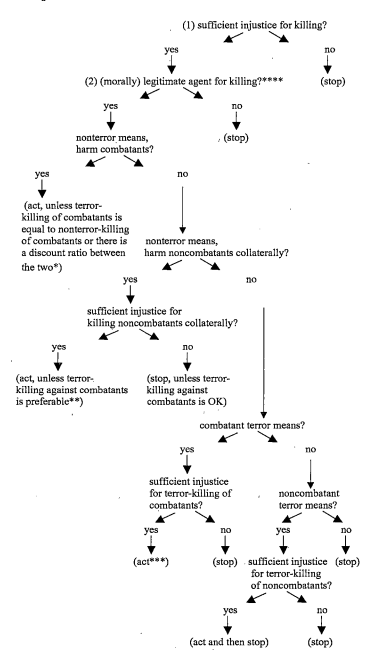

FIGURE 3.1

Legend: *As will be argued later, we might add "or there is a discount ratio between combatant and noncombatant deaths." **As will be argued later, we might add "or there is a discount ratio between nonterror-killing of noncombatants and terror-killing of noncombatants." *** As will be argued later, we might add "unless there is a discount ratio between terror-killing of combatants and terror-killing of noncombatants." ****Perhaps we should ask: Legitimate agent for each type of killing of each type of victim? If so, I am simplifying.

number of different children in order to terrorize the community into surrendering is impermissible. However, not all acts that meet the standards of the DDE need be permissible. It provides a necessary rather than a sufficient condition for permissibility. It is just that when its conditions are met, the reason an act is impermissible cannot be that the means to a greater good causes the lesser evil as a side effect.

It is important to keep in mind that a terror bomber of noncombatants is not necessarily someone who directly hits the noncombatants. For suppose that a terror bomber does not have enough fuel to get directly over the children. However, he knows that if he directly bombs an empty building that he can reach, its blowing up will certainly kill the children as a side effect. He hits the building only as a means of killing the children, which in turn is a means to ending the war through terror in the populace. This also qualifies as terror bombing. Notice also that there should really be two morally problematic aspects to terror killing from the perspective of the DDE. The first is that the individual who is intentionally killed as a means of producing terror is treated impermissibly. The second is that those who are intentionally terrorized as a means to ending war but are not otherwise harmed are treated impermissibly—for being terrorized is also an evil.

The DDE as presented depends on a conceptual distinction between intending X and foreseeing that X will certainly thereby come about (or, more narrowly, be caused by what we do). I think there is such a conceptual distinction; the question is whether it has moral relevance. What is known as the Counterfactual Test is commonly thought to isolate the conceptual distinction. It says the following: Suppose that, counterfactually, an evil would not occur if you acted but all else remained the same; would you, as a rational agent, have a reason not to act? It is said that the agent who intends the evil at least has some reason not to act, but an agent who merely foresees the evil would have no reason not to act.

It is important to realize that the DDE's prohibition on intending evil does not necessarily lead to minimizing harm to noncombatants since fewer noncombatants might be killed in terror bombing that brought a war quickly to its end than as collateral damage in a lengthy war. Rather, some argue, the point of the prohibition is to respect the dignity of the person. For example, Warren Quinn offered an explanation of the attempt to distinguish morally between intending evil and acting with mere foresight of its certain occurrence.[12] The former, he said, was objectionable when it involved treating other people as available to be used for our profit; it involved treating people as mere means in an objectionable sense. The latter involved not being willing to constrain the pursuit of our goals by legitimate means simply because of the harm to others that would result. It could involve objectionably failing to treat people as ends in themselves by not taking seriously enough their interests as constraints on pursuing our goals. Objectionably treating as a mere means involves not treating as an end, but not necessarily vice versa. Quinn thought that treatment as a mere means adds an additional morally objectionable element to merely acting despite harm to others, holding constant harm done in the two cases.

The DDE's other requirement that evil must be proportional to good does serve to limit noncombatant harm. This is because one is not permitted to achieve a good whatever the cost to noncombatants. But it must be combined with a general preference for killing combatants rather than noncombatants in order to achieve the fullest permissible reduction in noncombatant deaths. (This assumes that minimizing noncombatant deaths by terror killing some of them is impermissible.) For example, Michael Walzer argues that it is not enough for *jus in bello* that we not intend to kill noncombatants; we must also intend not to kill noncombatants (admittedly, without giving up war to do so).[13] That implies that even if we would kill noncombatants only as a side effect proportional to the good of our goal, we could be obligated to instead achieve our goal by doing what harms a greater number of combatants. This may include causing more deaths among one's own combatants, not merely those of the opposing side. (Walzer's view may just be another way of meeting the DDE's requirement that if a means that causes [dispreferred] harm is not necessary to achieve the good, we should use other means which cause less [or preferred] harm).

Walzer goes so far as to say that the DDE would not be defensible if it did not itself include this addendum.[14] This implies that he does not think that the distinction between TKN and strategic bombing (which kills noncombatants as a side effect) all by itself is morally important. But this position would imply favoring TKN that reduces noncombatant deaths and terror killing of combatants that reduces combatant or noncombatant deaths. This follows from rejecting the moral significance of intended versus merely foreseen deaths per se.

I have discussed the DDE and the Counterfactual Test elsewhere in more detail.[15] Here I will describe only a few problems with the DDE relevant to terror killing and side-effect deaths in just war theory.

A. WHEN THE DDE PROHIBITS THE PERMISSIBLE

1. *Attacking Threats in Order to Terrorize Others*

The first problem with the traditional DDE per se is its claim to be absolute, never overridable (though not all those who use the DDE in just war theory treat it as absolute). If intending evil were never permissible, one could not intend even in self-defense the death or terrorizing of a guilty aggressor, nor could one intend in self-defense the death of a morally innocent person who has been made into a fatal threat to oneself (e.g., a human missile). But intending an aggressor's death in ordinary self-defense often seems permissible. For example, adopting any criterion of death one thinks is correct, assume that you would have to repeatedly aim at the death of a malicious aggressor who will kill you unless he is dead. Intending his death seems permissible. Is terror killing also permissible sometimes? Suppose many combatants will shortly come at you with deadly force. Perhaps they would rather not be doing this, but they are under government orders (so they are *not* malicious aggressors). It would be permissible, I believe, for you to stop them if you can even by intentionally killing them. However, you have insufficient force to stop them all, and you would certainly be killed by those who remain. The only way to save your life is to kill one of the combatants at the back of the force (who might not otherwise have died). This helps because other soldiers at the back, as well as others in the surrounding population, ignorant of your true weakness, will believe that you can reach them. They will be terrorized into calling off the attack. (Notice that the surrounding population could have the power to call off the attack even if they did not originally order it.) Presumably one can defend oneself by doing this even though it involves killing a combatant in order to terrorize other combatants and noncombatants. Presumably, you could also defend the life of someone else who is similarly under attack by doing the same thing.

This case (call it the Distant Combatant Case) shows that killing in self- or other-defense and terror killing are not mutually exclusive. There can be cases in which one terror-kills in self- or other-defense, and this can be as permissible as ordinary self- or other-defense. It also shows that sometimes a soldier whose aggressive attempts would not have actually caused harm—as his comrades in front would have killed you before he ever could—can be used as a mere means to self- or other-defense.

Should there be a prohibition on terror killing persons who present threats when their being terror-killed would not stop the threat they themselves present but would otherwise be very useful? Or are the members of the force in my previous example liable to be used by me to end the war or win another battle just because they try to attack someone on my side in some way? To consider the latter possibility, imagine that nothing I do can stop the front members of the force from killing me. Nor does an attack on them prevent this force itself from threatening others in the future, as (I know) they will be retired from service subsequent to this attack and present no further threat to anyone. Before I die, may I kill a soldier at the back who will not otherwise die in battle if this will terrorize the surrounding population into stopping the war? I think it would be permissible to do this.

Might doing this be justified as follows? The reason I am under attack is that I am a member of a warring army, so an attack on me can be considered an attack on all members of the army. This might allow me to terror-kill a distant member of the force to save other members of my army from other enemy combatants who would attack them, assuming I could have terror-killed such a distant member in order to save myself or another person also under attack by the force, of which the distant member is a part. On this view, all attacking soldiers are, in general, susceptible to being permissibly killed for the general purpose of winning a war. Here is another possible justification. Suppose it is permissible for someone who will not be able to defend himself against an enemy's attack to uselessly kill, in hopeless resistance, those attacking him. (This is a rejection of the view that an attack on an aggressor must have some chance of defending the potential victim.) Then, in my example, I may permissibly kill members of the attacking force even if I would not take advantage of my moral option to kill if their deaths did not help to stop the war. For in this case, I kill the distant soldier who would not otherwise have been killed because I take advantage of a permission and capacity to resist him now in order to pursue a separate goal (ending the war) even if pursuing this goal did not itself give rise to the permission.[16] I do what I am permitted to do (hopelessly resist) for a reason that does not itself give rise to the permission.

This second justification would succeed if the force were composed of malicious aggressors, I believe. But suppose the force is composed of conscripted soldiers who might be construed as morally innocent threats.[17] Put to one side the view that one may harm any attacking soldiers for the general purpose of stopping the war. Is one permitted to kill conscripted, attacking, nonmalicious soldiers if this would be useless in stopping their attack? If not, there would be no right to kill that one could make use of in order to end the war merely by terror killing.

Now suppose that I am permitted to successfully defend myself against the conscripted attackers by killing the soldier at the back of the force. However, supererogatorily, I choose not to do so, as I do not want to kill a young conscripted soldier just to save my life. Then I learn that killing him would terrorize the surrounding population into surrendering, thus ending the war. Suppose it is not permissible, in general, to terror-kill attacking soldiers in order to end a war by means other than stopping their own attack. Nevertheless, because I could permissibly kill this soldier to save myself (or another person under his attack), I believe that I may exercise my option to kill him, when killing him will save me (or another) from his attack, for the separate goal of stopping the war by the terror resulting from his being killed.

In justifying terror killing in war in some of these cases, I have made use of the following idea: If the factors that would make my act permissible are objectively present (e.g., the act of killing an attacker can be permissible if it would save my life from the attack and it will save my life), then the act remains permissible if I do it for another reason (e.g., not to save my life but to terror-kill someone to stop the war). This is so even if I would not have done the act for the sake of the factor that makes it permissible (e.g., merely to save my life). Call this the Principle of Alternate Reason. In the cases I have given, the alternate reason concerns a good (i.e., ending the war) greater than the original good that made the act permissible. But in relying on the Principle of Alternate Reason, I am supposing that the greater good does not justify the act in the way that the lesser good does. Arguably, the act would remain permissible even if I acted only for a bad reason (e.g., I kill the soldier when doing so saves my life only because the soldier is short and I intend to eliminate short people). I would not have killed the young soldier to save my life had he not been short.

If the act remains permissible despite the reason given for it, it might still be that someone acts badly in doing the act for an alternate reason. Would this be true, however, if I kill the soldier when it will save my life but only in order to stop the war by terrorizing other combatants or even the civilian population? I do not think so. (Consider a domestic analogy. Suppose my apartment landlord is obligated to provide me with a parking space at cost to him. He need not incur costs so that tenants in other landlords' buildings have parking spaces. Suppose further that I was going to pass on using the parking space until I learn that if I take it, other landlords in the community will be influenced to provide parking spaces for their tenants. If I use the space for this good cause, I think I not only act permissibly but also do not act badly toward my landlord. Nor do I show that I am a bad person in parking for this alternate reason. This is true even though we could not justify costs to him just in order to help other landlords' tenants per se.[18])

2. Attacking Nonthreats

Perhaps it is easier to accept that the DDE is absolute if it applies only when one is intending serious physical harm to persons who are not threats or parts of threats (e.g., shields) even when they are technically combatants. (We have already considered intending the evil of terror to the civilian population in the Distant Combatant Cases.) Consider a case of sleeping Japanese combatants in World War II who are retiring from active service. Suppose we would be permitted to kill attacking Japanese combatants even if only to eliminate their potential for future attacks. Then we may, I believe, choose to exercise that option even if we would not otherwise do so in order to use these attacking combatants to create terror that will end the war. But the sleeping Japanese soldiers are not future threats. It is only if the status of soldier or formerly attacking soldier somehow made one liable to being used in any way necessary to help stop a war that it would be permitted to terror-kill these soldiers.[19]

Suppose, however, that there are people who are not now and will not in the future be combatants, yet due to current or previous acts carried out because of conscientious commitment to a cause, they are responsible for a current unjust war. Could they be terror-killed to stop the war? I have already said that I think this is permissible when they are former leaders. It may be permissible because someone who has acted sufficiently unjustly may be used to save his victims or potential victims. This case would show that noncombatants as well as combatants may be killed, contrary to the Principle of Discrimination. Consider a nonwar example along the same lines but involving a former attacker: Suppose A deliberately takes B's crucial organs. A is captured and is no longer a threat. However, the only way to save B is to transplant A's organs into B. I think doing so may be permissible.

Now consider a case in which the serious harm intended to a noncombatant would prevent an even greater harm to him. For example, suppose it is impermissible to intentionally paralyze A's legs as a means of ending a war by terrorizing others. It could still be permissible to do this as the alternative to permissibly killing A as a mere side effect. This is, in part, because it is much better for him to be paralyzed in a terror bombing than to be nonterror-killed. This is an instance of what I call the Principle of Secondary Permissibility.[20] It sometimes allows us to do an act that would not have been permitted in the first place when the act becomes the alternative, of all those that could reasonably be done, that minimizes harm that would otherwise permissibly be done to the same person. (The minimization condition rules out a somewhat less harmful act than would have been done even if it is not the least harmful one.) Indeed the least harmful act may become the only permissible harmful act. This principle implies that sometimes we need to know the alternative that would have permissibly been done before we can decide whether an act of a certain type is permissible. (Notice that this principle, unlike a general consequentialist justification, does not imply that if the consequences will be the same [or better], it does not matter how we bring about these consequences. For this principle does not claim that if it would be permissible to kill someone as a side effect, then it would also be permissible to paralyze him intentionally *even when we are not actually going to kill him*.)[21]

Consider another case in which intentionally seriously harming a noncombatant seems permissible. Suppose it would be permissible for us to produce a great good by innocent means despite the foreseen evil side effect of killing nonthreatening noncombatants Joe and Jim. There is an alternative, however: We could bring about the great good by intentionally killing Joe as a means and without harming Jim. I believe it is even permissible to kill Joe as a means, in part because he will be no worse off than he would otherwise permissibly have been made by us, and Jim will be much better off.[22] What if those who would die shortly anyway would not die as a result of a permissible act done by us or others, but of an impermissible act done by others? For example, during World War II, the Allies were asked to bomb trains carrying people to Nazi extermination camps. If it were certain that these people would soon die of wrongful Nazi acts and if our killing them would have been a means to saving others or ending the war (perhaps through terror produced), it would have been permissible to do so, I believe. These cases imply that, in order to achieve a just cause in war, when combatants or noncombatants will be no worse off than they would otherwise have been, it is sometimes permissible to kill them as means even to terror.

May bystanders who have never been and never will be threats be terror-killed in war when they will be made much worse off than they otherwise will be? Suppose that we have the capacity to permissibly bomb a munitions plant to achieve a great good despite foreseen deaths as side effects, but we choose not to take advantage of this option because we do not want to cause the deaths. Then we find out that we could achieve the same great good if we terror-kill one of the people whom we could permissibly kill as a side effect of bombing the munitions plant. He is one of those whom we have the capacity to and, I argued earlier, may permissibly terror-kill as the alternative to causing his and many more deaths as a mere side effect. Why should the fact that we decide not to exercise our option to do what will kill many people (including him) as a side effect stand in the way of our terror-bombing him? The only reason he will be worse off if we terror-bomb than he would otherwise have been is that we refrain from doing what it is both permissible and within our current capacity to do. If terror bombing in this case were permissible, it would require extending the Principle of Secondary Permissibility. This is because the permission to act does not depend on considering what we *would* otherwise permissibly do. It depends on considering what we can (in the sense of being within our capacity) permissibly otherwise do. So there may be an Extended Principle of Secondary Permissibility.

What if it would be permissible to bomb a munitions plant and cause non-combatant deaths as side effects but we have no capacity to do this (e.g., soldiers in the plant would shoot down our planes before we could bomb)? Would it be permissible to terror-bomb one of the bystanders if this achieved the same good result as our bombing the plant? In this case we do not merely refrain from doing what we have the physical capacity to permissibly do. Rather, we actually cannot do what we may permissibly do. This marks a moral difference. A reason to deny the permissibility of terror bombing the one person is that if we terror-bomb, he will be worse off than there was any possibility of his being in the absence of terror bombing. (Suppose someone else has the capacity to permissibly do what would kill the bystander but chooses not to do this. Does this give us license to do something harmful to the bystander where we lacked the physical capacity to do what it would have been permissible for us to do? I do not think so.)

Now consider a case in which we have the capacity to and are permitted to bomb a munitions plant, killing innocents as a side effect, in order to win a few battles where the opponent will lack munitions. We supererogatorily decide not to cause so many noncombatant deaths just for the sake of this goal. Then we find out that, if we do bomb the factory to get rid of the munitions, our causing deaths as a side effect will terrorize people into surrendering.[23] Hence, we bomb the factory and cause the deaths in order to use terror to achieve an even better goal, total surrender. Winning a few battles due to lack of enemy ammunition remains a possible step to winning the war if the terror does not occur. However, we know that the terror will cause the war to end sooner. In this case, we do the same act with the same side effects that we can permissibly do for one reason for another, terror-related, reason. This is still, I think, a permissible act even if no other act undertaken to produce surrender by terror would be permissible. It is a further instance of the Principle of Alternate Reason. However, in this case we know that the terror will prevent the further effect that justifies our act (winning battles) because people surrender first. Still, we should not be prevented from doing what could permissibly be our way to win a war (bomb munitions with side-effect deaths so as to win battles) just because we know that terror caused by side-effect deaths will end the war even sooner.[24] And, if we may bomb the munitions factory in these circumstances, doing so with the intention of producing the terror will not make the act impermissible, I think. (This is another case that casts doubt on the DDE claim that intending an evil makes an act impermissible.)[25]

Alternatively, imagine again that we supererogatorily decide not to cause so many side-effect deaths by bombing a munitions plant just for the sake of winning a few battles. Then we find out that if we terror-kill (by a means other than bombing the factory) just one of the noncombatants who would die as a side effect if we bombed the plant, we can achieve surrender. I believe it may be permissible to terror-kill in this case. (This is true even if we would not have been capable of achieving the surrender through a terrified response to the bombing we could permissibly have done. This might be because the populace would have been so angered at the blowing up of the munitions plant that they would not have succumbed to their terror at the side-effect deaths.) This is a case in which *both* our reason for acting and our act are different from what they permissibly could be initially; hence, it involves both the Principle of Alternate Reason and the Extended Principle of Secondary Permissibility.

In these cases, where we supererogatorily refrain from bombing to win some battles, the bystanders will be made worse off if we kill in order to produce terror than they would otherwise have been but only because we are more selective in choosing our goals and/or in causing deaths than we are morally permitted to be. Hence, it seems to me that it is permissible to terror-kill noncombatants in these cases. The fact that we are capable of permissibly causing the deaths (as side effects) for one goal can make it permissible to terror-kill (at minimum) for another goal if it would also be permissible to achieve that second goal when the deaths are side effects even if we lack the capacity to actually achieve the second goal when deaths are side effects.

3. *Causing Terror on Its Own*

Could the objection be raised against these examples that even if it were permissible sometimes to kill combatants and noncombatants to stop attacks or to end a war, it would still be impermissible to try to produce terror per se to stop attacks or end a war? For, it may be said, the DDE as an objection to terror killing does not sufficiently focus on the distinction between causing terror and causing harm, whether the terror is intended or merely foreseen. It might be said that terror killing is morally much worse than other forms of intentional killing because of the terror per se. Is terror even worse than death?

On one understanding of terror, it is fear of harm (to oneself or others) that can serve as a reason for prudence or altruism to end a war.[26] However, even if such fear is widespread,[27] it may be morally wrong to aggregate the fear of each and then claim that this huge amount of aggregated fear is a greater evil than the great loss suffered by an individual who is killed. After all, no one of the many who are terrorized suffers a loss as great as a person who is killed. On a second understanding of terror, it is a form of panic that undermines rational judgment and agency, and individuals surrender once their judgment is undermined, not through an exercise of judgment. It is this undermining of rational agency that, it might be said, makes terror morally worse than death. Further, such panic is associated with unpredictable killings of unpredictable targets and thus the undermining of order, which is necessary for civil society. But even if the second understanding of terror better accounts for its evil, are the panic and disorder really greater evils than the deaths of those killed? I do not think so. And if I have a choice between killing someone or terrorizing many without any death, I think I should often choose the latter.

However, even if being terrorized is less of an evil than death, it might be said that noncombatants do not have the characteristics that make it permissible to intentionally terrorize them even as a mere means to some other goal. The DDE could then be used to prohibit terror killing A in some cases on the grounds that killing A would be used to evoke terror in noncombatant B and it is wrong to act intending the lesser evil of terror to B. To argue in this way would, I believe, reveal another problem with the DDE. For, I believe, the big moral obstacle to terror killing is justifying the killing rather than justifying even the intentional production of terror in noncombatants per se. To support this claim, imagine that we find out that noncombatants on the unjust side, whom we could not permissibly harm in any other way, will experience terror leading to the country's surrender if we bomb some trees (not people). This is because they are irrational and worship the trees. If we bomb the trees, intending to terrorize these people as a means to ending the war, moral objections to terror bombing should be significantly reduced. Alternatively, suppose the people are rational. In destroying trees, we intend to convey that we have a powerful new weapon because we know the people will see this as raising the possibility that the weapon will be used on them; hence, they will be terrorized into surrendering. We actually have either no such weapon or no intention of using it on people. Could bombing the trees for purposes of terrorizing be permissible in order to stop a war, especially as the alternative to doing what will cause much noncombatant collateral harm? I believe it could be.[28]

4. The Absoluteness of a Narrowed DDE

Now consider the DDE's prohibition of intending evil when it is narrowed to intending the particular evil of death (not terror alone) to noncombatants who have never been and will never be threats and who cannot but be made overall much worse off by the evil than they would have been or than we are capable of permissibly making them. (It is only this sort of evil that I shall consider as the means to terror henceforth. It is also what I shall take to be represented by the last option in figure 3.1.) Is the prohibition now absolute? Let us suppose that the bombing of Hiroshima is a case of intentionally killing many noncombatants that fulfills this condition of a narrowed prohibition. John Rawls, in an article attacking the morality of the United States' bombing of Hiroshima, also claims that such a type of bombing could be morally permissible in some circumstances. For example, Rawls believes that if Britain had stood alone against the Nazis in World War II and was about to lose the war, and if such an attack on German noncombatants alone would have prevented the Nazi victory, it would have been permissible.[29] These are very high standards to meet, but if they do make terror bombing of noncombatants justifiable, then even a narrowed prohibition based on the DDE is not absolute.

I have mentioned Quinn's view that treatment of another as a mere means adds an additional objectionable element to conduct when we thereby treat people as available for our profit. But this element, on his view, does not make action absolutely wrong; it merely raises the bar for what will justify engaging in it. Hence, it seems to me that his view implies that it could be wrong to bring about many deaths in a group as a foreseen side effect when one could instead cause far fewer deaths in a different group by treating them as a mere opportunistic means, for example, in terror bombing.

Rawls and Quinn are examples of "threshold deontologists," who claim that avoiding some great cost beyond a threshold can override the deontological constraints. Rawls, as we have seen, considers a hypothetical case in which terror bombing is the only means to a just cause that is sufficiently important. By contrast, I have suggested that Quinn's approach to the DDE would permit overriding it even if there is an alternative way to achieve the just cause that has only side-effect deaths. So, in his reasoning, the cost that goes beyond the threshold is not necessarily only the defeat of one's just cause. The cost that goes beyond the threshold can also be the difference in the cost to human life of several possible courses of action. For example, the difference in cost between course 1 and course 2 might be too great to merit staying with course 1. This could be true even though it would be permissible to use course 1 if course 2 were unavailable. The point is that avoiding the difference in cost between the courses of action could itself be a goal that is sufficient to override the DDE constraint. Suppose for the sake of argument that it would be permissible for us to terror-bomb some hundreds of noncombatants rather than do what will kill a million different noncombatants as a mere side effect. Suppose it would be permissible for us to do what kills the million as a side effect if this alone would stop the Nazis. Then it should be permissible for us to terror-bomb hundreds to stop the Nazis, at least as the alternative to our stopping the Nazis by doing what kills a million different people as a side effect.[30]

5. *Preliminary Conclusion*

My conclusion at this point is that terror killing, even TKN, is not necessarily wrong from a deontological point of view. (Note, however, that there are cases in which it is not wrong for someone to resist what I may permissibly do to him. This, I believe, is often a mark of the fact that I can wrong someone in the course of doing what it is not wrong of me to do, in particular in the course of overriding some constraint that ordinarily governs my behavior toward others.[31]) Furthermore, it is consistent with there being one set of rules of war for everyone that on occasion terror killing can be permissible for one side but not another, just as on occasion causing side-effect deaths can be permissible for one side but not another. This is because what one may permissibly do depends on whether one has weapons to achieve one's goal that need cause no deaths at all. For example, one side may have precision weapons to meet its goal without killing any noncombatants as a side effect while the other side has only more primitive weapons that would cause side-effect deaths proportional to its goal. If the second side may permissibly cause side-effect deaths for a goal, then it could also be permissible for it, I have argued, to terror-kill only a few of its potential victims instead for the same goal. For the side with more sophisticated weapons, the secondary permissibility of terror killing does not arise as it will not permissibly kill any as a side effect.

I have been considering only deontological arguments bearing on terror killing. It is still possible that, from a consequentialist perspective, terror killing is impermissible. This would be so if there were an uncontrollable slippery slope from permissible to impermissible instances of terror killing once the absolute prohibition is not in place. Even a nonconsequentialist who denies that consequences are all that matter in determining what is right but gives some role to consequences might endorse a slippery-slope argument against TKN. The argument might be put as follows: "Suppose that terror killing is sometimes permissible. We would have to engage in very careful reasoning to decide when it is and is not permissible. Will people really engage in this careful reasoning, or rather, once they see that terror killing is permissible sometimes, will they conclude that it is just another way of bringing about a good end, with no special reasons having to be offered for its use? This will lead to a slippery slope toward deontologically impermissible uses of terror killing. If these impermissible uses would be more significant than permissible uses, then we should not even permit those terror killings that would be, in and of themselves, deontologically permissible." This may be a good argument if we have empirical evidence for the slippery slope. I have just been concerned to show that we will have to move on to considering further consequences if we want to object morally to some selected instances of terror killing.

6. The Problem of Narrow Intention

Let us assume that there is no absolute moral prohibition on terror killing even noncombatants who are not, have never been and will never be threats and who cannot but be made overall much worse off in being killed than they would otherwise have been or than we are capable of permissibly making them. Our question will now be whether it is the DDE that explains the existence of even a nonabsolute prohibition on TKN of this sort. The first problem with claiming that it does is the Problem of Narrow Intention, emphasized by Jonathan Bennett.[32] He notes that there may be a terror bomber who can truthfully say that his intention is only to make the noncombatants appear dead (i.e., to make them lie on the ground quietly for a while) until the war is over, as the mere appearance of their death is enough to frighten the enemy into surrendering. He does not intend that the noncombatants be dead even as a means to their appearing dead; he just foresees that the only thing he can do to make them appear dead (bomb them, as he has no sleeping gas) will certainly also kill them. His certainty as to their death is no greater than the certainty of the person who foresees deaths as a side effect of bombing the munitions plant to destroy weapons. The DDE might then present no objection to his bombing the children in order to end the war even though it seems a clear case of TKN.

One approach to dealing with this problem, suggested by Quinn, is to reconceive what is the inappropriate object of intention. The DDE so revised (DDE[R]) would say that it is inappropriate not only to intend an evil but also to intend the involvement of noncombatants (to which I would add never-threatening noncombatants) without their consent when we foresee that this will result in evil to them (to which I would add, evil that makes them much worse off than they would otherwise be or than we are capable of permissibly making them). Let us call this joint object of intention "evil*." The terror bomber, but not the tactical bomber in the standard case, intends evil* because he intends to involve the people knowing that harm will come to them. In the standard case, the tactical bomber only foresees evil*.

7. Deriving Permissibility from Intention

The second problem with the nonabsolute, narrowed DDE (and also for the DDE[R]) is more general: We cannot, contrary to the DDE, derive the impermissibility of an act by considering the state of mind (broadly construed to include goals, motivations, and reasons) of the person doing the act. Consider a case suggested by Thomson.[33] Assume that tactical bombing is permissible only if the bombardier merely foresees evil* as a side effect and the evil* is proportional to the good to be achieved. Suppose that the bombardier who is selected to bomb the munitions plant in tactical bombing is someone who would not have taken the job unless he knew that the children would be killed by the bombs as a side effect. This is because it has always been a goal of his to kill some children, and he sees his dropping bombs as a means of achieving that goal, not as a means of destroying the plant. Does the fact that he intends the evil* (here as a final goal rather than a mere means to a goal) and would not go on the mission if the evil* did not occur imply that it is impermissible for him to drop the bombs that will destroy the munitions plant? Must we wait to bomb until we find a bombardier who does not intend that the children die either as a means or a goal? I think not. Thomson thinks, and I agree, that (at least in many cases) an act is permissible because of properties other than the intentions—or, as Kantians would put it, the maxim—of those who perform it. One may do an act for a bad reason, not for the sake of the properties that make the act permissible, but those properties still make it permissible. Hence, the DDE is incorrect because it would often declare as impermissible acts that are permissible.[34]

Consider two possible responses to this objection. First, could we not say that it is permissible to do an act (with a wrong intention) so long as it is the type of act that someone with a good intention could perform? This too is a way to derive permissibility from intention. But in deciding whether someone with a good intention could do the act, we consider the properties of the act (e.g., whether it leads to a good greater than the evil* and whether the evil* causes or is required to cause the good) on which a good agent might focus, other than the intention with which he would do it. So we move from these properties of the act *to* determining that a good intention with regard to the act is possible, not vice versa.

The second response to the objection tells us to focus not on the intention of the agent who does the act—a soldier who wants to kill children—but on the intentions of those who planned the attack or of the government who runs the war: A bombing, it is said, will be permissible if the intentions of those in control are not bad. But suppose that the nation and its generals are committed to killing children, though they act on this intention only when they have the cover of acting in a way that leads both to a just cause being accomplished and to children's deaths. They do not act in wars that do not result in children's deaths, and they drop bombs on military facilities only in order to enable the bombs to kill the children in the vicinity. Contrary to what the second response implies, it is not impermissible for such a nation—call it Baby Killer Nation—to act due to its bad intention, I think.

8. *An Alternative Explanation*

What may justify the view that there is a crucial distinction between TKN and tactical bombing is the presence of a different, non-state-of-mind, property that we shall now try to identify. The bombing of the munitions plant, even if it were unaccompanied by the deaths of the children, is expected to produce some good that (supposedly) is sufficient to justify bombing even when it also produces this lesser evil*. Whether achieving this good is the aim or only a pretext of a particular agent when he does what produces the good but also kills children is irrelevant to the permissibility of the conduct. If we conceive of standard TKN cases as only ones in which someone directly attacks noncombatants, aiming to hit them to produce a greater good, we will probably be imagining cases in which nothing but hitting the children occurs that can bring about a good greater than the evil* of the childrens' deaths.

In these cases, *evil* is necessary as a cause of the greater good*. By contrast, in the cases where blowing up the munitions is (or leads to) a greater good, a means (dropping bombs) that is neutral rather than evil*, considered independently of its effects, is a cause of the greater good. This difference in the causal structure required—not an agent's state of mind—may help account for the sense that there is a difference in moral permissibility of tactical bombing and terror bombing in standard cases. (However, later I shall argue that the difference is neither sufficient nor necessary to show that tactical bombing is permissible.)

In another type of case, I suppose the bombardier has a terror-bomber's intention to use the children's deaths as a means (or even seeks the death of the children as a final goal). However, the bombs he drops blow up a munitions plant, whose explosion, independently of the involvement of the children, is (or can cause) a good to which the deaths of the children caused is proportional. Then his act is as permissible (or impermissible) as the act of a tactical bomber without these bad intentions. Suppose the ordinary tactical bomber's act is permissible. Then the deaths of the children are already justified by the good that results from bombs falling on the munitions. If a particular bombardier also intends those deaths, he merely intends deaths whose existence is already justified. That cannot make them be unjustified. However, there could be terror-bombing cases in which the destruction of munitions could not itself produce a great good and in which the harm to the children (or their involvement leading to harm) is necessary to produce the great good. Suppose it is these sorts of cases that have typically been contrasted with tactical bombing cases, and it is assumed that an agent intends the means necessary to his end. This would explain the mistaken conclusion that it is the intention of the bomber that makes the moral difference.

In the immediately preceding discussion, I say that neutral means "*could* be a cause of greater good" or "evil* is *necessary* as a cause." I say this because sometimes even when evil* *is* a cause, it need not be. This, I believe, can be important to making an act permissible.[35] To see this, consider how Thomson argues against the significance of the sort of causal structure that I have suggested is important to judgments of permissibility.[36] She says: "One possibility is to construe the doctrine [of double effect] as concerned, not with intendings, but with sheer causal order; I ignored this possibility in the text above, since I think it pretty obvious that the doctrine so construed has no future at all."[37] Continuing, she says, "Suppose a Good pilot bombed a place in Bad that contained both a munitions factory and a children's hospital, and that the Bads therefore sued for peace—not because of the loss of the munitions factory, but because of the loss of the children: the bombing terrorized the Bads, bringing home to them what war was going to have in store for them. It can hardly be thought that the fact that the causal route to the Goods' winning the war passed through Bad terror, rather than through Bad lack of munitions, shows that it was impermissible for the pilot to drop his bombs."[38]

But in Thomson's case, the permissibility of bombing may depend on the possibility that the bombing of the munitions that actually took place could have been justified independently of the results of terror produced by the children's deaths. Hence, the permissibility of bombing may depend on the fact that the actual bombing could permissibly have been undertaken even if there had been no possibility that the fear generated by the bombing of the children would lead to peace. The deaths and fear are *not* causally necessary to produce the effect that could justify the bombing. It is true that one may foresee that fear generated by the unavoidable deaths will cause the war to end. However, that does not mean that one cannot permissibly bomb the munitions when the bombing will cause deaths if destroying the munitions was also part of an alternative way our act could end the war that justifies dead children as a side effect.[39]

In my view, it is neither the agent's state of mind nor the actual causal structure that matters. Rather, what can matter is whether, if the actual evil* causal structure had not occurred as a result of an act, some other nonevil* event would have come about as a result of the same act, and it would have caused the greater good that justifies the lesser evil* also caused.[40] However, insofar as the DDE and DDE(R) emphasize only either (a) state of mind or (b) actual causal structure rather than the causal necessity of evil* for producing an outcome, they will be subject to both of Thomson's objections. Suppose we understood the DDE and DDE(R) or some other moral principle[41] as ruling out evil* as a necessary means, given our acts, to producing the greater good. The DDE and DDE(R) would still be subject to the next objection.[42]

B. WHEN THE DDE PERMITS THE IMPERMISSIBLE

1. *Inability to Justify Side-Effect Deaths*

Here is a third problem with the nonabsolute, narrowed DDE that it shares with the DDE(R): It does not correctly justify tactical bombing.[43] Indeed, it will not declare impermissible some acts that are impermissible. The DDE and DDE(R) are perfectly general moral doctrines that have been applied to a wartime context. But, as Philippa Foot pointed out long ago, the DDE leads to the wrong conclusion in nonwar cases.[44] This is because it is not true, as the DDE and DDE(R) hold, that it is no objection to neutral or good means to a greater good that a lesser evil* will occur as a side effect when no other better means are available that do not cause as much evil*. For example, suppose I must rush five people to the hospital to save their lives. On the road I must take is an immovable person (Car Case 1). May I run over him because his being run over is not a means to getting to the hospital but only a side effect of the means of getting there, and I foresee but do not intend the death, which is a lesser evil* in comparison to saving five lives? I think not.

It may be said in response that this Car Case 1 is not strictly analogous to what happens in strategic bombing. For though involving or harming the person in Car Case 1 is not a means, driving over the spot that he already occupies is a required means of getting to the hospital. A comparable strategic bombing case would involve having to drop bombs on a munitions plant when children are immovably lodged on the very spot that the bombs must go through to reach their target.[45] But that is not how strategic bombing is typically described.

However, this complaint, raised on behalf of the DDE's and DDE(R)'s ability to justify strategic bombing, does not eliminate the problem that these doctrines have with Car Case 1. That is, these doctrines do not imply that impermissible action in Car Case 1 is impermissible. Furthermore, they do not yet show that strategic bombing in the standard case is permissible. The complaint, however, does help us to see another problem with the DDE and the DDE(R), namely, that they do not deal with the various ways in which an evil* side effect might come about and the possibility that these differences might make a moral difference. Suppose another principle—call it Principle X— takes note of these distinctions and explains why action in Car Case 1 is impermissible.[46] If only a general moral principle like Principle X is needed in order to decide war and nonwar cases alike, then Principle X, unlike the DDE and DDE(R), might declare impermissible strategic bombing when bombs hit children who are immovably lodged in the plant.

Here are some other possible ways in which strategic bombing may cause death as a side effect: (a) Our bombs, before or after they hit the plant, also hit and kill the children who are not in the plant but near it; (b) the blowing up of the plant itself causes the death of the children near it; (c) our bombs hit not only the plant but also the roof of the nearby schoolhouse, which falls on and kills the children; and (d) the bombs that hit the plant also cause an avalanche of rocks, which causes the schoolhouse roof to cave in and kill the children.

I suspect that option (a) is the way strategic bombing is typically conceived. The DDE and DDE(R) would not rule it out. Would action be permissible in an analogous nonwar case? Consider Car Case 2: We have to rush to the hospital to save five people. The road is clear to the hospital, but there is someone immovable at the side of the road. We know that the car we must drive unavoidably emits deadly fumes. Hence, it will kill the person at the side of the road. May we proceed in this case because the death of one is a less bad side effect by comparison to the greater good we seek? I do not think we may proceed, but the DDE and DDE(R) would not find the death of the one a sufficient impediment. (I do not think that we may proceed even if the bystander is far away but will die from the fumes.)[47] If this is so, then we have another reason to think that Principle X, not the DDE or DDE(R), is necessary to account for permissible and impermissible action, at least in nonwar cases. However, Principle X, as applied to war cases, may permit bombing in options (b) and (d).[48]

It may be pointed out that Car Cases 1 and 2 omit features present in war and which, when added to nonwar cases, may result in Principle X not ruling out harm to bystanders even when caused in a manner analogous to option (a). One feature is that the country with just cause for war has to act in a way that endangers people because it is treated unjustly by another country. Hence, perhaps some or all of the evils that are necessary for its defense, though done by it, become the moral responsibility of the unjust country. Furthermore, in war a country confronts an unjust opponent, and it is willing to take risks to do so. In a nonwar context, trying to defeat rather than retreat from an unjust threat is not always right. But some (such as Michael Walzer) argue that when states are subject to unjust attack, it is not only permissible but morally required that they defend themselves. Those who take a stand against injustice may also contribute to strengthening a just world order. So, let us imagine Car Case 3, which has these features: It is morally required that several people try to defeat person B engaged in injustices against them, at least when their act is judged independently of its bad side effects. Furthermore, the strength of the rule of justice for all is greater if they take a stand. However, the car that they use to go to fight B emits deadly fumes that two bystanders breathe in. It may be asked, why should the bystanders pay high costs for a benefit they did not ask for on account of others doing what it is right for them to do?

Note, however, that it is too simple to think that the constraints on harming bystanders in *nonwar* cases arise merely because those who fight an unjust threat should never do what makes a bystander bear the cost of the fight or because the bystanders have a right to not be made to bear this cost. For if the five could redirect a mechanical threat away from themselves and toward where bystander C will be harmed by it, this might be permissible according to Principle X itself.[49] (Supporters of Principle X should explain the moral difference between these different ways of threatening C.)

But what if we think bombing in option (a) *is* permissible, though producing an analogous threat to bystanders in Car Case 3 is not permissible? (And recall that certain types of acts that also kill and terrorize people will be permissible secondarily only if bombing in option *a* is permissible.) Then we may have to consider the possibility that in the context of war, special factors are present that override or make inapplicable in some ways a general principle like X. (These factors are in addition to any general factors, such as extraordinarily horrific consequences, that account for the nonabsoluteness of Principle X.) This was the conclusion that Thomson reached as well, though she did not attempt to explain what it was about war that made bombing in option *a* permissible.[50] I shall return to this issue in section III.

2. Inability to Distinguish among Noncombatants

The Car Cases and their analogous Strategic Bombing Cases raise concerns that the DDE and DDE(R) could not rule out acts that are impermissible or might give the wrong reasons for permissibility. The fourth problem with the DDE and DDE(R) raises a version of this concern in a different way. Suppose that country A is waging a just war against country B, whose unjust acts make A's war just. Country B lies to the west of A. Bordering country B on its west is country C, which is permissibly neutral in this war. There are several ways in which a munitions plant in B can be bombed. In route 1, A bombs the plant, and the foreseen side effect is that some of its own children living on the border with B get killed. In route 2, A bombs the plant, and the foreseen side effect is that the same number of B's children in B are killed. In route 3, A bombs the plant in B, and the foreseen side effect is that the same number of C's children living on the border with B are killed. In all these cases, let us assume the evil* is proportional to the good to be achieved and that the way in which the side effect is brought about conforms to the DDE and the DDE(R). If we rely only on these doctrines to account for the permissibility of tactical bombing, then no moral distinction should be drawn between these different routes. Those who think that they may rush to the hospital in some of the Car Cases, thereby harming an innocent bystander, and who use this as a model for what may be done in war will have to allow themselves to treat the children in neutral C in the same way as they treat the children in enemy B. Furthermore, suppose that fewer children would be killed using route 1 (killing A's children) and route 3 (killing C's children) than in using route 2 (killing B's children). Then if we rely just on the DDE or DDE(R), we will have a duty to minimize noncombatant deaths in all permissible ways (given that no one route is necessary to achieve our goal), which should make it a duty *not* to choose route 2 (killing B's children).

The important point these cases bring out is that the DDE and DDE(R), considered on their own, treat noncombatants who are citizens of the enemy country the same as other noncombatants. They are not more violable. If those who support the DDE and DDE(R) balk at these conclusions, then this shows that they too must think that something besides the DDE and DDE(R) helps account for the permissibility and impermissibility of killing in war.

Supporters of Principle X also face this problem of distinguishing between different classes of noncombatants. I think this is a problem even if we use only a form of strategic bombing that Principle X permits because I do not think that all three routes are on a moral par or that country A must always choose the route with fewer deaths when this implies hitting A or neutral children. Indeed, I think that if the DDE, DDE(R), or Principle X implies that route 3 (hitting C children) is as permissible as the other routes, it would not rule out the impermissible option.[51] If this is so, then even if strategic bombing of some sort were permissible, and even if the DDE, DDE(R), or Principle X were the principle in part explaining such permissibility, some principle in addition to these (call it Principle Y) must play a role. Principle Y would have to explain why noncombatants in one country have a higher degree of inviolability than those in another country. Principle Y may explain other things as well, for example, why even combatants of one country are more violable than those of another and why different ways of killing than those allowed by Principle X are permitted when harming civilians in an opponent country.

If Principle Y does these things, it will help explain part of the idea of proportionality used when we decide that a goal justifies a certain number of deaths but not more. It will do this by helping us decide how many lives may permissibly be sacrificed in one country but not sacrificed in another country. It will tell us who is more inviolable and to what degree. Hence, understanding the proportionality component of a principle of just war can involve developing what I shall call "violability ratios among different groups."

III. Principles Special to War[52]

Let us now move beyond criticism of the DDE, DDE(R), and Principle X and consider some aspects of war in particular. This may help us distinguish morally among different noncombatants when acting in ways ordinarily judged to be permissible (or not impermissible) by Principle X (to be discussed in section IIIA). We will then see whether we can argue for extending the range of acts that are permissible in wartime beyond what Principle X ordinarily permits (or does not rule out) (to be discussed in section IIIB).

A. VIOLABILITY RATIOS

In this section, I shall consider only cases where I assume that some general moral principle like Principle X would permit certain ways of harming people (such as bombing in options b and d described earlier). The aim is to try to find (components of) Principle Y that should justify an agent's not being impartial with regard to the populations of countries A, B, and C. Consider first that the government of country A may have a special, strong, positive duty to care for its own citizens and that this duty interferes with its acting on a principle that equally permits causing harm to its citizens and to others. Analogously, suppose that a general moral principle implies that it is permissible to turn a trolley away from five people toward one. An agent may still have a duty not to turn it toward his own child because of a special, strong duty of care he has to the child; he should rather turn it toward someone else. On this view, while the inviolability of noncombatants in the enemy country B is not lowered relative to a standard baseline, special care owed by A to its own citizens raises the inviolability of noncombatants in A when A is acting. This explanation for treating people unequally gives rise to a duty not to harm one's own noncombatants rather than other noncombatants if some noncombatants must be harmed as side effects when one acts in an otherwise permissible manner.

However, there is an alternative explanation for A's preference for its own noncombatants. One may conceive of the situation as one in which country A must decide whether to harm itself or harm someone else, both options involving (we are assuming) permissible ways to harm noncombatants. It may simply be supererogatory (beyond the call of duty) yet not forbidden by a duty to oneself to direct a threat to oneself rather than send it to someone else to whom it is also permissible to send it. Analogously, suppose a trolley is headed toward five people whom it will kill, and it is permissible to redirect it along another track, where it will kill one other person instead. One track leads to Joe and the other to me. It is not impermissible for me to turn the trolley toward Joe rather than toss a coin in order to decide whether to send it toward Joe or me.[53] (I could also permissibly turn the trolley toward two people rather than toward me.) This conclusion is related to the view that there is a prerogative not to make big sacrifices in order to aid others.

Notice that the self/other asymmetry employed here is not being used as a complete way of showing that a certain course of conduct is permissible. It is being used only to show that once a general form of conduct that will harm others (e.g., redirecting with side-effect harm) is independently determined to be permissible, one may select a particular action by giving some preference to oneself. Furthermore, notice that it is not impermissible to turn the trolley to Joe even if, absent the side track going toward Joe, I would refuse to save the five at all by turning the trolley toward myself. Hence, it can remain permissible to harm others for some cause even though one would never be willing to undergo the same harm oneself to achieve that cause. This implies that it is not impermissible to cause noncombatant deaths to an enemy when one fights a just war merely because one would not impose the same losses on one's own noncombatants for the cause.[54]

But I also think that it is (nonabsolutely) impermissible for A to choose route 3, killing neutral C's children. Indeed, it may be a more serious wrong to choose route 3 than to choose route 1 (killing A's own children). This cannot be because A has a special duty of care for citizens of C, and it cannot be because of a self/other asymmetry that allows one to prefer oneself. Nor can it be because we have a duty not to bomb a neutral country since we are not bombing them in my hypothetical case. Rather, we bomb the munitions plant in B and (we imagine) the plant's blowing up sends deadly fumes into country C. This suggests that noncombatants in B and even in A have lower inviolability relative to neutral noncombatants. (I shall return to this issue later.)

Hence, based on these observations we can formulate a third proposal for explaining distinctions between noncombatants. In activities undertaken by A in its war against B, noncombatant bystanders in B and A may both fall below the violability baseline for noncombatants in general (as in neutral C), but either A's duty of special care to its own noncombatants or a self/other asymmetry partially compensates for this, making A's violability higher than C's but lower than B's. Therefore, threats should not go to C if they can go to B or, at last, to A instead (holding constant the numbers killed and otherwise harmed). On this view, war by its nature involves engagement between designated parties who are expected to absorb all costs. The appropriate analogy for war is a prize fight; people in the audience are not liable at all to being punched. This analogy, however, suggests that neutrals are even *more* immune to being harmed than bystanders in the Car Cases discussed earlier. For example, in war country A may not rely on it being permissible according to Principle X to redirect threats, in general, from more to fewer people in order to justify its constructing a defensive shield that redirects B's threat from its civilians to a neutral country instead. It may not redirect merely because this will reduce civilian deaths.[55]

This leaves it open that very large numbers of noncombatant deaths in, for example, B should be avoided by choosing route 1 if it kills a much smaller number in A. That is, there may be some ratio between A, B, and even possibly C, noncombatants such that when A acts, killing n people in C would be, for example, like killing $300n$ (but not more) in A and $500n$ (but not more) in B.

Next, keep in mind that in standard just war theory, a general moral principle like the DDE, DDE(R), or Principle X would be combined with a strong preference for killing combatants before noncombatants. (This is the Walzerian view, which states that one should intend not to kill noncombatants.) The strongest version of this view implies that no tactical bombing by A that will kill noncombatants (A, B, or C) as a side effect is allowed if A combatants can be sent in to fight B combatants instead.[56] (When A acts, C combatants can have the same degree of inviolability as C noncombatants even if they are fighting in an unrelated war with D.) A weaker version of the view that one should prefer killing combatants before noncombatants is that combatant casualties in A and B are strongly discounted relative to noncombatant casualties of both the homeland and of the country with which one is at war.

Consider an example of the latter discount view: When A is fighting a war against B, a noncombatant death in B (caused by A) counts as much as 300 A combatant deaths. Hence, on this view, A's combatants must take great risks and suffer big losses rather than do what kills B's noncombatants, but there is still a limit to what they must suffer for this purpose. This suggests that A's relying on an air war with imprecise targeting rather than sending ground troops may violate *jus in bello* unless the discount ratio has been met.

Even if A combatants are more violable than B noncombatants, they are less violable than B combatants, at least from A's perspective when A fights in a war. How much less violable they are may depend on how individually responsible for being a threat we think B soldiers are and on the context in which the issue of violability arises. The violability of A combatants relative to B combatants may decrease as the responsibility of B soldiers for acts increases. Standard just war theory, however, permits soldiers on the unjust *ad bellum* side to do exactly what soldiers on the just side may do. The theory holds that violability is not a function of whether one's acts are objectively for a just cause. *Jus in bello* is said to be separate from *jus ad bellum*. Why might this be true? Individual soldiers, at least those conscripted, may be more like morally innocent threats than evil aggressors, although they are in control of their actions and in this sense responsible. This is because sometimes it may be right for one to act as the agent of a state, especially a generally just and democratic one, even when the act one does is unjust, without one being held accountable for the injustice of what one is doing. (A nonwar example might be an officer carrying out an order to evict a poor family from a very rich person's property for nonpayment of rent.)[57]

One way of arguing for not holding the agent accountable for the injustice of his act is through a two-level moral theory that emphasizes rules or principles. Sometimes the right act is one that accords with a principle that is the overall best even if the act itself is not otherwise the best act one is capable of performing. It may be a correct principle that generally just democracies should get to carry out their policies even though they are sometimes unjust or at least that subordinate agents should not be permitted to individually defy those policies.

If enemy soldiers have reduced moral responsibility for their acts because they are in this way under orders, it may be appropriate for A combatants to take greater risks to reduce the number of B combatants killed and for B combatants to defend themselves against even appropriate threats presented in a just cause by A.[58] A nonwar analogy is the person who is morally innocent and yet a threat to us. He may be responsible for his actions in being a threat (e.g., a person who threatens us because he reasonably but mistakenly believes that we are a threat to him) or he may be nonresponsible (e.g., the person is hurled at us). Even in the latter case, if he will kill us, I believe we may kill him to defend ourselves. However, if we could avoid our death and his as well by suffering a broken leg or trying a maneuver that increases our chance of death by only 0.1 percent, we may have to shoulder this cost. We would not have to shoulder it for a malicious aggressor.[59]

Would this mean that there is some limit on the number of B combatants that A's side may kill in order to save one A soldier from certain death as B combatants attack? I do not think so. In nonwar contexts, it would be permissible (I believe) to kill many morally innocent threatening persons to save one's life from the threat they present. However, the reduced moral responsibility of soldiers could mean that A should choose from among various options for engagement so that each member of its large army assumes a slight risk of death in order to avoid killing a greater number of enemy soldiers. This is so even though it implies that some of A's soldiers who would not otherwise have died will perish.[60]

Suppose, by contrast, that A combatants need take no risks to reduce the number of B combatants killed. Then it is theoretically possible that, from A's perspective, A combatants should count for as much relative to B combatants as A noncombatants do. The latter ratio is very high (in favor of A noncombatants). The further question is whether it would be permissible for A to select an option for engagement in which it will have to kill any number of B combatants to certainly stop the attack on one A civilian rather than select a different option that limits B losses but imposes a slight risk on A civilian?

Notice that it could be true that A combatants and noncombatants have the same degree of inviolability relative to B combatants even though A noncombatants have greater inviolability than A combatants. That is, A combatants can have greater violability relative to A noncombatants but share the latter's status relative to B combatants. Let me expand on this point. First, note that it requires us to consider the topic of the violability ratio of one side's combatants to its own noncombatants. This, I believe, is a crucial topic, though it can be overlooked.[61] As shown in figure 3.2, although there are only four elements to compare, there are six comparisons to be made.

One of the A soldiers' tasks is to defend A noncombatants. Does this mean that any number of A combatants must die so that one of the A noncombatants does not die from a B attack? This seems unlikely if only because the A combatants must also fight for the just cause. More likely, there is some violability ratio such that the death of one A noncombatant is equal to, for example, the death of 100 A combatants, at least when it is a question of A choosing among possible engagements with the enemy or rescues of its noncombatants. It is also possible

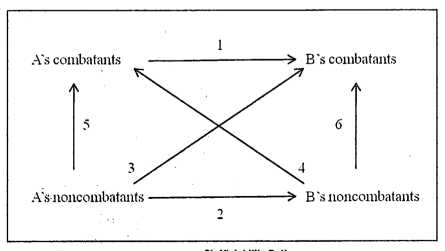

FIGURE 3.2 **Six Violability Ratios**

that, from A's perspective, the violability of its combatants is closer to the violability of its noncombatants than is the violability of B combatants to the violability of B noncombatants. This may be, in part, because it sees its soldiers as engaged in just warring and the difference between no warring acts and just warring acts is smaller than the difference between unjust warring acts (even permissibly undertaken by B soldiers) and no warring acts undertaken by B noncombatants. But drawing this distinction between different combatant/noncombatant ratios from one side's perspective seems to be inconsistent with the separation of *jus in bello* and *jus ad bellum* of standard just war theory. Another possible explanation of the different combatant/noncombatant ratios is that a self/other asymmetry is being drawn: That the combatants and noncombatants are both "our" people (from A's perspective) unites them in a way that effaces to some degree the difference in their roles. B combatants cannot be united with B noncombatants to efface the difference in their roles in the same way, given that from A's perspective they do not have the effacing property ("our own").

Now notice two important implications of the fact that there is a high discount on A combatant deaths relative to A noncombatant deaths. First, suppose A noncombatants will face counterattacks (e.g., terrorism) prompted by anger when too many B noncombatants (or even combatants) are killed. Then the fact that A noncombatants are more inviolable than A combatants gives A combatants another (indirect) reason to risk themselves rather than kill B noncombatants (and even combatants). For their taking such risks is a way of appropriately sacrificing themselves to save A noncombatants from subsequent retaliation. Attending to the violability ratio between combatants and noncombatants on the same side is important, in part, because it leads to this result. Second, if there is only a discount ratio between A combatants and A noncombatants, so not any number of A combatants must die to save one A noncombatant, it may also be true that A may do what saves many A combatants even though as a side effect this kills an A noncombatant. If this is permitted, it might give the other side (B) a reason to sometimes do what will kill a few A noncombatants rather than many A combatants. For it is not unreasonable to think that if some number of A combatants need not die to save a certain number of A noncombatants and may even in certain ways do what kills some as a side effect, then the opponent need not always favor A noncombatant lives to A combatant lives, either. (But violability ratios between combatants and noncombatants on the same side need not be the basis for attacks on the Principle of Discrimination with respect to deliberate targeting of noncombatants.[62])

In sum, from the point of view of A waging war, the order of increasing violability, seems to be as follows: neutrals, A noncombatants, B noncombatants, A combatants, and B combatants. But suppose there is only a discount ratio between combatant and noncombatant deaths rather than a lexical ordering. Then it is wrong to claim that if one has nonterror (or terror) means to use against combatants, one should always use them rather than have engagements that result in side-effect harm to noncombatants. The ordering reminds us that we should distinguish between harm to one's own combatants and harm to an opponent's combatants (or noncombatants) for the sake of one's own noncombatants. (Figure 3.1 would have to be modified to take this into account.)

This violability ordering depends, at least, on A's having a sincere (or perhaps reasonable, if not true) view of itself as satisfying *jus ad bellum*, after which, from its perspective, factors such as self-preference can permissibly enter in. For suppose that A is fighting an unjust war and B is its victim. *A knows this* but A should not stop fighting because this would lead to even worse injustices resulting from its having started the war. Then, I believe, A's own combatants and noncombatants have a greater responsibility to shoulder burdens of war than do those of B, and A should know this. A's duty of special care to its citizens should be replaced, I believe, by a concern that it and its citizens not unjustly harm others or be associated with injustice. (I shall say more about this in section IIIB.) Then violability in increasing order might be as follows: neutrals, B noncombatants, A noncombatants, B combatants, A combatants. Suppose this ordering were combined with a reconsideration of the preference for (1) combatant deaths even on the just side (when all know it to be just) over (2) noncombatant deaths on the unjust side. Then an ordering might put the violability of unjust A's noncombatants higher than that of B's combatants. The additional violability of A combatants and noncombatants may still be moderated to some degree if the combatants are only acting on a correct principle of obedience to a ruling authority (as discussed earlier) and the noncombatants have limited responsibility for the state's policies.

B. GROUP LIABILITY [63]

Suppose, as has been argued, that the DDE and DDE(R) are incorrect general moral principles. Suppose that the correct general Principle X rules out terror killing of noncombatants (with exceptions) and also some cases of tactical bombing (as where our bombs would directly kill noncombatants). While these prohibitions need not be absolute, in most circumstances the goals to be achieved by bombing would not override the prohibition. This implies that other means would have to be used unless some consideration present in wartime restricted the application of Principle X in some respects. What might such considerations be, and do they validate tactical bombing in manner(a) (as described on p. 55) and looser restrictions on TKN? In this section, I shall present two arguments for special circumstances restricting the application of Principle X in some ways. Both arguments, in different ways, imply that it is a mistake for A (believing its cause is just) to think of B noncombatants as analogous to the bystanders in Car Case 1, to whom Principle X applies. B noncombatants can have lower inviolability than these bystanders. (I argued earlier that C [neutral] citizens are not like such bystanders; they have even higher inviolability, as shown by the fact that they are not liable to redirection of threats.)

1. *The Liability Argument*

Consider the following argument, which I shall call the Liability Argument. Just states typically have the authority to draft some of their own citizens to become combatants. Having the right to send combatants to fight and perhaps be killed by the enemy is the right to intentionally put people in danger as a means to a goal, a right not typically held by just anyone. Hence, if just anyone sent people into danger, he would violate Principle X. Even the right to send people into danger is not exactly the right to deliberately kill one's own soldiers as a means to a great good. For example, a just state not in the most dire circumstances may not kill its own soldiers or noncombatants (who do not volunteer for death) in order to (somehow) terrorize the enemy and, thereby, win a war.

What might a just state do to its own noncombatants, including children? Suppose that it must deploy missiles from its own territory against the enemy or else surrender. However, the missiles sometimes backfire and cause deaths among civilians around the area where they are deployed. Efforts are made to minimize such harm, but some of it is unavoidable (Backfiring Missile Case 1). Presumably, a just state involved in a just war is permitted to use the missiles if the cause is important enough. Yet, if just anyone did this, he would violate Principle X. (In nonwar emergencies, perhaps a state may do similar things to its own citizens. Then the factor of war will be needed only to explain the permissibility of its doing these things to some noncitizens.)

A state is permitted to do these things to its combatants and noncombatants despite its having a special duty to care for its own citizens. I have not yet given an argument for the state having these powers. A possible argument follows.

A state may override Principle X to draft its own citizens and expose them (even children) to risks and harms (as in Backfiring Missile Case 1) because it is acting on their behalf as a collective. Citizens are to accept these risks and harms in wartime for the good of the collective of which they are a part. A collective is necessary in order that the benefit of civilized society be available to people. Even those, such as children, who have not yet reaped benefits from being a part of this collective are members of the collective, which is organized to be of service to these children should they survive.[64] This is a justification in terms of imposing risks and harms on people for their own collective good. Perhaps it is not strong enough. I shall assume for the sake of argument that it is adequate.

Now suppose one's own state is engaged in an *unjust* war. For example, suppose it has, without satisfying conditions for *jus ad bellum* or *jus in bello*, sent off a deadly missile toward another country and that it will kill many in that country. Suppose further that our state realizes right after it sent the missile off that it has been unjust. The only way for it to stop the missile is to send off another missile to destroy the first one. This second missile, like the one in our earlier example, will backfire and as a side effect kill some of our own noncombatants. We could imagine that it will kill fewer than, the same number as, or even more than those that would be killed unjustly in the other country if the first missile is not stopped (Backfiring Missile Case 2).

Would it be permissible and even obligatory for the government to send off the second missile despite its duty of care for its citizens and despite a self/other asymmetry that sometimes permits us to prefer ourselves? I believe it would be permissible and even obligatory to send off the second missile. If this is so, what is the justification for the state's right to endanger its own citizens in this case? It cannot be that the state's act is aimed at the greater good of its citizens collectively, as in the previous argument, because—assuming a distinction between being just and faring well—it is not the collective good of their nation that is being served. Rather, I believe, the justification is that citizens of a country are as liable to have risks and harms imposed on them so that their country will not be unjust as they are so that their collective interests will be promoted. I believe that they can have such liability even if they are not morally responsible for the injustice. (If one's country is unjust even to its own citizens, the citizenry is also liable to bear some costs to make its state internally just, insofar as this is possible. If this internal task has failed, the citizenry might still be liable, I think, for bearing costs to prevent its state from being unjust to others. Perhaps this is because the state is still one's state even when it does not treat one as a member should be treated.) This claim was also implicitly relied on in section IIIA when we revised the order of violability for a state that comes to realize that it began an unjust war but for reasons of justice should not stop the war.

We are already familiar with the idea that a country owes reparations to victims of its injustices even though those whose taxes will pay for the reparations are a new generation who neither participated in nor benefited from the injustice. The suggestion is that other costs besides money may be imposed to prevent the injustices of one's state, even on those who never participated in or benefited from the injustice. (I agree that much work in political philosophy would have to be done to justify such liability. I am only claiming that justifying it may be necessary in order to justify certain acts in war that endanger noncombatants.)

Admittedly, the citizens' liability for bearing costs may have to be moderated due to the opposing view that those who are not fully morally responsible for threats should be treated in some ways differently (as was said earlier in discussing conscripted combatants) from those who are fully morally responsible. If so, victims of injustice might have to accept some risks so that harm to noncombatants of the knowingly unjust side is reduced. I have already said that the group liability in my account does not depend on group responsibility for committing unjust action or policy. In this connection, note also that citizens' *being liable* for bearing costs is not the same as their having *a responsibility* to bear the costs since it does not imply that they must volunteer to suffer large costs, only that others may permissibly do what imposes the costs without wronging the citizens. Are they morally permitted to try to resist the harms that would befall them during the effort to stop their state's unjust war? (For example, in Backfiring Missile Case 2, may they shoot back at the second missile that will harm them?) If acting on such permission interfered with attempts to stop the injustice of their country, it would seem to be unjustified even if it were excusable.

It has been argued that a state may do some harmful things to its own citizens and, in essence, restrict the applicability of Principle X in some respects, for reasons of collective good or collective justice. Now we must continue the argument to show that a state may sometimes do similar things to the citizens of the country against whom it wages a just war. (For example, the case of bombs dropped on a military target that directly harm noncombatants of an enemy country as a side effect is supposed to be analogous to Backfiring Missile Case 2.) In order to show this, suppose we relied merely on the argument that a state may do things to its own citizens for their collective interest in order to show that a state may do similar things to citizens of an opponent state. Then it could be pointed out that this justification does not apply at all to the citizens of the opponent state. "Why," these citizens may ask, "should you impose risks and harms on us for your collective good when it is not for our own good?" In this question, there are two claims: (i) It is not for our good that risks and harms are imposed on us but for your good, and (ii) you are not our state and so cannot impose costs on us as you might impose them on your own citizens.

Here is a possible answer to the first claim that introduces a different argument. If one's country is engaged in a just war that satisfies *jus ad bellum*, then its enemy country has done something sufficiently unjust to provoke a war against it. Earlier it was argued (in dealing with the case in which our own country unjustly set off a missile) that citizens of a country should be liable for risks and harms in order that their country not be unjust, as much as in order that their country's interests be promoted. This implies that the citizens of the unjust country we fight when we are just should also be liable to risks and harms in order that their country not be unjust to us. (The fact that one country benefits from the end of another country's injustice does not mean either (i) that it should *take* the risks for these benefits any more than in Backfiring Missile Case 2 or (ii) that the victim country rather than the unjust country should *accept* the risks for the benefits to it of avoiding the first missile.)[65]

But now we have to deal with the second claim: Who are we—not their state—to impose losses on them? By hypothesis, their state continues to pursue its unjust ways, and so it will not do what imposes losses on its citizens in order that their state not be unjust. This may be either because it believes it is not unjust or because it does not care whether it is unjust. (It might be because it believes it does not have a duty to stop its injustice when its citizens will thereby be harmed. But I have argued that this is wrong.) In interpersonal relations, if someone has a duty to me to do something and does not do it, it is not necessarily true that I may interfere with him to enforce his duty. But I may sometimes go to some legitimate authorized agent, like the police or the state, to have the duty enforced. In international relations, there is often no international agency that will enforce the duties of one state relative to another. And, arguably, when that is the case, a state may itself try to enforce duties owed to it. Hence, when the just state conducts tactical bombing against the unjust state, knowing that noncombatants will suffer as a direct side effect of its bombs (in a way ruled out by Principle X), the just state may be seen as permissibly imposing risks and losses that the opponent state should be willing to impose on its own people to do what prevents its own injustice.[66]

Hence, a state that is at war, at least when it is the unjust state, loses with respect to its opponent the exclusive authority of a sovereign state over its populace. The citizens of the unjust state can be put at risk in the service of the state waging just war against it, as that state could put its own citizens at risk to stop its injustice were it unjust. (Hence, one is tempted to call this a "Shared Sovereignty Argument," but for reasons to be given later, I will not use this name.)

We can summarize the Liability Argument (so far) as follows: (1) Suppose our country is unjust to others. Then our government has a duty to stop the injustice, and our citizens are liable (in a sense which does not imply that they committed acts leading to injustice) for some costs imposed by our government to stop the injustice. (2) If another country is unjust to us, its government has a duty to stop the injustice, and its citizens are similarly liable to costs imposed by their government to stop its injustice. (3) Suppose the unjust country's government does not do its duty and there is no international policeman to enforce the duty. (4) Then we (or another country) may enforce the duty or stop the injustice, and we (or another country) may impose similar costs on the unjust country's citizens in doing so.[67]

An interesting further question is whether a country fighting a just war has something like the authority even to draft citizens of the country it is fighting so they work for the just cause. If so, it would have a right to expose those "draftable" citizens to dangers comparable to the ones to which it can expose its own combatants. Note, however, that its own combatants are permitted to defend themselves against the dangers presented to them by combatants they fight. But if a state may treat as drafted into its service some of the citizens of the state it is fighting, it will be drafting them to be exposed to harm presented by the very same state that drafts them, against whom defense seems problematic. Perhaps something comparable may occur when soldiers are subject to the risks of so-called friendly fire.

Recall that it was argued in section IIIA that a state does not have special duties of care toward the citizens of other countries the way it has toward its own citizens. Even independently of such a duty of care, it was said that a state's selecting its own noncombatants for harm rather than another state's noncombatants (when the manner of causing harm is permissible) is supererogatory as there is here a permissible self/other asymmetry. These points were supposed to help justify both selecting among both noncombatants to harm and some violability ratios. The Liability Argument as given so far now adds to an explanation of the increased violability of B citizens from A's point of view (at least if A knows it is just and B unjust). Special duties of care and self/other asymmetry could account for why A citizens (from A's point of view) should get better treatment than B citizens without lowering B citizens from a general inviolability baseline. Unlike these special duties and asymmetry, the Liability Argument helps explain why A sees B citizens as occupying a position lower than the general inviolability baseline. But the fact that A, in making war, acts to get a collective benefit for its citizens may help raise its citizens' violability relative to neutral C's citizens, whose violability is even less than that of ordinary bystanders, according to the prize-fight model discussed earlier.

Together all these factors reinforce the following claims: (1) If there is a choice between endangering its own noncombatants or those in the country it is fighting, a state that has a just cause may favor its own noncombatants at least to some degree. How much it may favor them is expressed by a violability ratio (or a discount rate) for the deaths of the other side's noncombatants versus its own. (2) If a country would prefer to forego a goal in its just war rather than permissibly harm its own noncombatants for the goal when harming them is the only way to achieve the goal, this need not mean that it is impermissible for it to impose such harm on its opponent's noncombatants when this is a way to achieve the goal.

Notice again that the self/other asymmetry has not been used to show that a course of conduct against an enemy country is permissible: It is used to decide only among courses of conduct that have already, on independent grounds, been shown to be permissible. The Liability Argument moved from what a state should do though it harms its own citizens to what it may permissibly do to an unjust opponent. However, if a state should do what causes its own citizens harm X, even in the presence of a duty of care, it is possible that it may cause harm $X + N$ to its opponent, to whose citizens it has no duty of care. Proving this would involve a further step. It would require showing that a citizenry's liability is not limited by what its own state may do to it in the course of the state fulfilling its duty to stop its own unjust acts.

So far, in expanding the scope of permissible killing beyond Principle X, we have considered noncombatant killings that are direct side effects of means we use in pursuing other goals. What about terror killing where this involves death and terror as necessary causes to produce a goal? Suppose a state is pursuing a just war that serves its interests. I said earlier that, except in the most dire cases, it is prohibited from terror killing its own nonvolunteering citizens, whether they are combatants or noncombatants, to achieve wartime goals. (There are exceptions described in section II that could also justify terror killing one's own citizens.) However, if a state engaged in a just war did (impermissibly) use its citizens in such a way, they would not be used to stop an unjust war but to pursue a just one. Hence, it is still possible that those who are noncombatants or combatants on the unjust side may permissibly be terror-killed to stop an unjust war. To consider this possibility we use the same strategy employed earlier in the Liability Argument. Suppose that a country is fighting an unjust war and comes to realize that it is unjust. Civilian leaders are prepared to stop fighting; however, military leaders in charge of the war will not stop it. The only way to stop the deadly missile it has unjustly sent to another country is for the president of the unjust country to deliberately harm some of its own combatants or noncombatants because, we may imagine, doing this would terrorize the military leaders into stopping the war. May this be done?

Possibly it is permissible to use one's own combatants as mere tools to stop the state's injustice. This suggests that stopping its own unjust war is an even more important goal than pursuing its just war would be. It can be more important that we not do injustice than that we avoid being the victim of injustice. Suppose, however, that it is not permissible to use noncombatants in this way except in the direst of cases (e.g., a whole other country will be destroyed by the unjustly sent missile). If a country may terror-kill its own combatants to stop its unjust war, the Liability Argument will imply that country A, fighting a just war, may terror-kill opponent B's combatants in similar circumstances to stop B's unjust war. (But, it may be said, A would then be terror-killing B's combatants to prevent its being a victim of injustice, and it was said only that A might terror-kill its own combatants to prevent its being unjust. It is permissible [if not obligatory, as is stopping its own injustice] for country A to terror-kill country B's combatants, I believe, if it does in fact prevent B from being unjust by means that B [like A] should be willing to use on its own combatants to prevent its own injustice. This is true even if A's motive for terror killing B combatants is to prevent injustice to itself.) This conclusion bears on the case of the sleeping Japanese soldiers that I discussed earlier. It is another way to argue that they could permissibly be terror-killed to stop an unjust war they are conducting if the costs of the continuing war were great enough.

Could it be that it is only the duty of special care or a permission based on a self/other distinction that stands in the way of a country terror killing its own *non*combatants to stop its own unjust war? If not, then the grounds for the prohibition may apply quite generally to citizens of the country it is fighting and will rule out terror killing its opponent's noncombatants except when general overriding conditions on Principle X ("direst circumstances") apply.

What about neutral states, like state C in our earlier example involving unjust B and just A at war? The theory now being presented distinguishes, I think, between what A may do to citizens of B and what A may do to citizens of C in regard to overriding Principle X. Not all states have an obligation to fight injustices to A or stop injustices that B commits. And even if it were good for C that A triumph over B, just as it is good for A and its citizens that A triumph, C has done nothing to lose its right to decide by itself what goods it will pursue and whether its citizens will be enlisted to help A. This is unlike B, I have argued. Hence, A's conduct toward C is at minimum still governed by Principle X and more likely by the code of prize fights. Suppose a certain type of tactical bombing against the plants in B is not permitted by Principle X or prize-fight rules because of the way in which it affects citizens in C who live on the border between B and C. Then A may not engage in such tactical bombing except to the extent that these principles and rules are nonabsolute for perfectly general reasons, such as horrific consequences.

Consideration of neutrals raises a question for the Liability Argument as so far developed. For suppose there are noncombatants of neutral countries living in A or B. The Liability Argument implies that they have greater immunity from harm than noncombatants of A or B. If this is true, it serves as confirmation of the argument, I believe.

Suppose an agent other than a state has passed the various just cause and moral legitimacy tests for killing. Could the same exemption from Principle X offered by the Liability Argument that applies to a state apply to this other agent in its relations with the combatants and noncombatants of its opponent? It would apply only if this agent has a moral (if not legal) authority to enlist and expose people on its own side to danger in order to pursue a just fight and especially to stop an unjust fight in which it might be engaged. But due to the implications of any special duty of care to its own people or the self/other asymmetry discussed earlier, its refusing to sacrifice people on its side for a goal that serves its interests need not imply that it is impermissible for it to harm citizens of its unjust opponent for this goal. (It is because the Liability Argument may also justify the behavior of nonstates that we should not call it the Shared Sovereignty Argument, for in these cases there is no sovereign state that could be said to exercise powers typical of sovereignty over its opponent.)[68]

The analysis in the Liability Argument has so far been framed in terms of what an agent who satisfies *jus ad bellum* may do. Of course, each side may think of itself as having the just cause, and either or both may be wrong about this. It might be argued that only if one is really in the right is one justified in overriding Principle X or even killing in a manner in accordance with Principle X. But there are at least two views on this matter. According to what we may refer to as an objective theory of permissibility, one's act is permissible only if one is acting correctly (e.g., as an agent with complete knowledge [empirical and moral] and with perfect moral motivation would act). Then no reason could possibly be given for having to act differently. For example, Judith Thomson imagines a case in which Bloggs presses a light switch that someone else has hooked up to a bomb in a neighboring house. Hence, Bloggs kills the person in the neighboring house. There was no way Bloggs could have known this would happen. Thomson says that Bloggs does not act permissibly. Indications of this, she says, are that if he could do it over, he should certainly do a different type of act and that if we know better than he about the bomb, we should interfere with the act that he actually does.[69] By contrast, Thomas Scanlon argues that the objective view abstracts too much from the agent's point of view, especially if there was no other way in which it would have been reasonable for him to act given everything he should have known.[70] On this agent-centered theory of permissibility, Bloggs did not act impermissibly. Scanlon's view of permissibility is one way to account for why two countries are both permitted to override Principle X in light of the Liability Argument. It is also a reason (in addition to the one given by a two-level moral theory) that soldiers on each side may be acting permissibly in killing combatants on the other side.

Given the agent-centered view of permissibility, one could add two steps to the four steps of the Liability Argument given earlier: (5) Each side in the conflict may not be unreasonable in thinking that it is just and the other side unjust. (6) Therefore, each side's citizens may be liable to costs as a result of the other side (or third party) stopping what it reasonably believes is the other country's injustice. Even on the objective view of permissibility, if it was not unreasonable (or only reasonable) for one to think that one's cause was just when it was not, then one's impermissible overriding of Principle X might still be excusable though not justifiable. But suppose it was not reasonable for leaders and citizens of a state to think their side was in the right or they knew it was in the wrong. Then on both views of permissibility, their killings are impermissible and may well be punishable.

2. The Shifted Responsibility Argument

There is a second argument that might be offered to override prohibitions supported by Principle X. I call it the Shifted Responsibility Argument. One form of shifted responsibility occurs when there is a transfer of an agent's moral responsibility (in the sense of accountability) for negative effects of its acts to another agent.[71] A disputed example is when a country puts its own bystanders in the way of what would otherwise be a just response by its opponents to a threat. In that case, some think the moral responsibility for deaths caused by A's bombing is attributable to B, who impermissibly moved people into harm's way. The moral option of redirecting a threat also suggests a morally clearer case. We could develop a device that conforms to Principle X and shifts moral responsibility for harm to an unjust agent. The device is a defensive screen that would deflect threats from B that would harm A's noncombatants back toward B's own noncombatants if the numbers of noncombatants thus killed would be minimized. (Recall that Principle X is neutral with regard to one's own noncombatants and one's opponents; hence minimizing is required). In this case, if the permissibility of A acting is not in question (as it might be in the earlier example), it is easier to think B is accountable for harm. If Principle X is combined with a violability ratio favoring A's noncombatants when A acts, a threat could be redirected even to a greater number of B people while still shifting responsibility to B for what A does to B.

However, the Shifted Responsibility Argument I will now consider has a different focus. Suppose the bystander, in what I will call Car Case 4, materially supports unjust person B, who threatens the five in the car. Then the bystander is not an innocent bystander but at least in part causally responsible for the threat. It is in this sense that responsibility is shifted to him; he shares it with B. Does this not diminish the bystander's immunity from harm? This Shifted Responsibility Argument does not claim that it is permissible for the just side to wrong an innocent bystander, with moral responsibility for the wrong going to the unjust person. Rather, it insists that the bystander is not wronged because at least causal responsibility for the evildoing is, in part, his. It might also be said that he is not really a bystander. The basis for the Shifted Responsibility Argument might also be the basis for an argument against the Principle of Discrimination if extended to deliberate attacks on noncombatants.

However, if someone materially supports a threat as a result of carrying out a superior duty, his liability to harm might not increase. An example might be a doctor who saves unjust combatants and so makes possible the continuation of the war but not because he supports combatants qua combatants. In addition, if the combatants' acts are justified by a two-level moral theory or by an agent's point-of-view theory of permissibility,[72] then the doctor who saved combatants' lives may not have his immunity to harm reduced just because he helps make possible their threat.[73] This doctor is more like the doctor of one prizefighter during a boxing match; he may not be punched by the opposing boxer.

Suppose someone was previously a supporter of the combatants. Might his immunity be significantly lowered because of his past causal responsibility for the threat? Only, I believe, if he was not a morally innocent threat. That is, his degree of responsibility for having helped a threat (or been a threat) seem to be relevant to whether his violability is now lower. (By contrast, a current threat who is morally innocent may be entitled to only minimal changes in how we react to his threat by comparison to a morally responsible threat, at least if it is a very serious threat.) This is a reason why conscripted soldiers who were threats but are retired now, unlike previous rulers who initiated aggression, are not liable to being used in terror bombing just because of their previous acts. Having moral fault for activities unrelated to the current war also does not reduce immunity. Hence, criminals serving sentences for civilian crimes do not, in virtue of these characteristics, have lowered immunity. But retired volunteer combatants for a clearly unjust cause might have decreased immunity for purposes of ending that very injustice.[74] Can we deny that there is diminished immunity simply by saying that it has been decreed that, in the "game" we are playing, only those who actually currently threaten a victim have diminished immunity to harm? I do not think so.

However, a moral objection to harming even a bystander who is materially supplying an unjust aggressor arises if he is situated among other bystanders who have not done this and if these bystanders would also be harmed. The protection that Principle X affords these other bystanders is not modified by the presence among them of an aggressor or by his supporters so long as the bystanders have had no option as to their location. Hence, I believe both the Shifted Responsibility Argument and Principle X fail to justify tactical bombing in which nonthreatening, nonsupportive noncombatants are killed by the bombs. Another argument, such as the Liability Argument, is needed to justify such bombing.

IV. Conclusion

My conclusion is that just war theory based on the DDE and the Principle of Discrimination fails in many ways. A further conclusion is that any other general moral principle, such as Principle X, will also fail as a sufficient basis for just war theory. If it is true that some types of strategic bombing are routinely justifiable despite harms caused in certain ways to noncombatants, what justifies them seems to be factors specific to war that modify the applicability of general moral principles. Hence, such factors, as identified by Principle Y, would be necessary in order to justify much conduct that is commonly thought to be part of *jus in bello*. Terror killing which is not commonly thought to be part of *jus in bello* can be most easily justified when it is done either to (1) those who are currently or were previously morally responsible for organizing the threats on behalf of the unjust cause that one is currently opposing, (2) those who are now in fact threats whom one can terror-kill in self-defense or to end a war, or (3) noncombatants whom we either would alternatively have permissibly harmed or have the capacity to permissibly harm to the same degree as side effects. The inviolability of neutrals, however, seems to be even greater than ordinary bystanders in a nonwar analogy.

Notes

This chapter is a revised version of "Failures of Just War Theory: Terror, Harm and Justice," *Ethics* 114 (July 2004, 650–692). That article was written for presentation at the conference on Terrorism and Justice at the Jean Beer Blumenfeld Center for Ethics, Georgia State University. It was also given as the annual Law and Philosophy Lecture at Columbia Law School and the Martin Benjamin Lecture at Michigan State University. I am grateful to the participants on those occasions for comments. For help on earlier versions of this article, I am also grateful to audiences at philosophy colloquia at City University Graduate Center, Oxford University, University of Nebraska at Lincoln, Princeton University, at the Conference on Just War, University of Illinois Law School, Urbana-Champaign, the Oberlin Philosophy Conference, and the Law and Philosophy Colloquium, University College London. I am indebted for written comments to Jeff McMahan and for conversation about his article on just war to R. Chang, S. Kagan, L. Temkin, and the Ethics Fellows Seminar at Harvard University. A shorter version of this article, entitled "Terror and Collateral Damage: Are They Permissible?", appeared in *The Journal of Ethics* 9 (October 2006): 381–401.

1. This case was suggested by Gertrude Ezorsky.
2. I shall discuss this issue in more detail in chapter 8, this volume. Some points made there are briefly raised in this chapter.
3. This does not necessarily imply that groups that lack certain legal rights that they should have, due to legitimate but wrong actions by a government rather than by way of illegitimate aggression, may kill to correct the situation.
4. As pointed out by Jeff McMahan.
5. I shall coin this verb for my purposes.
6. It was Peter Graham who emphasized this point to me. Of course, more would have to be said to justify this claim. I discuss "mere resistance" in chapter 9, this volume.
7. In what follows, I shall focus on means employed by states in standard war. I discuss terror by nonstates in chapter 8.
8. I also considered these cases in chapter 2, "Justification for Killing Noncombatants in War.".
9. It is the foundation of Catholic just war theory and used by secular theorists such as Elizabeth Anscombe in "War and Murder," reprinted in *Nuclear Weapons and Christian*

Conscience, ed. Walter Stein, 43–62 (London: Merlin, 1961); and Michael Walzer in *Just and Unjust Wars* (New York: Basic, 2000).

10. In chapter 8, I point out a different interpretation of the DDE that focuses on actual causal relations rather than intention. Endnote 11 in chapter 2 also mentions such an interpretation.

11. If not any evil less than the good is proportional to it, it will be a big problem to decide how much evil a good is worth. I shall not discuss this important issue here. An evil greater than the good can also be proportional to it, as when you do something that foreseeably kills a guilty aggressor in order to stop him from paralyzing you.

12. See Warren Quinn, "Actions, Intentions, and Consequences: The Doctrine of Double Effect," reprinted in his *Morality and Action* (New York: Cambridge University Press, 1994), 175–193. I argue that his is a revisionist account of the moral significance of the DDE in my *Morality, Mortality*, vol. 2 (New York: Oxford University Press, 1996), and discuss his proposal more fully in my *Intricate Ethics* (New York: Oxford University Press, 2006), chap. 3.

13. See Michael Walzer, *Just and Unjust Wars* (New York: Basic Books, 2000), pp. 155–157.

14. See ibid., p. 155: "Double effect is defensible, I want to argue, only when the two outcomes are the product of a double intention: first that the "good" be achieved; second that the foreseeable evil be reduced as far as possible."

15. See "The Doctrine of Triple Effect and Why a Rational Agent Need Not Intend the Means to His End," in *Proceedings of the Aristotelian Society* (2000), Supplement (74): 21–39, and my *Intricate Ethics*, chaps. 3–4.

16. This is a case that illustrates a point that will be made later: The permissibility of an act need not be affected by the reason for which an agent acts.

17. I discuss why they might be viewed this way later on.

18. I thank Agnieszka Jaworska for help in refining this analogy.

19. I shall return to this issue in section IIIA. What I say in section IIIB will also bear on whether our response should be different if the sleeping soldiers had previously been threats.

20. I discuss this in my *Morality, Mortality*, vol. 2, and in *Intricate Ethics*.

21. The Principle of Alternate Reason might be understood as a different form of secondary permissibility, in which the act done is the same as the act that would have been done, but a factor that would not have justified the act becomes one's reason for bringing about the act, given that factors that justify the act are present.

22. There are also other conditions that play a role in the permissibility of this act.

23. This case is based on one presented for a different purpose by Judith Thomson in her "Self-Defense," *Philosophy & Public Affairs* 20 (Autumn 1991): 283–310. She imagines that we are all along going to bomb the munitions plant to get rid of ammunition, but it turns out that it is the terror from side-effect deaths that actually ends the war.

24. This case has the causal structure of the Track Trolley Case mentioned in chap. 2, "Justifications for Killing Noncombatants in War," note 18.

25. When I originally wrote this, I seem to have thought that an act (such as bombing a munitions plant) that would not be terror killing if done for one reason, could become terror killing if done for a terror-related reason. I take a different view elsewhere. See chap. 8 in this volume and chap. 2 in my *Ethics for Enemies: Terror, Torture, and War* (Oxford: Oxford University Press, 2011).

26. I would now also emphasize that terror, like torture, is a way to try to manipulate someone's will so that he does something, not just a way to stop his act by interference. For this

aspect (and others) of torture see David Sussman's "What Is Wrong with Torture?" *Philosophy & Public Affairs* 33 (2004): 1–33, and my discussion in chap. 1 of *Ethics for Enemies*.

27. And, I would now add, the manipulation of will.

28. For further discussion of terror per se, see chap. 8.

29. See John Rawls, "Reflections on Hiroshima: 50 Years after Hiroshima," *Dissent* (Summer 1995): 323–327.

30. This leaves it open, I believe, that one may not terror-bomb the noncombatants in order to stop the Nazis when this would be the only way to stop them rather than the alternative to what we would (or could) otherwise permissibly do.

31. Though I do not think that the permissibility of resistance is sufficient for showing that someone is wronged. See the discussion in section III about combatants on the unjust side in war. Permission to resist is also not always available to someone wronged, in virtue of special obligations he may have not to resist.

32. See Jonathan Bennett, "Morality and Consequences," in *The Tanner Lectures on Human Values*, vol. 2, ed. Sterling M. McMurrin, pp. 110–111 (Salt Lake City: University of Utah Press, 1981).

33. See Thomson, "Self-Defense" and "Physician-Assisted Suicide: Two Moral Arguments," *Ethics* 109 (April 1999): 497–518.

34. I now think that there may be a distinction, insofar as the DDE is concerned, between the following two types of cases: (1) The bombardier intends to drop bombs. The bombs both cause the death of the children that he intends to kill and destroy the munitions plant as well. (This is the case I have described in the text.) (2) The bombardier intends to destroy the munitions plant only because its blowing up causes the death of the children that he intends to kill. In the second case, it is possible to construe the bombardier as intending something good (destruction of the munitions) with the further intention of producing something bad (the death of the children) (although there may be problems with thinking of the destruction of munitions as a good in itself; on this see chap. 2). In the first case, he intends a means (not good in itself) of dropping bombs with the further intention of producing its bad effect. In judging the second case, it is possible that proponents of the DDE might permit the action because the agent intends to do something good even if not because it is good. On the other hand, what is good is done only in order to accomplish a bad aim, and on these grounds the DDE might imply that the act is wrong. To avoid this problem in interpreting the DDE, I will use cases of the first type. If cases of the second type are also judged impermissible by the DDE, they too could be used to make my point. I failed to note this possible distinction between cases in discussing the relation of intention and permissibility in my *Intricate Ethics* but try to take account of it in "Terrorism and Intending Evil," in *Ethics for Enemies*, chap. 2. I think the distinction is also overlooked by Thomas Scanlon in his discussion of the relation between intention and permissibility in cases where someone intends something good (e.g., to save someone's life) but only for the sake of a bad further intention. However, this need not affect his conclusions. See his *Moral Dimensions: Permissibility, Meaning, Blame* (Cambridge, MA: Harvard University Press, 2010).

35. For an example of this, see the Track Trolley Case described in my *Morality, Mortality*, vol. 2, and in chap. 2, note 18, of this volume. (I owe the case to Keith DeRose.)

36. Thomson, "Self-Defense."

37. Ibid., p. 295 n9.

38. Ibid., p. 297.

39. Notice that Thomson's case is different from one in which, given our act, the deaths of the children are necessary to *sustain* the destruction of the munitions plant because grief over their death is what prevents the parents from immediately rebuilding the plant. This sort of necessary causal role in ending the war is, I believe, morally different from the deaths' being necessary to *produce* (rather than sustain) some effect that ends the war. For more on this, see chap. 2, this volume, as well as "Toward the Essence of Nonconsequentialism," in *Fact and Value: Essays on Ethics and Metaphysics for Judith Jarvis Thomson*, ed. Alex Byrne, Robert Stalnaker, and Ralph Wedgwood, pp. 155–182 (Cambridge, Mass.: MIT Press, 2001), and *Intricate Ethics*, chap. 5. For more on the distinction between TKN and tactical bombing see chapter 8, and *Ethics for Enemies*, chapter 2.

40. My own view is actually more complicated. For (as noted in n. 39) if evil* is causally necessary for greater good to occur but evil* sustains rather than produces the greater good, it can be permissible to bring it about. See chap. 2.

41. Such as the Doctrine of Productive Purity (DPP), which I discuss below, in chap. 10, and in my *Intricate Ethics*, chap. 5.

42. I have been discussing whether the DDE is correct to rule out terror killing. For additional types of acts in war that the DDE rules out but that seem to be permissible, see chap. 2, part 2.

43. I argue for the same conclusion in "Justifications for Killing Noncombatants," chap. 2, this volume, as did Thomson in her "Self-Defense."

44. Philippa Foot, "The Problem of Abortion and the Doctrine of Double Effect," reprinted in her *Virtues and Vices* (Berkeley: University of California Press, 1978).

45. I owe this case to Jeff McMahan. It raises the issue of whether we may shoot through a human shield to the aggressor he shields.

46. For an attempt to describe a principle of this sort, see chap. 2, and *Intricate Ethics*, chap. 5. I call it the Doctrine of Productive Purity (DPP). In chap. 2, part 3, I briefly describe its predecessor, the Doctrine of Initial Justification (DIJ).

47. That is, I do not think distance per se affects negative duties not to harm even if it may affect noncontractual duties to aid.

48. For a brief explanation of why option (b) might be permitted, see chap. 2, part 1. Option (d) might be permitted because it is not what we introduce into an environment (our bombs) that directly harms people or overlaps (occupy the same space as) what directly harms people. Rather, what we introduce into an environment makes something in the environment (with which what we introduce does not overlap) be a threat. For more on this, see my *Intricate Ethics*, chapter 5.

49. I do not think that the fact that one of the group that is threatened, rather than a bystander, redirects to C makes the redirection morally impermissible. However, C might also permissibly send the threat back toward the five as they were originally threatened, I believe. Note also that causing harm as one escapes an unjust threat rather than as one travels to defeat an unjust threat may be permissible according to Principle X. For this seems analogous to what I call the Lazy Susan Case. This case involves moving threatened people away from a threat coming at them with the side effect that fewer people get killed. I think turning the Lazy Susan is permissible. Now suppose that the five are trying to escape an unjust attack by B in a car, and they know the car will emit deadly fumes and kill bystander C. They are permitted to escape in this way if the Lazy Susan Case is any indication. I have discussed the Lazy Susan Case in my *Morality, Mortality*, vol. 2, and in *Intricate Ethics*, among other places.

50. Thomson, "Self-Defense."

51. A possible exception to this is if it were morally wrong for C to remain neutral. I owe this point to a member of the audience at the City University Graduate Center.

52. I would now say that such principles may apply in other circumstances that share the features present in war that justify the principles.

53. Jonathan Adler reminded me of the relevance of permissions related to self/other asymmetries rather than duties of special care in the war context. I had discussed them previously in connection with Peter Unger's views about the Trolley Problem in "Grouping and the Imposition of Loss," *Utilitas* 10 (1998): 292–319, reprinted as chapter 6 in *Intricate Ethics*.

54. Douglas Lackey disagrees. He informs me that he has argued that one must be strictly neutral between noncombatants of one's own country and an enemy's country in deciding who is harmed by tactical bombing. (Judith Thomson would now also disagree with what I wrote about the trolley case in the article on which this chapter is based. See her "Turning the Trolley," *Philosophy & Public Affairs* 36(4) (2008): 360–374, and a short response I make to her views in "The Trolley Problem," *International Encyclopedia of Ethics*, ed. H. LaFollette (Wiley-Blackwell, 2013).)

55. It may be suggested that neutral C is not to be harmed by A only because if A harmed C, then C would also go to war with A. But even if C were weak and could pose no threat to A, it seems to have greater inviolability.

56. Walzer's view makes it morally irrelevant that our soldiers are ours, at least when the comparison is with B noncombatants. But this view is compatible with the fact that they are ours being morally relevant in comparison to B combatants. It is possible that citizenship is morally irrelevant when comparing noncombatants with combatants even though citizenship is relevant when comparing combatant with combatant and also when comparing noncombatant with noncombatant. This is an instance of what I call the Principle of Contextual Interaction: A factor can matter morally in some but not all contexts. (Shelly Kagan's warnings about what he calls the Additive Fallacy also apply here. That is, it is wrong to think a factor always bears the same weight.)

57. These points arose in discussion with Ruth Chang, Shelly Kagan, Jeff McMahan, and Larry Temkin. McMahan argues that just cause can not be separated from violability of combatants in his *Killing in War* (New York: Oxford University Press, 2009), among other places. I discuss some of these views in "The Morality of Killing in War: Some Traditional and Nontraditional Views", in the *Oxford Handbook on Philosophy and Death*, ed. Ben Bradley, Fred Feldman, and Jens Johansson (forthcoming), which is chap. 4 of this volume.

58. This would be a case, I believe, in which a B combatant can permissibly respond to A's permissible attack on him, although B is not wronged by A's act.

59. I argued for this in *Creation and Abortion* (New York: Oxford University Press, 1992).

60. I would now emphasize that this paragraph discusses the possibility that risk of harm may be imposed ex ante to save a certain number of soldiers even though, ex post, at the time that an A soldier faces certain harm, he may kill the same number of B soldiers for whose sake he ran a small risk of harm.

61. Subsequently, I discovered that it was overlooked by Thomas Hurka in his "Proportionality in the Morality of Wars", *Philosophy & Public Affairs*, 33(1) (2005): 34–66.

62. In the original article on which this chapter is based, I mistakenly drew the opposite conclusion. If A combatants can be more violable than A noncombatants and yet (to A) have the same inviolability as A noncombatants relative to B combatants, does this lead to problems

when we face a choice among all three parties? For example, suppose that one A noncombatant death is equal to 100 A combatant deaths but not more and equal to 300 B combatant deaths but not more, at least in deciding when to engage with the enemy. Suppose that in a particular case, 350 B combatants will have to be killed if A is to rescue one A noncombatant stranded and under threat of death from natural causes. (If the A noncombatant were under attack from 350 B combatants, then I assume that he could permissibly kill them all if this is necessary to save himself and that A combatants may do in his defense what he may do.) Fifty A combatants could lay down their lives to save the one noncombatant by fighting off the 350 B combatants who would respond to any attempt to save an A noncombatant. May A engage with the 350 B combatants because the A combatant/B combatant ratio and the A combatant/A noncombatant ratio will be satisfied? Or may A not save the noncombatant because the A noncombatant/B combatant ratio is exceeded? (I am grateful to Ian McMullen for raising this issue.) To answer this question we should, I think, see what defense of whom would trigger the engagement. If we do this, we should conclude that an A combatant should not step in to defend an A noncombatant if saving him is not worth the number of B combatants. On the other hand, in another case suppose a possible engagement involves 110 A soldiers defending themselves against 350 B combatants, but B would be equally pleased to choose an alternative route to its goal that does not involve killing so many A combatants even though it kills one noncombatant as a side effect. What I have said implies that while one A noncombatant could kill any number of attacking B combatants if this were necessary to save himself, he need not be defended against B's use of the alternative route if this can be done only by sacrificing 110 A combatants (even assuming there is no shortage of A combatants for other goals). Now suppose A has to choose between (1) picking an engagement where it would have to kill 1,000 B combatants to save 200 of its combatants and (2) doing something to save those 200 combatants that would kill only one A noncombatant as a side effect. Do the ratios given imply that A should save A combatants by doing what kills its own noncombatant? Perhaps so. If the idea of finding actual ratios seems implausible, the points I have made could be put into terms of reasons. For example, that one will kill combatants rather than noncombatants (even when both are on the same side) is not always a definitive reason against a course of conduct with the opposite result. (I now think it is much too simple to speak about one ratio that relates, for example, A combatants and noncombatants. Much will depend on how their deaths would come about, for example, whether the A combatants must avoid killing a noncombatant or must save him from attack by B or whether A combatants must defend A noncombatants against B or instead simply "take a hit" for them. I discuss this a bit in "The Morality of Killing in War: Some Traditional and Nontraditional Views," chap. 4.)

63. I am here using liability without its implying that it is due to past conduct of those liable. The past-conduct condition is part of the sense of liability employed by Jeff McMahan in his *Killing in War*.

64. I owe this point to Stuart Swetland.

65. For an additional element in this argument, dealing with the difference between not being unjust and not being a victim of injustices, see p. 70.

66. Suppose it were only permissible but not obligatory for a state to stop its injustice against another state in a way that harms its citizens. Then the argument would have to claim that because it is permissible for the state engaged in such an injustice to do something, it is permissible for the victim of injustice to do it. Because this is not, in general, true,

it would have to be argued that it is true in the particular context where the two states are at war.

67. Later, two more steps will be added to this argument.

68. I owe this point to Ronald Dworkin.

69. See Judith Thomson, *The Realm of Rights* (Cambridge, MA: Harvard University Press, 1990).

70. Thomas Scanlon, "Moral Assessment and the Agent's Point of View" (presentation at Boalt Hall Law School, University of California–Berkeley, Feb. 28, 2002). See also his *Moral Dimensions*.

71. I discuss a possible instance of this in "Collaboration with the Enemy: Harming Some to Save Others from the Nazis," chap. 5, and in "Responsibility and Collaboration," which is chapter 10 in *Intricate Ethics*.

72. As discussed earlier.

73. Discussion with Ruth Chang, Shelly Kagan, Jeff McMahan, and Larry Temkin helped in reaching this conclusion. The issue of doctors in wartime was raised in a paper by Jeff McMahan, who took a different view of their role.

74. These are central claims of Jeff McMahan's "Innocence, Self-Defense, and Killing in War," *Journal of Political Philosophy* 2 (September 1994): 193–221. The possibility that people in the last class might be legitimate targets of terror bombing was also suggested by Gertrude Ezorsky.

4

The Morality of Killing in War: Some Traditional and Nontraditional Views

This chapter is about killing in war from a moral (not legal) perspective. It gives an overview of some "classic" views and some recent alternatives to these on selected issues. These views are derivative of deeper nonconsequentialist perspectives in ethics. The chapter raises questions, often without providing answers.

A. Some Aspects of Standard Just War Theory

1. *JUS AD BELLUM* VERSUS *JUS IN BELLO*

a. Standard just war theory's first stage is *jus ad bellum*, justice in starting a war. This includes having a just cause and meeting conditions of necessity (no other way to achieve the just cause) and proportionality (the costs of war in terms of harm to people would be proportional to the achievement of the just cause). Failure to meet these conditions (and others) can result in failing *jus ad bellum*. Standard just war theory is concerned with war between nation-states. But the question may arise whether a nonstate agent can satisfy the conditions of *jus ad bellum* and so be a legitimate agent for war. Similarly, the question may arise whether a nonstate entity may be the target of war.

b. According to the standard theory, questions of *jus ad bellum* are separate from the questions of *jus in bello* (justice in war), which are the primary concern of this chapter. On this view, a nation can fail the first and still satisfy the second because its combatants fight properly even if their side should not be fighting at all. Alternatively, on this view, an agent can satisfy *jus ad bellum* and fail *jus in bello* because its combatants fight improperly. Furthermore, according to the standard theory, the same conditions on justice in fighting apply to both just combatants (those on the just side) and unjust combatants (those on the unjust side), so what counts as a violation of *jus in bello* will be the same for all sides. This is referred to as the moral equality of combatants (which I shall abbreviate as the Equality Thesis).

2. WHAT DOES *JUS IN BELLO* PRESCRIBE ACCORDING TO STANDARD JUST WAR THEORY?

a. The discrimination condition distinguishes what combatants (Cs) may do on the basis of *to whom* they do it: to other Cs or to noncombatants (NCs). There is also a distinction between *what* may be done: Roughly, Cs on the opposing side(s) may be deliberately attacked and killed in order to achieve a military goal as well as killed as side effects, but NCs may not be deliberately attacked and killed. However, NCs may sometimes be killed as a side effect, even foreseen to certainly occur, of a deliberate action undertaken for military purposes. This is referred to as collateral damage. These elements are enumerated in figure 4.1 and discussed in what follows.

(i) Who are Cs? Standardly, they are thought to be members of a recognized fighting force who deliberately present a current threat to the physical well-being of opposing Cs or NCs. Cs are considered "noninnocent" in the sense that they are threats, not in the sense that they are at fault or to blame. Cs who are not threats at a given time (e.g., they are sleeping before an attack) may be attacked "preemptively" to stop their forthcoming attack. This suggests that "noninnocent" is used in standard theory more broadly than "currently presenting a threat" and closer to "part of a military operation," thereby also including commanders who only send Cs into battle.

As many opponent Cs may be killed as is necessary to achieve a military mission or save one's own people. Hence, it is not out of proportion to kill many opponent Cs to save one of one's own Cs. One way of understanding this is to see the determination of proportionality as involving a form of *pairwise comparison* between a victim and each of those who threaten him: If one opponent C is liable to be killed to save one's own C, then so is each opponent C. There is no aggregation of all the deaths of opponent Cs to determine the proportionality of one's response.[1]

If there is no restriction on the number of opponent Cs permissibly harmed when necessary to achieve military ends, there may still be restrictions on how they are harmed. Thomas Nagel has argued that, within *jus in bello*, Cs may be attacked only in a way that directly responds to the threat they do or will present, not in any way at all that furthers the defeat of their side. This implies, Nagel claims, that one may not starve them, deny them medical care, or use weapons that disfigure. These methods attack Cs simply as human beings, not as threats, even if attacking them as human beings is a means to stop them from being threats. But

Object of Harm	C		NC
Type of Harm	Deliberate	Side effect	Side effect

FIGURE 4.1

the complaint one has is not with their humanity but with their being a threat, and so Nagel thinks one's response should be directed at their threat itself.[2]

(ii) Who are NCs? They are thought to include all those who are innocent in the sense that they do not present current threats or who are not part of a recognized fighting force. In addition to civilian NCs, there might be noncivilian NCs (e.g., members of the military not part of a recognized fighting force). However, civilians who take up arms and become threats to Cs do not thereby achieve combatant status if they are not part of a recognized fighting force. NCs may be, to varying degrees, morally responsible for the existence of threats that Cs present (e.g., by voting to start and continue the war) and yet not be subject to deliberate attacks. It is said that even those who help to make others into threats by making munitions may not be targeted while they do their work but only collaterally harmed by attacks on munitions plants. Those who supply food to Cs and so keep the threat going are not subject to deliberate attack. (Nagel, however, distinguishes between deliberately attacking NCs whose activities support Cs as threats when they are engaged in these activities [e.g., making munitions] and attacking NCs who support Cs when they are simply acting as human beings [e.g., asleep] even though surviving as a human being is a necessary condition for being able to help a threat.)

(iii) What is the deliberate/side-effect distinction in standard *jus in bello*? Some (e.g., Michael Walzer) think it is based on the Doctrine of Double Effect (DDE),[3] which says that (1) it is morally impermissible to intend evil as an end or even as means to a greater good but (2) if we are seeking a good end, (3) we may deliberately (including intentionally) use means that (a) are not evil in themselves and (b) are necessary to achieve the good, and (4) the foreseen bad side effects (of the means or the achievement of the end) need not stand in the way of action if and only if the bad side effects are proportional to the good to be achieved. Conditions (3b) and (4) are the necessity and proportionality conditions of *jus in bello*. So sometimes causing the very same harm that was ruled out as a means to a good need not rule out achieving the good when the harm is a side effect. (It should be noted that the necessity condition does not refer to the necessity of pursuing the good. It may seem odd that the DDE nowhere requires one to consider whether pursuing some other, perhaps lesser good the means to which would cause no harm might be a substitute for the good one is actually pursuing.[4])

For the DDE, foreseen bad side effects to be considered in determining proportionality are primarily those that are direct effects of what is done to achieve some end in war and the effects of the achievement of these ends within war (for example, the direct effects of a bomb used to blow up munitions and the effect of the munitions blowing up). Such bad effects do not necessarily include those foreseen to come about but through the intervening agency of an opponent. For example, suppose one side drops bombs on a military facility that causes no harm to NCs. However, it is foreseen that the opponent will respond to the destruction of its munitions by engaging in activities that cause collateral deaths among its own

NCs. Though these deaths are foreseen, they do not have the same role in a pro-portionality calculation done by the side that would drop the bombs as would collateral harms from the bombs themselves. This is because they are most directly due to the opponent's acts.[5] The bad effects also seem to be limited to rights viola-tions, such as physical harm and property harm. Making people unhappy may be a bad effect but not one they have a right to avoid, and so it is not one counted in a proportionality calculation.[6]

Strictly speaking, the DDE can also be applied when dealing with Cs. So Aquinas[7] says that even though it is permissible to stop an attacker, foreseeing his death, one may not intend his death as a means of stopping his attack. Yet, stan-dard *jus in bello* permits intentionally killing Cs if this is necessary to stop their attacks and, in this way, does not conform to the DDE.

The DDE implies that it is wrong to intentionally kill NCs in terror bombing where some NCs would be deliberately killed in order to demoralize other NCs into pressuring their government to surrender. By contrast, the DDE implies that it may be permissible to bomb a munitions plant when either the bombs or the destruction of the plant foreseeably cause the same harm and terror to NCs as terror bombing, only as a side effect.

Walzer suggests what he sees as an addition to the DDE:[8] Not only must one *not intend* to harm NCs, one must also *intend not to* harm NCs (short of not fighting the war at all). So one should accomplish a military aim by intentionally killing *more* enemy Cs (or running greater risks to one's own Cs) instead of doing what would cause even a proportional number of deaths of NCs collaterally. Note however, if there are such alternative ways to accomplish one's aim that harm only Cs, this may imply that one has not met the necessity condition of the DDE, and so doing what causes even proportionate NC collateral harm may not be justified even according to the DDE. Intending not to harm NCs, however, may require one to also think about changing one's goal (e.g., to pursue a lesser good). In this respect, Walzer's proposal for a second intention may indeed modify the DDE.

Some think intended effects can be distinguished from side effects by the Counterfactual Test: Suppose, counter to fact, that harm to NCs would not occur. If we would then not proceed with our mission, this is said to be a sign that we intend the harm. There are well-known line-drawing problems involved in using the DDE. For example, perhaps one need not intend the death of a C when one rams a blade into his heart but only intend to incapacitate him until victory is won. Of course, one foresees with certainty that the C will die, but one can also foresee with certainty the deaths of victims in collateral damage. A revision to the DDE aims to deal with this problem by prohibiting *intended involvement* of someone without his consent even when one only foresees harm to him (in contrast to merely foreseen involvement leading to harm).[9]

To avoid the line-drawing problems raised by the intention/foresight distinc-tion, Nagel instead distinguishes "what we do to someone" from "what happens to someone as a result of what we do."[10] He thinks the moral constraints on doing harm to someone are stronger than those on doing what will result in harm. He argues that bombing an area where we know there are opponent Cs and NCs in order to get the Cs (without intending the involvement of NCs) still involves "doing something to" the NCs and should be ruled out on this ground.[11]

It is important to see that one cannot justify the intended/foreseen harm distinction (or something like it) on the grounds that it leads to fewer NC deaths overall. For it is possible that terror bombing a few NCs could end a war that will cause many more NC collateral deaths if it continues. This is one indication that we are dealing with a nonconsequentialist distinction (i.e., one not based solely on producing the best consequences, though perhaps required by respect for the worth of the person).[12]

b. Standard *jus in bello* has been interpreted to allow deliberate harming of NCs in a "supreme emergency."[13] Permitting such exceptions might be part of what is known as threshold deontology (or threshold nonconsequentialism): The prohibitions are not absolute but have thresholds and so may permissibly be overridden even if this involves infringing the rights of NCs. Nagel, however, calls deliberately killing NCs in a supreme emergency a "dilemmatic situation," by which he means that we do wrong if we kill the NCs and we do wrong if we do not kill them. Hence, he thinks this is *not* just a situation in which we *wrong someone* (by infringing his right) in the course of doing what is overall *not* a wrong act.

B. Some Alternatives to Standard *Jus in Bello*

Now consider some alternatives to the preceding claims. First, consider issues connected to killing Cs (in [1] and [2]) and then to killing NCs (in [3] and [4]).

1. REJECTING THE EQUALITY THESIS

a. Jeff McMahan has argued[14] that it is impossible morally to separate *jus ad bellum* from *jus in bello* and that, because of this, unjust Cs are not morally permitted to do whatever just Cs are permitted to do. McMahan attacks the Equality Thesis by rejecting the standard view of what makes someone noninnocent (and so liable to be intentionally attacked). That is, he denies that just Cs are noninnocent merely because they are threats to their opponents. On his view, what is crucial for being liable to attack is not presenting a threat but being morally responsible for an objectively wrong (impermissible) threat. (McMahan denies that objective wrongdoing is sufficient for being liable to attack in the absence of an agent's being morally responsible for such wrongdoing, and he does not require that an agent *be engaged* in the wrongdoing to be liable to attack so long as she is morally responsible for it, for example, by making someone else act wrongly.[15]) An objective wrong is what would be known to be morally wrong in a perfect epistemic state. Its opposite is objective right, including objective permissibility and, when there is a positive reason to act, objective justifiability. Emphasizing objectively permissible and impermissible (wrong) threats contrasts with, for example, holding that presenting a threat can be morally permissible when it is the result of beliefs that it is reasonable for a threatening agent to have even if the beliefs are in error. I shall call this alternative the nonobjective view of permissibility.[16]

Just Cs who have a just cause and act in accordance with discrimination, proportionality, and necessity conditions in war (and any other conditions of *jus in bello*) are not morally responsible for objectively wrong threats. Hence, McMahan believes that they are not liable to be attacked by unjust Cs who attack them even if they do so in self-defense. (He uses the analogy of a policeman who justifiably attacks a criminal but does not, he thinks, thereby become liable to any attacks on him by the criminal or others.[17]) McMahan thinks unjust Cs cannot satisfy the discrimination condition when they attack such just Cs because they then deliberately attack the innocent, which standard just war theory rules out. This is so even if unjust Cs reasonably believe the just Cs are unjustly attacking them. However, if unjust Cs are morally responsible for objective wrongdoing (in pursuing an unjust war), they themselves are noninnocent and liable to attack by just Cs. This is so even if it is reasonable for unjust Cs to believe they are just (and perhaps unreasonable for just Cs to believe they are themselves just). In attacking such unjust Cs, just Cs *can* satisfy the discrimination condition.[18]

McMahan further claims that unjust Cs also cannot satisfy the proportionality condition of *jus in bello* because: (1) The deaths of those who are liable to be killed (unjust Cs) do not count as bad effects in a proportionality calculation, but the deaths of innocents, including just Cs, do. (2) Many just Cs are killed intentionally by unjust Cs, not merely killed as side effects. McMahan believes that a higher degree of good is needed to compensate for intentional killing rather than for side-effect killing of the innocent. (He is not an absolutist about the DDE.) Hence, more good is needed to make these killings not be out of proportion to one's aim.[19] (3) But unjust Cs have no just cause whose achievement can be a good weighed against harms they cause, and saving unjust Cs who are liable to be killed is not a good that can be weighed against killing of just Cs or NCs. (4) Saving NCs from improper treatment by misbehaving Cs on the just side *is* a good that can be counted when achieved by unjust Cs. However, killing such Cs on the just side who violate *jus in bello* must also meet the necessity condition, and if the improper killing of NCs could also be prevented by unjust Cs' ceasing to wage war, killing misbehaving Cs on the just side is not necessary to stop the wrongs they do.

b. Consider possible objections to and implications of these arguments rejecting the Equality Thesis.

(i) In explaining the impermissibility of unjust Cs attacking just Cs, McMahan emphasizes that in rightfully defending themselves or pursuing some other just cause, just Cs have done nothing to make themselves liable to attack. However, he also considers the possibility that this is consistent with its sometimes being objectively permissible to kill them deliberately. For example, he supposes that

NCs will have their rights infringed if they die as a side effect of a C attack on a munitions plant that is justified despite collateral damage. He thinks these NCs might be permitted to target the just C (even when they know he is justified in his act) in order to stop his bombing and save themselves.[20] This case suggests that it is not sufficient for the impermissibility of killing someone and even for his not being liable to be killed that he bears no moral responsibility for a wrongful threat. What may be crucial is whether the victim of his threat was liable to that attack or instead would have his rights at least infringed if he were permissibly attacked. (Though I will later [p. 101] suggest that this too may not be crucial.) If the rights of unjust Cs responsibly involved in an unjust war would *not* be infringed if just Cs attack them, then it is this factor that should be emphasized in an argument for the impermissibility of unjust Cs' attacks on just Cs who threaten them.

(ii) One reason McMahan reaches his conclusions that unjust Cs may not (ordinarily) attack just Cs seems to be that he accepts the "objective account" of wrong, permissible, and justified. It might be argued that we need not reject many elements of the Equality Thesis if we accept the nonobjective account (as described earlier). Then, at least when unjust Cs are epistemically justified (even if wrong) in believing that their war is just and that actual just Cs are engaged in an unjust war, unjust Cs could permissibly attack just Cs. (McMahan, by contrast, would say that such unjust Cs may be excused but are still doing impermissible acts.) However, unjust Cs acting permissibly on the nonobjective view would *not* imply that it was (objectively or nonobjectively) impermissible for others (such as actual just Cs) to stop unjust Cs' attacks by killing them.[21] (The Equality Thesis speaks to whether opponents may do the same acts; this is consistent with it being permissible for third parties who know who truly has a just cause to attack *only* unjust Cs, not just Cs.) Hence, on the nonobjective account of permissibility, the unjust Cs and the just Cs could both satisfy at least nonobjective proportionality and discrimination requirements.[22]

To better understand the role of the objective account of permissibility in McMahan's rejection of the Equality Thesis, consider the following Debate Analogy: Suppose two people are debating an important issue to which no one yet knows the correct answer; they take opposite positions, and one and only one of the positions is correct though no one yet knows who is correct. Are these debaters moral equals who are entitled to do the same things in the debate? We know that one of them must be defending an untruth (though he is not lying), and he may influence other people to believe in an untruth on an important matter. We would ordinarily think that these debaters are moral equals and that it is permissible for each to do what the other does to defend his view and defeat his opponent in the debate. This is so even though an omniscient being (not us) might be correct in interfering with the debater who is in the wrong as he speaks but not interfering with the other. But it seems that on McMahan's view, the mere fact that one debater is objectively wrong means that he is not an equal in the debate.

Of course, there may be cases where a debater may not have good grounds for holding his position. But it is important to realize that on the objective view that

McMahan seems to employ, this is not necessary in order for one of the opponents to not be a moral equal. For that, it is sufficient that he is wrong even if he has good grounds for holding his position. (Not being reasonable in one's beliefs is a different ground [that McMahan may also accept] for not being a moral equal to someone who holds a correct position [even if his reasons for holding the correct position do not definitively prove the position is correct].)

(iii) If *jus in bello* were dependent on *jus ad bellum*, it is possible that most unjust Cs would not satisfy even the nonobjective account of permissible action in war. This is because they do not act on reasonable beliefs about the justice of their cause. Indeed, they may themselves recognize either that their side has no just cause or that they have only weak grounds for believing it has a just cause. It might be suggested that they are nevertheless the moral equals of just Cs with respect to being permitted to attack just Cs since just Cs may attack them. The argument for this might be that it is (even objectively) morally permissible (and perhaps obligatory) for Cs to carry out the directives of legitimate government officials. This could be true even if those officials mistakenly conclude that the war satisfies *jus ad bellum*. Indeed, especially in a democracy, Cs may have no right to interfere (by military inaction) with the democratic decision to go to war even though Cs will be the ones who do the killing. Similarly, a clerk who must carry out a legitimate democratic policy may have no right to disobey orders to carry out the policy even though it is the wrong policy and he will be the one who ultimately affects people by carrying it out. This is not to deny that someone might, on occasion, have the right to refuse to remain a C if he disagrees with the decision to go to war. However, remaining a C and then refusing to carry out orders, or undermining them, does not seem to be a right that Cs should have, at least when it is not a matter of their refusing to violate the requirements of *jus in bello*.

Suppose it is permissible (objectively or nonobjectively) to accept the role of a C who acts on orders in a system of government that is legitimate (judged objectively or nonobjectively). Then it might be permissible for people as Cs to do acts that it would be impermissible for them to do were they not in such a role (e.g., killing when it is not reasonable for them as individuals to think that their cause is just). And again, that it is permissible for them to accept and act in the role need not imply that it is impermissible for others to try to stop their action. Similarly, an adversary system of law might be justified, and in it a lawyer might be permitted to defend someone she knows to be guilty even though it might be wrong for her to engage in such a defense outside of the adversary system. Furthermore, another lawyer is also permitted to try to stop the success of her defense.

(iv) Suppose McMahan were correct that unjust Cs would act unjustly in intentionally killing just Cs because the latter are innocent. McMahan believes that it is harder to justify intentionally killing the innocent than to justify killing them as a side effect. If unjust Cs will do wrong whether they intentionally kill just Cs or kill them and NCs collaterally, should not those who believe they are unjust Cs but for some reason will not stop fighting entirely choose to do the less serious rather than the more serious wrong? If so, then McMahan's views seem to imply that such unjust Cs who continue any war should at least minimize the *intentional* killing of just Cs (as well as just NCs). This may mean carrying out a war by targeting only munitions or infrastructure sites and causing increased side-effect harm to NCs on the just side. Since just Cs are no more liable to harm than just NCs on McMahan's view, there also might be no reason to bomb military sites causing just C collateral damage rather than just NC collateral damage. (At a certain point, the constraint on intentional killing of innocents might be overridden, on McMahan's view, in order to minimize killing overall.) In principle, this would be a moral argument for waging war that involved no intentional killing of just Cs but only intentional killing of unjust Cs and targeting munitions and infrastructure with collateral harm to just Cs and NCs.[23]

These points bear on the following argument that McMahan gives for *a convention* permitting equal rules of *jus in bello* for Cs on all sides in the absence of the moral equality of all Cs:[24] (1) Each side will think it is the just side, and there is now no definitive way to alter this. (2) The just side might, in fact, be objectively and morally permitted to do even more to the unjust side than the content of current *jus in bello* permits either side to do to the other. (3) However, given (1), it would be dangerous to allow the just side to do more than current *jus in bello* rules permit because then the unjust side would do it, too. (4) So, (a) there should be (what could be called) a conventional equality of combatants (b) at a level that is actually lower than what morality would permit only to the just side (c) but that makes it at least possible for the just side to wage a winning war. (5) These considerations imply (roughly) the rules we have now.

However, recall McMahan's view that intentionally targeting just Cs is a more serious wrong than collaterally harming just Cs and also NCs, and combine it with the assumption that it is at least possible for the just side to win a war by a strategy that involves targeting munitions and other facilities despite collateral harm to Cs and NCs. This, in conjunction with accepting considerations (1)–(4), seems to imply a convention of equality that is very different from current rules that allow targeting of Cs. It would imply at least a convention with no intentional killing of any persons, C or NC (subject to any threshold that would apply to intentionally killing NCs), to eliminate the possibility of intentionally killing just Cs, whom McMahan treats as innocents.[25]

2. WHAT MAY BE DONE TO ENEMY CS ASSUMING EITHER MORAL EQUALITY OR CONVENTIONAL EQUALITY?

a. The usual concern is with what may be done to enemy Cs by opponent Cs. First, consider possible revisions to the limits that some, like Nagel, would put on what may be done to enemy Cs even if targeting enemy Cs is sometimes permissible.

(i) As noted earlier, Nagel objects to attacking enemy Cs as human beings per se rather than as Cs per se. The examples he gives of attacking Cs as human beings, however, arguably involve treating Cs worse than if their attacks were stopped directly even by killing them. But there could be cases in which attacking a person as a human being in order to undermine his military effectiveness treats him much better than an attack on his combatant activities. For example, suppose we could win a war either by (i) killing a thousand troops as they attack or (ii) putting a diarrhea-inducing substance in their food (or using a diarrhea-inducing spray on the battle-field instead of bullets), thus making them unable to fight. In the case I am imagining, it is certain that we will win the war by killing the thousand, and we consider substituting less harmful means to victory directed at the same forces for the same end. At least in such cases, I find it hard to believe that we should kill rather than induce the incapacitating condition.

What if it is not clear who would win with conventional means? If enemy Cs were ordinary wrongdoers or even fully excused wrongdoers, the diarrhea spray would seem a morally acceptable means by which to win what could not otherwise be won. But suppose unjust enemy Cs are appropriately viewed as engaged in something like a legitimate action as either moral or conventional equals to just Cs. This might make it wrong to undermine their capacity as human beings to use conventional means to try to win the war. (This assumes that from their point of view it is better to risk death and win the war than to suffer less personal harm but lose.) Hence, another reason Nagel may reach his conclusion about ways of fighting is that he takes such a view of Cs and considers only cases in which it is not known that one side is certain to win by conventional harming and killing.

(ii) Suppose that in order to win the war, we must destroy a munitions plant. However, we lack the bombs to attack the plant directly (with collateral deaths of enemy Cs). We can destroy it only by toppling enemy Cs onto it. The very same Cs would be killed by toppling as would have been killed collaterally had we been able to bomb the plant. Might it be permissible to make use of the Cs for this purpose? Similarly, suppose some NCs are about to be killed by enemy Cs coming from the right whom we cannot stop. However, we could drive in enemy Cs from the left, using them as a protective human wall between the enemy right flank and the NCs. Given that it is dark and the enemy cannot make out who will be harmed, they will kill their own Cs, not our NCs. Are these uses of Cs morally permissible even though they involve instrumentalizing some Cs and do not involve our attacking those Cs to eliminate any threat they do (or will) present?

(iii) Killing NCs for the purpose of creating terror in order to win a war is ruled out by standard *jus in bello*. But is it permissible to kill *Cs* for the purpose of creating terror either in NCs or in other Cs, thereby getting the enemy to surrender? This is an example of what I have called "nonstandard terror bombing."[26] Consider the Rear Combatant Case: Our Cs are fighting an enemy attack, and they cannot win simply by defeating the attacking forces. The rear of the force is near a village. Our Cs can kill some enemy Cs at the rear who actually present no threat to our Cs (and even in the future will not present a threat, as they are retiring after this engagement). Attacking them will terrorize the villagers, who fear they will die collaterally, and the villagers will stop their Cs from attacking.[27] It seems permissible to kill the rear Cs as a means of creating this terror. Alternately, we could suppose that killing the same enemy Cs at the rear of the force would be effective in stopping the attack only because it leads other enemy troops to think our capabilities are much greater than they actually are. (In this variant, no terror is created in NCs). This too seems morally permissible.

One way to characterize standard ways of killing enemy Cs, in contrast to the examples in (ii) and (iii), is as "eliminative agency," a term that Warren Quinn introduced.[28] Such agency could involve killing Cs in order to eliminate the threat they do or will shortly present that would harm us. By contrast, Quinn applied the term "opportunistic agency" to using people so that we thereby improve our prospects (perhaps by preventing others from harming us) even though the people used do not (and even will not) present a threat to us. Examples (ii) and (iii) seem to involve opportunistic agency on certain enemy Cs, using these Cs in order to stop the threat that other Cs present. Yet, I suggest, such action is morally permissible.

Suppose that only eliminative agency were permitted in dealing with enemy Cs. This would make the standard account of when we may target Cs and NCs more uniform to some degree. This is because if NCs do not (and will not) present threats, we can explain why we may not target them if only eliminative agency is permitted.[29] Further, prohibitions on opportunistic use of NCs (as in terror-bombing them) would not be unique to them, as the prohibitions would apply to enemy Cs (as in [iii]) as well.[30] However, suppose eliminative agency includes killing Cs who may be threats in the future. Then being restricted to eliminative agency should not alone rule out undermining Cs simply as human beings (e.g., by contaminating their food supply), for this too eliminates their future threat.

b. Related to deciding what types of acts may be done to Cs by other Cs is the question of how many enemy Cs may be killed to preserve one's own Cs or to pursue a military mission. This is an instance of what I have referred to as "violability ratios" among classes of people.[31] As Thomas Hurka points out, how many enemy Cs it is permissible to kill to achieve a military mission or to spare our own Cs bears on whether our conduct satisfies the proportionality condition of *jus in bello*.[32]

Hurka accepts close to what I have described as the traditional view, that there is "virtually" no limit on the number of enemy Cs (at least volunteers) that may be killed (as targets or side effects) if this is necessary to save even *one* of one's own Cs or to pursue a militarily necessary mission.[33] He bases this conclusion on the view, also described earlier, that in ordinary self-defense a person under attack by many aggressors may kill any number of them if this is necessary to save himself and a bystander is permitted to do the same in defense of another. (As noted earlier, I think the concept of pairwise comparison is a useful way of characterizing the view that killing so many is permissible.) However, also thinking of ordinary self-defense, McMahan considers cases in which our just Cs are merely defending their own lives and achievement of the just cause is not put in jeopardy. He argues (contrary to traditional *jus in bello*) that if enemy Cs have reduced moral responsibility for their actions due to duress and to epistemic limitations on knowing what cause is just, our Cs may have to absorb some costs to avoid killing those enemy Cs merely to save themselves. This implies that sometimes our Cs should bear more costs for the achievement of the just cause in order to spare enemy Cs whose behavior is to some degree excused.[34]

My own concern in the discussion of this topic is to emphasize a distinction between (1) what should be done to avoid exposing one's Cs to *risk* of death and (2) what should be done to prevent one's Cs' certain death.[35] Suppose one could achieve a military mission that would end a war in either of two ways. The first would present a 0.01 risk of dying to each of one's 5,000 Cs and a 0.8 risk of dying to each of the enemy's 5,000 Cs. This is the same as the certainty that 50 of our Cs will die and 4,000 enemy Cs will die. The second way would present a 0.012 risk of dying to each of our 5,000 Cs and a 0.4 risk of dying to each of 5,000 enemy Cs. Even if we are certain there will be ten additional deaths on our side with the second way, at the time we decide on the way (*ex ante*), there would be only a very small increase in the risk to each C of being one of the dead. This increased risk means that in choosing the second way, 2,000 fewer enemy Cs will die and each will have a much-reduced *ex ante* risk of dying. Some might argue we should use the second way. My concern here is not to argue that this choice is correct but only to suggest that this choice *could be consistent* with killing more than 4,000 enemy Cs if this were necessary to save ten of our Cs, each of whom would otherwise certainly (i.e., with a probability of 1) be killed by those enemy Cs. (There is a difference between it being certain *ex ante* that ten more Cs will die and it being true of ten particular Cs that they will certainly die. It is the latter scenario that most clearly compares to killing in self- and other-defense.) Put another way, the permissibility of saving ten of our Cs from certainly being killed if we can, by killing an enormous number of enemy Cs, need not be inconsistent with it being morally right to slightly increase the risk to each of our Cs to avoid killing an enormous number of enemy Cs. This is so even when increasing the risk will certainly lead to ten more of our Cs dying *when we will not be in a position to save them from the death each will then certainly face.*[36]

Suppose there were a requirement to reduce risks to one's opponent by having one's own combatants assume risks. This requirement need not apply if opponent soldiers would shortly be killed anyway or if reducing this risk to them in one operation actually increased their risk overall.

c. It is also important to consider what a given side in a war may permissibly do to its own Cs.[37] Assume that it is sometimes permissible to use enemy Cs opportunistically (not just eliminatively) for military purposes or to save one's own NCs. Is it also permissible to do something like this to one's own Cs? Consider analogues to the cases given earlier in 2a (i) and (ii). Suppose one may send one's Cs to destroy a munitions plant knowing that 100 of them will either be killed by enemy Cs or die from exertion. Would it also be permissible to fatally topple 100 of one's Cs onto the munitions plant (or topple more, knowing that 100 of them will die) if only this would destroy the plant? If enemy Cs were moving to kill our NCs and there was no way to protect them but station one's own unarmed Cs around them to take the hits, would this be permissible? Also, if one way to bomb the enemy munitions plant near our own border would result in collateral deaths to our NCs while another way would result in collateral deaths to our Cs, should we use the second way? (The Equality Thesis, which concerns the equality of Cs on opposing sides, is consistent with either side deciding what to do to its own Cs as a function of their status relative to NC cocitizens.)[38]

On what I call the "Bodyguard Model" of one's own Cs, they can be assigned to take a hit headed for an NC and, assuming there is no shortage of Cs to achieve the just cause, Cs should be the preferred victims of our bombing the munitions plant.[39] An objection may be raised to the Bodyguard Model: Our Cs are trained and have duties to defend our NCs and to further their compatriots' goals only *by fighting.* They are not resources to be used in just any way for military aims and for defense of NC cocitizens. On this view, lives of our Cs are not available for absorbing (rather than fighting off) enemy attacks or collateral damage.

Suppose that the permissibility of using *enemy* Cs opportunistically as mere resources would have to be argued for independently of the Cs being (presumed to be) on the unjust side. (The Equality Thesis [moral or conventional] implies that it would *not* be wrong of an opponent to use our Cs in comparable ways. This suggests that permissible opportunistic use of enemy Cs is independent of whether one is a C on the just or the unjust side.) Then the grounds of our not treating our own Cs opportunistically for the sake of our NCs will have to be their status relative to fellow citizens rather than their status as just Cs who may not be used in the way unjust Cs may be used.

3. DELIBERATELY KILLING NONCOMBATANTS

Standard *jus in bello* rules out (most) deliberate killing of NCs. However, it permits some military operations foreseen to kill NCs collaterally. The permissibility of such killings is *not* usually thought to rest on NCs' past acts having made them liable to be killed collaterally. (A possible exception is their choosing to remain near a military target when they could, at no great cost, have left.)[40]

a. An alternative view suggests that many NCs *are* liable to varying degrees of deliberate harm when a war is being fought. One ground of such liability is some degree of moral responsibility for having a role in causing an unjust war (as judged from an objective or a nonobjective view). On this alternative view, heads of state, politicians, or journalists who are fully morally responsible for having a large role in producing an unjust war are liable to be targeted and may permissibly be targeted if this is useful in ending a war (either militarily or by causing terror).[41] Indeed, sometimes Cs may be excused for actively presenting threats whereas NCs are fully morally responsible for sending those Cs into combat. Then, some argue, those with high moral responsibility for the existence of a threatening military force are liable to be deliberately killed rather than those Cs with weak moral responsibility for actually posing a threat. This is so even though Cs' act of posing a threat intervenes between NC behavior and the actual harm in war. McMahan provides the following analogy: A corrupt sheriff deputizes an uneducated local and misleads him into thinking that an innocent person is a criminal. The sheriff further puts great pressure on the deputy to kill the innocent. The innocent can defend himself by either shooting at the deputy (as the deputy shoots at him) or shooting at the unarmed sheriff (who watches the deputy and the innocent from behind a tree). The sheriff's death will lead the deputy to drop his gun. McMahan thinks it is morally permissible and preferable to shoot the liable sheriff.[42]

Many NCs, however, will have only minimal moral responsibility for their role in an unjust war (because, for example, they are nonnegligently ignorant of either the injustice of the war or the fact that what they do supports it). Or they may play only a small causal role in generating a threat (for example, by voting). Many NCs will have no moral responsibility or causal role (e.g., children). McMahan concludes that the deliberate killing of NCs is rarely morally permissible due to such facts,[43] combined with the further facts that the deliberate killing of NCs would (usually) involve opportunistic rather than eliminative agency, NCs who are liable are not isolated from those who are not liable, and killing NCs has low effectiveness in ending a war.

However, McMahan also argues (in discussing other issues) that when there is no way to avoid someone's life being lost, even slight moral responsibility in one party to a threat can imply that he should be the one to die.[44] Further, it is not clear that McMahan should think that opportunistic agency used on NCs who are *not* innocent is worse than eliminative agency. (In his case of the guilty sheriff, he himself says it would be permissible to make opportunistic use of the sheriff. For example, the sheriff can be made to fall on the deputy when it is foreseen this would kill the sheriff and stop the deputy's gun from going off.[45]) Hence, if big funders of war were separated from others at a political gathering and bombing a few of them would be effective in stopping the war, it seems McMahan should think it morally preferable to kill them rather than many conscripts, though the latter actually pose the threat of harm.

To support the conclusion that having a small causal role in bringing about a threat does not rule out NCs' being deliberately killed, Helen Frowe imagines a case in which each of many people eagerly contributes a small sum to hire someone to kill an innocent person. She argues that any one of the contributors is liable to be killed and that this would be permissible if it were necessary and useful to save the innocent person's life from the killer.[46] From this, she concludes that NCs who knowingly accept even small roles in war efforts are equally liable to be deliberately killed and that it may be permissible to kill them.

But notice that, ordinarily, it would be permissible for an innocent person threatened by thousands of evil attackers to *kill all of them* even if they threatened him only with significant paralysis, not death. This suggests that if those responsible for hiring the killer in Frowe's case are liable to attack, they all may be killed even if this were necessary only to prevent significant paralysis in the innocent person. Suppose that NCs' being morally responsible for small causal contributions to an unjust war (e.g., by knowingly voting for war or by buying war bonds) made them similarly liable to deliberate opportunistic attack. Then could targeting large numbers of such NCs be morally permissible even if this were not effective in winning a war or saving lives but only in saving a few Cs or NCs on the other side from significant paralysis? This is a radical implication that casts doubt on Frowe's argument.

(Liability to being deliberately killed as a result of one's acts is not the only sort of liability. McMahan notes that in virtue of having voted for war, NCs might become liable to the risk of death collateral to tactical bombing.[47])

b. An objector to these nonstandard views on deliberately killing NCs might try to derive liability to deliberate attack from moral responsibility for posing a threat (or simply posing a threat) rather than from moral responsibility for starting or supporting war. For example, suppose it is permissible for A members of country X to have agreements with B comembers that Bs will fight on behalf of As' policies. Could it then be wrong for country Y, with whom X is at war, not to honor that internal (supposedly permissible) relation between As and Bs by targeting As rather than Bs on the grounds of As' moral responsibility? Ordinarily, it is not impermissible to attack a Mafia boss who employs a bodyguard rather than to attack his bodyguard even if the relation between the two calls for the bodyguard to bear all costs. However, not all agents who make decisions to go to war, even incorrect decisions, are criminals like the Mafia boss.

Perhaps whether outside parties should honor the agreement between As and Bs depends on whether there are morally good reasons to insulate As from bearing certain costs even if they are to some degree morally and causally responsible for the war. For example, this might be true if As would be less likely to decide to go to war on the basis of only factors that make that decision right were they subject to personal attack for that decision. It is also possible that when members of a community are obligated to make certain decisions as best they can, moral responsibility for bearing the costs (what Scanlon calls substantive responsibility)[48] need not affix to them. To illustrate this point, we might re-imagine McMahan's sheriff as an administrator not licensed to shoot but who, to the best of her ability, carries out her obligation to stop criminals. She sends out her uneducated, pressured deputy to stop what the sheriff believes is a true criminal attack. Unfortunately, she is mistaken, and the deputy is about to shoot an innocent person who is defending himself against the deputy. Is it still true that the sheriff, sitting in her office and bearing moral responsibility to a high degree for the conflict between her deputy and the innocent person, may be killed by the innocent if this would be as effective in stopping the deputy's attack as directly attacking the deputy?

c. Let us now consider NCs on the opponent's side who have not acted in a way that would give them any moral or causal responsibility for starting or maintaining a war. Is deliberately killing these NCs always impermissible, as standard *jus in bello* claims (excluding only supreme emergencies)? Here are some reasons to think not.

(i) Suppose such deliberate killing is not the only way to stop a supreme emergency. However, the number of collateral NC deaths that would be caused by a permissible alternative means could be so great that a threshold is reached on the prohibition of deliberate killing.

(ii) Now consider a case in which this is not so. Suppose that 1,000 NCs will be killed and terrorized as a proportionate side effect of our bombing a munitions plant to achieve a military goal. The only alternative way to achieve our goal is to terror-bomb ten of the very same people who would otherwise have died collaterally. It might be permissible to terror-bomb in this case, in part because those killed and terrorized would have been killed and terrorized anyway at the same time and 990 other lives will be saved. Such terror bombing could be permissible even if it would have been impermissible to terror-bomb ten people who would not otherwise have died collaterally. Secondary to the expected deaths and terror of some people collaterally, terror bombing them that would otherwise have been impermissible becomes permissible. Indeed, it may become the only permissible harmful act. Being constrained by someone's right not to be treated in a certain way (e.g., terror killed rather than collaterally killed) may not have the same moral significance when it will not make a difference to whether he is harmed as it has when it makes such a difference. This as an instance of what I call the Principle of Secondary Permissibility (PSP).[49]

(iii) Now suppose that while it is permissible for us to bomb the plant, causing a thousand NC collateral deaths, we would *supererogatorily* refrain from killing so many. Then we learn that if we terror-bomb ten of the NCs who would die collaterally if we did bomb the plant—as it is still permissible and possible for us to do—we can also achieve our goal. In this case, the NCs we would kill would *not* otherwise have been killed by us, and there are no additional NCs who would otherwise have died who will be saved. It may nevertheless be permissible to terror-bomb in this case because we can still, though we will not, kill the people (plus others) in the initially permissible way and we would kill ten in the initially permissible way if this were possible.[50] This is an extension of the PSP (EPSP).

(iv) What if criminals within our opponent country were about to wrongfully kill NCs and we could not stop them? Would it be impermissible to deliberately kill a few of these NCs if this would somehow achieve an important military mission (e.g., their being killed confuses the opponent troops) when this also scares the criminals away and so saves many NCs who would otherwise have been killed?[51] This may be permissible even though we rather than others will kill. The constraint on our harming NCs in certain ways, I believe, stems less from a concern with whether we or someone else acts than from a concern that the potential victim be proctected from mistreatment and retain authority over himself.

d. Assuming that it *is* often wrong to terror-bomb or otherwise deliberately kill NCs, let us consider traditional and alternative views about what makes this so.

(i) As noted, some proponents of the DDE argue that *intending* to kill NCs makes an act that kills them impermissible. It is important to see that even this traditional view need not imply that it is impermissible to bomb some military facility *only because* NCs will be killed. That is, there is a conceptual difference between intending to kill NCs and acting only because (or on condition that) we will kill them. Consider what I call the Munitions Grief Case:[52] We need to bomb a munitions plant for military purposes and know this will unavoidably cause collateral deaths of children next door. Their deaths would be proportionate if the destruction of the plant were permanent. However, we know the community will quickly rebuild it better than ever—thus making bombing pointless and the collateral damage disproportionate—if not for the fact that they will be depressed by the deaths of their children. Hence, it is only because (we know) the children will die that we bomb the munitions plant; we would not bomb if they did not die as an effect of the bombing. I think bombing in this case is permissible and *not inconsistent with the DDE* even though we would act because the deaths help sustain the destruction of the plant. We here take advantage of an *unavoidable* side effect of bombing the plant; we do nothing extra that is not necessary to bomb the munitions plant merely in order to make it the case that the bombing does cause the deaths of children.

This case helps, I think, show that we can distinguish conceptually among effects that are intended, merely foreseen, and because of which we act. I have referred to a view that takes account of these three distinctions as the Doctrine of Triple Effect (DTE).[53] Suppose it is possible to act only because we will produce a certain effect and we will refrain from acting if we would not produce it, without thereby intending the effect. This would show that the Counterfactual Test (discussed earlier) for the presence of intention is inadequate.[54]

(ii) Contrary to what the DDE claims, some have argued that acting with a wrong intention need not make an act morally impermissible, and so it does not matter whether our acts in war are consistent with the DDE. Consider Judith Thomson's example:[55] We need to bomb a munitions plant for its military effects and the collateral deaths of NCs are proportionate. However, the bombardier who will carry out the bombing has always wanted to kill NCs, and he drops the bombs on the munitions plant only in order to kill the NCs (Bad Bombardier Case). If this morally bad bombardier behaves no differently in all respects from a good bombardier, who intends to bomb the munitions plant only for its military effects *despite* the side-effect deaths, is his act of bombing morally impermissible when the good bombardier's act is permissible? Thomson thinks not.

It might be said that the bad bombardier acts permissibly because he at least intends to bomb the munitions plant and this is a permissible intention even if he has this intention only as a means to killing NCs. But the bad bombardier need not intend to bomb the munitions plant; he may intend to drop the bombs only as his means of killing the NCs. He foresees that the bombs will also destroy the munitions plant and he would not act if they did not, for he needs a pretext for his actions. But this need not mean that he intends that further effect. Even with this revision, it seems that his dropping the bombs is permissible, if a good bombardier's dropping the bombs would be permissible. This revised case shows that the DDE is also wrong if it claims that only a good we are seeking (i.e., intending) can compensate for bad side effects. The unintended destruction of the munitions plant (and its further military effect) can also compensate for the NCs' deaths, at least if the intended destruction could so compensate.

(iii) Thomas Scanlon argues that deliberately killing NCs is impermissible because it serves no military purpose. He argues that "military purpose" involves reducing munitions and forces, not causing terror to NCs as a means to getting them to surrender.[56] But even if we have such a narrow understanding of military purpose, we can imagine cases where bombing NCs would serve that purpose: In the Stampede Case, we bomb some NCs so as to terrorize other NCs, leading them to stampede and destroy a military facility. In the Human Tinder Case, we bomb NCs who live near a munitions plant in order to set the plant on fire.[57] Alternatively, killing NCs who are the relatives of Cs could demoralize Cs, leading them to stop fighting. It seems to me that deliberately killing NCs in these cases (when the NCs do not have the characteristics discussed in section 3c[ii]) is wrong despite its usefulness in narrow military terms. (It is important to note, however, that as a matter of historical fact, such bombings of NCs may not have been ruled out in past wars and indeed may not have been considered "terror bombings.")[58]

(iv) A different account of the impermissibility of deliberately killing NCs in most circumstances claims that it is wrong to cause harm to NCs as a necessary means to produce effects if the harm results from processes whose other effects do not themselves justify the harm. To understand this proposal, consider a version of the Bad Bombardier Case. It might be that the intended harm and terror to NCs are what actually cause the country to surrender before the elimination of the munitions can have this effect, as Thomson notes. Yet this would not affect the permissibility of bombing because in this case the harm and terror are not necessary to produce surrender. Another effect of the bombardier's act, destroying the munitions, would have done this, too, and so would have justified the deaths of some NCs as a side effect. By comparison, in terror bombing cases standardly contrasted with strategic bombing, NCs are either directly bombed or some facility is bombed whose destruction will kill NCs, but neither type of bombing will have any other useful military effect, produced without a necessary causal role for NC deaths, that is sufficient to justify NC harm as a side effect.

How do cases in which harm to NCs is causally required for any good effect differ from the Munitions Grief Case (discussed earlier)? In that case a necessary causal role for NC deaths in sustaining the destruction of the plant did not, I claimed, make bombing impermissible. In Munitions Grief, unlike standard terror bombing cases, the deaths are caused by and sustain the very outcome (the factory is destroyed) that could justify the deaths if it were sustained. It may be that the permissibility of bombing can be affected by what causes the NC deaths and whether these deaths are necessary to "sustain" a sufficiently good effect already produced rather than "produce" such a new effect.[59]

4. COLLATERAL HARM TO NONCOMBATANTS

A. Let us first deal with NCs who would not otherwise shortly die or be seriously harmed anyway and who would in no way reap benefits from the loss of their lives.

   a. (i) As noted, a prominent traditional justification of some collateral killing in war is the DDE. However, it has long been thought by some that, in nonwar contexts, the DDE incorrectly licenses collateral harm that is morally impermissible.[60] For example, suppose you and four other people are unjustly attacked by a villain. The only way to stop the villain is to throw a bomb at him. However, fragments of the bomb will also penetrate and kill an innocent bystander (Domestic Villain Case). It is ordinarily thought that it is impermissible for you or any outsider helping you to use the bomb.[61] This is so even though the bystander's involvement and death would be unintended side effects, and a greater number of people would be saved. In a variant, setting the bomb to defeat the villain requires you to drive over a road where a person is immovably located. His involvement and death are foreseen but unintended effects, and a greater number of people would be saved, yet it seems impermissible to drive on. However, the DDE seems to permit acting in both these cases. The problem is that the DDE allows side-effect harm to some to be outweighed by greater good to others, as in any consequentialist calculation.

   As noted earlier, Thomas Nagel tries to account for the permissibility of some collateral killing of NCs by distinguishing between what we do to someone and what happens to someone as a result of what we do. This distinction would, I think, rule out driving over someone in the preceding case. However, it would not prohibit using the bomb whose fragments would kill the bystander.

   (ii) Another general principle for determining when harming innocent by-standers is permissible for the sake of a greater good for others distinguishes (roughly) between (1) side effects of achieving a greater good, (2) side effects of causal means that we introduce into a context in order to achieve a greater good, and (3) side effects that depend on interaction between causal means that we introduce into a context in order to achieve a greater good and what is independently present in the context.[62] This Principle of Permissible Harm (PPH) claims that it may be permissible to cause bad side effects in manners (1) and (3) but not in manner (2). Hence, condition (1) implies, in a further variant of the Domestic Villain Case, that it is permissible for the five people to escape the villain even if their moving into a safe spot causes a bystander to be pushed into a deadly ravine. Condition (3) implies that it could be permissible to attack the villain with the bomb even when it is foreseen that vibrations from it will cause a house in the area to collapse, killing a by-stander.[63] In the Domestic Villain Case, condition (2) rules out both driving over the person to get to the bomb and using the bomb whose fragments kill a bystander.

The question is whether it is plausible to think that there are comparable moral distinctions among the ways we produce collateral deaths in war. For example, is it impermissible to bomb a munitions factory when side-effect deaths result from fragments of our bomb but permissible when the deaths result from the munitions factory itself blowing up? If both *are* permitted (which seems likely), supporters of the PPH I have described will have to explain why side-effect harms are permitted in war that are ruled out elsewhere by the principle.[64]

b. Another problem with applying any general moral principle concerning side-effect harm (such as the DDE or the PPH) to innocents in war contexts is that such principles treat all innocent bystanders as equals. Hence, they tell us to select among permissible means to a greater good that are equally effective and otherwise the same on the basis of reducing deaths of innocent bystanders. However, suppose we must bomb a munitions factory that lies near the border between our country, the enemy, and a neutral country. We can bomb from any of three directions with the following collateral NC deaths: (1) direction 1 will kill 100 enemy NCs; (2) direction 2 will kill 50 of our own NCs; and (3) direction 3 will kill 25 neutral NCs.[65] A general moral principle, such as the DDE, would say that (3) is less bad than (2) which is less bad than (1). Yet, I believe, in war the reverse is true i.e., (1) is less bad than (2) which is less bad than (3) (at least when remaining neutral is a morally permissible option). This reverse ordering suggests that there are violability ratios between neutral NCs, our NCs, and enemy NCs, with the enemy NCs having highest violability. This could affect the proportionality calculation for wartime acts, as a given mission may satisfy proportionality if it collaterally kills enemy NCs but not if it kills the same number of neutral or our own NCs. And even if deaths of both our NCs and enemy NCs were proportional to the mission, it could still be morally preferable to choose the route that killed more enemy NCs rather than fewer of our own NCs.

(The ratios need not imply lexical priority among different groups. Suppose taking one route killed one of our NCs and taking another route killed a thousand enemy NCs. Even if both routes satisfied proportionality relative to achieving the military mission, it could be morally correct to choose the first route if the ratio of enemy NC deaths to our NC deaths exceeds the morally permitted violability ratio between these groups.)

It might be argued that direction (1) should be preferred to direction (2) because a government has a special duty of care for its own NCs. However, even if this is correct, a different explanation is needed for why direction (2) should be preferred to (3). Concern about making a neutral country into an enemy by harming its NCs is inadequate, as the order might apply even when the neutral is militarily insignificant.[66]

c. A form of "group liability," where liability does not depend on any actions of NCs, may explain both the higher violability of enemy NCs and the expanded range of ways it is permissible to harm enemy NCs (by contrast to what a general principle for harming bystanders in nonwar contexts implies [as discussed in section 4.a]). To consider this possibility, suppose our country has unjustly sent a missile to another country, where it will collaterally kill NCs. We realize the moral error of our ways, but the only thing that can be done is to send another missile to destroy the first one. Unfortunately, the second missile will backfire and collaterally kill some of our NCs (Backfiring Missile Case). I believe we are obligated to stop our unjust attack and that NCs of *our* country must be prepared to have certain costs (and the risk of certain costs) imposed on them in this way in order to stop the unjust behavior of their country. This is so even if they have done nothing to bring about the injustice. (Hence, this form of liability to bear costs has nothing to do with liability grounded in prior acts.) They are members of a community ordered for mutual benefit; as potential beneficiaries, they should also bear costs not only to achieve benefits for the country but also to make it not be an unjust country. (Its being permissible to impose such costs [and risk of costs] on them is not the same as their having a duty to volunteer for such costs.)[67]

When our country fights a war it considers just, it considers its enemy to have been unjust (e.g., in firing missiles at us). As the enemy is not stopping its own injustice (and there is no international police officer to stop it), we try to stop it. If enemy NCs who are not responsible for having started or supported the unjust war are still liable to bear costs in order to stop their country from being unjust, perhaps we may impose the costs when their government should do so but fails to.[68] (In this case, neither their government nor the enemy NCs may believe they are unjust, unlike what is true in the Backfiring Missile Case. This does not, I believe, affect the acceptability of the argument.)

d. Does this group-liability proposal bear on the relative violability of NCs and the opponent Cs who would harm them collaterally? For example, does it bear on whether NCs may stop collateral harm to themselves by attacking the opponent Cs who would be justified in doing what causes them such harm?

In a domestic villain case, suppose it is permissible (objectively or nonobjectively) to redirect a villainous threat away from five people in a direction where one other person will be killed as a side effect. This need not imply, I believe, that the one person may not try to stop the threat to himself even if this requires harming the person who permissibly redirected the threat *and* also results in the originally threatened five being killed by the threat. Now consider a war case in which an innocent NC of an unjust country wishes to prevent himself from being collaterally killed by a just C's permissible attack on munitions.[69] Suppose that if he kills the just C, this will interfere with the just C's mission (to whose achievement NC deaths were proportionate). Such defense by the NC seems permissible. This is so even if innocent NCs are *liable* (in virtue of group liability) to costs being imposed on them to stop the injustice of their country, and so they will not even have their rights infringed if the just C does what harms them collaterally. (By contrast, in the domestic case the person to whom the threat is redirected arguably has his rights infringed.) The permissibility of *imposing* collateral death on NCs need not imply that NCs must *volunteer* to let themselves be harmed or not resist being harmed just so that their unjust country will be defeated. (This is true even if they know it is unjust.)

This case suggests that having one's rights (at least) infringed is not necessary for permission to attack defensively due to the compatibility of someone being liable (via group liability) to having harms imposed on her and her permissibly resisting that imposition.[70] Yet it may also be permissible for the just C to defend himself to ensure the completion of his mission. Indeed, it seems that he might now permissibly *target* the NC (not just harm him collaterally) to stop the NC's attack on him. (In [e], we shall consider cases where he would act only to defend himself rather than pursue his mission).

e. More broadly, the question of the relative violability of Cs and the NCs whom they would collaterally harm concerns how much risk of harm Cs must take on themselves to achieve their mission in order to not collaterally harm innocent enemy NCs. (This question arises even when harm to NCs would satisfy proportionality and be permissible were there no other way to achieve the mission). Suppose an enormous number of Cs would be morally obligated to accept certain death to achieve a mission rather than impose some risk of death on enemy NCs by using alternative means to achieve the mission. This would imply that Cs are highly violable relative to enemy NCs that they would harm (and the NCs would be highly inviolable relative to these Cs, at least when it is a matter of the Cs not harming them).

Thomas Hurka argues that the fact that certain Cs "are one's own" (even if they are not irreplaceable for winning our war) counts in favor of their *in*violability. (Similarly, "one's own" NCs may have greater inviolability than enemy NCs.) However, he also claims that the fact that they are Cs, who have accepted exposure to risks as part of their C role, counts in favor of their violability in contrast to enemy NCs. Balancing these two factors, he concludes that from a country's point of view, its C lives and *enemy NC* lives have equal weight.[71]

An alternative to Hurka's view emphasizes that turning some of our citizens into Cs who threaten others might eliminate our right to count "one's own" in their favor, at least relative to the NCs they threaten. (This is a form of "silencing" the "one's own" factor. This means we cannot weigh it in the balance against "C" as we weigh "not ours" against "NC" when comparing enemy NCs with our NCs.) This is an example of "contextual interaction," wherein a factor that matters in one context does not matter in another. In another case, suppose a member of our family is a firefighter (who does not threaten others) and we have to decide how much risk he should take by comparison to shifting the risk to the victims of a fire who are not related to us. We should not balance "our relative" against his role and conclude that the victims and our related firefighter should bear equal risks. However, there might be some reason, such as group liability or liability through acts, to believe that enemy NCs are susceptible to having costs imposed on them so that their country is not unjust to others. It could be this factor, not Cs being ours, that would allow our Cs to impose some risks on enemy NCs rather than assume more risks themselves.

What would this alternative to Hurka's view imply for the following case? Our C will certainly kill the one hundred NCs near a military target as (proportionate) collateral damage to his military mission. During the course of the mission, it becomes clear that he can take another route to the military target and so harm no NCs. However, this will cost him his life after he hits the target (either because he will lose control of his plane or because he will be attacked by enemy Cs). Is he morally required to take the second route when there are no further bad effects of his dying?[72] Suppose these options had been known to our leaders initially. Would they have had to give up on sending the pilot on the first route and either command the second route or abandon the mission entirely because it would be wrong to require a "suicide" mission?

At the least, I think it is wrong to conclude that C must *volunteer* his own life when he pursues a just cause (objectively or nonobjectively) rather than *impose* a cost on NCs that is (independently determined to be) proportional to the military goal. It is not correct to say that in imposing the cost on the NCs, he is requiring the NCs to volunteer their lives in the way he refuses to volunteer his own. A loss may permissibly be imposed on someone (including on oneself by other parties) without this implying that a person must impose the loss on himself or not resist its imposition. If this is true, an argument for the permissibility of NCs killing the pilot in resistance to losses he would impose on them cannot always rely on the fact that they are only imposing a loss on him that he should have imposed on himself had he been able to.[73]

f. A complete discussion of the relative violability of NCs and Cs, when the issue is collateral harm to NCs, should consider how many of one's own Cs should die fighting to defend one's own NCs from death. Figure 4.2, which lays out in graphic form some of the topics we have discussed, makes clear that even if we just consider *four* types of persons—C_{our}, C_{enemy}, NC_{our}, NC_{enemy}—there are *six* possible relations between them.[74] If there are limits on the ways in which we may treat our Cs (by contrast to enemy Cs),[75] "sacrificing" Cs to spare our NCs would not *typically* involve our deciding to *kill* our Cs to spare our NCs (or vice versa). Rather, it could involve deciding how many NCs should be *allowed* to be killed *by enemy Cs* rather than risk our Cs' being killed by enemy Cs in order to save our NCs, holding

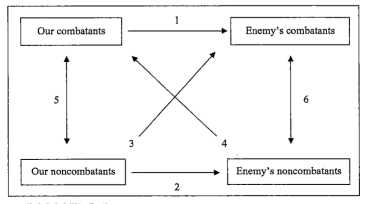

FIGURE 4.2 **(In)violability Ratios**

constant achieving military missions. Or, it could involve deciding whether to pursue a military mission in a way that reduces risks of death to our Cs but increases threats to our NCs (e.g., sending a very large force on a mission, leaving fewer Cs to protect NCs from attack by the enemy, holding constant achieving military missions).

Might the violability relation that should hold between our Cs and NCs in this context bear on whether enemy Cs should properly decide to wage war in a way that kills our NCs collaterally rather than target our Cs? For example, suppose we should not risk a large number of C deaths in fending off threats to a few NC cocitizens. Does this bear on whether enemy Cs should decide to achieve a military goal by (1) attacking a munitions plant, collaterally killing a few of our NCs rather than by (2) attacking and killing a large number of our Cs (other things being equal)? Probably not, for it may make a moral difference that enemy Cs would be *killing* NCs or Cs. By contrast, we would be deciding to *allow* enemy Cs to kill our NCs (by not protecting them) rather than allow the enemy to kill our Cs (by putting them in harm's way). In addition, the ratio between our C and NC lives may be relative to one's perspective. From our perspective, their violability may be closer both because we consider our Cs to be just and because we deny that they may be used in every way for NC benefit. From our opponent's perspective, our C's violability may be much greater than our NCs' violability because Cs are taken to actively pursue an unjust cause and so can be used more liberally. This also implies that, from our perspective, the violability of enemy Cs is much higher than the violability of enemy NCs.[76]

To summarize what has been said about the permissibility of both deliberate and side-effect killings, we can rank inviolability in decreasing order (or violability in increasing order) as follows, assuming we are not (or reasonably believe we are not) unjust:

$$NC_{our} < NC_{enemy} < C_{our} < C_{enemy}^{\ 77}$$

We might try to express the relative violability of enemy NCs and Cs in increasing order from our perspective as follows, assuming we are not (or reasonably believe we are not) unjust:

$$NC_{our} < NC_{enemy} < C_{our} <<< C_{enemy}^{\ 78}$$

The addition of "<<<" is meant to express how much more violable enemy Cs are relative to enemy NCs than our Cs are relative to our NCs (from our perspective). However, this does not yet capture the fact that while in a pairwise comparison our NCs are less violable than our Cs, relative to enemy Cs they are equal (from our perspective). That is, from our perspective, as many enemy Cs may be killed to save each (and possibly also to save enemy NCs). This relative violability in increasing order, from our perspective, may be represented as follows:

$$NC_{our} < NC_{enemy} < C_{our}$$

$$\wedge \qquad\qquad \wedge \qquad\qquad \wedge$$
$$\wedge \qquad\qquad \wedge \qquad\qquad \wedge$$
$$\wedge \qquad\qquad \wedge \qquad\qquad \wedge$$

$$C_{enemy}$$

B. Now let us consider collateral killing of enemy NCs who would die shortly anyway and/or who will be benefited in some way by being exposed to a risk of death (or even benefited by death itself).[79]

Intuitively, it seems that harm to such enemy NCs should weigh less in any proportionality calculation to determine whether one may proceed with a military mission. For example, consider the Scare the Criminals Case. We need to bomb a munitions factory, but this will cause one hundred enemy NC side-effect deaths which would ordinarily be out of proportion to the good to be achieved. However, we learn that these NCs along with many others will shortly be killed by criminals. If we bomb the munitions plant, this will scare the criminals away. The NCs who die due to our bombing are no worse off than they would have been, and the lives of many others are saved. The bombing now seems permissible. This case shows us that what seems like unproportional collateral NC harm when considered on its own is no longer unproportional harm when we consider what would have happened to the very people we harm had we not bombed.

In another type of case, those who will be killed would not in fact have otherwise died. However, the *ex ante* risk of their dying is higher (e.g., due to criminals in their neighborhood) than it is if we engaged in a military mission (and scare the criminals away). So it seems reasonable to think that it is better even for each of those who die that we engage in the military mission since it lowers their risk of death. Once again, NC deaths that on their own seem out of proportion to a military mission can be seen to be proportional once we compare the probabilities of these very people being killed at the same time if we bomb and if do not bomb.

Finally, there may be cases in which those NCs who die are themselves compensated for the risk of death and their ensuing deaths, which our military mission imposes. The good to the very people who die can be weighed against the risk of harm and the actual harm to them so as to make deaths that would otherwise be out of proportion for a military mission be in proportion for it. For example, consider the Parents Case: Suppose parents would be willing (and even have a duty) to risk death to prevent the deaths of their children. There has been an avalanche in the area near the munitions plant we would destroy. The avalanche has buried the children of the people whom we would risk killing collateral to bombing the munitions plant. It will be a further good effect of bombing the munitions plant that the rocks will be moved, freeing the children who would otherwise shortly die. The parents' risk of death that our bombing imposes is no more than they should take to save the lives of their children. This could mean that even though the actual number of parents who die is out of proportion on its own to the military mission, it is not out of proportion once the good to them of having their children saved is taken into account.[80]

Notes

I am grateful to Johann Frick, Jens Johanssen, Shelly Kagan, Jeff McMahan, and Larry Temkin for comments on earlier versions of this chapter. It will also appear in *The Oxford Handbook of Philosophy of Death*, eds. Ben Bradley, Fred Feldman, and J. Johanssen (2013).

1. The idea of pairwise comparison is commonly used as a nonutilitarian decision procedure in deciding on the justice of outcomes and in allocating resources. I am suggesting its use can be extended to explain certain aspects of self- and other-defense against aggressors. Notice that there is also no use of the method of "balancing"; that is, the death of a victim is not simply balanced against the death of an attacker, the former thus having its moral weight used up and leaving the potential death of other aggressors to rule out the permissibility of responding. For more on these decision procedures, see Thomas Nagel, "Equality," in his *Mortal Questions* (New York: Cambridge University Press, 1979), pp. 106–127, and my *Morality, Mortality*, vol. 1 (New York: Oxford University Press, 1993).

2. See Thomas Nagel, "War and Massacre," *Philosophy & Public Affairs* 1 (1972): 123–144.

3. Michael Walzer, *Just and Unjust Wars* (New York: Basic Books, 1977).

4. Jeff McMahan discusses the implications for the permissibility of action of possibility of different goods and what it would cost to pursue them in his "Proportionality" (unpublished).

5. Some theorists seem to deny the significance of an intervening agent's act. For example, Jeff McMahan has argued that if one foresees that a bad effect will occur if one does an act, it should be irrelevant to deciding to do the act that the bad effect would not occur but for another agent's intervening act. He argued in this way in his Appignani Lecture at the University of Miami on Apr. 10, 2009 and in his "Responsibility, Permissibility, and Vicarious Agency," *Philosophy and Phenomenological Research* 80(3) (May 2010): 673–680, criticizing my views in *Intricate Ethics*. More recently, in his "Proportionality," his view seems to have changed somewhat.

6. I discuss this issue in my "*Jus Post Bellum*, Proportionality, and Compensation," which is chapter 7 in this book.

7. Thomas Aquinas, *Summa Theologica.* English trans. by Fathers of the English Dominican Province, in three vols. (New York: Benziger Bros., 1947).

8. Indeed, he doubts that the distinction between intention and foresight that the DDE draws would be of moral significance in itself. See *Just and Unjust Wars*, p. 155.

9. Such a suggestion is made by Warren Quinn in his "Action, Intention, and Consequences: The Doctrine of Double Effect," reprinted in his *Morality and Action* (New York: Cambridge University Press, 1994): 175–193.

10. In "War and Massacre." He is more favorably inclined toward the DDE in his later *The View from Nowhere* (New York: Oxford University Press, 1986).

11. Note that this distinction might also rule out bombing a munitions plant when this kills NCs working in it, if they were to be treated like ordinary NCs.

12. For one discussion of the relation between certain sorts of permissibility and the worth of the person see my *Morality, Mortality*, vol. 2, chap. 5 (New York: Oxford University Press, 1996).

13. For example, see Michael Walzer's *Just and Unjust Wars*, chap. 16.

14. For example, in his *Killing in War* (New York: Oxford University Press, 2009).

15. McMahan distinguishes being liable (in his sense) to attack from the permissibility of an attack, as possibly some who are not responsible for wrongdoing may sometimes be permissibly attacked. Neither of these notions implies that a person deserves to be attacked rather than that he may be attacked only if this is necessary to achieve an end. Unlike McMahan, some think that even a completely nonresponsible person (e.g., someone who has been turned into a human missile or someone who acts out of a drug-induced psychosis) may be liable to be killed (and this is also permissible) if this killing is necessary to stop the lethal threat he presents to an innocent victim. See, for example, Judith Thomson, "Self-Defense," *Philosophy & Public Affairs* 20 (1991): 283–310, and F. M. Kamm, "The Insanity Defense, Innocent Treats, and Limited Alternatives," *Criminal Justice Ethics* 6 (1987): 61–76, and *Creation and Abortion* (New York: Oxford University Press, 1992).

16. The objective view is defended by Judith Thomson in her *The Realm of Rights* (Cambridge, MA: Harvard University Press, 1992). What I call the nonobjective view is defended by Thomas Scanlon in chap. 2 of his *Moral Dimensions* (Cambridge, MA: Harvard University Press, 2008). Scanlon notes that this view is not merely subjective since it is not enough that if what someone actually believes were true, his act would be permissible. Someone must satisfy an objective standard of what it would be reasonable for him to believe.

17. Note, however, that McMahan also believes that if one does an act that is otherwise objectively permissible for evil reasons, one does not act permissibly. Given this view, a C who satisfies conditions of *jus in bello* such as proportionality and necessity still does not act permissibly and is not innocent in achieving an objectively just cause if he actually *intends to do something* unjust. Is such a C liable to be killed because he acts impermissibly? I doubt that McMahan would want to conclude this. If this is correct, then on his view not all Cs who kill impermissibly are liable to be attacked. Henceforth, I shall put such cases to one side.

18. Doubts have been raised, however, about whether unjust Cs are morally responsible agents. Many of them may be under duress to become Cs and to carry out attacks, and they may have limited access to information about the justice of their cause. If someone who does something wrong is fully or partially excused on these grounds, and if these excuses eliminate or reduce the attacks to which they are liable, would it be impermissible for just Cs to kill unjust Cs? McMahan argues that if unjust Cs' excuses are strong, just Cs might have to absorb some costs in battle rather than place all costs on unjust Cs (McMahan, *Killing in War*, 192–198), but they should not do so if it jeopardizes the just cause. Furthermore, he thinks that given any moral responsibility at all on the part of unjust Cs for their objectively wrong conduct, they become liable to being killed if this is necessary to prevent the death of just Cs they attack. In support of this, he considers an analogy: Suppose a resident believes completely reasonably that the innocent identical twin of a mass murderer *is* the mass murderer who is about to kill the resident. The resident may himself be killed if this is necessary to prevent his killing the innocent twin (see ibid., 164 and 175–182).

19. McMahan holds a nonabsolutist version of how evil intentions can make acts impermissible. In particular, he thinks evil intentions have negative moral weight that needs to be overridden. Independently of disagreeing that evil intentions can make acts impermissible, one might think this is too consequentialist an interpretation even of a *nonabsolute* nonconsequentialist side constraint. It does not capture the idea of a side constraint by contrast to something of negative value that weighs against other factors.

20. McMahan, *Killing in War*, 45–47. A possible explanation of this, which he attributes to me, is that the just C should have been willing to do what would cost him his life

in order to attack the munitions without causing collateral damage to NCs. When there is no way he can do this on his own, the NCs may impose the cost on him to stop the collateral damage (at least when this does not interfere with the military success of the mission). However, this explanation (which I suggested but do not necessarily support) would be inconsistent with McMahan's view that the just C may defend himself by firing on the NCs to stop their attack on him. For if the NCs are only imposing a cost on the just C that he should have *imposed on himself* had he been able to do so, it does not seem that he should be permitted to defend himself against their attack.

21. This corresponds to McMahan's view that fully excused but mistaken attackers may be killed if this is necessary to save their innocent victims.

22. There is another element that can be added to this nonobjective account: Each warring side could not just be reasonable in thinking it is just and the other side is unjust, but each side can (and perhaps should) realize this about the other side. McMahan suggests that it is reasonable for each side, after it has done its best to determine the justice of its cause and has concluded it is just, to doubt that it is correct, given knowledge of the history of errors made by others. (See McMahan, *Killing in War*, 152.) I think this is too "external" and skeptical a view for an agent to take of his own thought processes and conclusions. Once he concludes—for the best reasons he can find and taking into account the history of past errors—that his cause is just, it is inappropriate for him to act as if his conclusion is more likely than not to be false. In commenting on this point, Johann Frick says, "The possibility of error evinced by the past errors of ourselves and others may (and *should*) feature *internally*, as a pro tanto reason against believing that our cause is just. But it isn't also a reason for 'externally' calling into question one's all-things-considered judgment about the justice of our cause, into which the possibility of error has already been factored" (in personal correspondence).

23. Notice that this is not like the view that intentional harm, even if it is a more serious wrong, is to be balanced against the fact that it is a C who will die, which diminishes the seriousness of the wrong. On McMahan's view, killing just Cs is not a fact that diminishes the wrongness of killing in comparison to killing NCs, except possibly because it involves eliminative versus opportunistic agency. (This distinction is discussed in the text. Notice also that it is not a "balancing" view to hold that while it is prima facie wrong to intentionally kill, it is not wrong at all to kill a C.)

24. See McMahan, *Killing in War*, 108–109.

25. McMahan's argument could be extended in order to further reduce what *jus in bello* as a matter of convention permits if one weighed the avoidance of wrong acts (such as unjust Cs collaterally killing just Cs or NCs) more than the promotion of right acts by just Cs without totally eliminating the possibility of achieving the just cause. Once one limits what acts are conventionally permissible for fear the unjust side will do them, it is no longer clear what the content of *jus in bello* should be.

26. I first used this term in "Terrorism and Several Moral Distinctions," *Legal Theory* 12 (2006): 19–69.

27. I first discussed this case in "Failures of Just War Theory," *Ethics* 114 (2004): 650–692.

28. In "Action, Intention, and Consequences."

29. This need not imply that all eliminative agency is permissible. For example, Noam Zohar has considered cases in which an NC stands in the way of our killing someone who threatens to kill us (or an NC blocks our escape from such a threat). Zohar argues that

this NC is an indirect threat to us and killing him would also involve only eliminative agency, yet it is still impermissible. If this is correct, then eliminative agency would not be a sufficient condition for permissibly killing someone who is a threat to one's life. See his "Collective War and Individualistic Ethics: Against the Conscription of 'Self-Defense,'" *Political Theory* 21 (1993), 606–622.

30. This way of distinguishing what may be done to Cs and NCs does not rely on the distinction between intentional and nonintentional killing because intentional opportunistic killing of both Cs and NCs would be ruled out. It also does not rely on the idea that military advantage in a narrow sense (e.g., reducing military supplies or fighters) is to be achieved by attacking only Cs and not NCs. For it is physically possible to achieve narrow military advantage by opportunistic use of Cs (in case [ii]), yet this would be ruled out.

31. I introduced this term in "Failures of Just War Theory." For a representation of some possible entities between which violability ratios could hold, see figure 4.2. Contexts in which saving our own Cs could arise include preserving them from an attack by enemy Cs, rescuing them from being held captive by enemy Cs, rescuing them from a natural disaster by means that kill enemy Cs, and using a military plan that kills fewer of our Cs and more enemy Cs than other possible plans.

32. See Thomas Hurka, "Proportionality in the Morality of War," *Philosophy & Public Affairs* 33 (2005): 34–66.

33. Ibid., 58.

34. See his *Killing in War*, 192–198.

35. I first made reference to this distinction in "Failures of Just War Theory."

36. Comparable issues arise in nonwar contexts. I discuss some of those that arise when allocating scarce funds or scarce medical resources in *Intricate Ethics*, chap. 1, p. 35, and in "Health and Equity" (revised) in my *Philosophical Bioethics* (unpublished). For example, I argue that each of many people may choose to bear a small risk of dying of a rare disease in order to invest in a medicine for commonly recurring headaches. But it is not inconsistent with this to hold that, if someone were dying of the rare disease and only all of the headache medicine could save him, it should be given to him. I discuss these issues more generally in "Should You Save This Child? Gibbard on Intuitions, Contractualism, and Strains of Commitment," in Allan Gibbard, *Reconciling Our Aims: In Search of Bases for Ethics* (New York: Oxford University Press, 2008), pp. 120–144, and in a longer, unpublished version of that essay. More recently, Johann Frick has argued for morally distinguishing between (a) risk that will certainly lead to some deaths and (b) some particular individuals facing certain death. See his "Contractualism and the Ethics of Risk" (unpublished). He argues against Alex Voorhoeve and Marc Fleurbaey, who deny the moral significance of the distinction in their "On the Evaluation of Expectedly Beneficial Treatments That Will Disadvantage the Worse Off" (unpublished).

37. I first raised this issue in "Failures of Just War Theory" when I considered violability ratios between one's own Cs and NCs, by which I meant how many of one's own Cs should be sacrificed to save a given number of NCs from attacks by enemy Cs.

38. It is a different question whether Cs should fight for or otherwise be sacrificed for enemy or neutral NCs.

39. I assumed something like the Bodyguard Model, without naming it this, when discussing violability ratios between Cs and NCs on one side in "Failures of Just War Theory." The objection to this model described in what follows was raised by Craig Neuman. Even if

one rejects the Bodyguard Model of Cs, the issue of violability ratios between Cs and NCs on one's own side can still arise when deciding how many Cs can be required to lose their lives in *fighting* to save cocitizen NCs. I discuss this issue in section 4f.

40. See Walzer, *Just and Unjust Wars*.

41. Helen Frowe argues that liability is not sufficient for permissibility if usefulness and necessity are not present. See her "Noncombatant Liability," unpublished. By contrast, McMahan argues that there is no liability at all to harm if it is not useful. (This is part of his view that liability has a proportionality condition involving consideration of what good can be achieved internal to it.) See his *Killing in War*.

42. In ibid., chap..5.

43. However, Helen Frowe argues that McMahan does not distinguish minimal moral responsibility from minimal causal responsibility. Ibid.

44. Ibid., for example, in his discussion of a driver of an out-of-control car. In such cases, he uses a slight difference between people as a tiebreaker. I have doubts that such small differences should be relevant when a great deal is at stake for each person. This may relate to my discussion of "irrelevant goods" in my *Morality, Mortality*, vol. 1 (Oxford University Press, 1993).

45. Ibid., 226–227.

46. See Frowe, "Noncombatant Liability."

47. McMahan, *Killing in War*, 219–221.

48. See his *What We Owe to Each Other* (Cambridge, MA: Harvard University Press, 1999).

49. I first discussed the PSP in my *Morality, Mortality*, vol. 2. This case was first presented in "Failures of Just War Theory."

50. I first presented this case and the EPSP in "Failures of Just War Theory."

51. This case is modeled on my Scare the Criminals Case (which involved only collateral harm to NCs) presented in "Reasons for Starting War: Goals, Conditions, and Proportionality," which is chap. 3 in my *Ethics for Enemies: Terror, Torture, and War* (Oxford: Oxford University Press, 2011).

52. I discuss this case in *Morality, Mortality*, vol. 2, and *Intricate Ethics*, chap. 4, among other places.

53. See my "The Doctrine of Triple Effect and Why a Rational Agent Need Not Intend the Means to His End," supplement, *Proceedings of the Aristotelian Society* 74(1) (July 2000): 21–39 (reprinted in my *Intricate Ethics*, chap. 4), among other places.

54. Ibid.

55. See her "Physician-Assisted Suicide: Two Arguments," *Ethics* 109 (April 1999): 497–518.

56. See his *Moral Dimensions*, chap. 1.

57. I introduced the Stampede Case, which I described as nonstandard terror bombing, and the Human Tinder Case in my "Terrorism and Several Moral Distinctions." Notice that the permissibility of deliberately bombing NCs would not eliminate all distinctions between Cs and NCs, as we might still be required to harm Cs before harming NCs or require that more good be done in order to justify harming NCs than Cs. Note also that even if it were permissible to deliberately kill only Cs as a means of producing terror in NCs (as in the Rear Combatant Case), this would imply that deliberately terrorizing NCs (even if not terror bombing them) could be a permissible means to winning war. If such terrorizing of NCs were permissible, it is not clear how the fact that NC terror that leads to surrender is not a "narrow" military advantage could explain the impermissibility of deliberately killing

NCs, contrary to what Scanlon says. In this regard, see also the Trees Case in my "Terrorism and Several Moral Distinctions" and in "Terrorism and Intending Evil," *Philosophy & Public Affairs* 2 (2008): 157–186, a revised version of which is chap. 2 in *Ethics for Enemies*.

58. I owe this information to Professor John Lewis, Ashland University (in conversation). For more on this issue, see my "Types of Terror Bombing and Shifting Responsibility," in *Action, Ethics, Responsibility*, ed. J. Campbell, M. O'Rourke, and H. Silverstein (Cambridge, MA: MIT Press, 2010): 281–294.

59. For more on these distinctions and their possible significance, see *Intricate Ethics*, chap. 5.

60. Philippa Foot pointed this out in her "The Problem of Abortion and the Doctrine of Double Effect," *Oxford Review* 5 (1967): 5–15.

61. Judith Thomson uses this example in her "Self-Defense." However, Thomas Hurka seems to think it is permissible to save one's own child by doing what will harm bystanders in the domestic case. See his "Proportionality in the Morality of War."

62. I propose a general principle of permissible harm that makes these distinctions in *Intricate Ethics* and other places.

63. Furthermore, there are means that have what I call a noncausal (in contrast to a causal) relation to producing the greater good. For example, suppose we turn a threat that a villain has sent toward killing five people away from them though it will kill a bystander instead. The five being saved (the greater good) is just the noncausal flip side of turning the threat away from them, not a further effect caused by turning it. So turning the threat is a *non*causal means to the greater good. In such cases, I believe, the harm caused to the bystander by redirecting the threat is as permissible as the harm caused by the greater good itself (option [1]). For more on this, see *Intricate Ethics*, chap. 5.

64. I first discussed this issue in detail in "Justifications for Killing Noncombatants in War," *Midwest Studies in Philosophy* 24 (2000): 219–228, and then again in "Failures of Just War Theory." Thomas Hurka subsequently raised the concern in his "Proportionality in the Morality War." Note that the factor that accounts for the permission in war may be present in some nonwar contexts as well.

65. I first introduced cases of this form in "Failures of Just War Theory." I am here discussing certain individuals who will certainly die, not just the imposition of risk on them or tradeoffs between, for example, the risk of killing neutral NCs and the certainty of killing other NCs.

66. McMahan suggests it is relevant that our NCs, not neutrals, would benefit by reduced risk of harm from our winning the war. See his "Just Distribution of Harm Between Combatants and Noncombatants," *Philosophy & Public Affairs* 38, no. 4: 342–379.

67. I believe that one problem with Judith Thomson's argument for the impermissibility of a bystander turning a trolley headed toward five people when it will then kill one person on another track is that she does not allow for a distinction between imposing costs on the one person and his volunteering for them. See her "Turning the Trolley," *Philosophy & Public Affairs* 36(4) (2008): 359–374. I discuss this briefly in my "The Trolley Problem" (*International Encyclopedia of Ethics*, Wiley-Blackwell (2013)) and in more detail in "Who May Turn the Trolley"(unpublished).

68. I first proposed such an account in "Failures of Just War Theory." Such group liability may apply outside war to groups whose members are incorporated in ways similar to the members of a nation state.

69. McMahan discusses such a case in *Killing in War*.

70. This contrasts with the view proposed earlier (p. 87).

71. See Hurka's "Proportionality in the Morality of War." Johann Frick has pointed out that one's own Cs have accepted risk to defend their compatriots. That alone does not imply that they have agreed to bear risks for enemy NCs. A more extreme view than Hurka's, that Cs' being our citizens implies that they should accept few risks rather than impose harm on enemy NCs, is presented in Asa Kasher and Amos Yadlin, "Assassination and Preventive Killing," *SAIS Review* 25 (2005): 41–57.

72. This case is reminiscent of discussions of self-other choices by Peter Unger in his *Living High and Letting Die* (New York: Oxford University Press, 1996), and Judith Thomson in her "Turning the Trolley." I respond to Unger in *Intricate Ethics*, chap. 6 (among other places) and to Thomson in work cited in endnote 66.

73. In contrast to the earlier suggestion in endnote 20.

74. Hurka fails to consider the relative violability of Cs and NCs on one side and the implications this has for proportionality in "Proportionality in the Morality of War."

75. We considered this issue in section B2, including whether we should redirect an enemy threat headed toward our NCs to our Cs instead even if we should redirect it to enemy Cs.

76. I pointed this out in "Failures of Just War Theory," p. 678. Hence, Hurka's claim that "our" should be balanced against "C" may be true when comparing our Cs with our NCs from our perspective even if not when comparing our Cs with enemy NCs they would kill. This is another example of "contextual interaction"; a factor can matter in some contexts and not in others.

77. I provided this ordering in "Failure of Just War Theory." If we know we are unjust, as in the Backfiring Missile Case, the order of increasing violability from our perspective could be as follows:

$$NC_{enemy} < C_{enemy} < NC_{our} < C_{our}$$

78. I am indebted to Beatrice Franklin for suggesting the addition of "<<<."

79. I discuss such cases (including the ones following in the text), as well as cases in which collateral harm to some only benefits others in "Reasons for Starting War: Goals, Conditions, and Proportionality," which is chap. 3 in my *Ethics for Enemies*.

80. For further discussion of such cases see *Ethics for Enemies*, chap. 3. Suppose neutral NCs or Cs would similarly have reduced harm or risk of harm as a result of our action that causes them collateral harm. Then some harm to them could become permissible.

5

Collaboration with the Enemy: Harming Some to Save Others from the Nazis

Recent philosophical discussion by nonconsequentialists of when it is permissible to harm some in order to help others and when it is permissible to collaborate with evil may help us to morally evaluate the behavior of some who collaborated with the Nazis. I have in mind those who tried to reduce the total amount of harm the Nazis did by themselves helping to produce lesser evil.

Harming some to save others raises very basic questions: When we must choose between saving a group containing a greater number of people or a group containing fewer people, why is it morally preferable to save the larger one? Are there characteristics that distinguish people (such as age or health) that should play a role in our deciding whose life to save? I believe that recent philosophical discussion of these issues could be relevant to the evaluation of decisions made by those who collaborated with Nazis in order to save the lives of people who would otherwise have died due to the acts of the Nazis.

In this chapter, I shall not survey in detail recent philosophical discussions of permissible harm, collaboration, and principles for saving lives.[1] Rather, I shall briefly characterize what have been central areas of concern for nonconsequentialists (sometimes also called deontologists). Act consequentialists think that we may always do what is necessary to produce the best outcome. By contrast, nonconsequentialists argue (often from judgments about individual cases) that there are distinctions among the *ways* in which we bring about an outcome and that these may be important for whether it is permissible to act. In section II, I consider whether nonconsequentialist analyses of cases where some are harmed to save others show how we might argue for the permissibility or impermissibility of certain types of acts that collaborators may have undertaken. (I say "may" because I am not attempting to be historically accurate and judge actual historical agents.)

I. Overview of Issues

A. *SAVING THE GREATER NUMBER*

Consider two groups of people, one larger than the other, where there are no morally relevant differences between the people. We face *the choice of which group to save* and which to let die. (This case does not involve harming some to save others.) Why does the fact that we would save a greater number of people give us reason to abandon a smaller number of other people rather than save them (or give each group an equal chance to be saved)? One argument might be that we thereby produce a greater good without abandoning anyone who would be worse off than any individual we save would have been. In response, some have argued that in conflicts like this, it is worse for the greater number if they die but worse for the lesser number if they die, and there is no impartial point of view from which to judge that we produce a greater good if more are saved. However, the following Argument for Better Outcomes suggests that this view is flawed: (1) Using Pareto optimality, we see that it is better if both B and C are saved than if only B is saved (i.e., B+C>B). Though it is not better for B, it is better for C and not worse for B. (2) It is better to a still greater degree if B, C, and D are saved rather than just B. Our judgment that the world is better to a greater degree by saving the additional person (D) by comparison to what is true if only B and C are saved, although it is also only better for person D, seems to be made from a point of view outside that of any person. (This goes beyond Pareto optimality.) (3) A world in which A dies and B survives is just as bad as a world in which B dies and A survives. This is true from an impartial point of view even though the worlds are not equally preferred by A and B. (4) Given (3), we can substitute A for B on the right side of the moral equation in (1) and get that it is better if B and C are saved than if only A is saved.

Although it would be better if B and C are saved than if A alone is, that does not necessarily mean that it is right for us to save B and C rather than A. A nonconsequentialist says that we cannot automatically assume it is morally permissible to maximize the good, for this may violate justice or fairness. Some might claim that if we save B and C on the basis of (4), we abandon A to save the greater number without giving A an equal chance and this is unfair.

But is it really wrong to produce the best outcome in this case (i.e., that in which the most people are saved)? The argument I prefer for the conclusion that it is not wrong does not appeal to the greater good we would produce. It considers what we owe to each individual person. I call it the Balancing Argument.[2] The Balancing Argument claims that, in a conflict, what we owe is that each person on one side should have her interests balanced against those of one person on the opposing side; those in the larger group that are not balanced out help determine that the larger group should be saved. If we instead toss a coin between one person and any number on the other side, giving each person an equal chance, we would behave no differently than if it were a contest between one and one. If the presence of each additional person would make no difference, this seems to deny the equal significance of each person.

Sometimes, however, there may be differences in the individual characteristics of persons that are morally relevant to deciding whom to save. Here are two possibilities: (1) One person has lived a full life already; the other is quite young and would die not having had anywhere near as much good life as the other has already had. (2) One person, if saved, will live a long time (or has a high probability of this); the other person will not live long anyway.

B. *KILLING BYSTANDERS*

Now consider the additional element of *killing* some rather than merely letting some die and saving others. There are many possible scenarios in which the issue of killing some to help others survive may arise. Here are some: (1) We would have to kill some of a group of innocent, nonthreatening people who would soon die naturally or be unjustly killed in order to save the larger part of the group from dying naturally or being unjustly killed. Bernard Williams's much-discussed case of Jim and the Indians is of this type since Jim must kill one of the twenty Indians who would soon be killed in order to save the nineteen others.[3] (2) We would have to kill some people who are under threat of dying but who we are not sure will die soon anyway in order to save a greater number of the group of which they are a part from soon dying natural deaths or being killed. (In one case in this category, *each* person we would kill would have a *higher* probability of being killed if we did nothing, though it is possible that the person we kill would not actually have been killed if we did nothing.) (3) We would have to kill innocent, nonthreatening people who we are sure would otherwise not die soon, in order to save a greater number of people from soon dying natural deaths or being killed. (Call this the Bystander category.)

The Bystander category could be divided into two subclasses: (a) We must either redirect a threat from the greater number to the lesser number or redirect the greater number away from a threat when this results in the lesser number being threatened. The most-discussed version of this subclass is the Trolley Case: A runaway trolley is headed toward killing five people, and we can redirect it to a track where we foresee that one person will be killed.[4] Even many nonconsequentialists believe redirection is permissible.[5] (b) Alternatively, we may save the greater number from a threat by doing something that kills the smaller number in some way other than those described in (a). The most-discussed version of this case is known as Transplant: We must kill someone to get his organs in order to save five other people from organ failure. Nonconsequentialists, at least, believe it is impermissible to kill in Transplant. Much effort has been spent in trying to explain why killing a bystander could be permissible in Trolley but not in Transplant.

Killing in these types of scenarios need not involve collaborating with any evil persons (villains) who are responsible for the original threat to the greater number.

There might not even be any villains responsible for the initial threat, only a natural disaster. Or, if there are villains, we might just know of their threat and have to decide on our own whether to save the greater number without collaborating with those who initiated the threat. However, we could also imagine variants on all these cases in which we must collaborate (i.e., engage in jointly intended coordination) with the villains who began threats in order to save the greater number.

II. Particulars related to the Nazis

A. *DIFFERENT TYPES OF AGENTS*

Consider the hypothetical case of someone who stayed in Germany and undertook the construction of death camps when he, as a non-Jewish German citizen, was free to leave. He did this only in order to cause fewer deaths than his substitute would have caused. (Assume that he did, in fact, cause fewer deaths.)[6] On the other hand, we have Jews in the *Judenräte* (the Jewish community's governing bodies during World War II) whose members were assigned by the Nazis to select people to be taken either to work or to concentration camps, where they would eventually die or be killed. It is said (suppose correctly) that at least some members of the Judenrat selected these Jews for the Nazis in order to make it the case that there was less suffering and damage overall than the Nazis would have caused if they had done the task themselves. I shall refer to these Jews as the Selectors.

There are, of course, many differences between the German Case and the Selector Case. One is that the Selectors were themselves already, and likely to continue to be, victims of Nazis. This might mean that if the Selectors' behavior was wrong, it is partially excused by duress. But we should be clear about the exact nature of the duress. It is possible that they would be harmed sooner if they did not select others, but they would not be set free for selecting. So what they stood to lose comparatively by not cooperating with the Nazis may not have been so great. However, they may not have known this. In addition, their lives were constantly in jeopardy by virtue of being Jews, and a state of misery and panic can affect judgment.

On the other hand, whether the acts of the German and the Selectors were correct or incorrect, only the person—most likely, the German—who did *not* act under duress could probably be said to have acted solely for the good of others and not also for himself. This means that while an excuse based on duress may be relevant to the Selectors, only a necessity defense (that justifies, not merely excuses, conduct) might be relevant to the German (as well as to the Selectors). The necessity defense can justify harming some to save others in some cases, whether or not the agent himself is under a threat. It is also possible that some Selectors intended only to save themselves and even to harm enemies they may have had among their fellow Jews. Nevertheless, this could be consistent with their act still being permissible, for the permissibility of an act may not depend on the motive or intention with which it is done.[7] For example, someone may put himself at risk to save someone else only in order to frighten those who care about him. This reason need not make his act of saving someone else impermissible.

However, the Selectors, unlike the German, would be doing what results in harm to their *fellow* victims. Their actions would thus raise issues like those raised by black overseers during slavery. The peculiar satisfaction members of an evil system may take when they divide a subjugated group and turn some victims against others might be relevant to the permissibility of the Selectors' action. But it is also possible that a member of an oppressed group may have greater authority to consent to the sacrifice of some of the group for the sake of others, in contrast to an outsider agent such as the German. I shall return to this latter point, as well as the distinction between acting from necessity and duress, near the end of my discussion.

B. *CERTAINTY AND NECESSITY OF EVIL*

Both the German and the Selector Cases differ from a case like Jim and the Indians. Unlike Jim, neither the Selectors nor the German actually kill their victims, but they assist a process that does kill them. In the Jim and the Indians Case, we can be sure that a greater evil will come about (including harm to the very person we harm) if we do not produce the lesser evil. In the German and Selector cases, we cannot be sure that the Nazis would themselves do greater evil if the German and the Selectors did not act. For example, it is said that in Denmark, where Danes refused to help select Jews, the Nazis simply did not proceed with their plans for harming Jews.[8] Another real-world factor is the possibility that collaborators help increase the total evil done by freeing up villains to engage in *other* wrong acts they would not have otherwise undertaken.[9] The major point here is that if the Nazis could not have killed so many victims unless Jews helped them as Selectors, then no Jew should have collaborated as a Selector. There should have been a rule of noncollaboration and positive steps taken to prevent collaboration.[10]

However, what if one knew that the Nazis would certainly find some Jew to help them? (It is assumed that this person is not per se interested in Jews being killed, as the Nazis are. He may collaborate because he is coerced by the Nazis or because he is rewarded by them or because he himself assumes that *someone else* will certainly collaborate for these reasons and that other person will do more harm than he will do. I assume that none of these is an adequate justification for his collaborating if a rule of not collaborating should be in place.) May other Jews then serve as Selectors if this would result in fewer people being harmed?[11] Is there a moral difference between (i) selecting some Jews in order to stop a Nazi who will definitely kill these and more and (ii) selecting some Jews in order to stop another Jew who *should not have agreed* to collaborate—because without collaboration, the Nazis will not kill so many—from definitely selecting these Jews and more? In both cases someone (the original villain or wrongful collaborator) will definitely bring about great harm that need not occur. And if each acts as he should (not being a villain, not collaborating), no harm will occur. In the case of the villain, there is noncompliance with ideal moral conduct. In the wrongful collaborator case, there is noncompliance with the noncollaboration solution to the villain's noncompliance with ideal moral conduct. In both (i) and (ii), those who try to remedy the situation would have to abandon the same rule of not participating in a process that kills innocents that the villain and wrongful collaborator abandon.

And yet, in the case where there is wrongful collaboration, the necessity of evil occurring, in contrast to the certainty of its occurring, seems absent. That is, there was a noncollaboration solution to the problem of evil. Nothing bad had to happen, though, of course, it will happen. Further, it is only because the rule not to collaborate was broken that the Nazis had the power to do wrong. Hence, in collaborating to diminish the effects of wrongful collaboration, one would be doing the same type of act—breaking the no-collaboration rule—that empowered the Nazis to begin with. This seems especially hard to do, I think. By contrast, in the case where a villain who intends the evil has the power on his own to do the evil, the necessity of its occurrence seems greater; it is not due to someone's mistake but to someone's goal. And the collaboration that a Selector would engage in to eradicate the harm is not the type of act that made the villain capable of evil conduct to begin with. Perhaps this is grounds for thinking that we should not collaborate in order to correct incorrect collaboration. This reason leaves it open whether we should collaborate to diminish the evil a villain would do without collaboration.

Henceforth, I shall assume that in the absence of any collaborators, the Nazis would have proceeded to do greater evil and that collaboration does not increase total evil.

C. *DIFFERENCES BETWEEN PEOPLE*

One of the most important distinctions between the Selector Case and both the German and the Jim and the Indians cases is the way in which collaboration makes the outcome better than it would be otherwise. Fewer people are killed in Jim's case, and I have stipulated that fewer are killed in the German Case. But the Selectors may not have been in a position to reduce the *number killed,* only the *number who died.* For example, suppose they selected for concentration camp those (e.g., old, sick, very young) who would not have survived long anyway in the ghettos even without being killed. In selecting such people with the knowledge that they would be killed, they thereby tried to save the lives of those who could survive in the ghettos (e.g., healthy workers) but might otherwise have been killed. The number killed would then be constant, but more people overall would survive. Selectors may even have known that they could not reduce either the number killed *or* the number who died, for eventually even the ones who lived longer in the ghettos would die there. If this were so, in selecting they would only be trying to increase time lived before death. How much good the Selectors would achieve can be relevant to deciding whether it is permissible for them to collaborate, for it might be permissible to collaborate if they would make a significant difference for the good but not if they made only a small difference. Let us assume, for the sake of discussion, that they could make a significant difference.

Would it have been a fundamental moral mistake to select for concentration camps on the basis of characteristics such as age (i.e., to select someone who will have had more life than someone else at time of death) or expected outcome (i.e., to select someone who would have *less* time alive if she were *not* selected than someone else if he were *not* selected)? Some of these choices seem not unlike choices we might be asked to make in distributing a scarce, life-saving health resource, thereby determining who lives and who dies. In the latter case, I do not think it is always immoral to select on these grounds. We might save the young rather than the old (other things being equal) because it is morally more valuable to give life years to someone who would have had fewer life years at death.[12] Indeed, this could be true even if the younger person will not thereby have as many additional years as an older person would have if he were saved. Expected additional length of life in itself, however, can also be a factor of moral importance. If a young person will die in a few months anyway if saved now, it might be right to instead save a sixty-year-old who would live for a few years instead.

Still, the context of sending someone to a concentration camp or to be brutalized or immediately killed (rather than just not saving him with a scarce medical procedure) may make choosing on the basis of age at time of death and outcome morally more dubious. This is because brutalizing or killing will deprive someone of what he is *equally entitled to keep*, that is, whatever period of life, unmolested, that he would have if not interfered with. He is entitled not to have this taken from him even in order to save others from being similarly maltreated, though he may not be entitled to some benefit like a scarce resource. Certainly, we should ordinarily raise a moral objection to sending an old person who does not have much time left to live to be killed in order to prevent the killings of young people who will then have long lives. (Such an objection to killing is consistent with the permissibility of providing scarce medical resources to young people who will then live long lives rather than providing the resources to the elderly.) Does this objection not also apply to selecting the old for concentration camps to save the young?

I believe not. It is true that, in the Selector Case, each victim will be deprived of life to which he is entitled when he is killed by the Nazis. But *if* and when it is permissible to decide who will be wronged in this way, it will also be permissible to use the same characteristics for selection as we could permissibly use in distributing a scarce drug. The crucial question is whether and when it is permissible to help choose in any way who will be wronged.[13]

We can also show that it is permissible to use differential, morally relevant characteristics to select among victims by considering the various *different* things Selectors might have done. I have said that they decided who would go to the Nazis' concentration camps. However, they may have selected in the first instance who would *not go* (e.g., because certain skills were necessary in the ghettos). If this is so, then they would be distributing a scarce benefit (e.g., work passes) with foreknowledge of the fact that those who do not get this benefit would be subject to the Nazis' own selection mechanisms for the concentration camps. In distributing this scarce benefit, I believe they might often permissibly have used criteria that would permissibly be used in a very different context, where injustice would not be the ultimate cause of the death of those not saved by the scarce, lifesaving benefit.

An additional problem arises when the differences between people that bear on selection reflect only the *instrumental* role people have. For example, suppose we must choose whether to save a doctor who can save other lives or save someone who is the same age and will live as long but cannot save others. In medical contexts, such as distributing a scarce organ for transplantation, if our duty is the proper distribution of organs and not maximizing lives saved overall, the fact that one candidate is a doctor who is indispensable for saving lives should not by itself lead us to prefer her over another candidate who will not save lives. However, if the Selectors' duty was simply to maximize Jewish lives saved (without acting immorally), saving the doctor who can save others seems to be a means of their fulfilling their duty. Similarly, suppose our duty is just to properly distribute a scarce drug, and only one of the potential recipients, if he is saved, can go on to deliver the drug to more people that we cannot reach. I believe we may take this as a reason to save him.[14]

If there were no morally relevant differences between people in the context, it would have been permissible for the Selectors to give work passes to some but not others by using a random-decision technique.

D. *SELECTION AND THE REDIRECTION OF THREATS*

Let us now abstract from the issues of uncertainty about whether a greater evil will be done if one does not act and whether a greater good will occur if one does act and also from the existence of differential characteristics among people who need to be saved. Imagine a case in which one knows that significantly fewer individuals with the same morally relevant characteristics will be killed (or otherwise die) if the German or the Selectors act. It is still true that we cannot be sure that if the German and the Selectors act, the smaller number who will be killed will be selected from only those who would have been killed anyway, as is true in Jim and the Indians. Does this threaten to make the German and Selector Cases more like a Bystander Case, where someone who would not shortly have died anyway will be killed? This would be so if the selectors' choosing implies that some people who will be killed were *not* under a threat and would not otherwise have been killed or have died had the Nazis selected more people.

However, recall that there are (at least) two types of Bystander Cases. One involves redirection of a threat to a bystander (as in the Trolley Case). Another involves using a bystander to save others (as in the Transplant Case). Perhaps we can conceive of what the Selectors did on the model of the redirection of threat cases: Either the Nazis select and kill people H–Z or the Selectors *redirect the Nazis* who are the threats to people A–G. Redirecting a threat from harming more people to harming fewer people who were not originally under any threat—even if a villain started the threat to the greater number of people and even when redirecting amounts to oneself being a killer (which is not true in the Selector Case)—is commonly recognized as morally permissible in the Trolley Case. This is so even in a case in which we must choose not only whether to send a trolley away from a larger number of people but also to which of multiple tracks with different people on them to send the trolley.[15] It may also be permissible to act in the Selector Case if this is the same type of redirection case.

However, in the Trolley Case, the threat that is redirected is a mechanical device, not a responsible agent who intends to kill people and whose acts are under his control. The issue is whether such agents may permissibly be redirected as well. Some think that it is permissible to redirect the trolley because one only foresees but does not intend the death it will cause. But the Selector only foresees that a Nazi will intentionally kill; the Selector does not intend that the Nazi do so. This point *also* highlights the fact that Jim or the redirector of a mechanical device such as the trolley would himself kill someone; by contrast, when the Selectors redirect the Nazis, the Nazis, not the Selectors, *do the actual killing.* This may speak in favor of redirecting. Nevertheless it is possible that moral problems arise simply because the Selectors' collaboration is appropriately conceived of as redirecting a responsible person who will kill. This would be in addition to the objection to the collaboration per se.[16]

Perhaps, however, the Selector Case is not a redirection-of-threat case. For suppose that the Nazis had not yet selected any people they would kill but had the Selectors do so initially. This would mean there was not *re*direction but only direction of a threat. This is not a crucial moral difference, I think, given that in either case Selectors intervene when the Nazis are still in control of the threat they will present. Suppose that a villain has a trolley threat stationed at a cross-point, and you know he *will shortly direct it* to some large, not-yet-identified group of people (Cross-Point Case). You are able to direct this stationary trolley where you know it will kill a small group who would not be part of the larger group. Is it as permissible to direct the threat to them as it would be to *re*direct it to them when it is headed to the larger group out of the villain's control? If dealing with "responsible" threats were as permissible as dealing with out of control threats, what could be the reason for the permissibility of either?

This is a complicated issue at the heart of what morally distinguishes Trolley from Transplant. All I can hope to do here is state (in an oversimplified form and without defense) what I believe, very approximately, is the reason for distinguishing these cases.[17] Harming some who would not have been threatened in order to help others is permissible when either the greater good (of, for example, a greater number removed from a threat) itself causes the lesser evil (in this case, harm to the lesser number) or means that have the greater good as their *noncausal* flipside cause the lesser evil. (Call this a Principle of

Permissible Harm.) When we send a threat to person A, the noncausal flipside of this is the greater good of its not being sent to people B and C. By contrast, if we were to push A in the way of the threat, blocking it from hitting B and C, stopping the threat to B and C would be a causal consequence of a lesser evil (where lesser evil is understood as involving A, against his will, in a way we know will lead to significant harm to him). This way of producing the greater good would be prima facie impermissible, and it is present in the Transplant Case.

However, there is another truly significant problem with applying the redirection of threat analysis to what Selectors would do. In most redirection cases—for example, the Trolley Case, as described earlier—the involvement of the bystander, leading to his death, is not causally necessary in order for the greater number to be saved; it is merely a foreseen effect. However, if the Selectors redirect (or direct) Nazis, it is only if the Nazis get the people to whom they are directed that they will not take those the Selectors are trying to save instead. Therefore, at the very least, the Selectors would redirect *because* they believe those people to whom they direct Nazis will become victims of the Nazis. Does this make their redirection impermissible?

Interestingly, there is a version of the Trolley Case, known as the Loop Case,[18] which involves acting because we know the bystander will be hit. The trolley is headed toward killing five persons. We can redirect it but only toward a track that loops back to the five anyway. However, there is a bystander on that track, and his being hit stops the trolley from looping. We would not bother to turn the trolley unless we expected the bystander to be hit since there would be no point in turning the trolley if it were not stopped from looping. I believe turning because (on condition that) someone will be hit is permissible in the Loop Case, and that is not the same as acting with the intention that someone be hit.

Accepting this conclusion would, however, require revising some of the earlier explanation given of the permissibility of redirecting in the original Trolley Cases, while retaining its spirit. We can do this once we see two things. First, the bystander's being hit *sustains* the five's being free of the trolley threat, an outcome which we managed to achieve temporarily in getting the trolley away from hitting them originally. Second, we do nothing to harm the bystander besides what is necessary to get the trolley away from originally hitting the five. That is, we do nothing to establish the connection between what we do to get the trolley away and its hitting the bystander; we merely take advantage of the connection being there. This latter fact helps us see that we need not intend the bystander's being hit even if we act only because it will happen.[19] Suppose the Selectors do something similar when they make the Nazis' harming one group of people a condition of their own action because the Nazis' being satisfied is necessary to sustain the rescue of another, larger group of people. Then this would not make the Selectors' act impermissible, I think.

However, Selectors may have been prepared to do more. For suppose those to whom the Nazis were redirected tried to escape. If they escaped, the Nazis would go back to take the other, larger group of people. If Selectors interfered with the escape of the small number of people they had selected so that the Nazis would be satisfied, I believe their behavior would not be justified by any principle that justifies redirection even in the Loop Case. (Similarly, in the Loop Case, blocking the escape of the bystander from the side track so that the trolley would hit him would not be justified by whatever principle justifies redirection in the Loop Case, I think.)

E. *SELECTION AND THE REDIRECTION OF PEOPLE*

Now we come to a deeper objection to the analogy with redirecting threats. It might be argued that the Selectors were not directing or redirecting a threat; rather, they were moving around the victims who would be confronted by a steady threat. That is, they were not sending the Nazis to one group of people rather than another; they were sending one group of people rather than another to the Nazis. However, consideration of other variants on the Trolley Case suggest that, in some cases, it can be permissible to send one group of people to a threat in order to save others. For example, suppose a trolley threat is coming at many people who are seated on a large swivel table, and we cannot redirect the trolley. It is permissible, I believe, to turn the table, thereby moving the many away from the threat. This is so even if this moves a different, smaller group of people seated on the other side of the table into the trolley. (I call this the Lazy Susan Case.[20]) Here, the good of the greater number being removed from the threat leads to the lesser number facing the threat, so it satisfies the Principle of Permissible Harm I described earlier. (A much simpler case involves permissible ducking; that is, a large number of people who stand between a smaller group of people and the threat duck, and the smaller number then face the threat. This is a simpler case because, in ducking, the greater number just deny their protection [cover] to the smaller number; the shift in their position, in which they move what is theirs, does not alter the position of the smaller number, as happens in the Lazy Susan Case.[21])

However, there are types of cases in which placing in harm's way a bystander who is not otherwise threatened in order to save a greater number from the threat is not permissible, I believe. For example, suppose a Monster will go to people A and C, but if we throw person B in front of it, this will stop the Monster from reaching A and C. In this case, B is not thrown in as a consequence of moving A and C away from the threat (as in the Lazy Susan Case). Instead, A and C are saved as a further causal effect of sending B in because killing him causes the Monster to stop. Similarly, what is known as the Fat Man (or Bridge) Case involves stopping the trolley headed toward killing five people by toppling a fat man from a bridge in front of the trolley that kills him.[22] This is thought to be as impermissible as what is done in Transplant.

However, A and C *would* be saved as a noncausal flipside of sending in B if we sent in B as the alternative to sending in A and C. And the model closest to what some Selectors would have to do *is* sending person B to the Nazis rather than sending A and C. Here, as I see it, the greater good—A and C being away from the threat—is the noncausal flipside of sending in B. They send in B as the alternative to sending in A and C; they do not send in B as a means of (in the sense of a causal route to) saving A and C, as in the Monster Case.[23]

Is sending in B in such a case permissible? Is sending in B necessary in order that A and C not be sent in? Theoretically, A and C could be spared without sending in B in their stead just by not sending in A and C. But if A and C will definitely be selected to go to the Nazis if B is not, sending B instead is a necessary means to saving A and C that has their being saved as its noncausal flipside. Still, sending some people or others to a threat of death is not something anyone usually has the authority to do (unlike generals in an army, who have the authority to send some soldiers rather than others into a battle). Whence could the Selectors have gotten the authority over persons such that they could appropriately have sent in either A and C or B?

Here may be one part of the answer to this question: The Selectors might get into the position of having the authority of sending at least A and C to the Nazis if the Nazis would have killed them anyway, Hence, there may be nothing wrong with the Selectors exercising authority over A and C in order to save lives. The second part of the question is the real problem: How did the Selectors get authority over B, who (we are assuming) would not have been killed otherwise? Further, when the Selectors deliver B to the Nazis instead of A and C, it seems that they will have to try to prevent B from escaping. This was something we said no principle justifying redirection would let them do. Redirection of a threat and even movement of persons into a threat in ways that the Principle of Permissible Harm determines to be permissible do not require the same authority over the person who will be harmed. The problem for delivery of B arises, in part, because we are selecting a person rather than either selecting an alternative route along which a threat will go or sending someone to a threat as a consequence of moving the greater number away from a threat (as in the Lazy Susan Case).

To make this clearer, consider two analogies involving the trolley. (1) The trolley headed toward five persons will stop temporarily if I step in to make the *choice* between sending it in the direction in which it will hit the five or the other direction in which it will hit one. If I do not make the choice, the trolley starts up again toward the five. (This is in some ways like the case where I find the trolley that will soon be sent by a villain toward the five but is now at the cross-point (p. 121).) It is at least as permissible for me to direct the trolley to the one when I have a choice between directing it to one or to five, as when I had no choice whether to *direct to* the five (in the ordinary Trolley Case) as it was already headed to them. (2) The trolley headed toward the five will stop temporarily if I step in to make the choice between sending the five *into* the trolley (with an impact that will kill them) or sending some bystander into the trolley (with an impact that kills him). If I do not make the choice, the trolley starts up again toward the five. We can, I think, see how it might be permissible for me to send in the five who will die anyway if my doing this makes their deaths easier or if this helps other people. But it is impermissible to take a bystander who would not die and send him at the trolley instead of the five even if doing so were noncausally related to not sending in these five.

Taking control of a person without his permission and putting him in a position where this will lead to harm to him is wrong in itself (unlike turning a trolley or pushing a Lazy Susan). The fact that doing so is necessary to produce the greater good (of A and C being okay) as a noncausal flipside cannot make the act permissible. By contrast, when the greater good is the flipside or aspect of a neutral means (such as turning a trolley or swivel table), the harmful effects of that means, I would claim, are morally tolerable. Hence, not only lesser evils that are a causal means to a greater good are ruled out. Even evil means that have a greater good as their flipsides can be ruled out.[24]

I conclude that, even bracketing the distinction between responsible threatening agents and out-of-control mechanical threats, principles justifying direction or redirection of threats and movement of persons into threats would not justify the behavior of Selectors if they delivered up some who would not be killed in order to prevent a greater number of others from being killed. Some other ground would have to be found for the Selectors having authority to control someone like B in order for it to be permissible for them to deliver B to a threat.

F. WHENCE MIGHT AUTHORITY COME?

To consider whether the Selectors could have the authority to send some people rather than others to the Nazis, it might help to now reintroduce considerations from which we abstracted in the previous sections. First, probably no one could know who would be selected by the Nazis, and there was probably no class of Jewish people known to not be in danger from the Nazis. If this was so, no Jewish person could be certain that he would not be selected by the Nazis, and it could be in each person's interest *ex ante* to have a smaller rather than a greater number die. That is, each person's chances *ex ante* of dying would be reduced if a smaller number of people were picked by Selectors rather than a larger number by the Nazis even if some would eventually die who would not otherwise have died. If this were so, perhaps it could help account for the authority of the Selectors to deliver up people. However, this description of the facts is not quite accurate. If it were known that Selectors with authority would first send to die the old or sick or very young who were unlikely to survive for long anyway, then it does not reduce these people's chances of dying *ex ante* for the Selectors to have the authority to choose people. Their having authority might actually increase some people's chances of dying or of dying sooner rather than later.[25] Even if their fate is not made worse to a great degree, we still cannot say that *ex ante* it would be in *everyone's* interest or even not against anyone's interest to have the Selectors acquire the authority to choose. The *ex ante* interests of some *would* be sacrificed for the sake of others.

Suppose the sacrifice imposed on those selected would be minimal. Then it might be argued that the Selectors get their authority to deliver up such people, even independently of considering the *ex ante* interests of the people selected, because delivering them makes little difference in outcome to those to whom it is done, and it produces much good for others. Alternatively, this problem could be eliminated if the Selectors used a random-decision procedure to select people rather than criteria such as age or future prospects.

It is important to remember, in considering whether an *ex ante* decision model could yield authority, that Selectors would not be delivering up people who are like those in the Bystander Case, that is, people who it is reasonable to believe would go on living unharmed for a long time if not selected. Furthermore, in the Selector Case, even at the very time someone is selected to be sent to the Nazis, it is not known that he would have avoided this fate had the Selectors not acted. In this way, the case differs from others in which each person's *ex ante* probability of dying is lower if someone will be selected for death but at the time the one person is to be killed, we would know he would not have died shortly. For example, in a version of the Transplant Case, all those in a society would lower their probability of death if we had a policy of killing someone for his organs, but we would kill someone when he is known to be healthy. Hence, in order to think that *ex ante* benefit might be a way to justify Selector authority, we need not assume that the *ex ante* self-interest of each can justify anything we might do to a person. For example, I do not think it justifies delivering up someone to be killed in this version of Transplant.

A second factor that might bear on the authority of the Selectors is whether they represent a group of Jews, each member of which actively consented to the Selectors having authority to select. Selectors would have authority to move people around because those people authorized them. (By contrast, someone not actually authorized by those threatened could only try to give a justification for his act, such as those previously considered.)

Suppose we could justify the Selectors' delivering people to the Nazis. Would this also encompass their preventing B from escaping when they chose B to go instead of A and C? Suppose B could truly escape to freedom (and not just back into uncertainty as to whether he will or will not be killed by the Nazis.) Such true escape would make the case more like Transplant or other Bystander cases, in which we know at the time we kill someone that he would not otherwise die. If anything, only actual *ex ante* consent by all those affected to be treated in this way could justify the Selectors' preventing escape. However, if escape were only escape back into uncertainty, then Selectors would have the same authority (if any) to prevent such escape as they had to select someone uncertain to be sent to the Nazis to begin with.

If Selectors may deliver B instead of A and C, may they send B in as a means whose causal effect is to stop the threat from reaching A and C? May a general who has the authority to send B into battle instead of A and C do this other thing to B as well? If so, this suggests that Selectors also are permitted to do such things.

G. COLLABORATION.[26]

Might the fact of collaboration itself bear on the permissibility or impermissibility of either selecting or actually killing (in Jim's case)? Collaboration has negative aspects (for example, dealing with evil people as if they were legitimate authorities). Some have suggested[27] that quite independently of the problem of doing things to victims, collaboration raises the problem of having to treat villains respectfully. That is, one enters into communication and other normative relations (such as promising and bargaining) with people one should shun. Suppose that this is a morally bad aspect of collaboration that contrasts with acting independently (though I think it pales by comparison to being involved in harming victims). Nevertheless, it might be that collaboration sometimes not only reduces harm but also keeps moral discredit where it belongs and preserves a certain sort of moral purity in an agent who, in collaborating, selects victims or even kills them. If this is so, collaboration may sometimes morally release us to do what we should otherwise not do quite so easily.

Strictly speaking, both the German and the Selectors would be considered collaborators since they worked with the Nazis. But I am concerned that *how* they came to work with the Nazis may be morally significant. In the Selector Case, the Nazis arguably offered to let the Selectors do something rather than have the Nazis do it. They might also have given them an order. If selection was more favorable to the victims if the Selectors did it, then even though the Nazis were not responsible for intentionally "offering a better outcome" or threatening a worse outcome if the Selectors did not act, the Nazis made an offer that could have led to a better outcome.[28]

In the German Case, the Nazis (it is assumed) neither made an *offer* to the German nor threatened to do worse if he did not act. The German simply believed (we assume) that he would cause fewer deaths, and he therefore initiated the collaboration with the Nazis that involved him in causing deaths.

I believe there may sometimes be a morally significant difference between taking up an offer or acting on an order and either initiating an offer or acting on one's own to produce less evil than would otherwise be produced. Consider this claim as it applies to agents who are *not* members of the group that is under threat.

Suppose one takes up an offer from a villain who plans great harm, that one do a less harmful act that already has certain characteristics in favor of its being permissible. For example, suppose the act gives every potential victim a greater chance of survival because every victim would have been killed and now only some will be. Then, I suggest, full moral responsibility and accountability for any negative consequences of one's act will belong to the villain who would otherwise have done worse. This is so even though the person who acts is *causally* responsible for the negative consequences, and he is morally responsible for choosing to do the act.

Here is one way of understanding why moral responsibility and accountability for any negative consequences of the act will belong to the villain who would have done worse.[29] When one does such an act in response to an offer or order, one makes oneself the Agent (note the capital "A") of the villain. By Agent, I mean someone chosen by the villain to carry out his will, as a lawyer who is hired to evict tenants is the Agent of his employer. (This is distinct from being an agent [note the lowercase "a"] in the sense of anyone who performs an act.) One is morally responsible for one's choosing to become an Agent, but the person for whom one acts becomes morally responsible for the negative consequences of one's act, at least if one's act is within certain bounds.

Suppose that, in order to save a greater number from the Nazis, someone kills an innocent bystander who had no chance of being killed by Nazis and who did not consent to a policy permitting this or to the act itself. Here there are no factors such as we discussed earlier that speak in favor of this act being permissible. This makes moral responsibility for the death remain with the person who causes the death. This is also true of those who do acts that cannot be justified and who were "only following orders." Here moral responsibility can be had to the highest degree by both the villain who gives the order and the person who acts. Suppose Selectors could not have had the authority to send some people rather than others into a Nazi threat. Then responding to a Nazi offer would not have transferred responsibility for such acts from the Selectors to Nazis.

However, if that moral responsibility for the lesser number of deaths can sometimes lie with the villain who makes the offer, this has at least two implications in cases where an Agent actually does a killing: (1) The villain gets moral responsibility for unjust deaths, not merely moral responsibility for creating circumstances where others face the choice of having to kill some to save a greater number of people. Hence, the villain can correctly be punished for murders. (2) Often, even when one does an overall right act, there are negative aspects of the act that are justified by its positive aspects but nevertheless leave what is called a "negative residue." For example, one may wrong someone in the course of doing an overall right act by telling him a lie. One can have responsibility for those negative aspects and for trying to compensate for them. Hence, even though one is "morally pure" in the sense that one did the right act, one's purity is diminished as an agent in the sense that one becomes morally responsible for negative residue. We might call this a loss of "hyperpurity." (An example of this is breaking a significant promise to someone in order to save a life instead, and then one still owes an apology or compensation to the first party.) But if it is permissible to act as an Agent, one retains even one's hyperpurity because moral responsibility for negative aspects of one's act lie with the villain who made the offer. On this account, in the case where the Agent does not actually kill but only selects who will die, moral responsibility for their selection and for the deaths of the victims will be had by the Nazis who made the offer or gave the order.

By contrast, suppose one initiates an offer to the villain or one acts on one's own to kill and/or select a smaller number before the villain selects and kills a greater number. Suppose one's act is still permissible. (I do not want to deny that it might be permissible, for example, to kill on one's own one of those who would otherwise die anyway as a result of the Nazis' acts in order to save a greater number of lives.) Then, I believe, moral responsibility for the negative consequences of one's act is either shared with the villain (in the case where one initiates an offer to the Nazis to collaborate and they accept) or responsibility for the negative consequences of one's act remains one's own (when one acts independently). When one acts independently, the most obvious reason that such responsibility remains with one—for the killing and/or selection—is that the villain did not license one's act. In the case where one initiates a plan with the villain, I believe such responsibility is not totally transferred to the villain because one acts (in proposing the plan) at an early point before the villain has done all that he can do that is sufficient to bring about the cause of deaths.[30]

Notice that in this latter case one is still an Agent of the villain. Ordinarily, offering one's services does not increase one's responsibility for negative consequences if one becomes an Agent. For example, if a lawyer offers his services to someone, he need not have greater responsibility than a lawyer who accepts an offer to be an Agent. Yet I think that in the wartime case I am discussing, actively seeking rather than being responsive to an offer of collaboration may make a moral difference. This suggests that there is another way of understanding why moral responsibility and accountability shift to the villain. When an offer is made to a specific person and not sought, the Agent is himself put under pressure that he did not seek. Further, his refusal to help will now have a positive causal role in the villain's decision-making process that leads to more harm. This suggests that the Agent is himself under duress even if he is not a member of the threatened groups.[31]

In any case, I believe it is understandable that an agent would prefer to act if there will be a transfer of full moral responsibility for the negative aspects of his act to the villain. If this is true, some non-Jews who got an offer from the Nazis to select may correctly have felt morally freer than the German to collaborate.[32] This is not to deny that the Nazis share responsibility for the deaths that the German helps cause; after all, he works for them and does some of what they want, while he tries to minimize the damage they do. It is just that the German would, I believe, also have moral responsibility for the negative consequences of his acts because he initiated his participation. It is not true of him that if he does what leads to people being killed, the negative consequences of his acts are only being added to the moral account of the Nazis, as I have suggested might be true of someone who got the offer. I have not, of course, claimed that this is a decisive reason for his not acting. But if there is a bias of the sort I have described in favor of not acting when moral responsibility for negative consequences cannot be completely transferred to the villain, then this is one reason, from the German's point of view, to think his actions would be more morally problematic than those of a German non-Jew who got an offer to select.

Now, let us suppose that the non-Jew got no Nazis offer but was authorized by each member of the endangered Jewish group to select whom to send to the Nazis. Furthermore, suppose he is to do this when there is continuing uncertainty as to who would be selected and killed by the Nazis if there was no Selector. (As discussed earlier, this was a very problematic situation in which to justify sending some rather than others to the Nazis.) Suppose the group, like the German, received no offer or order from the Nazis. The group had the non-Jew either initiate the offer to select to the Nazis or act independently of the Nazis to substitute some people for others that the Nazis had selected. This selector becomes the Agent of those who have proper authority over their own lives (the Jews). I believe that full responsibility and accountability for negative aspects of his act (sending some to be killed) shift to the group for whom he permissibly acts. Would the group itself, like the German, lose the cloak of hyperpurity provided by the Nazis having full moral responsibility for those selected and killed? I believe not.[33] The Nazis need not make any offers to members of the group they persecute (e.g., "If you ask someone to be a selector, I will not kill all of you") in order for the selecting and killing of the smaller number to be the Nazis' moral responsibility. This is because the Nazis threaten these Jews who act in permissible self-defense against the Nazis. This seems to be enough to shift full moral responsibility to the Nazis for the negative consequences of acts that those threatened authorize a non-Jew selector to do if they are necessary in order to diminish the Nazis' threat. We can say something like "the Nazis made the Jews do it," although they did not specifically tell them what to do, and the Jews could have chosen to do nothing. But someone in the original German's situation, with the possibility of doing something to help others, is not being threatened by the Nazis. The German cannot say "the Nazis made me do it" in the way the Jews can.

Now return to the case where Selectors are fellow Jews threatened by the Nazis who also offer them the selector role. These Selectors are not imagined to be merely helping themselves by selecting from among a consenting group of Selectors. They are imagined to be helping the whole group and, in particular, nonselectors. Being under duress to save themselves and being made an offer by Nazis are not sufficient to justify their making decisions about sending some to the Nazis if what was said about sending earlier is true. However, if the Selectors were authorized to select by each member of the very group from which they must select, their choice to send some who might not have otherwise died could be justified. Further, the fact that they act on a Nazi offer and for those who are also threatened by the Nazis implies that the Nazis bear full moral responsibility for the Selectors' necessary threat-reducing acts.

III. Conclusion

I have argued that some of the ways in which Selectors might have acted in order to save a greater number of people are permissible. These ways include giving work passes to some (even if not all can have them) nonrandomly. Redirecting the Nazis to a smaller number of people even *because* they know the Nazis will then harm the smaller number of people could be permissible if the analogy to redirecting mechanical threats is correct. Some other ways in which Selectors may act are even harder to justify. These include sending some people to the Nazis in order to save a greater number of other people when it is not clear who would otherwise have died and preventing the escape of those they select.

In focusing on these issues, I have not meant to imply that saving lives even by permissible means should have been the paramount aim of victims of Nazi injustice. Resisting the Nazis may have been preferable whether it saved lives or not. Doing this would raise a whole different set of moral issues. In conclusion, I shall just mention some of them.

When one is attacked, self-defense is commonly thought to be permissible. But what if one knows in advance that one cannot successfully defend oneself against the enemy? That is, one may succeed in harming the attacker to some degree but not sufficiently to defend oneself or defeat him. Is it no longer permissible to attack the unjust aggressor? No, since one may be saving others who would also be attacked by the aggressors. What if there is no hope that one's acts will do even this? May one give up the aim of stopping the bad consequences of aggression or defeating the aggressor and just resist as an inherently appropriate response to aggression?[34] I believe so.[35] Do the acts become mere punishment of villains undertaken without legally instituted investigation of guilt and innocence? No, because unlike punishment, one would resist aggression while it is still ongoing. This factor, I believe, leaves the aggressor open to attacks on him even when one knows that these attacks will not defeat him, will not succeed in stopping the harm he will do, and may themselves produce the same harm (e.g., one's death). Such an argument that can justify resistance apart from any further good consequences may be required if one is to justify uprisings like the one in the Warsaw Ghetto.[36]

Notes

This chapter is a revised version of "Harming Some to Save Others from the Nazis," in *Moral Philosophy and the Holocaust*, ed. E. Garrard and G. Scarre (London: Ashgate, 2003), 155–168.

1. For lengthy discussion, see my *Morality, Mortality*, vols. 1 and 2 (New York: Oxford University Press, 1993, 1996). For shorter discussions, see my "Nonconsequentialism," in *Blackwell's Guide to Ethical Theory*, ed. H. LaFollette (Oxford: Blackwell, 2000), 205–226; "Toward the Essence of Nonconsequentialism," in *Fact and Value: Essays on Ethics and Metaphysics for Judith Jarvis Thomson*, ed. A. Byrne, R. Stalnaker, and R. Wedgwood (Cambridge, MA: MIT Press, 2001), 155–182; "Responsibility and Collaboration," *Philosophy & Public Affairs* (Summer 1999): 197–202; and chaps. 1, 5, and 10 based on these articles in my *Intricate Ethics* (New York: Oxford University Press, 2007).

2. I first presented this in "Equal Treatment and Equal Chances," *Philosophy & Public Affairs* (Spring 1985): 177–194.

3. See J. J. C. Smart and B. Williams, *Utilitarianism: For and Against* (Cambridge: Cambridge University Press, 1973), 98.

4. One version of this case was introduced by Philippa Foot in "The Problem of Abortion and the Doctrine of Double Effect," *Oxford Review* 5 (1967): 5–15; and another by Judith Thomson in "Killing, Letting Die, and the Trolley Problem," *Monist* 59 (1976): 204–217. In Thomson's case, "bystander" refers to someone other than the trolley driver who is capable of turning the trolley. In this chapter, "bystander" refers to whom the trolley would be redirected.

5. Recently, Judith Thomson has raised objections to this view. For a short response to her, see my "The Trolley Problem," *Encyclopedia of Ethics* (forthcoming).

6. I discuss the hypothetical case here because I am not sure there really was anyone like this, although I believe Albert Speer (Hitler's architect) may have conceived of himself in this way. Oskar Schindler collaborated with the Nazis in order to save Jews, but he did not collaborate on projects that involved him in sending Jews to be killed, killing Jews, or building means for killing them.

7. For one defense of such a view, see Thomas Scanlon, *Moral Dimensions: Permissibility, Meaning, Blame* (Cambridge, MA: Harvard University Press, 2008).

8. I am grateful to Susan Wolf for this information.

9. I owe this point to Richard Arneson.

10. Suppose that on a few occasions, the Nazis need collaborators or else evil will not occur. One may not know whether one is in such a situation when deciding whether to

collaborate. If one gave lexical priority to not helping to cause evil that would not otherwise exist, one should then never collaborate. But suppose one should not give this lexical priority and that the probability of producing evil that would not otherwise exist is small relative to the probability of reducing evil that would otherwise exist. Then it may not be clear that one should not collaborate.

11. Sebastian Martens emphasized to me (in personal communication) the difference between cases in which a villain will kill if I do not and the case where the villain cannot kill without help but somebody else is bound to help. In the first case, a villain threatens to kill ten people if I do not kill one of them. In the second case, a villain threatens that if I do not kill someone, he will certainly find someone else to do it and that person will *also* kill even more people. (Of course, as already noted, the Selector Case differs from the Jim and the Indians Case in that the Selectors do not themselves kill Jews.)

12. Kimberley Brownlee suggests that the Selectors would have had reason to save the young in order to try to ensure a future for the Jewish people.

13. Similarly, Carlos Soto has argued (in unpublished material) that if it is permissible to turn a trolley away from killing a greater number of people toward killing a smaller number of different people, then it is permissible to choose to send it to a smaller number of older people rather than a smaller number of younger people.

14. See *Morality, Mortality*, vol. 1, where I first discussed such a distinction between cases.

15. I have discussed the Trolley Case in *Morality, Mortality*, vol. 2, and more recently in chap. 5 in my *Intricate Ethics*.

16. I distinguished between intervening to prevent a threat (1) after the agent who threatens has done all he can do to present the threat and (2) before he has done so in "Responsibility and Collaboration." Subsequent to the publication of the article on which this chapter is based, I became more concerned about the role of the distinction in the Selector Case and have tried to investigate the general issue elsewhere.

17. I have dealt with this issue in detail in the other sources cited in note 15.

18. First presented by Judith Thomson in her "Killing, Letting Die, and the Trolley Problem."

19. I argue at length for the distinction between intending harm and acting because we will bring it about in "The Doctrine of Triple Effect and Why a Rational Agent Need Not Intend the Means to His End," supplement, *Proceedings of the Aristotelian Society* 74(1) (July 2000): 21–39, and in chap. 4 in my *Intricate Ethics*.

20. I discuss this case in *Intricate Ethics* and other places. In another variant, the turning Lazy Susan would push a bystander near the Lazy Susan into the trolley. Here he does not share the Lazy Susan.

21. Notice that it can be permissible for a smaller number who stand between a threat and a greater number of people to duck even if this leaves a larger number facing the threat. This is because ducking involves people terminating the assistance (cover) they provide to those behind them just by removing themselves. Those behind them may have no right to such assistance and no right to control the bodily movements of the people in front of them. By contrast, it does not seem permissible to move a smaller group of people on a Lazy Susan so that a larger number are moved in front of a threat. Even if it is permissible for *greater* good to cause lesser evil, it is not permissible for a lesser good to cause a greater evil.

22. Judith Thomson introduced this case in "Killing, Letting Die, and the Trolley Problem."

23. It is a mistake in considering this issue to treat the paperwork representation of what a Selector would do as governed by the same moral principles as apply to the actual

treatment of people. Consider three possible types of paperwork, where "A," "B," and "C" are letters representing three different people. (1) "A" and "C" are on a written list, and then someone writes in "B" ahead of them. (2) "A" and "C" are at the top of a list, with "B" next. Someone crosses the first two out, so "B" is at the top of the list. (3) "A" and "C" are alone on a list; someone crosses them out and puts in "B." There need not be any moral difference in what one may do based on which list one starts with and what one does to it.

24. This bears on the view that it is permissible to turn the swivel table to remove the greater number from the threat even though this pushes the smaller number into the threat. In the light of our recent discussion, we can see that it matters how we do this. If we have to take hold of the table (not owned by anyone) or take hold of the five we will save, this is permissible. But what if we must take hold of the one person (who will be pushed into the threat) in order to move the table? This seems impermissible. Similarly, if that one person owns the swivel table, taking hold is a violation of the person's right over his nonthreatening property when this will lead to something very bad for him.

25. If the Selectors picked the old and sick to go to the Nazis, but the Nazis would have taken these anyway, the arrangement is at least no worse for those selected than it would otherwise have been.

26. I first discussed collaboration in my "Responsibility and Collaboration." A revised version of that article appears as chap. 10 in my *Intricate Ethics*. The following section relies heavily on those discussions.

27. For example, Christopher Kutz, in conversation.

28. In Jim and the Indians, Captain does offer Jim an opportunity to stop the Captain doing the worse act he was going to do before Jim's arrival. A slightly different (and perhaps worse case from Jim's perspective) is the Captain's threatening to do something worse that he would *not* otherwise have done because Jim refuses to do something less bad. That is, we could imagine the Captain was not going to kill any of the Indians, but if Jim refused the offer to kill one, the Captain would kill that one and nineteen others. Here it is Jim's presence that triggers the potential for harm.

29. I shall suggest another later.

30. In fact, I think that the first explanation—one acts without being made an offer by the villain—can be subsumed under the second explanation, that one acts very early before the villain has fully done his part.

31. This alternative understanding was suggested by Elinor Mason and independently by John Gardiner.

32. I am not, however, claiming that they had a duty to collaborate, as my remarks in the conclusion should make clear.

33. Here I repeat what I said about the Captain and the Indians in discussing Bernard Williams's case in "Responsibility and Collaboration."

34. It was Peter Graham who raised this issue for me (in conversation).

35. Barbara Herman seems to agree. See her "Murder and Mayhem," reprinted in her *The Practice of Moral Judgment* (Cambridge, MA: Harvard University Press, 1996), 133–131.

36. See Chapter 9 for further discussion of these issues. I thank Prof. Doris Bergen for information about the *Judenräte*. This chapter was originally a paper that was presented to the Department of Philosophy at the University of Pennsylvania, the University of Chicago Law School, and the Conference on Complicity, Corpus Christi College, Oxford University. I am grateful for comments on these occasions to Cass Sunstein, Martha Nussbaum, Stephen Perry, and Kimberley Brownlee (among others).

6

Moral Improvisation and New Obligations: The Case of Truth Commissions

After the end of a conflict between states or within a state where one side wins, how should the losing side be dealt with when it is accused of crimes either in the conflict or in conditions that led to conflict? In this chapter, I consider Barbara Herman's arguments for a particular answer to this question.[1] Her arguments concern the moral justification of the Truth and Reconciliation Commission (TRC), established in South Africa after the conflict to end apartheid. It is an example used to illustrate her views about how creative solutions to moral problems can come about and, thereby, generate new obligations.

In the first section, I begin by considering what I take to be Herman's view of morality and how it allows for creativity in the form of improvisation. Then, I consider how she understands the particulars of the South African situation. In the second section, I offer some reflections on her discussion. I claim that one of her arguments can be simplified and that focusing on that simplified argument lets us characterize in general terms (which Herman does not employ) one strategy that those seeking new, morally acceptable solutions to problems can pursue. However, this strategy, I conclude, removes much of the sting that Herman initially sees in our uncertainty that we may face new obligations at any time. I shall also consider other aspects of her argument that I find problematic, including her notion of obligation, and her views on balancing arguments and on retributive punishment.

I.

A. HERMAN'S VIEW OF MORALITY

I think that Herman believes that the basic components of a universally required morality (such as respect for persons) do not amount to principles that deductively imply particular conclusions in particular circumstances (e.g., what acts or intentions are permissible or obligatory). I believe she refers to this as contingency at the high level of morality, in that there is no principle or rule from which we simply deduce conclusions. She differentiates between the universally required components of morality and what she calls "lived morality." The latter are the

134

norms that people accept as correct at a given time and place. These may change into new norms that are also in accord with components of universal morality because people see—but do not deduce—a new way to be true to the universal components in dealing with a new problem. The nondeductiveness and the newness of the solution amount to the creative, improvisational aspect of morality, in her view.

She thinks that there is also contingency at the ground level of morality in that there may be more than one way in a given situation to be true to components of required universal morality. (This sort of contingency could also, I believe, be present in a system in which conclusions were deducible from principles, for it is possible to deduce a disjunction of equally good alternatives from a principle. So I do not think contingency at the ground level is necessarily connected with contingency at the high level that Herman describes.)

Her further claim, which she investigates in detail, is that even when there are several genuine moral options in dealing with a new problem, people can come to have new obligations that "impose significant burdens" (p. 21) in virtue of the acceptance by others of one of the merely optional routes. These obligations can even eliminate certain of the moral rights they previously had. That we might face new, unexpected obligations in life, she emphasizes, can be unsettling, as morality is valued in part because of the predictability it introduces into social life. A standard way in which unexpected ground-level moral change occurs is our discovering that conduct we have taken to be permissible or even obligatory is wrong. (This description seems to apply to the case she describes where people discover that behavior they had "thought charming comes to be regarded as demeaning, even an expression of aggression or dominance" [p. 24]). Changing such bad behavior can be very unsettling and burdensome but still necessary. However, these are not the cases on which Herman focuses. She wants to focus on change when there are genuine options, not change away from doing what is shown not to be an option at all because it is morally wrong. In particular, she wants to focus on changing from one permissible option to another permissible option.

B. HERMAN'S VIEW OF SOUTH AFRICA

The TRC allowed amnesty for those confessing to crimes that were politically motivated. Herman thinks the TRC is a morally justified alternative to retributive justice (RJ). She also believes that the TRC was not required, as RJ was also a morally permissible option. But given the acceptance of the TRC, all citizens (even those opposed to it) lose a moral right held under the previous "lived morality" to seek RJ, and they acquire a new moral obligation not to pursue RJ against politically motivated crimes that amnesty covers.[2] (That is, if someone requests amnesty, his victim is not at liberty to refuse to allow him to get it. Amnesty is not granted merely on condition that one's victim is willing to go that route.) Furthermore, she is most concerned to argue that the moral right to seek RJ is not merely overridden or outweighed by the necessity of pursuing some greater good. Outweighing or overriding would leave a residue of maltreatment of those who wish to exercise the right, and she denies that this residue exists.[3] Now let us consider in greater detail how Herman argues for her views about the TRC.

II.

A. AVAILABLE AND UNAVAILABLE OPTIONS

Herman first reminds us of cases in which either of two options is perfectly morally acceptable, such as driving on the right or the left. We must choose one, however, and when we do, everyone acquires a new obligation to drive on the side chosen even if it is not chosen by everyone. However, she notes that, in the driving case, the chosen option does not conflict with a status quo right in the way that moving to the TRC conflicts with people's recognized right to seek RJ. But what if a society already had a rule requiring one to drive on the right and then decided to change this rule? Presumably, it would not be difficult to generate a new rule in this case, either. Herman's real concern is, I think, that the right to seek RJ is not as easily changed as the right to drive on the right because RJ has nonarbitrary moral content.

We might ask whether there are also other differences between the TRC case and the driving case. Consider two:

1. *Combining Approaches*

In the case of driving, a choice *must* be made; we cannot have people driving in both ways at once on pain of too many accidents. Must a choice be made between amnesty and RJ? Theoretically, a society could permit victims who are willing to allow amnesty for their accused oppressors to do so but also permit victims eager to pursue RJ against their accused oppressors to do that. Then the society as a whole would not pursue one policy. Herman's argument, therefore, would have to make clear why only one of the two options must be chosen. For if both could be combined, the complaint of those who wish to pursue RJ would seem to be even greater when they are not permitted to do so. I do not think that Herman makes it entirely clear why the two options could not morally and legally be combined, though, as we shall see, she presents facts that suggest why this was not a realistic possibility.[4]

2. *Civic Benevolence*

A second difference between the driving case and the TRC is suggested by Herman's description of Nelson Mandela's refusal to seek RJ even if his accused oppressors would not confess under amnesty. She describes what he did as an act of "moral heroism" that exemplifies "civic benevolence" (p. 37). It was his act, she believes, that made it possible for many people to do something somewhat less heroic but also an instance of civic benevolence: namely, giving up RJ for amnesty plus confession by the accused oppressors. Herman's glowing characterization of Mandela's act might suggest that the TRC is morally superior to RJ. By contrast, in the case of driving, neither the right side nor the left side is morally superior. Although the TRC but not Mandela required confession, if agreeing to the TRC still involves civic benevolence, this suggests the TRC is morally superior to RJ.

At least two issues are raised by the possible moral superiority of a choice involving civic benevolence.

(a) The first is that superior conduct need not be obligatory in principle. Herman agrees. However, Herman also seems to take the position that when many in a community are willing to take a nonobligatory superior course, then for them "can implies ought" (p. 43). This suggests that she thinks that at least for these many, the less noble course is, in fact, impermissible. (If adopting only one course [rather than a combination] is necessary, the fact that many [supposedly] find themselves with an obligation to pursue the TRC because they are willing to do so will be an additional reason to allow only the TRC.)

To conclude that for many, in this particular way, the noble cause becomes obligatory and the less noble impermissible would be a more radical move than Herman acknowledges. It is another way, which she does not emphasize, in which her account might give rise to new, contingent obligations. That is, if one in fact feels capable of and wants to do a nonrequired, noble act, one acquires an obligation to do it. I think this radical conclusion would not be correct. Suppose I find myself psychologically able to give up my kidney to a stranger, and I even desire to do this truly noble act. I do not think it becomes impermissible (wrong) for me not to act on my desire. For suppose that I let my desire to go back to sleep interfere with my capacity and desire to give my kidney to save a life, when giving it just then is necessary. I do not think I thereby fail in an obligation to give my kidney. The capacity and even desire to do a noble act do not turn the merely permissible into the obligatory.

Notice also that if a new obligation were generated in this radical way, it would not have the unsettling characteristics Herman thinks are associated with unexpected changes in obligations. For the existence of the new obligation would depend on a change in one's own desires and capacities and stem from and be consistent with them.[5] In this way, at least, they would be less problematic.

(b) A second issue raised by "civic benevolence" involves its exact definition and whether it is a nobler course. Suppose that only a few people had committed politically inspired crimes and it would have been possible to use RJ to punish them. It would have been benevolent of black South Africans to use TRC instead, but it is hard to believe that they would have done so. (Herman agrees that the TRC was not about the superiority of forgiveness by individuals.) Perhaps this is because "civic benevolence" is really at stake only if the *society is the real object* of people's benevolence. For example, civic benevolence may lead people to institute amnesty because they do not want RJ to lead to civil war when large numbers of contested, politically inspired crimes are at issue. However, Herman also notes that the police and military would never have allowed RJ against their members. This is one reason to believe that widespread RJ was not in fact a real possibility, and so civic benevolence to avoid civil war due to contested trials was not really needed.

In such a context, I think it is better to say that the TRC *could have been* the creation of people who were motivated by civic benevolence but that, in fact, the TRC may not have been the product of such motivation and, indeed, may not have been what most people preferred. Its objective properties might make it the nobler course even if its use does not signal noble motives of those who participate in it, when widespread use of the other (RJ) option would be blocked by powerful forces anyway. (One reason to worry that the TRC is not the nobler course is that it may cheapen the value of South African citizenship. This is because even if one has committed grave crimes, amnesty means that one need not forfeit any of the rights that other citizens have.)

B. JUSTIFICATIONS FOR RULING OUT RETRIBUTIVE JUSTICE

I have further characterized the options in the South African case (though not necessarily in the way that Herman does). Now consider one argument Herman presents for the justifiability of the TRC even when it removes the option of a realistically possible exercise of a right to RJ once someone requests amnesty for a politically motivated crime. First, as already noted, she thinks that Mandela's example changed the TRC from a nobler option that was a theoretical possibility to a psychologically real possibility for many in the populace. Second, she also thinks the TRC was a way to change the status of blacks from "victim" to "citizen." (Of course, it was also a way of turning accused oppressors into ordinary citizens.) She seems to think that the TRC could have this effect because she believes that the confessions would provide a shared moral history, presumably endorsing the black cause as the foundation of a new community in which blacks would be full citizens.[6] The only drawback Herman sees with endorsing the TRC as the *only* system for dealing with political crimes for which amnesty is requested is that it seems to conflict with the rights of those who still want to pursue RJ. The justification of the TRC will not be complete, she thinks, until this problem is dealt with. She considers some ways to deal with it.

1. Balancing

One possible way is to argue that a greater good justifies imposing a cost (of an infringed right) on some. This is what she calls a balancing argument, wherein we weigh the right against the greater good, the right loses, and some people have to bear the cost. Herman tries to avoid this balancing approach quite generally when seeking to explain either why a right does not stand in the way of a greater good (as in the TRC case) or why it does.[7] However, it seems especially important not to override rights in the South African case, for one is attempting, for the first time, to recognize the equal rights and citizenship of black South Africans.

As an example of a case where a right does stand in the way of a greater good, Herman discusses why it is not permissible to kill someone in order to stop many other people from being killed. Her nonbalancing answer has two components. First, she says the wrong involved in killing does not add up, so more killings are not necessarily worse than fewer. By implication, avoiding more killing would not necessarily be a greater good. I do not think this is correct. For if I had to go to one island where I could prevent ten wrongful killings or to another island where I could prevent one wrongful killing (other things being equal), I should go to the first island. I think that this is because it is worse if there are more rather than fewer *people killed*. (Preventing ten more killings might even weigh more than preventing ten deaths through natural causes or deaths from criminal acts already completed. Admittedly, I do not think it is for the sake of preventing more rather than fewer agents from becoming killers that I should go to one island rather than another.) Furthermore, if I have a forced choice between going in one direction where I will kill ten people with my car or another direction where I will kill one other person, I think I should do the latter. The second component of Herman's answer to why it is not permissible to kill one person to stop other people from being killed is that the reason why it is wrong to kill someone is different from whatever reason there is to not allow people to be killed. I think this is correct. However, I do not think that the particular reason she isolates for not killing is quite right.

She focuses on the faulty relationship killing creates between me and the person I would kill. But suppose I have set a bomb that will kill ten people unless I throw another person on it who will be blown up instead. I will be involved in ten faulty relationships if the bomb goes off, yet I should not use the one person to prevent this even though it is only one faulty relationship. I do not think this is because faulty relationships do not add up. I think it is wrong to kill the one person because if doing this were permissible, then he would not be the highly inviolable person that he really is. Furthermore, this would be true of every person, including those who would be saved from being killed (in the same way to save yet others). By contrast, if we do not prevent others from being killed, and they are, in fact, violated, this does nothing to show that it is permissible for them to be killed or, in other words, that they are not highly inviolable. The requirement to not kill one to save others from being killed shows, I believe, that respect for the inviolable status of persons may take precedence over what actually happens to people (i.e., that many people will be wrongly killed). This is also a nonbalancing argument insofar as we would not respect a value we might be trying to protect (inviolability) if we killed the one. (It does, however, balance lives saved against respecting the status of all. In this sense, Herman's argument would also balance saving lives against interpersonal relationships.)[8]

2. *Equally Good for the Victim*

Having rejected a balancing argument, Herman proposes another solution to deal with the problem of rights to RJ that might stand in the way of the TRC. She argues that when a victim gets from TRC everything significant that he would have gotten from RJ, there is no longer a ground for his claiming the right to RJ, and there is also no cost (which is supposedly outweighed on the balancing model) imposed on those who lose the right. A right to RJ may have been part of the lived moral life of the community without the TRC, but it is not a right that is a part of fundamental universal morality. This is because something else may accomplish for the victim what RJ is meant to accomplish for him.

(a) Let us consider this solution in more detail. Herman suggests that RJ is meant to help a victim regain his status in the moral community and that the TRC does this, too. My first concern with her solution is that this is not the distinctive point of RJ. For the victim may regain his status simply by everyone agreeing that he has been wronged and someone else is indeed the criminal (even without confession by the criminal). Hence, while RJ may help a victim regain his status, it is not necessary for doing this. Rather, RJ is necessary in order to make the criminal pay for his crime with some nonmonetary loss, and this is its distinctive point. Possibly, the victim even has a right to have the person who wronged him pay for his crime in this way, and only RJ could satisfy this right.[9]

If the victim has such a personal right to have the criminal pay for his crime, then the TRC will not provide a victim with all he is personally entitled to have. So it is important for Herman's approach to the problem of depriving people of RJ that there be no such personal right to have the criminal pay. Suppose there is no such right. Then even if the point of RJ is to have the criminal pay (though not because the victim has a personal right that this happen), his not paying need not be a personal wrong to the victim. Hence, even if Herman's view of what RJ is about is not complete, it is still possible that *the victim can also get under TRC what he is entitled to get from RJ*. This can be so even if not everything that should be gotten from RJ for society can be gotten under TRC (because the criminal does not pay for his crime in a nonmonetary way) so long as, in failing to get what RJ alone can give, the victim would not be made to bear any cost that *he* has a right not to bear or lose anything that *he* has a right to have.[10]

(b) We can raise another concern about Herman's solution by making clear how it may contrast with an alternative proposal. On Herman's proposal, the right to bring a wrongdoer before a TRC is a direct interpretation of (if not a deduction from) some component of universal morality. It need not depend on anyone (including society) having a right to pursue the punishment of a wrongdoer for RJ, for RJ is a different direct interpretation of a component of universal morality. The alternative proposal I wish to consider now, by contrast, emphasizes that the right to insist that someone appear before a TRC, confess, and only then receive amnesty depends on someone's (including society's) prior right to seek RJ.[11] The right to set up the TRC and to grant amnesty may "piggyback" on the right to seek RJ. Indeed, amnesty literally means release from punishment that others had a right to impose. Hence, one might object that because, on Herman's proposal, the right to establish a TRC does not depend on a prior right to pursue RJ, it does not even seem appropriate to speak of the TRC granting *amnesty* (i.e., release from punishment that one had a right to impose) at all!

Some analogies may help us to better understand the contrast between Herman's approach and what I will call the Piggyback Alternative. Here is Analogy 1: Suppose that we do not allow any physical violence or threat of it against wrongdoers, but we do claim the right to restrict a wrongdoer and to try to persuade him to apologize and change. If he fails to do these things, we still would have no right to use physical violence within this social system. However, if we found this "pacifist" system a complete failure at social control, we do think it is permissible for us to institute a different system involving the use and threat of physical violence. This analogy fits, I think, with Herman's views of the relation of the TRC to RJ: They are completely alternative systems that interpret some fundamental moral concern.

Here is Analogy 2, which is meant to represent the structure of the relation between the TRC and RJ on the Piggyback Alternative, though the analogy is about capturing criminals: Suppose we have a right to shoot a criminal if this is necessary to stop the threat he presents. Because we have this right, we also have a right to threaten to shoot him in order to get him to put down his weapon peacefully without our shooting him. If he puts down his weapon and there is no more threat, we no longer have the right to shoot him or threaten him with violence, for we get everything we are entitled to get by his desisting from crime that we would otherwise get from shooting him. We are not entitled to have him shot per se. However, if he fails to desist, it would be permissible to use violence as the alternative.

I suggest that it is the Piggyback Alternative's explanation of the relation between the TRC and RJ that more accurately represents the situation in South Africa. Although it must be admitted that it was probably unrealistic for South Africans to think that they could have actually carried out their right to seek RJ, the permissibility of their doing so could have been the ground for the permissibility of setting up the TRC. Notice that the Piggyback Alternative, like Herman's approach, implies that if the TRC can be made to work, South Africans do not lose a right to punish that they are entitled to exercise per se. Hence, the Piggyback Alternative, like Herman's approach, would succeed in justifying the TRC with no residue, at least on the supposition that there is no right to make the wrongdoer suffer nonmonetary punishment per se, for which nothing can substitute.

(c) Now consider Herman's approach again. Though Herman does not say so, her way of dealing with the problem of the supposed costs to the victim of using TRC rather than RJ seems to me to be an instance of a common strategy for turning supererogatory acts into obligations: Reduce the Cost of the act. (The same could be said of the Piggyback Alternative.) It is also a common strategy for turning unjust impositions into permissible ones. That is, we can sometimes turn a supererogatory act (or an omission such as not taking advantage of RJ) into an obligation (not to take advantage of RJ) by reducing the costs of the act (or omission). Similarly, an imposition on someone that makes it impossible for him to seek RJ might be unjust if this is very costly to him. However, we can sometimes make such an imposition not be unjust by reducing the costs of the imposition. The costs get reduced because an alternative (TRC) provides as well all that one had a right to have. (Consider an analogy: It would be unjust of me to interfere with someone to the extent of killing him to save others' lives, but it might not be unjust to pinch him to do so.) Herman adopts an extremely demanding version of this cost-reducing strategy in that she wishes there to be no costs to those who give up RJ. But notice that even if the person imposed on pays some cost (e.g., in being pinched), there may be no *moral* cost or negative *moral* remainder, for it may clearly be someone's duty to undergo such a small cost for the sake of the end in question. If this is so, there is also no mere overriding or balancing going on.

This Reduce the Cost strategy of creating new obligations (with no costs or with a small cost) shows us the difference between (a) having new obligations because there is now no large sacrifice associated with doing certain things that previously would have involved big sacrifices and (b) having new obligations because big sacrifices not previously required are now required. That one has many new obligations that come about in manner (a) is not a source of complaint or worry. For example, previously we may have had no obligations to those at a great distance because the cost of helping them would have been high. But now, with rapid and cheap transport, the cost has gone down, and so we may have new obligations but not ones that are burdensome. Similarly, it is said that with great wealth come great obligations. Suppose that prior to being wealthy one would have had an obligation to give away 1 percent of one's income if this would help the needy. Suppose that such a small amount of money in absolute terms would not have helped them, and so one actually had no obligation to give it. Now one may also have an obligation to give away 1 percent of one's new wealth if this would help the needy. But this amount in absolute terms will be useful, so one comes to have new obligations. But in reality there has not been much of a change in the burden imposed on one, given one's new wealth.

That we can identify such a general strategy suggests that so-called creativity and improvisation in generating new obligations may conform to certain patterns. It suggests that certain universals (e.g., turn a high cost into a low one to make an obligation) play a part in the transformation rules for going from one moral solution to another. It also suggests that one could discover more structure in creativity and that there may be a limited set of general moves that one could try when thinking about new moral solutions to problems even though many different institutions or acts might satisfy these moves.

Notice, however, that the cost-reducing strategy for creating a new obligation is designed to make *the existence of uncertainty as to what our obligations might turn out to be very nonthreatening.* For the new ground-level moral regime is allowed to come into existence only if it makes us not significantly worse off (in ways that we are entitled not to be made worse off) than we were under the old regime. So it defuses some crucial concerns associated with instability that Herman emphasizes at the beginning of "Contingency in Obligation" when she speaks of new obligations that "impose significant burdens" (p. 21). (Earlier we saw that this nonthreatening character of new obligations could be true for a different reason if it were the case that new obligations arose only when they were consistent with our desires to do what is ordinarily supererogatory.) But then this means that the explanation and justification of the TRC that Herman gives show it *not* to be a case of the sort she was supposed to be discussing, namely, one where significant burdens are imposed and "difficult obligations of this kind . . . come about . . . where creative solutions to moral difficulties are . . . attempted" (p. 21).

The example and the explanation that she has given of how to bring about a new contingent obligation raise the following possibility: Generating in other people new, unexpected obligations in selecting one of two permissible options is permissible only when it does not impose significant burdens. This is only a possibility, however, as there may be other permissible ways of bringing about new obligations as a result of choosing one of two permissible options despite severe dislocations it produces. For Herman says (only in passing, p. 22) that when some in a community find it possible to do heroic acts that do great good (e.g., saving victims from persecution at great risk to themselves), then while others do not have to do as the heroes do, others may not go about their lives as they always have if this would interfere with the heroic acts. This suggests that these others might have to bear significant burdens as a result of not being able to do what they have always done. They do not merely have to do things differently while not being made much worse off than they would otherwise have been.

This passing remark of Herman's seems to involve the balancing that she rejected in arguing for the TRC, for there are residual costs some must bear. What might distinguish cases where balancing is permitted from those where it is not? Perhaps, in the former the burdens do not involve any denial of someone's *right*. After all, we do not have a right not to be made much worse off, for example, by heroes refusing us access that we previously had to their property because they are now hiding victims of persecution. Hence, there may be another class of cases where significant burdens not involving transgression of a right may be justified via a balancing argument, at least in order to choose a permissible option that is morally superior to another permissible option.

3. *Psychologically Real Possibilities*

We have considered the solution to the problem of eliminating RJ that Herman gives when she assumes that RJ is not only morally permissible but also a real possibility and that some want it, but most do not. In discussing civic benevolence, I raised the possibility that RJ was not a real possibility because powerful forces would have stood in its way. Now let us consider that aspect of her discussion in which Herman *retracts* her original assumption that RJ was a real possibility, though not for the reasons I gave. First, having said that both RJ and TRC are theoretically moral possibilities, she claims (p. 44) that, in fact, only the TRC option was *psychologically* a real possibility for most people. (It is not clear to me why this is so, assuming that just preferring one alternative does not make another alternative psychologically unreal for one.) Indeed, she thinks that they "experience it [the TRC] (hear it) as obligatory" (p. 43). One explanation for why Herman thinks that they "experience" the TRC as obligatory is her view, examined earlier, that "can implies ought" when one finds oneself with the capacity to do a noble deed. (Earlier, I argued that "can implies ought" is not true, at least if "ought" is understood as "obligated.") A second explanation for only the TRC's being a real possibility is suggested by Herman's discussion: South Africans are obligated to do either TRC or RJ, many are psychologically unable to do RJ, and hence those people are obligated to do TRC. On the first explanation, RJ becomes, in fact, impermissible because the psychological reality of the nobler TRC imparts a duty to do it. On the second explanation, the TRC is experienced as obligatory merely as a consequence of RJ having no psychological reality.[12]

When does Herman think people cannot do something (in a sense that relates to the claim that *ought* implies or presupposes *can*)? Her account seems to heavily imply that contingency in obligation can result from theoretically permissible options not being "psychologically real" for people. (Notice that in this respect the contingent obligation is not that some people must not pursue RJ but that the greater number (supposedly) must *use* the TRC. This is another type of contingency in obligation that her account implies but that is not her primary focus.)

I think Herman overpsychologizes "can't." For a psychopath, all morally permissible options might be psychologically unreal. Does this mean there is nothing he is actually morally permitted or obligated to do? Presumably not. Some people might be unable to conceive of themselves as responsible voters. Does this mean they are not permitted or obligated to vote? Presumably not. Those who want RJ might have a complaint against those who want the TRC exclusively because RJ's being psychologically unavailable to the latter group does not make them unable to support RJ in a way that would neutralize obligations to those who have a supposed right to RJ. This is one reason that we have to give another argument (as described in B[2]) for why those who have to forego RJ have no complaint. When an option is psychologically unreal for someone, this is more like his being unwilling to do it than his being unable to do it, in the context of the view that "ought" implies or presupposes "can."

It is still true, however, that if someone will not do one of only two permissible options, he comes to have an obligation to do the other one, and this obligation is contingent on his choice. But, again, since this new, contingent obligation arises from a predilection or choice of the agent himself, such contingent obligations should not be threatening for agents seeking to avoid dislocations associated with changes in ground-level moral life. Such contingent obligations are not instances of the difficult contingent obligations for which Herman was supposed to be arguing.

Another reason Herman offers for thinking that RJ was actually impossible goes beyond its psychological unreality for many in the community. It implies that RJ was not even theoretically possible in the circumstances, though not because RJ was a morally inadmissible option. For she says (p. 46) that a constituted community may commit itself to pursue RJ, but the problem in South Africa was to constitute the community (implying it was not yet constituted). This suggests that she thinks RJ requires a community to pursue it, and there was no community that could pursue RJ; she may even think that there were no citizens who could pursue it but only victims and other remnants of a previous community.[13] (This would seem to be the real meaning of her view that victims had to be turned into citizens.) If only after one is a citizen of a community could one pursue RJ, one would need something else to make one a citizen besides RJ. Herman seems to think that one can create a community by way of the construction of a moral history for a community, from those who give testimony and confessions during amnesty proceedings. She finally suggests, therefore, that as a *conceptual matter* TRC is the only possible route when a community is being formed.

I do not think that this could be correct. Suppose Jewish people who had been abused citizens of Nazi Germany tried to hold trials of their persecutors in a postwar Germany in which no amnesty was available and no confessions served as the basis for a historical narrative of the new state. I think there could already be a new state with former victims as citizens who could, as a conceptual matter, pursue RJ. They need neither the results of RJ nor the TRC in order to be full-fledged citizens. This would be so even if there were no community in the sense that those to be tried themselves accepted the legitimacy of the new order. Why should the legitimacy of the new order depend on its acceptance (via signs such as participating in a TRC confessional proceeding) by people accused of crimes in the old order? Citizens may think it right to bring such people into the new community as full-fledged members (rather than as convicted criminals) by civic benevolence and amnesty but not because it is literally impossible to do anything else if a new state capable of RJ is to exist.

Even if ordinary courts could not pursue RJ for practical reasons, this need not mean that RJ could not and should not be pursued. For nonstate courts, such as international war-crimes tribunals, could still be convened to pursue RJ. Indeed, Herman herself says (in footnote 33, pp. 51–52), "Analogous claims [to those about the TRC] are made about the need for international war crimes trials. . . . The justification for abnormal judicial activities is more commonly that some moral possibility needs to be opened (or closed) that exceeds the orbit of ordinary justice." Hence, contrary to Herman's view, RJ is not ruled out as a conceptual matter even if it must be pursued in an "abnormal judicial context" such as an international court.

Conclusion

I conclude that if it were true that victims have no fundamental right to have criminals pay for their crimes in nonmonetary ways, Herman will have provided an argument for TRC that eliminates a significant complaint made by those who lose

RJ. However, I think that if her argument is correct, it also shows that the TRC is *not* a case of the sort she had intended to investigate, namely one where "significant burdens" are imposed on some in virtue of new obligations that they have when others choose one of two permissible options. This is because her argument depends on showing that the TRC, as much as RJ, gives victims all they are entitled to have, and if they get all they are entitled to have, they do not bear significant burdens. I also do not think she shows that RJ was not a possible option (either on its own or in conjunction with the TRC) because of its actual (versus theoretical) impermissibility for those who were capable of a nobler option, either because of its psychological unavailability to them or because of its conceptual impossibility in transitional contexts.

More generally, I isolated and focused on three ways (not all emphasized by Herman) in which Herman's account suggests that new, contingent obligations can arise consistent with deeper, universal elements of morality: (1) When some people want to do something, this can create new obligations for others. (This is the one to which she gives the most attention.) (2) If one is capable of and wants to do something noble, this may make one obligated to do it. (I argued against this.) (3) If one of (only) two permissible options is psychologically unavailable to you, you acquire an obligation to do the other option. (I suggested problems with this claim.) I argued that none of Herman's examples of these ways of generating new obligations should worry people who are concerned about the dislocations and burdens of ground-level moral change. This is, in part, because certain transformation rules (e.g., unjust impositions can be made just by eliminating costs) may be part of the deeper, universal elements of morality. It is also, in part, because a desire or psychological predilection to fulfill a new obligation reduces the burden of fulfilling it.

Notes

This chapter is a revision of "Moral Improvisation and New Obligations," in *Moral Universalism and Pluralism*, ed. H. S. Richardson and M. Williams (New York: New York University Press, 2009), 64–80. It is a response to Barbara Herman's "Contingency in Obligation," published in the same volume (17–53). Page references for Herman are to that volume.

   1. See citation to Herman, above.

   2. Herman does not discuss the fact that people are at least encouraged to give up another right—that against self-incrimination—and to bear witness against themselves with the establishment of the TRC.

   3. One immediate possible objection to her claim that the citizens acquire a moral obligation not to pursue RJ is made by Frank Michelman in his comment on Herman in *Moral Universalism and Pluralism*, "Moral Improvisation, Moral Change, and Political Institutions: Comment on Barbara Herman," pp. 54–63. He says that the legal possibility of pursuing RJ was eliminated once the TRC option was chosen, and it does not make sense to say that people acquire a moral obligation not to do what it is legally impossible for them to

do anyway. I think one could respond to this objection as follows: Suppose it can be shown (for one reason or another) that South Africa is morally justified in pursuing the amnesty option alone and that one would have a moral obligation not to do what conflicts with this *even if it were* legally possible to do so (for example, because all legal loopholes had not been closed to RJ). Then if pursuing RJ would conflict with the amnesty, one would have a moral obligation not to pursue it even if it were legally possible to do so. On these grounds, one might justify taking the further step of making what would be morally impermissible to do into what it is also legally impossible to do (by closing the loopholes).

4. She herself notes that South Africa did permit civil suits as well as amnesty for politically motivated crimes.

5. However, it is possible that when someone says that "can implies ought" for those who can do the morally superior act, the *ought* does not signify obligation in the ordinary sense. For example, some (such as Allan Gibbard) think that failure to fulfill an obligation merits guilt on the part of the agent and resentment by others. But even if one ought to do a supererogatory act that one is willing and able to do, the failure to do it through laziness need not, in a reasonable agent, result in guilt (though it might trigger shame). (On these grounds, I have suggested that Allan Gibbard's characterization of "ought" judgments as signaling the appropriateness of guilt, if one fails to do what one ought to do, is too broad. A distinction should be drawn between what one ought to do and what one is obligated to do, and only failure to do the latter triggers guilt. (See my "Should You Save This Child? Gibbard on Intuitions, Contractualism, and Strains of Commitment," in Allan Gibbard, *Reconciling Our Aims: In Search of Bases for Ethics* [New York: Oxford University Press, 2008].)

6. One danger of the confession process, I would note, is that the shared moral history will then not be based on firmer evidence that might result from a trial.

7. However, elsewhere in "Contingency in Obligation," it is not so clear that Herman would always reject such a balancing approach. For she says (p. 22) that when some in a community find it possible to do heroic acts that do great good (e.g., saving victims from persecution at great risk to themselves), then while others do not have to do as they do, these others may not go about their lives as they always have if this would interfere with the heroic acts. This suggests that these others must bear costs as a result of not being able to go about their lives as they have always done in order that a great good may be accomplished. Perhaps Herman is opposed to imposing costs in this way only when the costs stem from transgressing a right to do something and not otherwise. I shall have occasion to repeat this point in the text later.

8. My discussion here draws on my discussion of this topic in other places, for example, in "Harming Some to Save Others," *Philosophical Studies* (November 1989): 227–260, in *Morality, Mortality*, vol. 2 (New York: Oxford University Press, 1996), and in *Intricate Ethics* (New York: Oxford University Press, 2007).

9. Perhaps the victim's right might be better thought of as his right to pursue such payment by the criminal or his right to have society pursue it. I shall assume these alternative readings in using the phrase "right to have a criminal pay."

10. Of course, if the victim supports RJ on grounds independent of what he has a right to just because he thinks the criminal deserves to pay, he will not be satisfied by the TRC. But he would have no personal right to have the community decide for RJ unless victims have rights to have the perpetrators of crimes against them "pay."

11. This alternative was raised by Philip Pettit and Thomas Scanlon in public remarks.

12. Problematically, Herman raises the second explanation *before* she presents her solution to the problem of eliminating RJ, which I have already described in B(2), namely that everything important gotten by a victim from RJ can be gotten from the TRC. I think this is puzzling because if the community were actually incapable of pursuing RJ, and if *ought* implies or presupposes *can*, how could those who lose out on RJ complain that they failed to get something to which they had a right from the community (i.e., how does the community fail to give them something that the community ought to give them if the community cannot give it to them)? A possible answer to this is that Herman does not think that *ought* implies or presupposes *can*. Another answer is that our sense of what the community owes victims is identifiable independently of the means by which it can be achieved. So we can know what the TRC should give independently of whether any other means can give it.

13. She says, "[I]n the circumstances of transition . . . the restitutive moral function of retributive justice could not be realized" and that there was an "absence of conditions of civility and trust that allow ordinary systems of justice to perform their status-securing functions" (p. 46).

7

Jus Post Bellum, Proportionality, and Compensation

Traditionally, discussions of justice and war have focused on justice in starting a war (*jus ad bellum*) and justice in carrying out a war (*jus in bello*). This is, in part, because it is thought that only a limited set of causes justifies starting a war and that not everything is morally permitted in carrying out a war. A more recent addition to these discussions is a concern with what justice requires following a war (called *jus post bellum*). In this chapter, I shall consider several recommendations made for justice after war mostly concerning the victors' duties postbellum. Assuming the just side wins, these include duties to punish those responsible for unjustly starting and/or unjustly carrying out war, duties to rehabilitate the loser and help civilians harmed by war, and duties not to cause harm to civilians after war is over. It may seem that there being such duties postbellum would make it harder to justify starting a war and so may reduce instances of war. One of my additional concerns will be to see whether attending to *jus post bellum* might actually make it easier to justify starting a war and doing things in war.

I. Principles

A. *OREND'S ACCOUNT*

Brian Orend has been a leading developer of *jus post bellum*.[1] He provides an outline of proper aims and the means that may be used to secure them after a war is concluded. He suggests that these aims and means should be modeled on a standard checklist of items describing justice in starting and pursuing a war from a moral (if not a legal) perspective. For example, *jus ad bellum* enumerates only certain aims as just causes for starting a war. So his outline for *jus post bellum* says that only certain aims are just causes to be sought after war. In addition to having a just cause postbellum, we cannot proceed unless we use means to accomplish it whose bad effects are proportional to the good to be achieved. This is analogous to a similar moral requirement of proportionality in starting a war.[2] Orend also thinks we must abide by a principle of discrimination comparable to one that is said to govern proper conduct in war (*jus in bello*). The traditional *jus in bello* principle of discrimination distinguishes morally between causing harm to combatants and causing harm to noncombatants, where the latter class includes civilians who do not take up arms. (There might be noncivilian noncombatants, as when military personnel are not part of a fighting force.) For example, according to *jus in bello* it is permissible to deliberately cause harm to combatants, and harming any number of combatants may be proportional to achieving a just cause. By contrast, causing harm to civilians who do not take up arms can be permissible only as a side effect of strikes on military targets (so-called collateral damage), and the amount of such collateral harm may be limited in order to not be out of proportion to pursuing missions within war. (This leaves it open that civilians might be deliberately attacked if they fight even though they do not then acquire the status of soldiers. While there have been objections to the traditional principle of discrimination, I shall assume it for the sake of argument.)

Analogously, Orend thinks that in pursuing a just cause postbellum we should have a postbellum principle of discrimination, distinguishing whether harms postbellum would come to those responsible for an unjust conflict or to those who were civilians in the war and whether we impose harms deliberately, as in punishment, or only collaterally, as side effects of other actions. (It may be that former combatants who were reasonably following noncriminal orders are to be classified postbellum with the civilians who had no part in fighting the war at all.) Having a right reason to go to war (i.e., going to war for the sake of the just cause that exists), having a reasonable chance of success in achieving a just cause, and the necessity of war to achieve the just cause—factors found on standard checklists for *jus ad bellum*—also find their analogues in *jus post bellum* in Orend's account.

He believes that one just cause postbellum is to bring the leaders responsible for an unjust war to trial and to prosecute war crimes committed by combatants on any side in the conflict, winners or losers. He sees this at least in part as a matter of retributive justice (RJ), not just as a matter of deterring future wrong acts and otherwise producing best consequences. However, he thinks that pursuit of these just aims is governed by a proportionality condition. He notes (p. 53): "[S]ometimes such leaders . . . retain considerable popular legitimacy, and thus bringing them to trial could seriously destabilize the polity. . . . Care needs to be taken, as always, that appeal to proportionality does not amount to rewarding aggressors. . . . Yet this care does not vitiate the need to consider the destruction and suffering that might result from adhering totally to what the requirements of justice as retribution demand."

Other just causes postbellum give permissions, not requirements. So the original victims of a state that began an unjust war may seek rectification and compensation for themselves but need not. (This is different from seeking RJ of aggressors or criminals in war.) The principle of discrimination, Orend thinks, implies that rectification and compensation of this sort may be sought only from leaders, not from those who were innocent enemy civilians, and so economic sanctions aimed at rectification and compensation of the victor are not permitted if aimed at a whole population. Even if seeking rectification and compensation may permissibly affect a whole population just as a side effect, there should be limits on such postbellum collateral damage based on proportionality.

It is worth emphasizing that Orend is concerned with duties and permissions postbellum that could arise independently of purely consequentialist considerations such as what will win hearts and minds of citizens of an enemy country. Yet, in his discussion of RJ, Orend is also engaged in *balancing* the claims of retributive justice against consequences of pursuing it. As such I think it is worth noting some concerns about balancing raised by Barbara Herman in her discussion of postconflict justice in South Africa.[3]

B. *HERMAN'S ACCOUNT*

Orend does not consider whether a truth and reconciliation committee (TRC) such as was used in South Africa for dealing postconflict with noncapital offenses would be a satisfactory alternative to RJ if having a TRC diminished the threat of destabilizing the polity. Barbara Herman focuses on this issue. Like Orend, Herman is aware that seeking RJ postconflict can have negative effects on a postwar society, in particular where there was intrasocial conflict. She begins by assuming that what makes the pursuit of wrongdoers postconflict something like a just cause is that there is a moral right on the part of victims to have wrongdoers subject to RJ. She then considers how these victims come to have a new obligation not to pursue RJ if they are offered a TRC as an alternative.

Unlike Orend, Herman refuses to rely on the idea that a right or an obligation to pursue RJ may be merely balanced against and *overridden by* greater goods such as reconciliation, social peace, or the avoidance of violence. She objects to the "negative residue" that overriding rights, in particular, will leave. Hence, her way of reasoning is very different from the balancing of good and bad effects involved in standard proportionality calculations, where the failure to pursue justice may be seen as regrettable but necessary so that other worse effects do not occur. Her way of reasoning even differs from a version of balancing that gives greater negative weight to overriding rights or justice than to other effects. Instead, she hopes to explain why replacing RJ with a TRC involves no outweighing by or balancing against social costs *at all*.

My understanding of how this can happen, which differs somewhat from her own understanding of it, is as follows: We first identify what it is about RJ (for example, what it provides) that gives victims and their vindicators a right or even a duty to pursue it. If the TRC as much as RJ provides these things, then there is *no cost at all* to those who must give up RJ for the TRC, so we need not think of balancing and outweighing justice by other things. I have argued that this form of reasoning is an instance of a general strategy for turning what could be a supererogatory sacrifice (e.g., waiving a right to have RJ done) into an obligation (e.g., to have only a TRC) by eliminating or reducing the costs of giving up RJ.[4]

In general, nonconsequentialists tend to be very careful about using balancing. Nonconsequentialists are those who deny that right conduct is determined solely by expected consequences; they do not deny that consequences may be relevant to determining right conduct. One reason they are careful about using balancing is that they focus on how outcomes come about, not just on whether the ultimate outcome is on balance good. For example, from a nonconsequentialist perspective we may not simply balance the death of one person against the deaths of five others if we have to kill the one person to save the five. Nor may we always balance our killing one person against our killing five people even if we must kill the one person as a means of preventing us from killing the five. For example, suppose we are driving a trolley that is headed toward five people, whom it will kill. The only way to stop the trolley is for us to use a device to topple a man standing on a footbridge onto the trolley tracks so that he falls in front of the trolley. This would stop the trolley but kill him. Doing this to one person to save the five seems impermissible from a nonconsequentialist perspective. This is because the right of the one person not to be toppled and killed is seen as a side constraint that stands in the way of our even minimizing overall the violations of comparable rights.

However, it may sometimes be permissible even on a nonconsequentialist view to balance saving five against killing one. For example, suppose the death of one person would be a consequence of a bystander redirecting the trolley away from five onto another track, where it hits the one. Then it may be permissible to balance one death against five. It may also be permissible to balance saving one person against saving five different people when it is a question of whom we aid. This is in part because nonconsequentialists distinguish morally between failing to aid someone so that we may help others and harming someone so that we may help others. The general point is that from a nonconsequentialist perspective, *how* outcomes come about will be relevant to whether balancing goods and bads in an outcome is a permissible way to decide what to do. This is especially true when the goods come to some people and the bads to other people (interpersonal balancing). There will be less concern when the bads and goods (including avoiding other bads) come to the same person (intrapersonal balancing).

II. Proportionality

A. *RIGHTS AND ROUTE TO EFFECTS*

With this as a background, my primary concern now is to consider Orend's approach to balancing the pursuit of RJ as a just cause postbellum against other considerations. It is not clear that Orend adheres to the internal logic that *jus ad bellum* and *jus in bello* proportionality arguments seem to have when they balance achievement of the just cause or a particular military mission against bad effects. For example, consider what is standardly involved when proportionality arguments dealing with collateral harm are used to defeat the right to pursue a just cause (such as defense against aggression) in *jus ad bellum* or the right to engage in a particular military action in *jus in bello*. First, the negative effects that are counted in a proportionality calculation relative to the aim to be achieved are typically what I shall here call *direct* effects either of the means necessary to achieve the aim or of the achievement of the aim itself rather than what I shall here call *indirect* effects. Second, especially in *jus in bello* these negative effects would involve the violation of the *rights* of others. (I believe it is harder than commonly believed to explain why collateral harm is permissible in war. I shall not discuss this issue here but have considered it elsewhere, for example in chapters 2–4 in this volume.)

By "direct" I here mean only that negative effects such as civilians being killed collaterally would be caused by weapons we would use in a war or in a particular military action without the intervention of agents not acting for our side.[5] Not all effects of our acts are direct in this sense. For example, suppose some civilians in an opponent country will respond to our defending ourselves against their country by killing other fellow civilians. Here the intervening acts of other agents not acting under our auspices but responding to our military action or success cause the deaths. Even if such a civilian action would be a certain and foreseen result of our responding to aggression, the deaths the civilians caused are not attributable only to our war or military attack in the way direct effects, as I am now using the term, are. Because of this these effects might not outweigh our right to defend ourselves even if our causing the same number of side-effect deaths "directly" would stand in the way of our defending ourselves.[6] Here is a domestic analogy: An aggressor hurls a deadly bomb at you. Suppose the only way to save yourself is to redirect it, but it will then hit a group of ten people who will be killed. Redirecting is, I believe, impermissible. Alternatively, suppose you can save yourself by redirecting the bomb to the aggressor. This is permissible. But what if you know the aggressor will then impermissibly further redirect the bomb away from himself and in a direction where ten people will be killed? I do not think foresight of this intervening wrong act makes your self-defense by redirecting to the aggressor impermissible.

In addition, even direct bad effects need not always involve violation of rights. For example, no one, including civilians, has a right not to be made unhappy or somewhat poorer by their side losing a war, and such a direct bad effect need not stand in the way of military action to defeat aggression. Note that individuals may have the right to pursue happiness or wealth. This is what is known as a liberty right. Someone's liberty right need not imply that he has what is known as a claim right against others that they not do things that interfere with the success of his efforts to achieve wealth or happiness (for example, others may successfully compete with him for scarce resources). By contrast, a right not to be killed involves a claim against others not to interfere with one's life in certain ways. It is the concern over violating such negative claim rights that usually stands most prominently in the way of military action in *jus ad bellum* and (especially) *jus in bello* reasoning.

Suppose that postbellum we are considering whether to seek RJ for leaders responsible for aggression or genocide when a TRC is not an option. Do the characteristics of (1) directness and (2) negative claim rights violation just described apply to the factors that Orend believes should enter a proportionality calculation about proceeding with RJ? Orend suggests that instability of the society might count against pursuing RJ. Consider first whether causing instability itself is a rights violation in the relevant sense: Is stability in itself something to which people have a right, so that their rights would be violated just because their society is made unstable even by such means as RJ against aggressors? It seems that people have a liberty right to pursue stability, but that need not mean that they have a claim against others to not act in any way that could interfere with their achieving stability. Furthermore, suppose one has achieved stability. One does not seem to have a negative claim right against others that they not interfere with it per se.[7] Arguably if a society is undergoing major changes, such as moving from communism to democracy or from segregation to integration, there may be instability. Are such changes permissible only because a negative claim right to retain stability is overridden by other rights or good effects involved in pursuing just causes? I am inclined to think that there is no claim right to retain stability per se.

Of course, if instability results in violent criminal attacks, then people will suffer rights violations. However, we have to consider whether characteristic (1), directness, applies to these rights violations following on RJ. They do not seem to be direct effects of pursuing RJ against leaders. The rights violations are direct effects of criminals who act in the absence of a stable government. (This might also be true in the case described earlier in which civilians kill other civilians after we bomb a military facility in order to defend ourselves.) It might also be said that the absence of a stable government is itself only an indirect effect of RJ if it is more directly attributable to citizens failing in a duty to find appropriate leaders to replace the wrongdoers. Rather than avoiding the rights violations which are indirect results of instability by continuing to support a regime of wrongdoers, one should prevent rights violations by finding new leaders or increasing police protection. However, in this case, even wrongful omissions by other parties only fail to stop the bad effect of RJ (instability); they do not start a new harmful cause, such as criminal activity. This may be morally significant.[8]

In sum, my theoretical concern is that the negative effects of pursuing RJ may be neither claim rights violations nor directly caused by pursuing RJ. Hence, they may not play a comparable role to the direct rights violations that are often involved in *jus ad bellum* and especially *jus in bello* proportionality calculations.

It might be suggested that all types of negative effects, not just rights violations, regardless of whether they are direct or indirect, should be allowed to play the same role in a proportionality calculation postbellum. One issue is whether this would retain the analogies with *jus ad bellum* or *in bello*. The more important issue is whether this suggestion is correct from a nonconsequentialist perspective because it ignores how the bad effects come about and may not sufficiently distinguish the role of claim rights violations from other bad effects.

Now suppose that innocents will suffer a lack of needed lifesaving drugs as a result of society pursuing RJ instead of drug research. Even such severe effects may not be claim rights violations or direct effects of pursuing RJ. But might the victims give the following nonconsequentialist-sounding argument? "We do not have to give up our drugs and die of a disease in order to bring aggressors to RJ any more than someone has to give up his life to save five others. This is the wrong route to RJ. Hence, it is wrong to pursue RJ if this results in our lack of lifesaving drugs and subsequent death." Instead of equating dying through lack of provision of drugs with being directly killed by the pursuit of RJ, this argument equates dying through such lack with people having to give up *their* medicines to help prosecute criminals. But I think that from a nonconsequentialist perspective it is a mistake to equate (i) taking away people's lifesaving drugs in order to be able to pursue RJ with (ii) pursuing RJ even though society will not then be able to provide people with lifesaving drugs. In (i), we would take from people drugs that they are imagined to have already gotten by means unrelated to not prosecuting wrongdoers in order to pursue the wrongdoers. In (ii), not pursuing the wrongdoers is required if we are to help produce drugs for people. People may have a right in (i) to refuse to give up their drugs or not to have such a loss imposed on them without it being true that they have a right in (ii) to our producing drugs for them rather than do something else, such as pursue RJ. This difference in how RJ would come about and how their survival or death would come about may be morally relevant, and it is not captured by just considering how many will die if we do or do not pursue RJ.

Proportionality calculations postbellum (and also *ad bellum* and *in bello*) that do not take into account these nonconsequentialist distinctions concerning how bad and good effects come about before weighing the effects would be flawed, I believe. Let us call this the Route to Effect Objection.[9]

Finally, in this connection, suppose that it would be right for a society to prevent deaths by producing drugs rather than pursue former aggressors for RJ. This is compatible with its being wrong not to pursue RJ just because RJ would prevent former aggressors themselves from using knowledge they alone have that is necessary to produce the drugs. In the first supposition, we are imagining spending *our* time and effort on one task (drug research) rather than another (pursuing RJ). The wrongdoers who are not pursued by RJ play no necessary causal role in producing the drugs. In the second scenario, we are imagining that the wrongdoers are spared so that they can produce the drugs. The Route to Effect Objection might rule out bypassing RJ only in the second scenario. (On the other hand, it might be the reverse: Former wrongdoers being used to help people is seen as an appropriate substitute for RJ. This would most likely be true if the people they help are the very ones who suffered at their hands.) The general point is that the Route to Effect Objection prevents us from just looking at outcomes in doing a proportionality calculation to decide whether to pursue RJ. For in both scenarios—whether we or the wrongdoers produce drugs—people will have drugs when there is no RJ, and people will have no drugs when there is RJ. Yet there might be a moral difference between the scenarios.

III. *Jus Post Bellum* as a Side Constraint

A. *OREND'S ACCOUNT*

We have been considering some essentially non-consequentialist reasons pro and con for counting harms and benefits in deciding whether to pursue RJ post bellum. Let us now consider another aspect of Orend's view. Orend believes that one may not begin fighting a war, although one meets traditional conditions for *jus ad bellum*, if one knows that one will not be able to fulfill the conditions for *jus in bello*. Similarly, he thinks that one may not begin fighting a war, although one meets traditional conditions for *jus ad bellum* and can fulfill *jus in bello*, if one knows that one will not be able to fulfill the conditions of *jus post bellum*. His position might be analyzed into two components: (i) One should not consider these conditions on just war sequentially, when the time for each is present, but together at the time one decides whether to start a war; and (ii) one should take each condition as a side constraint on starting a war (i.e., the ability to satisfy each is necessary for permissibly starting a war). I shall call this position Simultaneous Constraints.

The particular implications of this position will vary depending on what *jus post bellum* substantively involves. According to Orend, some of the just causes postbellum involve requirements. As we have seen, according to Orend, victors have at least a prima facie duty to seek RJ of unjust leaders and war criminals. Orend also thinks that another required just cause of victors postbellum involves rehabilitating the aggressor country and helping its civilians who were harmed as a result of acts in the war. In general, it seems natural to think that the more requirements one can foresee having to fulfill, the harder it will be to satisfy the simultaneous constraints before we may start a war and the less likely we are to be justified in starting a war.

Let us consider some problems with this view.

B. *PROBLEMS*

Given what Orend thinks is substantively required by *jus post bellum*, his proposal that one include *jus post bellum* into *jus ad bellum* decision making as a side constraint does not seem correct. For Orend's position seems to imply that in order for it to be permissible for a victim of aggression to defend itself by going to war with an aggressor, the victim of aggression must believe that it will be able to (a) seek RJ of wrongdoers postbellum and (b) rehabilitate the defeated country and help civilians whom it harmed collaterally even when the harm would be caused in a manner and to a degree consistent with *jus in bello* and *jus ad bellum*.

It is highly implausible that (a) (seeking RJ) could be a side constraint on going to war. Surely one need not forego defending oneself against aggression simply because one will not be able to bring those who are responsible for the aggression to justice. For example, suppose one foresees that one will lack resources postbellum to pursue RJ. Then even if one would have a duty to pursue RJ if one had the resources, one cannot be constrained from going to war.

Now consider (b) (help and rehabilitation). Suppose that a victim of aggression knew in advance of war that it would be impoverished by fighting its defensive war and that the aggressor country's leaders would not be able to compensate it postwar. This means that it knows it would have no resources with which to rehabilitate civilians it had harmed, collaterally and to a proportionate degree, on the aggressor's side. On Orend's view, this seems to imply that it is impermissible for the victim to defend itself against aggression. I do not think this is correct.

Consider a domestic analogy involving individuals. Suppose innocent A is about to be unjustly killed by B. If A is to respond to the attack, he must use a weapon that will, as a side effect, destroy the tires on a parked car that does not belong to him. It seems permissible to do this because the side-effect harm is proportional to the self-defense. Now suppose that A is very poor and knows that he cannot compensate the owner of the car. This does not change the permissibility of his defending himself, I think.[10] This is consistent with it being true that if A had the capacity to compensate the owner, he would have a duty to do so. In this case, a requirement of postconflict justice is not a side constraint on self-defensive actions that cause proportional harm to bystanders.

Consider a further variation on this case: B has a family, and if he is killed by A (or even just goes to jail), the family will suffer emotionally and financially. It would seem that if the only way A could defend himself against B's attack is by killing B, it is permissible for him to do so. The fact that A is poor and cannot support B's family afterward or compensate them does not imply that A may not permissibly defend himself against B. This is consistent with it being true that if A had the capacity to support the family, he would have a duty to do so. (That it is consistent with such a duty, of course, does not show that there would be such a duty. Indeed, it seems less likely that he would owe it to B's family to compensate them for their loss of B's support than that he would owe compensation to the car owner, whom he directly harmed, in the earlier scenario.) Furthermore, given that B unjustly put A in the position of having to defend himself, it is more likely that B has a duty to compensate *everyone* if he survives.

Domestic analogies, therefore, do not suggest that postbellum duties to rehabilitate the loser and repay civilians for proportional harm we cause constrain starting a war against aggression. Victims who are poor to begin with or whose poverty will be caused by the aggressor do not lose a right to self-defend. (By contrast, duties related to how one fights a conflict do seem to impose constraints on going to war. A domestic analogy confirms this. For example, suppose that the only weapon one could use in order to defend oneself against a criminal's deadly attack would kill many bystanders as a direct [in the sense described earlier] side effect. Self-defense would be impermissible.)

We have been considering whether a victim of aggression might be constrained from going to war by what it would owe its defeated opponent. What about a country that is not attacked but is, as Orend says, a vindicator of another country that is unjustly attacked? We may imagine that the vindicator was permitted but not obligated to attack the aggressor. Suppose the vindicator would cause only proportionate harm to civilians, according to standards of *jus in bello* and *jus ad bellum*. Would the vindicator have to refrain from involving itself in the conflict if it foresaw that it would be unable to fulfill whatever duties to rehabilitate and help its former opponent that it would have if it had greater capacities? I do not think so, any more than a comparable third party would have to refrain from entering a conflict on the side of a victim in the domestic case. The general point is that what is true of the victim who self-defends can be true of his vindicator who other-defends.

In sum, I believe that satisfying what Orend thinks is involved in *jus post bellum* is not, contrary to what he says, a condition of engaging in a conflict. There are several possible explanations of this. First, it is possible that Orend is wrong about there being duties postbellum or about what they substantively are. Second, even if he is not wrong about postbellum duties, it is possible that he is wrong that we have to consider them (at all) at the time of deciding whether to go to war. Third, it is possible that he is wrong that being able to satisfy *jus post bellum* duties is a necessary condition of starting a war (i.e., a side constraint), though they should be considered.

Let us examine the third possibility in more detail. Often there are provisos on the fulfillment of duties. For example, sometimes one may break a promise rather than suffer a great loss even if one knows that one will not be able to compensate the person one has let down. This does not mean one need not consider one's duty to keep the promise *at all* in deciding what to do or that one does not really have a duty that will go unmet. It is only that the duty does not trump all else. I suspect this could be true at least of the postbellum duties that Orend believes exist to rehabilitate the former opponent and help its civilians. Notice that if being able to fulfill postbellum duties were a constraint on starting a war, side-effect harm within war might not really be judged justified merely by considering it relative to some military goal; if it will go uncompensated or uncorrected, it will be impermissible to bring the harm about. By contrast, we ordinarily think that some harm might infringe an innocent person's right so that he is owed compensation, and yet it could be permissible to cause the harm even if compensation or correction were not possible.[11]

IV. Content of *Jus Post Bellum*: Limits on and Grounds for Compensation, Help, and Rehabilitation

Suppose now that a victorious country was able to rehabilitate a defeated wrongdoer nation and/or help relieve proportionate side-effect harm. Is Orend correct that it would have a duty to do so as a matter of *jus post bellum*? If not, this will be another reason why these considerations fail to be side constraints on starting war or performing acts in war. Previously we dealt with cases of self- and other-defense from aggression. We can now broaden the cases considered to include those in which a vindicator fulfills a prima facie duty to stop genocide of a subpopulation by the subpopulation's own government.

A. *THOSE TO BE MADE BETTER OFF*

Consider the potential victims of genocide, each of whom a vindicator makes better off by preventing their death even if the vindicator harms them in the course of intervention. Suppose that there were no wrong acts done by the vindicator that led to the side-effect harms. Then, it seems, there may be nothing more which a vindicator must, as a matter of justice, provide those whom it has rescued. They are each better off overall than they would have been and unavoidably harmed to avoid the worse harm of genocide. There also seems to be no claim on the vindicator, *just in virtue of vindicating*, to rehabilitate those it has rescued to a better condition than existed for them before the intervention, independent of eliminating the prospect of genocide.

However, this argument may have to be supplemented. For suppose a vindicator would have been required to accept more harm to himself rather than cause side-effect harm to those he rescued. Then even if he could not, in fact, have done this during the rescue, it might be that he should accept harm (in the form of costs) to himself after the rescue in order to compensate for the harm he caused.[12] So it may be crucial whether the vindicator would have had a duty to accept harm to himself in the course of rescue, had he been able to, to prevent collateral harm to those he rescued. In response to such a possibility, Jeff McMahan has argued that, in fact, if there is a choice between a vindicator suffering harm to save a victim—even one unjustly endangered by others—or the victim himself suffering such harm in order to be saved from worse harm, having the victim accept the cost of his own rescue is permissible, other things being equal.[13] If this is correct, then the argument that vindicators do not have a duty to compensate those they rescue from worse harm would be complete, assuming no factors such as negligence on the part of the vindicators apply.

What if a vindicator carried out the invasion in a negligent manner or did a poorer job than would have been done by some other vindicator who offered to act instead and with whom he interfered? Then the vindicator might become obligated to improve further the condition even of those who are individually better off due to his intervention, making up the difference between where they are and where they would have been without negligence or with the help of other vindicators. Also, suppose *ex ante* it was reasonable to believe that certain people would be better off if intervention removed the threat of genocide, even taking into account the harm caused by intervention. However, these people are in fact made much worse off due to the harm of intervention than they would have been facing genocide. For example, suppose each had a 50 percent chance of dying in genocide, but due to unforeseeable factors each now has a 75 percent chance of side-effect death due to an intervention. Furthermore, more die during the intervention than would have died without it. Perhaps in this case the vindicator is obligated to compensate in some way the survivors of, and among, those it has made worse off than they would have been. This is because it mistakenly, though not unreasonably, believed it was justified in pursuing a just cause. That is, it should not have tried to eliminate genocide if the means of doing so would make the situation even worse for the potential victims unless for some good reason they consented to this.

On what other grounds, besides compensation for harm caused, would those saved from genocide be owed more by their vindicators than they have already been given? Suppose vindicators had humanitarian duties or duties of distributive justice that they could not have fulfilled before an intervention. This might be because being in the country is necessary to fulfill these duties, and intervention for reasons other than stopping genocide would have been wrong. Now that a vindicator is already justifiably in the country, it can fulfill the humanitarian duties or duties of justice. Alternatively, vindicators could come to have a new duty of assistance they did not have before simply because they are now not distant from people in need. This assumes that mere distance could affect whether there is a duty to aid.[14] However, neither of these duties arises solely because one has first stopped genocide and caused proportionate bad side effects. Furthermore, the duty to aid arising from humanitarian considerations or distributive justice is one that other countries besides the vindicator could have, too. These other countries fulfilling the duty does not now require them to impermissibly intervene but only to assist the vindicator or to get permission to enter the country from those now controlling it. Hence, they may have as strong or stronger obligations to provide the humanitarian aid or meet the demands of distributive justice as the vindicator, and once in the country they can acquire any additional duties arising from no longer being distant.

What if the vindicators themselves received large overall benefits from their actions? They were able to engage in these actions only at the cost of some harm to those whose rights they vindicated. Might it be argued that it would be exploitative not to share those benefits with those they helped? After all, in other cases Pareto improvements to all parties as a result of actions are not enough to show that there is a fair distribution of benefits or harms. It could certainly be true that causing a harm to someone that is proportional to achieving a goal is still exploitative if there is a way of distributing the harm more fairly (e.g., instead of having one of those vindicated bear a proportional harm, one should distribute smaller components of the harm over all those vindicated, other things being equal.)[15]

In sum, the postbellum duty that Orend thinks exists to rehabilitate and help civilian victims may not exist in many types of cases of humanitarian intervention if all civilians are made better off than they would have been without intervention.

B. *THOSE MADE WORSE OFF*

Now consider innocent civilians of an aggressor or a genocidal country who were never the potential beneficiaries of a rescue and who are made worse off as side effects of the acts of either a self-defending or vindicating country. Suppose the civilians are made worse off only to a degree that was proportionate to military goals and otherwise in accord with *jus in bello* and *jus ad bellum*. Could they be owed compensation or rehabilitation in virtue of being harmed if the victors are capable of doing this?

First, it seems to matter with respect to which baseline these civilians are worse off. Suppose that the civilians' prior good economic condition or stability came about as a result of a regime that either used the enslavement of one part of the population to create good conditions for others or instigated aggression against other countries to benefit its own citizens. The good conditions civilians had were not ones to which they were entitled, given how the conditions were achieved. Hence, these past conditions may not provide the relevant baseline, by reference to which we should determine that the civilians are now worse off, for purposes of determining duties of compensation or rehabilitation.

A more problematic case is presented by a regime that engages in conduct worth stopping (e.g., genocide or aggression) but is also doing other things properly (e.g., it provides stability and prosperity through appropriate routes for at least part of its citizenry). The ideal is to stop the wrongs one is justified in stopping by war without stopping the regime's permissible good effects. Suppose, however, that one must do what stops the whole regime from functioning in order to achieve a just cause for war or intervention. This might result in civilians losing things that they are entitled to retain, and yet this could be a proportionate bad side effect. A more radical view is that not engaging in grave wrongs is a side constraint on a regime's existence. Hence the population might have not been entitled to retain the goods acquired for it by the regime even in a legitimate fashion.

In both these cases, however, the actual existence of the formerly unjust regime may have interfered with other means of justly achieving goods such as stability and prosperity, and the population may have been entitled (in some sense) to a better regime. Should the baseline for compensation be the level at which a benign counterfactual regime would have kept its people? It is not clear why a victorious victim or vindicator has a duty to provide the populace with what a hypothetical benign regime should or would have provided merely because it has removed an actual nonbenign regime that should not have been kept on. It might be that there is a duty, *independent of having justifiably removed the unjust regime*, to help people who have had unjust regimes now achieve stability and economic security through morally appropriate means. Such a duty could apply to every country with the capacity to help, not only to the victorious former victim or vindicator, especially since helping need not require additional physical invasion not already accomplished.

Still, suppose that people's not having been physically harmed prior to war as they were harmed in war is a condition they were entitled to retain whether or not it was due to the unjust regime. And suppose that if a self-defender or vindicator had been able to make reasonable extra efforts (which were in fact not possible at the time) in carrying out the war, it would not have caused side-effect physical harm. Should it have made these extra efforts?[16] Traditionally, both *jus ad bellum* and *jus in bello* require that one not aim at harming civilians and that harm caused by means necessary to achieve a just cause be proportionate to the cause. Michael Walzer has argued that even if harm to civilians is not intended and is proportionate to a just cause, one should still *intend not to do* harm.[17] This might mean taking risks or paying a monetary price to find some other way to accomplish one's goal. Failure to take on the additional costs when it is possible to do so might be an instance of negligence. (Of course, if one can accomplish one's aim in some other way less harmful to civilians, the means that harmed them more were not really necessary to achieve one's cause. Thus, failing to meet Walzer's additional condition may actually involve failing to meet the "necessity condition" for the use of harmful means to one's goal, which is a standard part of traditional just war theory.)[18]

However, suppose it was not possible to do anything differently to reduce harm at the time of action. Might it be required of the self-defender to pay costs postbellum to undo harm that it could not prevent, to the extent it should have paid (had it been possible) *in bello*? If so, this implies that one's duty is not merely to do what one can (within reasonable limits) to avoid harming civilians (Duty 1). One also has a duty not to be causally responsible for an outcome in which people are in a harmed state (Duty 2). One can fulfill the latter duty by accepting costs either *in bello* or postbellum, holding upper limits on costs constant. Duty 2 could account for there being duties to rehabilitate and compensate, if a victor has the capacity to do so, even when harm caused by the victor was proportionate and the result of acts necessary to achieve a justified aim.

It might be responded that, with the exception of strict liability, we ordinarily think that compensation is owed only if one could have exerted oneself at the time of action to avoid harming someone (not if there was no way to do so at the time). As Duty 2 denies this is so, the duty is contentious. However, we are dealing with cases in which one could have avoided carrying out a war or intervention entirely even if one could not have pursued them in a less harmful way. It may have been reasonable to decide to act but, to consider an analogy, when someone breaks into another person's cabin as the only way to avoid starvation, that, too, is morally reasonable, and yet compensation is owed if possible.[19]

An additional factor may be relevant to deciding how much the victorious victim or vindicator owes to prevent or compensate for proportionate civilian harm, namely, what duties enemy civilians had to suffer losses in order that their country not be unjust either to other countries or to its own subpopulations. That is, suppose that what these civilians stand to lose as a result of collateral harm are not benefits of injustices. Still, it might be argued that, unlike either bystanders and family members in the domestic analogies considered earlier or citizens of a neutral country, citizens of an aggressive or domestically unjust country may be liable to suffer collateral harm if this is necessary to stop their country from being unjust. What I have in mind is that civilians who have done nothing wrong (e.g., have not supported an unjust regime) may be liable merely in virtue of being citizens to bear some costs or risks in order that their country not be unjust. This duty might at least imply that they may have imposed on them the risk of side-effect collateral harm in the course of actions necessary to defeat their unjust country.[20] If they were really liable in this way to such risks, they might not be owed efforts to prevent or to compensate for these side effects of war, even if the victor were able to provide it.

V. The Effect of Postbellum on *Ad Bellum* and *In Bello*

We have been considering some essentially nonconsequentialist reasons pro and con to rehabilitate and help a former enemy after a war. Our discussion so far should alert us to some ways that Orend does not consider in which the possibility of compensating and rehabilitating postbellum relate to the permissibility of starting war and to the permissibility of acts *in bello*. Beginning a war may fail the proportionality test because of the harms to civilians to which war would lead. Likewise, many acts that we need to do in war may fail the proportionality test because of the harm they cause to civilians. But if we include the effect of efforts made after the war in order to help and rehabilitate—whether we are obligated to do this or just plan to do it—this may well negate some of the items in the "harm column" of an *ad bellum* or *in bello* proportionality calculation. For example, the negative effect on people of economic destruction might be outweighed in an *ad bellum* or *in bello* proportionality calculation by rapidly rebuilding and even improving the economic infrastructure immediately after the war *for the very same people*. I am not suggesting that one may cause destruction whenever one intends to fully reconstruct. If one has no independent just goal to be achieved, planning such reconstruction does not justify destruction. But when there is an independent just goal (such as ending aggression), it seems to me that the reconstruction (as well as certain other good effects) may weigh against the destruction that would otherwise stand in the way of pursuing the goal.

In this case, the harm done is of the same type as the greater benefit to come, and both are economic. Physical harm to some people might also be outweighed if it is foreseen that advanced medical procedures that would be present in an opponent's country due only to our winning the war will cure even worse preexisting physical conditions of the very same people we collaterally harmed. Then harm that would have been disproportionate may not be. In all these calculations, the negative effect of simple disruption and its duration should be included even if it is followed by postbellum rehabilitation of the very same people. Lives, of course, cannot be replaced. An important question is whether it might be permissible to weigh against side-effect deaths of some *other* lives that would be saved from preexisting conditions by new medical procedures that would not have been present had we not won the war. The fact that this involves tradeoffs between different lives makes it most dubious for a nonconsequentialist.[21]

In sum, if causing harm to one set of people may permissibly be balanced by preventing worse harm or even producing some other benefits to the very same people, then we will have provided a new reason to consider *jus post bellum* simultaneously with *jus ad bellum* and *jus in bello*. But requiring such simultaneous considerations may result in its being easier to justify war rather than harder.

A second proposal for how *jus post bellum* could affect *jus ad bellum* and *jus in bello* relies on the view that a victorious victim or vindicator has permission to pursue compensation for itself from those responsible for aggression or for other injustices that triggered a duty to intervene. Going to war and engaging in it could involve depriving one's citizens of goods and services, and a country might decline to do so for this reason. However, if it expects to be compensated for its efforts, this may make it willing and morally permitted to go to war or to intervene. Again, simultaneous consideration of *jus post bellum* with *jus ad bellum* and *jus in bello* may result in its being easier to justify war rather than harder.

I have argued against Orend's view that a war would become impermissible if one could not fulfill *jus post bellum* obligations (should they exist). I have now suggested two alternative ways in which *jus post bellum* could fit into decision making about whether to go to war and what to do in war. In particular, it could imply that some wars or acts of war that would otherwise be impermissible could be permissible if we commit to performing certain reconstructive postbellum actions for others and/or seek compensation for ourselves. In this way, thinking simultaneously about *jus ad bellum, jus in bello*, and *jus post bellum* could make it easier to morally justify war and acts of war.[22]

Notes

The text of this chapter is from a previously unpublished paper written in 2008. It was revised for delivery as an August Comte Memorial Lecture at the London School of Economics in March 2011, then delivered as the Goutman Lecture at George Washington University, April 2011; at the Department of Philosophy, Union College, May 2011; as a 2011 Chancellor Dunning Trust Lecture at Queens University, Kingston, Ontario, November 2011; and as the 2012 Roseman Lecture at Toronto University. For comments on those occasions, I am grateful to Jeffrey Brand-Ballard, Rahul Kumar, Michael Otsuka, Joseph Raz, Arthur Ripstein, Alex Voorhoeve, Leo Zaibert, and members of the Philosophy Department at the London School of Economics, George Washington University, Union College, Queens University, and Toronto University.

1. See his "Justice after War," *Ethics and International Affairs* 16(1) (2002): 43–56. All references to Orend are to this article.

2. Typically the good with which the bad effects are compared is the just cause being achieved or a particular military mission being accomplished. However, some have argued that other goods achieved by or in war (perhaps some side-effects goods) should also be weighed against negative effects when doing a proportionality calculation. I discuss this issue in *Ethics for Enemies: Terror, Torture, and War* (New York: Oxford University Press, 2011), chapter 3. Here I will first follow the typical view and later reconsider it.

3. Herman's discussion is in her "Contingency and Obligation," in her *Moral Literacy* (Cambridge, MA: Harvard University Press, 2007). Herman discusses the issue in the context of justice after intrastate conflict (such as occurred in South Africa), while Orend confines himself to discussion of postbellum justice following interstate conflict. Indeed, he specifically says that intrastate conflict may require different principles. Nevertheless, I think it is useful to consider what Orend's principles suggest for the issue of RJ in general.

4. See my "Moral Improvisation and New Obligations," reprinted in this volume as chapter 6, for my discussion of Herman.

5. In the sense of "direct" used here, even a far-off effect caused without intervention by agents acting independently of us is being considered "direct."

6. Thomas Hurka also makes this point in his "Proportionality in the Morality of War," *Philosophy & Public Affairs* 33 (2005): 34–66.

7. I am grateful to James Sedlak and David Kanaan for discussion about rights that helped me clarify these points.

8. Thomas Hurka makes this point in "Proportionality in the Morality of War."

9. The concerns this objection reflects would apply to calculations within war and in starting war as well. I have been suggesting that Orend's proposals may not adhere to principles governing *jus ad bellum* and *in bello* proportionality calculations. However, it is possible that the Route to Effect Objection applies to the way calculations are actually done in all circumstances. Subsequent to my writing the original version of this article in 2008, Jeff McMahan has written about the possible failure of *jus in bello* proportionality calculations to take account of how bad effects come about. See his "Proportionality" (unpublished). (Possibly the criticism might be extended to how good effects come about.)

10. At least in most cases. We can imagine exceptions: for example, if the bystander would be killed by the tires' destruction.

11. This is true of cases that Joel Feinberg discusses (e.g., breaking into a cabin in a blizzard). See his "Voluntary Euthanasia and the Inalienable Right to Life," *Philosophy & Public Affairs* (Winter 1978): 102.

12. I first discussed this possibility in contexts where people nonnegligently cause harm in my "Insanity Defense, Innocent Threats, and Limited Alternatives," *Criminal Justice Ethics* 6(1) (1987): 61–76. I will discuss this issue further later.

13. See his *Killing in War* (New York: Oxford University Press, 2009).

14. On the issue of whether distance could affect the duty to aid, see my *Intricate Ethics* (New York: Oxford University Press, 2007), chaps. 11 and 12.

15. Note that self-defenders also stand to benefit from defeating an aggressor. But their benefit may just be retaining that to which they had a claim of noninterference. The special nature of this benefit may call for different treatment from larger overall benefits to vindicators.

16. We asked the same question earlier when discussing a case where people harmed were saved from greater harm.

17. See his *Just and Unjust Wars* (New York: Basic Books, 1977), 155–56.

18. But see chap. 4 for an additional role that Walzer's "second intention" might play in changing one's goal.

19. I first discussed Duty 2 in my "Insanity Defense."

20. I suggested this in "Failures of Just War Theory," *Ethics* 114 (July 2004): 650–692, reprinted as chap. 3 in this volume.

21. There are different ways in which our pursuing a military mission could make the people harmed collaterally less badly off than they would otherwise have been. Here are some hypothetical cases to illustrate: (1) in war our bombing that harms them collaterally might scare away criminals who would otherwise have killed them; (2) our bombing in war that harms them collaterally is necessary in order for us to win the war and so be present in their country with advanced medical equipment that cures their pre-existing conditions which are worse than the harm we would do to them; (3) the act that causes collateral harm to them is unrelated to our being in a position to help them; for example, we could have brought them to our country to cure them at any time and we do so now merely to outweigh harm that we did to them. I thank Kerah Gordon-Solomon for pressing me to enumerate ways in which I imagined postbellum aid coming about as differences among them may be morally significant. I discuss (1) in *Ethics for Enemies*, chapter 3.

22. For more on this issue, see my *Ethics for Enemies: Terror, Torture, and War*, chap. 3

8

Terrorism and Several Moral Distinctions

I. Introduction

In this chapter,[1] I examine several distinctions that may be relevant to the morality (and conceptual characterization) of terrorism. Some of these distinctions are commonly thought to be relevant, while others are not: (1) the state/nonstate agent distinction; (2) the combatant/noncombatant distinction; (3) the intention/foresight distinction; (4) the means/side-effect distinction; (5) the interrelated necessary/nonnecessary means and produce/sustain distinctions; (6) the mechanical/nonmechanical use distinction; (7) the military/political distinction; (8) the harm/terror distinction; and (9) the harm-for-terror/terror-for-goal distinction. I conclude that some of the factors in these distinctions (though not those most commonly cited) account for the prima facie wrongness of terrorism and that the nondistinctive properties of terrorism (which it shares with some nonterrorist acts) are what make it most seriously wrong. Before considering these distinctions, I shall begin with a conceptual examination of terrorism as we commonly think of it. In the course of discussing the distinctions and also in concluding the article, I shall consider why terrorism may sometimes be morally permissible.

II. Conceptual Examination of Standard Terrorism

A.

This is not intended to be a set of necessary and sufficient conditions but only characteristics of terrorism on which we tend to focus. In standard terrorism (ST), the victim is a noncombatant (NC). I shall take this to mean not only that the victim is not a fighting agent but also that the victim is innocent in the sense of not presenting a threat to anyone, not even as a nonresponsible human missile. The victim is typically a random member of the group that the terrorist agent is against and someone who is not otherwise shortly to die. The bad (broadly construed) that is done to the NCs in ST is (1) harm to some NCs of a severe sort, such as death or grave injury, and (2) terror in other NCs (due to [1]) put in fear of death or grave injury to themselves or to yet others.

This understanding of what goes on in ST implies that some in the community are harmed and others are terrorized. This is in contrast to a form of nonstandard terrorism (NST)—which is still terrorism—where the victim who is harmed is himself also terrorized. It also contrasts with just random killing of NCs that does not terrorize anyone.

The agent in ST is a nonstate agent and is not engaged in standard war between nation-states. I shall leave it open that the nonstate agent receives support from a state but is not merely a subpart of it. This agent intends rather than merely foresees the harm and terror to his victims either as a means or as an end in itself.[2] His actions are also thought through rather than impulsive.

Furthermore, all of this harm and terror is supposed to be bad for the NCs, at least in the sense of being against their prudential interests. This contrasts with a painful means of doing what *is* in their self-interest (as when we terrorize someone to get him to escape a flood). However, this is consistent with the thinking that harm and terror serves the NCs' moral interests if it is seen as a way of preventing their being too passive with respect to moral wrongs that their country is committing.[3] For example, suppose that German NCs had been bombed to awaken them to the existence of Nazi extermination camps. Even if such means were impermissible, the goal of setting people on the right moral track is in some sense in those people's interest.

The further aims of the terrorist agent could be various. For example, he might have political or religious goals and be trying to draw attention to his cause or aiming to eliminate what he sees as injustice. He might simply be aiming to show the mighty that they are vulnerable and also thereby create some equality between himself and his opponent. (It is unfortunate but often true that respect for an opponent may be greater when he shows that he has the ability and will to harm you, and that respect may lead to negotiations.) He might be punishing the opponent for wrongs he believes have been done to his side. Or he might be trying to create political pressure by the populace on its government or directly create pressure on the opponent government in order to change its policies. A famous example of such ST—as odd as it sounds—is the God of the Old Testament sending the plague of death on Egyptian children.[4]

My characterization of ST allows that it might sometimes be justified, though it is prima facie or pro tanto wrong in the sense of being prima facie impermissible. That is, it might always have negative properties that count against its permissibility, but other moral considerations might override or efface these. My characterization contrasts with what has become a common use of the term "terrorism" to imply that such an act is always ultimately impermissible. On this common use, if the act is not wrong in the sense of being ultimately impermissible, then it cannot be terrorism. I think that we should rather use the term to designate a type of behavior that is prima facie wrong without implying any final moral judgment of impermissibility. We might still conclude that terrorism is always impermissible, but this question should remain open for now.

B.

1.

Let us compare ST with standard murder (SM). The murderer in SM is typically an individual rather than a group. He also intends death but not necessarily to terrorize others. Standardly, he has something against the particular person he would kill rather than selecting him at random and killing for political purposes. The killing could be impulsive rather than thought through. It is typically done for personal (or perhaps, if done by the Mafia, for business) reasons.

It is standardly thought that SM is by definition morally wrong. But possibly even murder is only prima facie or pro tanto wrong.[5] For imagine that, in order to save the life of a twenty-year-old person who will then live a normal life span, I kill a ninety-year-old person who will die in thirty seconds anyway but who wishes not to die before then. This may be murder and yet be justified.

Is it possible that in the case of ST and SM, the person harmed/terrorized is always wronged even if we wrong him in the course of doing an act that, all things considered, is not wrong? (Often a sign of someone being wronged is that he may permissibly resist what is being done to him even if this interferes with the goals of the agent that justify his act.) Consider a variant of the possibly justified murder case described earlier: If I do not kill the elderly person, someone else will torture him in the last thirty seconds of his life. Suppose that he knows the details of his prospects but refuses to consent to being killed by me thirty seconds earlier. It seems that, in this case, if I kill the man, I would murder someone in his own best interests. Do I also wrong him? Perhaps not. If not, then someone need not always be wronged in being murdered. By contrast, ST as described earlier is never in the prudential interests of those harmed/terrorized. On these grounds one might think that ST, but not SM, always wrongs its victim even if the act is ultimately right. But what if it were in the moral interests of at least those who are only terrorized to be jolted from passivity in the face of the crimes of their government? Must we always be wronging these people if we put their moral interests before some of their strong prudential interests?

C.

1.

Let us consider possible implications of some of the differences I have pointed out between ST and SM. Do the differences bear on the issue of whether stopping terrorists is a "war" rather than merely a "policing of (prima facie) criminal activity"? I have suggested that ST is not SM. But this does not mean that ST could not be criminal activity of any sort. If ST is a form of criminal activity, then might it be better to think of policing it rather than of being at war with it?

We should examine the war model. If we are at war with those who use terrorism, then this will be a war against the use of (let us suppose) improper means per se. This is a deontologist's dream in a sense. But is a war against improper means not merely policing rather than a war? No, because there is a sense of "war" in which it seems appropriate to speak of a war against crime. This is when we do not go piecemeal after criminals. Rather, we go all out and try to extirpate criminal activity. So it may be the metaphorical sense of "war" that is used by those who speak of a war on terrorism (or a war on poverty). Terrorists, of course, do not think of themselves as engaged in a metaphorical war; they have declared real war on certain countries. But if white supremacists in the United States had also declared real war on the United States, would this mean that fighting them is more than policing criminal activity and that it is metaphorical war at most?

Consider another possibility. Perhaps terrorists are war criminals, and this is why it is appropriate to speak of being at war with them. But that suggests that there is a real war ongoing about something besides the use of improper means of fighting (for example, about the forms of government that should exist in the Middle East). In that real war, there are those who use means that are ruled out by the rules of just war, and they are the war criminals. But going after war criminals is itself usually a policing activity rather than a war. We might, however, make it a metaphorical war by adopting the all-out, extirpating approach discussed earlier. Then there would be two sorts of wars going on simultaneously.

Employing the second model of war, in which we are at war over issues besides improper means of fighting, we could say that we are at war with people over a particular substantive issue (e.g., the nature of political arrangements in the Middle East). It happens that all of the warriors on the other side use (seemingly) improper means in pursuing the war. If they are really unjustified in using those means, then they are war criminals. This model, unlike the first war-against-crime model, does not allow us to ignore the political/religious aims of the opponents and the differences between us and them over a particular substantive issue as well as over the means used in fighting.

Neither sort of war I have described implies by itself that there is a national emergency in a country at war (even an attack on one's home ground need not always imply a national emergency). Perhaps it is the presence of an emergency rather than merely real or metaphorical war that might permit infringement of civil liberties and constitutional protections in order to stop terrorism.

2.

The second model of war—involving substantive disagreement—brings us to a possible implication of the difference made by the political/religious motivation of the terrorists. Suppose that we came to see merit in some of their views about the very important issues that divide us (e.g., political arrangements in the Middle East) and also recognized that we would never have changed our views in this crucial way but for their terrorist acts. Then we might think that it is not morally inappropriate to forgive their use of improper means rather than to punish the terrorists as criminals. This seems to have happened with Menachem Begin of

Israel and Yasser Arafat of Palestine, who were terrorists but became recognized leaders of their national groups. Forgiving or even excusing such terrorists may require them to forswear ST means but not necessarily to deny the legitimacy of their past behavior.

By contrast, if Begin had been found to be an ordinary murderer and user of terror (e.g., he killed his wife to terrorize women in his family), then he would probably have been put on trial and told to resign his premiership. This raises the possibility that even planners of the 9/11 attack could theoretically come to be seen neither as mere criminals nor even as war criminals. But this could be so only if it turned out that they had been to a large degree in the right while we had been seriously deluded (and resistant to change except by terrorism) about crucial issues that divide us.

III. Some Morally Relevant Characteristics of ST

What makes ST at least prima facie wrong in the sense of prima facie impermissible? The obvious answer is that it involves killing, for all killing is prima facie wrong and requires justification. But those who ask about ST in particular are really concerned with why it may be prima facie wrong even when other forms of killing, such as killing in self-defense, have been justified. In discussing this question, we should keep in mind the possibility that what distinguishes ST conceptually from other forms of killing is not what is primarily responsible for its wrongness. What accounts for its prima facie wrongness could be some property it shares with some other killings. We should also keep in mind that factors may make ST prima facie wrong singly, added together, or in interaction with each other. Furthermore, even if ST were permissible in order to achieve a very important end, it is not only the absence of such an end or the nonnecessity of ST to achieve it that may make terrorism prima facie wrong. Properties of the act itself or how it brings about consequences may help make it prima facie wrong.

Suggestions as to what might make ST prima facie wrong include the nature of the agent and/or victims, the fact that harm and terror are intended, the role of the victims (e.g., harm and terror to them are causally useful means), and the type of harm that occurs to people. Let us investigate some proposals related to these factors.

A. THE STATE/NONSTATE AGENT DISTINCTION

One proposal is that ST is prima facie wrong because of the nature of the agent. The agent is not a legitimate state but a self-appointed group. Terrorism, it is said, would be at least somewhat improved morally if it were done by a legitimate state, other things being equal. (This would make it NST, not ST, of course.) This is one way to emphasize the state-versus-nonstate agent distinction.

Some might want to rule out this position by declaring terrorism to be by definition an act of either a nonstate or a nonlegitimate state agent (such as rogue states); the same type of act done by a legitimate state would not be terrorism. This position would not be correct, however. For suppose that someone blew himself up in a crowded area in order to kill NCs and terrorize others. We could know that this was a terrorist act without knowing whether it was a nonstate agent or a legitimate state such as France that directed the occurrence of this event. Hence I shall assume that it is possible for even a legitimate state to be the agent of terrorism. We can consider, however, whether being done by such a state could change the act's moral status.

I do not believe that terrorism would always be morally improved if done by a legitimate state whenever other things are equal. Other properties of the act could make it wrong to such a degree that who or what carried out the act would be a morally irrelevant consideration. Nevertheless, there could be cases in which other properties of the act, including a justifying goal, create a context in which it is morally permissible for a politically legitimate state to act but not for a self-appointed group to do so. Not just anyone may permissibly carry out acts that are justified when carried out by a politically legitimate state. But, of course, things other than whether there is a state or nonstate agent are not always equal. For example, a state may (arguably) be nonrepresentative of its people and yet be politically legitimate, while a nonstate agent may (arguably) be representative of people. Possibly a state may be morally illegitimate even if it is politically legitimate, and even a nonrepresentative nonstate agent could be morally legitimate. This would be true, for example, of a resistance group fighting a Nazi state when that state represents a supermajority of the population. These differences might count in favor of a nonstate rather than a state agent as the morally preferred perpetrator of terrorism.

I think we should conclude that being a nonstate agent is neither necessary for the prima facie wrongness of terrorism nor sufficient for the prima facie wrongness of ST, though sometimes the fact that a legitimate state acts could be morally relevant.

B. THE COMBATANT/NONCOMBATANT DISTINCTION

A second proposal is that ST is prima facie wrong because of the nature of the victim. The victim is an NC who, it is imagined, has not, does not, and will not threaten to harm to others, unlike combatants. By contrast, it seems not to be prima facie wrong to intend harm to combatants for the purpose of creating terror in other combatants in order to get them to surrender; this is an example of NST.

To consider whether NCs are always immune to attack, suppose that NCs voted directly to authorize their leaders to do harmful things to others. For example, suppose that in a vote that requires unanimity, the NCs vote to authorize their leaders' military attack. This makes the NCs materially responsible for an attack on others. (I shall assume for argument's sake, along with standard just war theory, that we need not consider whether the attack is just in order to decide whether those attacked may permissibly counterattack.) They are still neither combatants nor direct threats to others, but they are directly responsible for such threats and, arguably, from a moral point of view subject to counterattack.

This case differs from a second one where the NCs unanimously vote for a government whose policies they know will lead enemies to attack even though these policies do not themselves involve harmful attacks. (For example, the policies involve instituting governments of a certain sort in the Middle East.) Are the NCs then also subject to being attacked by enemies? (Let us again try to put aside the question of whether the government's actions are just or unjust.) I do not think so, as they were not directing the sort of attacks on others that make a violent response permissible.

To avoid the issues raised by certain cases involving responsible adult NCs, let us suppose that the terrorist agent would attack only babies and children (good babies and children!). I believe this is prima facie impermissible in part because of the nature of the victims. However, in ST these children would still be members of the community that is being opposed by the terrorist. By contrast, suppose that the country opposed by the terrorist had impenetrable defenses, and so the terrorist attacked the children of a neutral country. For example, the terrorist attacks Swiss children because he can get at them in order to get Switzerland to pressure the United States to change its policies. Is this attack on Swiss children and NCs an even more serious wrong than one on U.S. children even when both are impermissible? I suggest that it is. This seems to be so even if the children who would be attacked in each country are unloved orphans, allowing us to factor out the (possibly) different moral significance of grief in Swiss adults from grief in U.S. adults. If this were so, it would indicate that even nonresponsible NCs of the country opposed are not quite as immune to attack as neutral NCs.

But now notice that all of the harm to NCs, which the proposal we are considering says accounts for the wrongness of ST, could occur as a foreseen side effect of nonterrorist attacks. That is, the deaths could result as a side effect of attacks on military targets for military purposes, and people could be terrorized by these deaths and even be led to surrender as a result. Here is a hypothetical example. Suppose, contrary to fact, that there were ongoing military operations in the World Trade Center (WTC) on 9/11 and that it was instrumentally useful for Al Qaeda to attack them. Suppose also that the Al Qaeda pilots could not hijack earlier planes in order to strike when no NCs were in the building. The NCs killed both inside and outside the building, and the resulting terror, would be only foreseen side effects. (Call this the WTC-Military Case.) Would this action be less objectionable than ST even if it is also impermissible in virtue of the harm to certain sorts of NCs? Could other acts with collateral damage to highly immune NCs be permissible when ST is not?

C. THE INTENTION/FORESIGHT AND MEANS/SIDE-EFFECT DISTINCTIONS

To answer these questions, we should consider the next proposal as to what factors make ST prima facie wrong. The claim is that the attitude of the agent—his intending harm and terror as a means or an end (rather than merely foreseeing them)—contributes to the prima facie wrongness of ST. The intention/foresight distinction is sometimes associated with a separable distinction relating to the causal role of the victim's harm or terror. The claim is that the harm to NCs being a means to terror and the terror being a means to other things (rather than harm and terror being side effects) contribute to the prima facie wrongness of ST.[6]

The doctrine of double effect (DDE) is one view that relies on the intention/foresight distinction in determining the permissibility of acts, for it claims that when an agent intends the harm/terror as a means or an end in itself, the act is impermissible. (On some interpretations, the DDE also involves the causal-role distinction independent of intention.) Furthermore, it is widely thought to be grounds for the impermissibility of an act that it treats people as mere means to one's end. This, it is said, can make an act wrong even when an act that has the same bad effects on people but does not employ them as mere means to one's end is permissible. And even if the latter type of act were impermissible because we act despite the harm to others, it is said that it is not as serious a wrong. It is more seriously wrong to treat persons as available to be used as mere means to one's end when this is seriously against their self-interest, they neither deserve nor are liable to such treatment, and they do not consent to it.[7]

In evaluating the intention/foresight proposal, first consider cases where the terrorist seeks to punish the NCs or simply make them suffer as he feels his side has suffered. While he here intends the harm and terror, these cases do not involve intending harm and terror to people as mere means to some further end. They also do not involve treating the people themselves as mere means (tools). This is because the agent believes that the NCs deserve to suffer as an end in itself, and the receipt of punishment by those who deserve it is a good and not an evil. Punishment commonly involves intending harm. The objection to punishing NCs in this way is not that it is wrong to intend harm or that punishing treats NCs as mere means to some end but that the NCs do not deserve punishment.

Hence, let us distinguish terror as punishment from other forms of ST. Let us consider cases where there is intended use of harm and terror to NCs, where harm and terror are treated as mere means to a goal such as surrender, or where harm and terror are sought as ends in themselves and separate from hatred (not for punishment). The general conclusions for which I shall argue in this section are as follows: (1) When an act is otherwise morally permissible despite the harm and terror it produces, intending the harm and terror as means or ends can make the act morally worse, but it need not make the act impermissible, whether the act is appropriately called terrorism or not. (2) When the act is otherwise impermissible, intending the harm and terror as means or ends can sometimes make the impermissible act be a more serious wrong.

1. Conceptual Issues

Let us begin the detailed discussion leading to these conclusions by considering whether intending harm as a means to terror, which terror is in turn intended as a means to something else, is sufficient to make an act be ST when NCs are seriously harmed against their self-interest and without their consent. This is just a conceptual question independent of whether the act is a more serious wrong than causing collateral damage.

Consider this question first in cases in which it is assumed to be permissible to bomb a military facility, causing death and terror as collateral damage. The act will be permissible if we use standards developed in just war theory, when the military goal is sufficiently important, the bombing is a necessary means to that goal, it has a significantly high probability of bringing about the goal, and the collateral damage is a proportionate evil relative to the goal to be achieved.[8] I will further suppose that there is an objectively just goal in the following imaginary cases which involve permissible (P) acts.

P(i) Suppose that the United States is controlled by Nazis. The Resistance's aim in bombing the WTC is to destroy ongoing military operations in it. Suppose that this would be morally justified despite the side-effect deaths of and terror inflicted on nonresponsible NCs. However, the only pilots willing to fly the planes and drop the bombs on the WTC are those who are interested in bringing about the side effect of this, killing and terrorizing NCs. Would the pilots' intentions change the operation from military bombing with collateral damage to terrorism? To focus on the intentions alone, I assume that these pilots are definitely unable to kill and terrorize any people other than pilots who lacked the bad intention would, given that they would bomb the military facility in exactly the same way as the other pilots and would have no option to do otherwise.[9] I do not think their intentions would change the operation to terrorism.

It may be said that there are two acts here: the act of the pilot and the act of the authority in the Resistance who authorizes the attack. The former is an act of terrorism; the latter is not. It may also be said that in this case an authority uses terrorists to carry out a nonterrorist mission (at least if it knows of the pilots' intentions).[10] Possibly these points are correct. If so, then a minimal claim might be that we determine what type of event (terrorism or not) blowing up the Nazi WTC is by reference to the authority's intentions. It is for this reason that we can know that the United States did not engage in terrorism in World War II when it bombed munitions factories though children were killed as a side effect even if we do not know as a matter of biography whether some U.S. bombardier intended to hit the munitions as a mere means to killing children. It is also for this reason that we cannot conclude that the authority seeks to kill and terrorize whenever we have a pilot who confesses to his intentions to kill and terrorize.

P(ii) Now suppose that there is no Resistance movement that will bomb the WTC in the Nazi United States. Instead, the bombing is planned and done by Baby Killer Nation, a group that takes an interest in destroying the Nazi's military operations in the WTC only because it is a means to satisfy its own desire to harm and terrorize NCs. This is a desire that Baby Killer Nation's members act on only when there is such a type of act in a just cause that can serve as a cover. Furthermore, they would never perform any acts in bombing the WTC that would cause more side-effect damage than would be caused by bombers who lack their bad intentions. Should their act of bombing the Nazi WTC be classified as an act of terrorism rather than a military operation? I do not think so. This conclusion goes beyond the claim stated earlier, for the intention of the authority is not determinative here. Rather, the new claim might be that the conditions under which the authority will allow itself to act on its intention to harm and terrorize NCs and its doing no more than what others seeking to destroy the military operation without bad intentions would do are determinative of the category into which we should place the act.

I believe that the conceptual issue that we are dealing with in P(ii) is analogous to a problem in the philosophy of law. Suppose that A intends to murder B but deliberately waits to do so until B attempts to murder him, so that A's act is no different from what C would permissibly do in self-defense if B attacked C except, of course, that A's intention is different from C's. Indeed, we can suppose that A would supererogatorily have refused to defend himself against anyone's attack on him but B's. In other words, his act is not overdetermined in the sense that he also has a constant intention to save himself. I believe that, even in this latter case, A's act should be classified as self-defense because his act is what is actually needed to prevent his murder. (This will be true whether A intends B's death as an end in itself or as a means to, for example, making B's organs available to save D.)

Of course, in P(ii), unlike a self-defense case, Baby Killer's actions that destroy the Nazi regime may not help save Baby Killer Nation itself. Rather, they save others from the Nazi regime. An analogue to this is what I call the Bad Man Trolley Case. Suppose that a trolley is headed toward killing five people, and it would be permissible for a bystander who wants to save the five to redirect it toward killing one person instead. Imagine, however, that the bystander is a bad person. He would not bother to save the five lives but for the fact that he recognizes that the one person who will be killed if he redirects the trolley is his enemy. He turns the trolley only in order to kill his enemy but only because he is in a context where the five will be saved by his turning the trolley. His turning the trolley, exactly as a person who merely wanted to save the five people would turn it, is not, I think, a murder (understood as described on p.169).

It might be suggested that the unwillingness to characterize P(ii) as terrorism is linked to a deeper point about the characterization of terrorism. Perhaps it involves the agent's not only intending harm and terror but also intending that those harmed and terrorized know that it is his intention to harm and terrorize them. Bombing only on the condition that there is a militarily useful target to hit (which will cause harm, leading to terror) may conceal the intention to harm and terrorize people. If making clear to the populace one's intention to harm and terrorize were a part of terrorism, then that would explain why P(ii) is not thought of as terrorism.[11] Possibly one could go further and claim that if Baby Killer Nation would bomb only on the condition that there is a militarily useful target, then it cannot even form the intention to make it clear to those harmed and terrorized that it intends them to be harmed and terrorized.[12]

I do not think that the latter claim is true. It would not be inconsistent with bombing only on the condition that there is an appropriate military target to also put on one's plane a sign that says "Aiming to harm and terrorize you." (Call this the Baby Killer Message Case.) I think we should still refuse to characterize the Baby Killer Message Case as terrorism. But if this is true, then it weakens the claim that the reason we would not classify P(ii) as terrorism is that the agent does not make clear to its victims that it intends them to be victims.

P(iii) Suppose next that Baby Killer Nation would have bombed the Nazi WTC even if there had been no military significance to its destruction; it has an unconditional intention to act just to produce the harm and terror. Suppose further that such an act would have been impermissible. But, in fact, there are Nazi military operations worth destroying in the WTC, and Baby Killer Nation knows this. Further, it does nothing in bombing the WTC other than what a genuine resistance lacking intentions to harm and terrorize would have done. Its bombing could then be categorized as a military bombing rather than terrorism, I believe. What the nation would have done—bomb in the absence of the military operations—does not bear on our description of what it actually does in this case. Hence, we should move beyond the claim made in P(ii) that the conditions under which the authority will allow itself to act are always relevant to deciding whether an act is terrorism.

In an analogous Bad Man Trolley Case, the same is true. That is, suppose the bad man would have turned the trolley on his enemy even if doing this would not also save the five, but in fact turning will save the five, the bad man knows this, and he does only what someone who wanted to save the five would do. Then his act should not be classified as murder. In a self-defense case, suppose that A would have killed B even if B were not attacking him, but B in fact is attacking A, A knows this, and A does only what C could permissibly have done in self-defense. Though A acts only intending to kill B as an end, his act should be classified as an act of self-defense, I think.

P(iv) What if we assume that Baby Killer Nation was ignorant of the Nazi military operations in the WTC and bombed it with the intention of harming and terrorizing NCs? Nevertheless, if members of the nation actually destroy the ongoing military operations and do no more than what a genuine resistance lacking their intention would have done, I think that their act should be characterized in the following way: They attempted to perform an act of terrorism but succeeded in doing something else. In an analogous trolley case, when the bad man does not know that five could be saved by redirecting the trolley, I think he attempted to murder his enemy but succeeded in doing something else. In an analogous self-defense case, A does not know that B is trying to attack him. When A attacks B, trying to murder him, A actually succeeds in defending himself, though he may have attempted murder.

P(v) So far, Baby Killer Nation has been presented as intending harm and terror as ends in themselves while it is bombing the military operations in the Nazi WTC. Most terrorists do not intend harm and terror as ends in themselves but as means to achieving other goals. So let us suppose instead that Baby Killer Nation intends the death and terror as possible means to the surrender of the Nazis. And indeed, it is as likely that the populace will surrender from terror as that the army will surrender from lack of munitions.

Nevertheless, Baby Killer Nation acts on the intention to cause harm and terror leading to surrender only when there is another possible route to victory, namely, stopping the military operations in the WTC. I believe that its act is then not terrorism. For suppose that members of a resistance movement foresaw but did not intend that people would surrender as a result of being terrorized by collateral deaths from the resistance's bombing of the Nazi WTC, and all this would occur before the military effect of bombing the WTC was decisive. This would not make their bombing the WTC terrorism. (Nor would it make the bombing impermissible if bombing the WTC is permissible when the deaths and terror are merely foreseen side effects.)[13] After all, if they did not bomb the WTC, then they would not engage in the only act that might be useful (even without its causing terror or harm) to end the Nazi regime. Baby Killer Nation might sign up for just wars only when this same scenario was true, do nothing but what a resistance movement that would never harm and terrorize people as a means would have done, and yet intend the harm and terror as means. (Henceforth, I shall assume that all points about intending harm and terror as means can be made by discussing intending harm and terror as ends in themselves in cases where what one does also involves another possible means [e.g., getting rid of munitions] to an end [e.g., ending Nazi rule] that can justify one's behavior.)

I have been considering primarily the conceptual question of whether intentions to harm and terrorize NCs are sufficient to make an act that harms and terrorizes NCs terrorism and have so far suggested "no." Now consider the means/side-effect distinction separately from intention. Suppose that in all these WTC-Military cases the harm and terror to which they lead are, in fact, the causal route through which the downfall of the Nazis comes about, as the terrorized citizens overthrow the Nazi government independently of any military effect of the destruction of the military operations. As I noted in discussing P(v), the actual causal significance of harm and terror are not enough for us to call the bombings of the WTC acts of terrorism. How people react to what may just be a side effect is not enough to determine the character of the agent's act. Would the combination of intending harm and terror with these being the actual causal route to surrender be sufficient for terrorism if neither alone is sufficient? Not in a variant of P(ii): Baby Killer Nation bombs the Nazi WTC, intending the deaths and terror of NCs, and such terror actually leads to surrender. These facts do not imply that its act is terrorism given that destroying the military facility, its condition for bombing at all, could also be a means to surrender.

2. Moral Issues

Let us now consider the moral rather than conceptual significance in P(i)–P(v) of an agent's intention to harm and terrorize and then, separately, the moral significance of the causal role for harm and terror in bringing about an agent's goal. (I shall return to the conceptual issue.)

Consider intention first. I believe that acts are morally worse when the intention is wrong, in the sense that there are morally wrong attitudes toward persons present and they are also efficacious in leading to acts. I think that it is worse to seek harm and terror (even as means rather than as ends in themselves) rather than act despite their occurrence (or even on condition of their occurrence) but not seek them, other things being equal. However, this is not the same as saying that the intention makes an act impermissible when another act like it in all respects except for the intention is permissible. Nor is it the same as saying that the intention makes an act a more serious wrong, in the sense, for example, that there is a higher threshold of good to be achieved that must be met in order to override the prima facie wrongness of the act and make it permissible.

In particular, in P(i)–P(v), we need not require the resistance movement or Baby Killer Nation or their pilots to refrain from bombing the military target even when we know the latter two will act only for bad reasons. Furthermore, I think we need not require them to refrain even if we would require individuals to refrain from doing acts against the Nazis that were impermissible on grounds other than the agent's intentions. (That is, we need not merely be allowing any impermissible act for the greater good.) Nor need we require the bad man in any of the trolley cases to refrain from turning the trolley. Nor need we require A to refrain from attacking B in any of the self-defense cases even if we knew he would act for bad reasons and we had no reason to favor the outcome in which he defended himself over the one in which he did not. We certainly should not require these agents to refrain from attacking a target or saving the five if it were the agents' duty to do these acts. Even Kant would have agreed. He argued that a shopkeeper should give the right change to a child from concern with fulfilling his duty to do so rather than from mere prudence. But suppose a shopkeeper would return the change merely from prudence. Kant would not claim that his returning the change was morally impermissible even if his act would have no moral worth.[14]

Furthermore, I think that we should not tell Baby Killer Nation, the bad man, or A to refrain from their acts even if it were not anyone's duty to take out the target, save the five, or defend oneself but merely permissible to do so. Nor does the amount of good that would come from bombing the military facility, turning the trolley, or killing B have to be greater in order to justify these acts when the intentions of the agent are bad.

Now consider the means/side-effect distinction separately from the intention/foresight distinction by considering the actual causal route to surrender. Does the fact that the actual causal route to surrender will be through harm and terror mean that it is impermissible to bomb the Nazi military facility whose destruction could also have helped bring about surrender for military reasons? I do not think that this is so even if it would have been wrong to bomb in the absence of any facility whose destruction was of military use. One need not be required to refrain from destroying a military facility whose destruction could promote an objective good (such as ending Nazi rule) when doing this is justified despite side-effect deaths and terror simply because people will respond to these side effects by surrendering. Nor does the good that one can achieve by destroying a military facility have to be greater in order to justify one's act when it is one's intention that the collateral harm and terror actually cause surrender.

Finally, returning to the conceptual issue, suppose that some of my conceptual suggestions in C(1) about P(i)–P(v) are incorrect and that some of these cases should be categorized as terrorism. Thomas Scanlon has argued that intentions can change the meaning of acts.[15] A meaning of Baby Killer Nation's bombing the WTC in P(i)–(iv) is that it seeks to destroy and terrorize civilians as an end in itself. In P(v), a meaning of Baby Killer Nation's act is that people are available to be harmed and terrorized as mere means to some end. Whether their victims know of these meanings or not, these are what their acts mean. Suppose we should apply "terrorism" to acts that have these meanings even when the agent conditionalizes acting with these intentions on being able to destroy some military target, as in P(ii) or P(v). Then the fact that the acts are nevertheless permissible will imply that there are permissible acts of terrorism (though this does not mean that the aspects of these acts that make them terrorism are justified). Indeed, surprisingly, it will be possible to show that there are permissible acts of terrorism that are justified by even rather small good effects. This will be so if the act that harms and terrorizes is a means to produce a good effect independently of any causal role for harm and terror, and the harm and terror that result as side effects, relative to this other way of producing the good effect, are proportionate to the good achieved. For example, suppose that bombing a small Nazi munitions factory should proceed because it reduces Nazi power a bit even when ten innocent NCs will certainly be killed as a side effect. Suppose Baby Killer Nation bombs the factory in order to kill the ten people as an end or a means, and its act is terrorism because of its meaning even though it does nothing other than what those lacking this intention would do. Then this terrorist bombing will still be permissible so long as it is also a reasonable means to reduce the Nazis' power a bit through the destruction of the factory itself.

These results would imply that on the meaning theory of terrorism we could not rule out the permissibility of terrorist acts without first considering other possible effects of the acts (such as destroying military targets) that could justify the acts even when the harm and the terror turn out to be causally efficacious to the good effect (e.g., surrender) that justifies the destructive act.

I have been dealing with hypothetical cases where the act of destroying the Nazi WTC is assumed to be *permissible* (P). I argued that the intention to harm and terrorize (as ends or merely means) even when the harm and terror are actually the means that achieve one's end does not account for the supposed distinction in moral permissibility between bombing that involves collateral damage and terrorist bombing. However, I also noted that the intention to harm and terrorize people can be additional bad elements of the act. It can lead to justified indignation because of people's the attitudes toward other people and the considerations they take to justify acts (such as death and terror) that do not justify acts. Nevertheless, this need not imply that the act they perform for bad reasons is a wrong (impermissible) act.

3. Impermissible Acts

Now let us consider the role of intention and also the actual causal role of harm and terror in deciding what type of wrong act is done (a conceptual issue) and how serious a wrong it is when the act is assumed to be *impermissible* (abbreviated "I").[16] The act of bombing the military facility will be impermissible, at least, if the death and terror it leads to as side effects are out of proportion to the military goal to be achieved. First consider imaginary cases.

I(i) Suppose that it makes military sense for Al Qaeda to blow up the WTC in a United States not controlled by Nazis because of military operations going on in it. However, it is morally wrong for it to attack because of the side effects of death and terror. (It could also be that, given the type of conflict Al Qaeda is involved in, it is not permissible for it to destroy an opponent's homeland property even when this harms and terrorizes no one.) No pilot is interested in taking the job for the purely military reasons. However, some pilots are interested in doing the job because it will kill and terrorize people. Does hitting the military WTC with this intention, carried out in exactly the same way as pilots who do not intend to kill and terrorize would carry it out, become an act of terrorism when Al Qaeda's leaders authorize the mission in order to destroy the military operation? Even though the destruction of the WTC would be impermissible, I do not think that its impermissibility should alter our conclusion from what it was in P(i), namely, that the pilot's intentions do not determine how we should categorize the bombing. However, in this case, where we are considering which *wrong* act was committed, it will be the wrong of the impermissible bombing of a military facility rather than the wrong of terrorism.

I(ii) Suppose that all is as in I(i) except that Al Qaeda (including its pilots) is not interested in doing what it makes military sense for it to do. It is interested only in killing and terrorizing NCs. Nevertheless, it will not cause death and terror unless military factors are present to create a militarily rational cover for its operation.

If it bombs only on this condition and does no acts that would not be done by someone interested only in getting rid of the military operation, is its act terrorism rather than impermissible military bombing?

I have mentioned the view that an authority's intention can change the meaning of the act and that "terrorism" should be applied when the meaning of the act is that people seek to harm and terrorize. If this view were correct, I(ii) would be terrorism.

Alternatively, we might get support for the negative answer by considering a self-defense analogy.[17] In order for it to be truly relevant to I(ii), we would have to imagine that the self-defense is impermissible (for example, when the defensive act would have very bad side effects on bystanders). This is a new extension of the philosophy-of-law problem discussed earlier. So suppose that C would be engaged in impermissible self-defense against an attacker B in killing him even though his aim is only self-defense. If A does only what C does, can we classify his wrong act as impermissible self-defense when A aims only to murder B but waits until B's attack on him to kill him? Here is the issue at stake: May we ignore intention in characterizing the type of act done when the act is impermissible (as one view holds we might when it is permissible)? Might we focus instead on the condition that sets limits on when the bad intention will be acted on rather than on the intention itself (as was at first proposed in discussing P[ii])? Might the answer depend on whether there is a "core of appropriateness" to the act even if it is ultimately impermissible? That is, defending oneself in the face of an attack is appropriate but is made impermissible in virtue of some other factor, such as that the only available response is excessive. However, attacking a nonthreat does not have the same core of appropriateness. Attacking military supplies to be used unjustly against one is appropriate even if ultimately impermissible due to collateral damage. Attacking a public garden does not have the same core of permissibility.

In all of these cases, the agent should refrain from his act. Possibly this makes it appropriate to refer to intention to characterize the act's type. If so, in cases I(i)–(ii) the conceptual results will be closer to those of the "meaning" approach to categorizing acts. It is also possible that the seriousness of the wrong done is determined by reference to intention. If this were true, it would indicate that the role of intention in determining the type of act could be different for permissible and impermissible acts. Nevertheless, the impermissibility of the act is still established on grounds other than the presence of the intention to harm and terrorize.

Consider how we might reason in more detail about the relevance of intention in cases I(i)–(ii). Suppose that A, like C, would have impermissibly defended himself against attacking agents other than B even though he did not begin with the aim of killing them as he did with B. Suppose also that A set the self-defense scenario as a condition of killing B. I suggest that we might then classify A's act in killing B the same way as C's wrongful self-defense. This is because the case suggests that A has two intentions in the circumstance when he kills B—to defend himself and to eliminate B—and the self-defense goal is primary in that it suffices on its own as a reason for action and also sets the conditions for acting on the intention of killing B.[18] Similarly, in our variants on imaginary examples I(i)–(ii), suppose that Al Qaeda would have bombed the WTC military operation even if NCs would not have been killed, and it would have killed NCs only in attacking a building with military facilities. This suggests that where it intends to kill NCs, it has two goals. That is, it also intends to destroy the WTC for military purposes, and more than this, harming and terrorizing are not necessary for it to act. Then, if the impermissible self-defense analogy is to be trusted, Al Qaeda's wrong in this imaginary case would be classified as the wrong of causing impermissible collateral damage even when it also intends harm and terror. (Even the meaning approach to characterizing acts might lead to the same conclusion, for we have now introduced two intentions.)[19]

But if A, unlike C, would not have impermissibly killed any other attacking agent except B, this suggests that he is completely uninterested in self-defense even though he conditionalizes acting in order to kill B on self-defense being possible. This suggests that his impermissible act should be classified as a different, more serious wrong than C's. Analogously, in I(ii), if Al Qaeda has no interest in the military target per se, then the wrong in bombing will be terrorism even when it is made conditional on bombing a military operation. Finally, suppose that in variants on cases I(i)–(ii) Al Qaeda is interested both in destruction of the military WTC and in harm and terror, but the harm and terror are necessary (if not sufficient) conditions for its acting. That is, Al Qaeda would not fulfill its intention to destroy the military WTC unless it also achieved this other goal. Here, attacking the military is a goal of action but is not sufficient on its own for action. Harming and terrorizing are also goals of action but are not sufficient on their own. In this sort of case, I think that the impermissible act would be terrorism, at least in part.

For completeness, let us now consider I(iii) and I(iv).

I(iii) Suppose that all is as in I(ii), except that although Al Qaeda knows about the military usefulness of destroying the WTC, it would have destroyed the WTC merely in order to produce death and terror even if there had been no ongoing military operations there. Its wrong is thereby the wrong of terrorism.

I(iv) Suppose that all is as in I(iii) except that no one in Al Qaeda knows of the actual military operations in the WTC and it aims to destroy the WTC in order to kill and terrorize. Here again, I think that the wrongful act is terrorism.

Should the actual causal route (independent of intention) to an end affect how we categorize an impermissible act or the degree of its wrongness? I do not think so. For example, suppose bombing the WTC military facility for military reasons would be impermissible at least because of collateral harm and terror. Does the act become terrorism or a more significant wrong just because the populace actually surrenders due to the harm and terror? I do not think so.

Suppose this analysis of when we should apply the term "terrorism," arrived at by considering I(i)–(iv) and variants, is correct. Then it will be important in describing the actual bombing of the WTC (where no military operations were ongoing) on 9/11 to consider whether bombing the WTC is something Al Qaeda would have done even if no deaths or terror would have occurred. The bombing would certainly be useful to show the vulnerability of one's opponent and perhaps to destroy some of its economic power. We could certainly conceive of some other agent (analogous to C in the self-defense cases) who did not intend to harm and terrorize NCs as a means or an end yet would exhibit instrumental (though not moral) rationality in bombing the WTC for such reasons. Of course, such a bombing would be morally impermissible. It would be impermissible either because of the collateral damage or because it is not true that one may destroy the homeland property of one's opponent in just any sort of conflict. Nevertheless, the wrong would not be classified as terrorism. Suppose Al Qaeda would have bombed the WTC on 9/11 if no people would have been harmed or terrorized. Suppose that in its actual bombing on 9/11 it did nothing other than what someone who was interested only in destroying the WTC would have done. Then if what has been said about I(i)–(iv) is correct, even if Al Qaeda also intended the harm and terror and it was harm and terror that actually had the biggest useful effect for its cause, its impermissible act would not be terrorism.[20]

D. HARM AND TERROR AS NECESSARY TO ACHIEVE ONE'S END

I have argued that neither intention to harm and terrorize (as ends or means) per se nor the actual causal route to an outcome through harm and terror per se (nor the combination of these) determines the impermissibility of an act. However, all this does not mean that the impermissibility of an act might not be determined by the necessity, given one's act, of a route through harm and terror to a chosen outcome (including the mere occurrence of the harm and terror in themselves) in the absence of any possible effects of the act not causally requiring harm and terror that could justify harm and terror that is caused. This might be grounds for asserting that terror bombing is impermissible when bombing with comparable collateral damage is permissible. This is a fourth proposal to account for the prima facie wrongness, in the sense of impermissibility, of ST. It is different from proposals that focus on intention and the actual (but not necessary) causal route through harm and terror.

1. The Necessary/Nonnecessary Harmful Means Distinctions

Intending harm and terror is necessary, I think, to make one's act be terrorism, but it is the conjunction of this intention to bring harm and terror about when they alone are effects of one's act that could be a means to one's end, in the absence of any other good effects of the act not requiring harm and terror to cause them that could justify harm and terror, that could make one's act be an example of impermissible terrorism. Cases that have been standardly used to illustrate terrorism have this characteristic. For example, they involve a pilot who drops bombs directly on children or on buildings whose destruction serves no military purpose per se and who intends the resulting harm and terror as means to surrender when no other effect of his act can help cause surrender without causally requiring harm and terror. It has been mistakenly thought that the intention and/or actual causal route through harm and terror were the crucial characteristics of impermissibility. But if the harm and terror are effects that do bring about one's end when something else one brought about through one's act could independently have also brought about one's end or some other sufficiently good effect, we may not yet have either terrorism or an impermissible act even in the presence of a bad intention that causes action. This was true in the case where hitting military operations in the Nazi WTC could also have brought about surrender by way of reduced munitions if harm and terror had not actually led to surrender. Further, the fact that harm and terror would be the only effect of one's act that could produce the outcome at which one aims (as in Baby Killer Nation's case) implies that it is necessary, given one's act, for them to have a causal role in achieving one's goal. Yet even then the effect of destroying Nazi munitions, which could justify harm and terror caused as a side effect, makes Baby Killer Nation's act permissible. (Note that the necessity of a particular causal route to achieve one's goal, given one's act, is not the same as the necessity of that causal route tout court. The fact that one might have done many different acts to bring about one's end that did not require harm and terror is consistent with the act one actually does leading to one's end only through harm and terror.) But is the necessity of a role for harm and terror, given one's act, in the absence of some possible effect of one's act not requiring harm and terror to cause it that could justify the harm and terror, sufficient to make the act impermissible?

2. The Produce/Sustain Distinction

There is reason to doubt this, as is shown by the following cases.[21] In the Sustain Destruction Case, the Resistance bombs the military facility in the Nazi WTC, foreseeing the collateral damage and terror. However, it also knows that these facilities will be quickly rebuilt unless the collateral harm and terror to NCs keeps people otherwise occupied. There will be no point in bombing the facility if it is quickly rebuilt. In this case, the harm and terror are causally necessary for the achievement of the Resistance's goal because they sustain the destructive effects of its bombing. The Resistance bombs the WTC only because it knows that the harm and terror will occur unavoidably as side effects; it will not act if the side effects do not occur, for the military facility will then be quickly rebuilt. This need not imply that the Resistance intends the harm and terror or bombs in order to produce them. For there is, I believe, a conceptual distinction between acting only because one will produce an effect—on condition that one will—and acting in order to bring about that effect.[22] However, Baby Killer Nation might join the bombing of the Nazis on this occasion, and it would intend to cause harm and terror. Whether it is the Resistance or Baby Killer Nation acting, it would still, I believe, be permissible to bomb the WTC in the Sustain Destruction Case. This is so even if the route to the Nazi surrender, given the destructive act, is through harm and terror sustaining the destruction of the WTC. Why is this so?

A key point in distinguishing the permissible from the impermissible cases where harm and terror are necessary to achieve one's goal is the different way in which the harm and terror come about and, as a consequence, the different causal roles of harm and terror. In the Sustain Destruction Case, the harm and terror are brought about by the destruction of the WTC, which would, if only it could be sustained, be the goal that could justify the existence of collateral harm and terror. This contrasts with the harm and terror being necessary means to the initial destruction of the WTC, not produced by that destruction and merely necessary to sustain the destruction. I believe that it is these differences that can account for the impermissibility of some terror bombing (for example, when harm and terror are necessary, given one's act, to produce an outcome at which one aims, and the harm and terror are effects of one's act in the absence of any other justifying effects).

I conclude that intending harm and terror as means or ends is necessary for a case to involve ST, but it is not this intention that contributes to the prima facie impermissibility of the act that causes harm and terror. Furthermore, neither an actual nor a necessary role, given one's act, for harm and terror in achieving one's goal makes for the prima facie impermissibility of the act that harms. Rather, what can be crucial for the prima facie impermissibility of an act is that the harm and terror have a necessary role, given one's act, in *producing one's end in the absence of any other justifying effect not requiring harm and terror to produce it. This contrasts with harm and terror being the effects of achieving one's goal and having a necessary causal role in sustaining it.*[23]

The results of section D imply that a modal operator (such as the necessity of harm and terror, given one's act, as a means to producing the outcome at which one aims or the possibility of doing without them in producing this outcome) should sometimes play a role in characterizing the impermissible or permissible act. These results also imply that, even when someone does not intend to harm and terrorize NCs, we could condemn his act as impermissible because it involves harm and terror as the only possible means to producing his end, given his act, in the absence of other justifying effects not requiring harm and terror to produce them. This is true even if the act is not terrorism because there is no intention to harm and terrorize. For example, consider the Cow Case: Suppose that a pilot mistakenly believes that the people on the ground are cows. He has no intention of harming and terrorizing people but only of bombing a nonmilitary building in order to harm some cows in order to terrorize other cows into trampling a munitions site. Still, we could say that his act is impermissible because it would actually require these things being done to people if the munitions are to be trampled. This is consistent with its being permissible to destroy a building to eliminate its military use, though as a side effect this imposes the same harm and terror on people, and these would actually lead them to surrender.[24]

E. THE MECHANICAL/NONMECHANICAL AND MILITARY/ POLITICAL DISTINCTIONS

Is there something else that contributes either to the prima facie wrongness of ST or at least to its increased moral badness (if this does not affect its impermissibility)? I think that we should consider how the effects of being used (in being harmed or terrorized) function, for possibly this will distinguish ST morally from other cases where there is improper use of harm and terror as means or ends.

1.

In order to make this clearer, consider the Human Tinder Case: An agent bombs people as a means to starting a fire that will blow up a military target. Or consider the Stampede Case: An agent bombs people as a means to creating terror in others so that they will stampede and trample a military facility, thereby terminating a military operation. In these two cases, terror and/or harm are mechanical means to military ends. I say "mechanical" because the destruction of the military target in the Human Tinder Case could be produced by any burnable substance. And the terror involved in the Stampede Case is like a fright-and-flight instinctive response and is in this sense mechanical.

By contrast, it is often true in ST that the harm and terror are meant to influence people's judgment and will, especially in the political sphere. Here, fear gives rise to a prudential or an altruistic judgment (that one should save oneself or others) that is meant to provide one with a reason to alter one's behavior or policies. The fear is not a factor that causes one to bypass the exercise of judgment and reduces one to an instinctive fright-and-flight response. In the Stampede Case, people act in a panic. This form of terror is somewhat like torture without the already ongoing physical abuse insofar as the torturer tries to undermine the victim's will rather than give him a reason (namely, the avoidance of additional pain) to change his willed behavior.[25] We might call this the mechanical/nonmechanical distinction.[26]

In the Human Tinder and Stampede cases, the attacker *fights with* the people harmed and terrorized in the sense that he uses people as tools in defeating the military. But in standard terror bombing, the agent could be seen as trying to terrorize people in order to bypass the need for a purely military victory that he may be incapable of achieving: In the Standard Terror Bombing Case, people are imagined nonmechanically to decide to get their government to change policies or petition for peace. It is also possible that the aim of producing nonmechanical terror is to get people to alter their social and economic behavior in ways that their government finds unacceptable. Then the government, without fear having led NCs to petition their government, surrenders or otherwise changes its policies without

Table 1

	Military	Political
Mechanical	MM	MP
Nonmechanical	NM	NP

the other side having to win military victories.[27] So there may also be a distinction to be drawn between the military use of harm and terror and their political use. Table 1 lays out the possible combinations of these distinctions.

Notice that there could be a nonmechanical use of people to defeat the military, as when fear leads people, as a matter of prudence or altruism, to consider sabotaging their own country's military operations. And there could be a mechanical use that affects the political realm, as when people's terror leads them to stampede and interfere with an election.

2.[28]

One of my purposes in considering cases involving mechanical and nonmechanical terror and/or harm to achieve military victory has been to show that they too involve wrongs to NCs. However, my further purpose is to bring to more prominent attention the fact—to me very surprising—that such cases may not have been considered "terror bombing" at all by the same governments who would have been concerned about standard terror bombing. That is, though philosophers typically focus on standard terror bombing, many of their criteria for condemning it could also lead them to condemn the Human Tinder and Stampede Cases. But many practitioners of war would not have followed them in this conclusion, it seems. I first became aware of this as a result of a PBS documentary on World War II.[29] It reported that the Allied forces' deliberate bombing of German civilians in order to stop them and frighten away others from rebuilding a road (because the repair would threaten a military aim) was not considered terror bombing. It might be said that, in this case, unlike my Human Tinder or Stampede cases, the NCs who are harmed and terrorized are doing something that indirectly impeded a military aim, and for this reason, harm and terror to them to achieve a military goal do not raise the moral problem of terror bombing. However, subsequently I presented my Human Tinder and Stampede Cases to an historian of war.[30] His initial response was to deny that these would be considered terror bombing. I believe this is because they were directed at achieving a military goal in a declared war rather than simply being directed at undermining the will of the population in order to bring about a surrender without needing to achieve military victory. If this is so, then the fact that deliberate killing and terrorizing of NCs take place and that these are necessary to achieve a goal are not the characteristics that military leaders are focusing on in condemning standard terror bombing. Rather, the attempt to harm and terrorize people solely to bring about a surrender without military victory may be seen by them as crucial to impermissible terror bombing.[31]

I believe that moral philosophers should object to such a determinative role for the political versus military goal factor in demarcating morally problematic terror bombing. Instead, they should emphasize acts that require a productive role for terror and/or harm in NCs in order to achieve a goal, political or military, in the absence of other effects of the act, not produced in this way, that could justify harm and terror. If this is correct, it raises the possibility that from the point of view of moral philosophers, many acts in, for example, World War II that have not been classified as terror bombing and therefore have not been thought to be morally problematic in the way that standard terror bombing is were indeed morally problematic terror bombing. It is important to investigate this for historical accuracy. It is also important for purposes of future conduct in war that this issue be clarified, as there may well be disagreement about not only a conceptual matter (whether something is terror bombing) but also about whether achieving a military goal can morally justify terror and/or harm to NCs as a necessary productive means.

3 .

Let us consider the use of mechanically produced harm (killing some people) to produce nonmechanical terror for political purposes (NP) in more detail. When the aim is to create terror that will lead people to put political pressure on their government, the terrorist is trying to change people's judgment and deliberately willed political behavior.[32] Unlike soldiers, NCs are often not prepared to die for a cause, both in the sense that they are not trained to fight to the death for it and also, possibly, in that they would not be willing to fight to the death for it. The home front is often willing to commit to a policy only if it can rely on others who are soldiers to do the fighting and sustain the losses for it. (So the agent's attempt to pressure or fight people who are not prepared to die does not apply if those affected are soldiers who are not in combat.) This would help explain why ST agents are considered cowards even when they risk their lives. For they are bypassing fighting the military to win a war, relying instead on attacking NCs, who are not trained to sustain attacks. This idea—perhaps somewhat inaccurate—of a coward is of someone who does not fight someone else prepared to fight. He is concerned with easy victory in this sense even if it costs him his life.

The terrorist in the type of case we are considering is also trying to get people to behave in ways that exhibit a lack of the virtue of courage, it might be argued. When an agent harms people, she may be trying to make them unable to fight. When she terrorizes them for nonmechanical purposes, she tries to make them unwilling to support a fight or otherwise stay the course, though they are not unable to do so. (The Stampede Case involves a mechanical form of terror that makes one psychologically unable to control oneself, so it differs from the unwillingness to stay a course that I am now considering.) It would be better if people did not give in to fear, as doing so leads them to take factors on which one focuses merely because of fear as reasons to change policy. They cannot be proud of their behavior when they change a policy merely because of fear and independently of merit. This is especially true when the fear is out of proportion to the real increase in the probability of death and destruction (for example, when there is a much higher probability of dying in a car accident than from a terrorist attack).[33] Hence, ST of this type raises the specter of a war of cowards on both sides. (Suppose, though, that people mistakenly overestimate the probability of death, and the fear is proportional to the imagined probability. Then there may not be cowardice on their part but a form of irrationality that is also not admirable.)

Focusing on these factors in ST raises the issue of whether and when it is in fact cowardly to give in to fear as a reason for seeking a change in policy. It seems reasonable to surrender from fear when a criminal says, "Your money or your life." But pressuring one's government out of fear to give in to terrorist demands is more like calling off the police from catching the criminal (to whom one gave one's money from fear) out of fear. And this is wrong. It is also more like giving in to a criminal when what he asks for violates one's principles rather than just diminishes one's wealth. An analogy here might be calling off the police on criminals whose goal in killing and terrorizing is to stop racial integration from taking place.

In response to this last point, it may be argued that U.S. foreign policy (if that is what the terrorist is trying to change) is a matter of national self-interest, not principles, and so if changing the policy to stop terrorist attacks were in the U.S. national interest overall, then there would be nothing morally objectionable (or cowardly) in doing so.[34] (Of course, in the long run it might not be in its interest to do this, but suppose it were.)

However, even if the substance of U.S. foreign policy were only a matter of self-interest and not principle, giving in to ST would not be like ordinary action from self-interest. In ST (and in criminal threats) the agent takes or threatens to take something from people (e.g., their lives) to which they have a right, in order to make it be in their interest to trade something else (e.g., their foreign policy) in order to get back (or avoid losing) what they have a right to have without such a trade. Contrast this with a nation that says, "We will not give you our oil unless you change your foreign policy" (the Oil Threat Case). This, too, may be done in order to cause fear in people and lead them to pressure their government to change its foreign policy. But such a threat does not involve taking U.S. oil (or anything else to which U.S. citizens are entitled) and then trying to trade it back to them for a change in U.S. foreign policy. Indeed, if a threat of withholding oil were intended to produce terror, then it might be an instance of morally permissible NST. (One might resent such an attempt to alter one's policies, but this would not be enough to show that it is impermissible. It is like the embargo that the United States used to try to alter Saddam Hussein's policies, at least if we abstract them from the objective merits of the good sought.) The moral objection to the attempt to make something be in one's self-interest seems appropriately greater in the case of threatened ST than in the Oil Threat Case even if the deaths that might result from each threat are held constant.

Perhaps this claim might be challenged in the following way:[35] Whether or not U.S. foreign policy is motivated purely by national self-interest, the United States also uses impermissible means to pursue its policies, for example, helping maintain unjust autocratic regimes. The terrorist tries to make it be in the United States' self-interest to alter its foreign policy by raising the costs of this policy. Perhaps he does so by immoral means, but as the United States uses immoral means in pursuing its aims, it is asked, how can it complain when the terrorist does likewise? Hence, the United States should treat the terrorist acts as just another cost when deciding whether to change its foreign policy; it should not think in terms of either morally impermissible means being used or of cowardice in giving in.

Consistently or inconsistently, however, the United States rejects both the view that ST is just another way of raising costs and the view that, given its own conduct, it is not in a position to argue that there are moral constraints on pursuing aims. Indeed, given that ST actually increases the likelihood of death and serious injury to NCs very little, it is probably resentment against what it considers the terrorist's impermissible means, combined with the view that U.S. foreign policy is to some degree principled and the immoral means it employs are not as seriously wrong as ST, that may be underlying the attempt to extirpate ST. So we are back to the view that changing principled foreign policy from fear, when this requires giving in to pressure produced in immoral ways, is morally objectionable.

I conclude, therefore, that if ST is an attempt to give people a reason based on fear to give in to impermissible types of pressure and to change principled policies when the actual increase in the probability of death or serious injury is and is perceived to be small, then ST is an attempt to get people to behave in a cowardly manner. (If it is expected that people will unreasonably overestimate the increased probability of death, then there is at least an attempt by the terrorists to get people to behave in an irrational way.)

Giving in from fear is not the same as reconsidering the merits of a policy after ST, when one sees how strongly some people object to the policy. I suggested earlier that ST agents might be trying to set their victims on what they see as a morally right path. They may induce cowardice and irrationality to do this, but they may also seek conversion, a reconsideration of the merits of a policy. (To do this, harm and terror should be accompanied by dissemination of arguments for their side.) Suppose that one changed one's policy because, on reconsidering it, one saw its flaws. (And not only in the sense that one sees that the policy is not really in one's self-interest because it leads to terrorism. One sees its flaws independently of that effect.) Will others believe that one changed the policy because of fear instead (that is, that one would have changed it even if it were not flawed)? If so, this might encourage ST as a tactic. Indeed, even if others believe that one changed the policy on grounds of merit only after ST, then ST might seem to be a successful tactic for getting one to attend more closely to the merits of one's policy! This, too, could encourage ST.

If these things might happen, then it is no longer a simple matter of changing one's policies on the merits. The additional possible effects of encouraging ST might have to be considered and weighed in the balance. Here lies the poignancy of the Spanish case in 2003. The majority of the Spanish people all along thought that the policy of supporting the U.S. war with Iraq was wrong (and not just on self-interested grounds). But they seemed to put real pressure on their government after an ST act, and so some causal chain from ST against Spaniards was suggested. But should they have gone on paying with their lives for what they always thought was wrong just so as not to be thought to be giving in—or even being responsive in some other way—to ST? This is a hard question.

4.

(a). Suppose that an act of ST is an attempt to make people act cowardly, to prey on their weakness or on their less-than-optimal rationality in calculating risks. Does this help make the ST act prima facie wrong in the sense of being impermissible? I believe so. This is because it is prima facie wrong to play a role in undermining

people's judgment and will. It is also because these effects are, given the agent's act, necessary to produce his further end (rather than only side effects). However, these factors are also present in the Oil Threat Case, but they do not make that threat overall impermissible. Do these factors make an act that is impermissible on other grounds (e.g., it involves impermissible killing) be a more serious wrong? One way to test for this is to hold constant in all cases the amount of harm and terror and their causal necessity in producing an outcome and ask whether the agent does a more serious wrong in an NP case than in either an MM case or an MP case. One problem with this approach is that we might not be able to equalize for terror, for the terror that will undermine judgment entirely and produce panic (a mechanical case) must, it seems, be more intense and hence greater than the terror that does not.[36] One response to this objection is to imagine that the less-intense terror lasts for a longer period of time than the more-intense terror. In this way, we equalize total terror. Let us assume that this is possible and proceed with some comparisons.

Is it a more serious wrong to try to influence politics and thereby win a conflict than to merely influence the military when both are done through a mechanical use of harm and terror? Perhaps. Is it a more serious wrong to influence politics through the effect on judgment described earlier rather than mechanically? I think that it is in some ways "uglier," but I do not think that this makes it a more serious wrong. Why is it uglier? It may be because it shifts responsibility for the change in policy or the failure of military action from the terror bomber to the civilians. Hence it may make ST a morally worse event for its victims. After all, they will act in a morally wrong way (e.g., in a cowardly way). The responsibility for any wrong behavior by the victims will be theirs when they let their judgment be swayed by fear. They have the option of not doing this. To some degree they even have the option of not feeling fear, as we have more control over this emotional response than over physical harms, at least when there is no panic attack (as in the Stampede Case). For this reason the victims may prefer to be used mechanically, for then the responsibility for the outcome lies solely with the ST agent. (Notice that this sort of ugliness can be increased further by offering inducements rather than threats in order to achieve surrender or a change in principled policies.)

However, I do not think that it is the responsibility of an agent involved in a conflict, when he decides whether to use harm and terror mechanically or nonmechanically, to choose on the basis of sparing his opponents from their own bad decision making (if this will be bad only for his opponents). (By contrast, in nonconflict situations, I think that we should act to promote and support each other's good reasoning and moral virtues.) Similarly, we need not correct the errors of our opponents when this will harm our side even when they consult us for advice. However, the victim's desire to avoid being placed in a situation where he will behave badly is an added incentive for him to try to extirpate ST even if not because it makes what the ST agent does a more serious wrong.

Suppose that an agent does want to help the people he harms and terrorizes to avoid cowardly behavior or bad risk assessment so that they will not later be ashamed of their conduct. He could make their behavior not exhibit these defects by increasing the harm he does so that it would be truly reasonable for them to fear great further damage and be reasonable for them to surrender. But this has several problems. First, it would do more harm to people, and that seems too great a price to pay in order to make one's opponent's conduct reasonable and noncowardly. Second, it seems unnecessarily solicitous toward someone in a conflict to want to cushion the blow of choices they are responsible for making.

The first problem could be remedied[37] not by increasing the harm one actually does but rather by threatening to do much worse than one would actually do or by falsely magnifying the damage and frequency of attacks one has actually undertaken. Here, too, it could be only reasonable for others to be taken in and surrender. However, in these scenarios the agent takes it upon himself to appear to be much worse than he actually is or possibly would be. From the agent's point of view, this can be too great a moral sacrifice to make just to spare his opponent shame.

(b). So far I have argued that, due to the role of NC responsibility and the lack of a duty to be solicitous of one's opponent's behavior, achieving one's end via non-mechanical terror does not make an agent's act a more serious wrong than achieving the end via mechanical terror. Can we also argue that using the nonmechanical route—even though it will depend on eliciting poor judgment or cowardice on the part of one's opponent—is morally better than producing the same effects through mechanical means (holding the amount of harm and terror and their causal necessity in producing an outcome in both cases constant)? That is, if it were a more serious wrong to use the mechanical, rationality-undermining means, then this, rather than merely the refusal to be solicitous of one's opponent, should lead one to use nonmechanical means.

In answering this question, recall the claim that mechanical terror is like some types of torture, without physical abuse of the one terrorized. (There is, of course, still physical abuse in ST of those whose deaths lead to terror.) Indeed, psychological torture is a bona fide category of torture that does not require physical abuse.[38] So let us consider a certain aspect of interrogational torture.

Would it be morally worse to try to get a person to divulge information by breaking the person down to a nonrational, panicked state or by threatening him so that reasons of self-interest stemming from fear overcome his moral impulse to keep a secret? Even though the second course involves trying to corrupt someone, I think that it could be permissible to take it when reducing someone to a nonrational, panicked state is impermissible. This is so even if the corrupted person becomes less worthy of respect and the reduced person would be only an object of pity. This would explain why corrupting (by unpleasant or pleasant prospects) is considered a morally permissible interrogation procedure but psychological terror is not.

It might be suggested that the fear leading to panic is greater than the fear that gives one a prudential reason to divulge information, and this is why the former is prohibited when the latter is not. To deal with this possibility, we should imagine that the panic period is short and the lesser fear is extended in time. Alternatively, we could imagine options involving no fear at all. Suppose that we could for a brief duration give someone a truth serum that made it impossible for him to exercise self-control, so that he blurted out everything he knew. The alternative way to get information is to bribe the person with the prospect of rewards rather than punishments. Again, I suggest that it is no solution to the problem of corrupting someone to undermine his rational agency instead, even for a short while in the way described.

Why might it be true that it is preferable to avoid mechanical psychological means? This is a difficult question. I suspect that rather than be corrupted, it may be better for the person to lose control in a way that, in a sense, reduces his functioning to a nonperson level for a short while. However, it is contrary to the importance of being a person to try to elicit responses from him by bypassing his rational control in this way, and those who do so bear full responsibility for his state and what he does in it. The alternative will involve encouraging him to make choices that reflect badly on his moral character. But the outcome, whatever it is, will be a function of his full humanity being exercised, not short-circuited, and more responsibility for his ultimate state will lie with him. We might say that while the short, tortured period could be (comparatively) better *for* him, it is more at odds with the importance *of* him. For similar reasons, it might be morally worse to create the mechanical panic response in a population rather than the fear that corrupts their judgment even if we could equalize the fear involved.

Hence I conclude that in conflict situations, contributing to an opponent's moral corruption or poor judgment does not play a big role in accounting for the wrong of terror bombing.

F. THE HARM/TERROR DISTINCTION

The degree and type of damage (loosely construed) done to the NCs, of course, also plays a role in making ST prima facie wrong. But it might said that a distinction in the types of damage—that is, harm or terror—must be examined in order to isolate what makes ST, in particular, prima facie wrong. (In using "harm," I mean to focus on physical damage. However, psychological dysfunction of a more than temporary sort [e.g., continued panic attacks or debilitating depression] can be considered harm, too. "Terror" is not meant to include such long-term, debilitating psychological conditions.) Some have actually said that terror is worse than harm, whether it is foreseen or intended, whether the terror is used as a means or an end. Traditional emphasis on the intention/foresight and means/side-effect distinctions ignores the harm/terror distinction as a possible explanation of what is wrong with ST. (Indeed, in many accounts that rely on the traditional distinctions, the emphasis is on the intentional killing of someone that leads to terror in others without even focusing on the fact that there is also an intention to cause terror and that it is being used for a further end.) Let us, therefore, consider terror and harm separately, narrowing the type of harm to being killed. We shall focus on two questions: (A) Is what happens to those who are terrorized worse than what happens to those who are killed? (B) Is a more serious wrong done to people who are terrorized or to those who are killed?

1. Terror

(a). Its Significance per se. In order for terror to be not unreasonable, what must its object be? Could it be a broken leg (in an ordinary person)? I doubt it. It must be fear of something very bad, such as death or grave injury to oneself or others. However, such terror could come from seeing someone else being harmed only to the extent of having his leg broken if one thinks, "That's only the beginning." There seem to be two major types of terror, as noted in section IIIE: nonmechanical (N), fear that gives one a reason of prudence or altruism to alter behavior, and mechanical (M), fear that undermines rationality so that one does not act for reasons of prudence or altruism as one is no longer reasoning; rather, one acts in a panic. The conditions that lead to each type of terror might be temporary or permanent and (in each category) frequent or infrequent. (Permanent, infrequent conditions of terror would occur, for example, if the world were never again without ST, but it occurred no more than once a year.) As noted earlier, the M form of terror is like torture without physical abuse insofar as torture tries to undermine the will rather than give one a reason to change one's behavior. M is involved in the Stampede Case mentioned earlier.[39]

Is either type of terror worse for its victims than death or grave bodily injury, keeping constant the number of people affected? Neither temporary N or M terror nor N or M terror caused by permanent conditions, if they are infrequent, are as bad as death. But perhaps permanent and frequent M terror would be as bad as or worse than death or grave bodily injury.

To confirm some of these judgments, consider the significance of temporary N terror all by itself. That is, suppose that we aim to produce such terror but without any harm. We bomb some trees because we know that people will interpret this as our trying to kill them, and they will then become terrorized and pressure for a change of policy. However, we do not and would not harm anyone. Call this the Trees Case. (A Trees-Stampede Case could be imagined involving M terror, where we bomb the trees in order to produce fear of death, leading to a panic that causes a stampede.) Or we might spread rumors that we have weapons of mass destruction (WMD) in order to terrorize people, though we have no such weapons (the Rumor Case). Are these cases of terrorism? I believe so, but they are NST, as no physical harm would be either intended or caused.[40] Is this sort of NST as bad as death for its victims? I do not think so. Is this sort of NST, even if it is impermissible, as serious a wrong as impermissibly killing people? I do not think so. Even employing nonharming terror that is necessary, given one's act, as a means to producing an outcome seems morally preferable to killing as a side effect. If we had to choose which to do, we should do the former rather than the latter. These results are consistent with there being a stronger objection to (1) killing NCs as a required means to causing terror that is itself a required means to achieving a goal than to (2) killing NCs as a required means to achieving a goal when no terror is produced, holding constant deaths. There are at least two possible ways to account for the view that (1) is morally worse than (2). First, there are two bad things happening in (1), killing and terror, and therefore there is a stronger moral objection to doing (1). Second, killing is itself worse when it also serves as a means to terror rather than directly producing a goal. The first account is correct, but the second is dubious, I think. Let us assume, therefore, that a very serious wrong is done to NCs in the Human Tinder and Stampede cases and that Stampede is the more seriously wrong of the two for reason (1) but not because terror is per se worse than death.

Of course, worse events can come from terrorizing without harm than can come even from killing if the reaction to the former will be much worse than to the latter. So suppose that Saddam Hussein had terrorized people in manner N with rumors of WMD when he had none and that this led the United States to go to war, which resulted in many deaths on all sides. This could be a worse outcome than that achieved by an instance of ST that did not produce such an extreme response. Even an M terror stampede not caused by harm to anyone could result in more deaths and injuries than a few deaths that alternatively would have been caused by deliberately harming people. But the reason it will be a worse outcome is that it produces serious harm rather than just more temporary N or M terror.

I have been arguing that terror per se is typically less bad and that causing it has less moral significance than killing or gravely injuring, other things being equal. But this need not be true simply because being harmed is always morally worse than being wronged in nonharmful ways. For example, I think that killing a person against his will when it is for his own good is nonharmful but seriously wrong. It is more serious than harming him in some minor way. So, possibly, if one has a choice, one should do what wrongfully breaks an arm in each NC rather than what wrongfully terrorizes each without harm.

.However, in deciding which to do, one must not only consider how terror compares with less serious harms: One must also consider the dynamics of responsibility for both harm and terror. (This issue was referred to in the discussion of victim responsibility in section IIIE.) That is,.when we harm someone even in a small way, it is we who are responsible for the harm. When we terrorize nonharmfully, and N terror leads someone to change his conduct from fear, the responsibility for the change seems to be in large part his. For when we cause N terror, its victims have the option of not responding to it in certain ways. Indeed, in the case of N terror, people may have control even over whether they become terrorized. (For example, if they stay calm and remember that the objective probability of future harm is not much increased, then they may not be terrorized.) An agent might reasonably prefer not to be responsible for causing harm and prefer to do what shifts responsibility away from himself and onto his opponent for any harm that does occur. He may choose between nonserious harming and N terrorizing on these grounds. Hence the prospect of achieving one's end with less responsibility for harm might attract an agent to NST that involves his using N terror. However, as I argued in section IIIE, it is hardly the responsibility of an agent, when he decides whether to harm an opponent or cause him nonharmful N terror, to choose on the basis of sparing others from their own bad decision making. The victims who behave badly may ultimately prefer to have been harmed instead, thus avoiding responsibility for bad conduct. But this will not be an additional factor that makes it wrong for an agent to use harmless terror instead of harm.

What if an agent is morally responsible for either the truly unavoidable (M) or perfectly reasonable terrified responses by others to the agent's harmless act (such as bombing trees)? For example, suppose that Iraq had provided strong evidence of its having WMD (stronger than what was actually pointed to in launching the war against it), and it would have been completely morally appropriate to respond to this evidence with fear leading to war even though war would harm many. Then there would be less difference between an agent's causing harm and his opponents' causing harm in responding to the agent's doing what merely N terrorizes them.

(b). We have been comparing causing terror and causing harm on the assumption that we are dealing with cases where it is wrong to do either one. Before considering challenges to what I have said, it is worth considering the way in which it clearly seems permissible in a conflict to use terror on NCs (when one causes no harm) even when the terror is a required means, given one's act, to producing an outcome and there is no other sufficiently good effect of one's act. In a conflict-free context, it is most often wrong to terrorize people even by telling them a truth. But in a situation where one faces an opponent in a conflict, this may not be true. Consider briefly some ways in which we might permissibly N terrorize NCs in a conflict, intending to do so: (i) We tell them the truth (for example, that their children will die as soldiers, their supplies are low, and we have superior arms). N terror is a reasonable response to these truths. It is permissible to cause N terror in this way, I think. (ii) Intending to create N terror, we do or threaten to do other things it is permissible to do when we know this will reasonably lead to terror. For example, in the Oil Threat Case, someone threatens not to sell oil. Causing terror in this way seems to be permissible in a conflict. (iii) We tell opponents truths that we know will unreasonably lead them to N terror. This involves taking advantage of their irrationality and so is demeaning in a way that reasonable, truth-produced terror is not. Trying to get people to behave in a cowardly way is also preying on their imperfections. If the victims act shamefully, then they may wish they had been harmed instead of terrorized in this way. But this does not mean that, in a conflict, using tactics that depend on the opponent NCs' defects of rationality and character makes the otherwise permissible act of telling truths impermissible, at least if it is N terror we produce. In cases (i)–(iii), terror per se is not only a less serious imposition than significant harm but is also permissible.

Is it permissible to threaten to do what it is impermissible actually to do as a way of N terrorizing? Some have argued that it would be permissible to threaten to use nuclear weapons on NCs if this would deter nuclear war. This is so even if one intended never to use the weapons on NCs because doing so would be impermissible. However, the nuclear deterrent is supposed to benefit at least some of the NCs who are to be threatened, on the assumption that they would be harmed in a non-deterred nuclear conflict as a side effect of either their own side's releasing nuclear weapons or of our responding to such an attack by attacking only military sites. This type of overall benefit to victims would not be present in the cases of NST that I am considering now. So perhaps producing terror by threatening to do what it is impermissible to do is wrong if it will not also benefit some of those terrorized.

Is it permissible to do what one knows will give rise to an expectation that one will do what it is wrong to do, intending to give rise to such an expectation, when one does not actually threaten to do something wrong? This is what happens in the Trees Case (described earlier) when we seek to establish a false terrorizing belief that we will bomb NCs as a means to producing our goal. It seems to me that this sort of terror might sometimes be permissible. It is also present in the following Terror in Other-Defense Case: A military division is under attack. It cannot beat back the opponent. Someone not under attack realizes that if he kills a combatant at the back of the attacking force, close to where villagers live, then the villagers will think they are going to be attacked. This will lead the villagers to interfere with the attacking force. Intentionally creating the terror in NCs (by harming the combatant) in this way seems permissible in a conflict.

Now consider whether it is always impermissible in a conflict to produce M terror of a temporary sort as a means that, given one's act, is necessary to produce military or political ends when there are no other sufficiently good effects of one's act. It may be that even though creating panic is "cleaner" than N terror, it is more rarely permissible. This is an implication of our earlier argument in which we compared using torture without harm that reduces people to a nonrational state with doing what elicits incorrect judgments and moral weakness. Even dropping leaflets with truths on them that will cause a mindless panic or destroying trees that will cause a mindless panic in NCs seems impermissible in many cases where these same means to causing N terror would be permissible. Still, if the only way to stop an attack on our side is for a bystander to do something harmless that creates a harmless terror stampede by an opponent's NCs, then I think that this may be permissible.

On the basis of cases of permissible and impermissible terror we can, I think, conclude the following. Terror (and the inappropriate weakening of one's resolve) is certainly something people would like to avoid, and it can make an act prima facie wrong. But people do not always have a right not to have these states deliberately brought about during conflict. They may have a right that certain means, such as killing NCs, not be used (and even not be threatened to be used) to bring about these states even in a situation of conflict. But this is because the people killed would be improperly treated if their involvement is, given someone's act, a necessary means to producing the terror when there are no other effects of the act not requiring harm and terror to produce them that could justify the occurence of the harm and terror.[41]

I also conclude that what happens in ST to those who are killed is usually worse and a more serious wrong than what happens to those who are only terrorized.

(c) Challenges. I have downplayed the badness and seriousness of even wrongfully causing terror per se (when no physical harm is done) relative to causing serious harm such as death. Consider some challenges to this view.

(i) It may be said that it is wrong merely to compare terror with death in the same number of people, for terror typically affects many people, but killing via ST affects only a few. Terrorizing many is worse and can be a more serious wrong than killing a few.

A response to (i) recognizes that terrorizing more people is worse than terrorizing a few (other things being equal), and terrorizing many can be a more serious wrong than terrorizing a few. This is consistent with its not being as bad or as serious a wrong to terrorize many as to seriously harm a few. This is because it is a mistake, in two ways, to aggregate much smaller impositions on each of many people and think this outweighs much graver losses to a few (assuming that each person's baseline condition is the same). First, it is not as bad an outcome if many people suffer terror as when a few die, for no one of the many suffers as great a loss as death. Second, if we have a choice of killing a few people or instead producing terror in many, then it would be wrong to do the former.

(ii) It may be said that it is wrong to focus on terror per se rather than on its wider effects, independently of weakening commitment to policies. Terror undermines civil society in a way that even thousands of deaths do not. For example, people are afraid to lead lives in public and congregate with others, at least when the harm that people fear is random and does not occur at predictable times (unlike the nighttime bombing of London during World War II).

A response to (ii) recognizes that undermining civil society can make an act prima facie wrong (though not all means to this effect ultimately may be wrong). However, it is only if the absence of civil society and public life leads to death and grave losses to individuals (e.g., serious medical conditions are left untreated because people are afraid to go to hospitals) that the loss to individuals will be as great as it is to those killed in ST (or nearly so). And only this is morally relevant if we are to avoid the mistake of aggregating much smaller losses to many individuals so as to outweigh grave ones to fewer individuals (as discussed in the response to [i]).

So the response to (ii) implies that an outcome with a few deaths is worse than one where people are terrorized (without any actual harm to anyone), and so there is no civil society providing non-life-preserving benefits to people. It also implies that if a terrorist agent has a choice, it would be wrong to produce the few deaths rather than the terror and collapse of non-life-preserving aspects of civil society through nonharmful means. (Henceforth I will assume that "civil society" involves only non-life-preserving benefits.)

(iii) Now consider a general objection to the view (embodied in the response to [ii]) that death to a few is worse than many being affected by both terror and the absence of civil society but with no deaths. We each often take a small risk of death in order to participate in civil society rather than certainly eliminate our civic involvement. (This is an intrapersonal calculation we make independently of numbers of people.) For example, we increase our risk of dying by driving to a café rather than staying home. Should we not then think that the small risk of dying in a harmful ST attack to which everyone would be exposed by terrorists is less bad than an outcome in which terror per se, without harm, causes people to cease participating in civil society? (In the case where each runs a risk of death by driving [in order to participate in civil society], we are imagining that those who might benefit from civil society are also the ones running the risk of death. This is a simplifying assumption. Let us suppose that it is true in ST scenarios, where harm leads to terror, that those who would benefit from civil society are also the ones who run the risk of death because it is in public venues that agents of ST attack.)

The risk to each is small, in the ST case, if terrorists can kill only a few of many people at random. An important difference between the one-person and the many-person cases is that only in the latter can we be sure that someone will be killed. Hence if many people avoid public activities, then each certainly loses civic life, and there is also no civic life, but death(s) will be avoided that would otherwise have occurred. By contrast, in the single-person case, the person might never have been killed even if he had not retreated from civic life. Suppose the possibility of no deaths occurring can sometimes also be a characteristic of many-person cases. Then the fact that people are each willing to take a small risk of death rather than give up some good does not show that the occurrence of the death is less bad than the absence of the good per se. For example, each may be willing to risk a devastating nuclear explosion in order to have cheap energy that increases the standard of living. This is consistent with the nuclear devastation being far worse an outcome than many living with a somewhat lower standard of living. What is needed to make taking this risk a rational choice is the belief that the devastation need not certainly occur—that we really may all escape it.

But as noted, in some cases someone will certainly die, though each runs only a small risk of it happening to him. This seems to be true when many drive in order to participate in civil society. It is these cases that support objection (iii), for they support the conclusion that people think that the state of affairs in which something very bad happens to a few (such as dying in car accidents or terrorist attacks) and not just the state of affairs of running a risk of dying is better than a state of affairs in which the deaths do not occur but many people are afraid and go without the good of civil society.

One response to this objection questions whether we can decide which outcome is worse by considering which one people would choose to live with. If each person decides to live with an outcome in which a few die, on the basis of the low risk that each person has of being among the dead, this may just mean that each one does not care about how bad the outcome will be but only about the risk each faces. And this might be a morally permissible basis for decisions. But it still could be that the outcome in which people die is worse and that it is morally appropriate for an agent, who has a choice of whether to bring about one outcome or another even by simply creating risks to each *person* that will certainly eventuate in a certain number of deaths, to care about which outcome is worse.

Let us suppose, however, that willingness to live with an outcome tells us about its relative badness. A second response to objection (iii) raises what we can call the Paradox of Risk. That is, suppose the outcome is worse when we are afraid and do not participate in civic society than when each has a small risk of death *and* some eventually die. Then why would the terrorist, in increasing the risk of death to each a small bit that will eventuate in the deaths of some, thereby produce terror sufficient to stop people from engaging in civil society? That is, why would he succeed in bringing about (what objection [iii] claims is) the worse state of affairs? Is it because a more serious moral wrong would occur if one were deliberately killed in ST than if one were killed in a car accident? But if it is fear that causes people to flee civil society, the fear should presumably be in proportion to the probability of being killed or dying rather than to the moral seriousness of the death. In order to confirm this conclusion, consider the following two imaginary variants of driving cases:

> **D1.** We have always believed that people die accidentally in highway collisions. Now we learn that villains have been operating in car manufacturing plants, weakening brakes slightly and thereby creating a greater risk of collision on the highways. All deaths that occur on highways have been and will be for some time due to this cause, though the villains no longer work in the plants.
>
> **D2.** We have always believed that people die accidentally in highway collisions. Now we learn that there are villains who use magnetic devices at long distance in order to cause collisions. All deaths that occur on highways have been and will be due to this cause as the villains are still operating.

In these cases, the risks that drivers face and the deaths that actually occur are due to deliberate villainy. Would we think that this was a worse state of affairs than when people die in accidents? I believe we would. Should we stop driving and give up participating in civil society? I do not think so. But it is worth pointing out two factors that complicate giving this response. First, D1 and D2 may differ slightly in a morally significant way. In D1, the villains have already done the dirty work that will lead to collisions. Hence it may be that we have no concern that our driving and some being killed will encourage villains to engage in further tampering to achieve their aims. By contrast, in D2 the villains are still active (which is more like the situation with ongoing ST). Hence going out on the road and giving villains successes may encourage them to continue to create collisions; our actions might fuel the creation of new risks of death and additional deaths. This effect on the villains may add another factor that makes the deaths in D2 worse from our point of view and may encourage one not to participate in civil society. However, a second factor may move one in the opposite direction, for not participating in civil society will give the villains who continue to operate the power to alter one's behavior in another significant way. This additional factor could make giving up on civil society a worse outcome than it would otherwise be per se.

Suppose we would be willing to have villain-caused deaths happen rather than give up civil society when abstracting from these last two factors; this would suggest that we think it is a worse state of affairs not to have civil society for many than for each to run a risk of death and have a few villainous deaths. Then it is only if people want not to encourage villains with successful killings that there would be a reason why what the terrorists do in ST would make people avoid civil society. Alternatively, their avoiding civil society may (again) raise the question of whether people are responding irrationally when they fear death from ST but not from driving on the road (even in D1); perhaps they see the risk from ST as greater than it is. Perhaps they see the risk as so great that if they had to undergo the risk in order to participate in civil society, then they would reasonably forego civil society. But this would not mean that the actual uninflated number of deaths involve a worse state relative to the loss of civil society.[42]

(iv) The objection we have been considering to the claim that a few deaths are worse than fear that leads to the absence of civil society can be rephrased so that the objection avoids the Paradox of Risk. Assume that in reality there is a small risk of death to each of many (in driving or from terrorist attacks). The objection (rephrased) claims that the outcome in which some people die as the fulfillment of this risk is not as bad as the outcome in which deaths do not occur but people are afraid and avoid civil society. However, many people would give up civil society and stay home through terror because they *over*estimate the probability of death. They would run the risk and tolerate some of them being killed rather than give up civil society *if* they did not overestimate the probability of death. Now we must deal with this objection.

In all of the driving cases considered so far, the deaths occur to people who are trying to participate in civil society. Many deaths also occur to people while or as a consequence of participating in civil society. ST typically kills people on the occasion of their participation in civil society, which is why avoiding civil society is a response to the fear of death, as it eliminates the occasion for the deaths. We might describe the causal route as follows: Participating in civil society (or means to it) leads to deaths, while not participating in civil society (or means to it) eliminates these deaths.

By contrast, we could imagine other cases in which it is also true that only those who try to or do participate in civil society are put at risk but without it being true that they are at risk on the occasion of trying to or participating in civil society. Rather, undergoing some risk that will eventuate in death for some is just a condition of the availability of civil society. We might describe this causal route as follows: Accepting risk of death and some actual deaths allows us to participate in civil society, while not accepting risk of death and some deaths prevents us from participating in civil society. Consider the following two cases as illustrations:

D3. Villains control the route that people must take in order to reach civil society. The villains will allow people to pass only if they are permitted to select a few people every month at random to be killed in their homes. The risk to each person of being killed is no greater than his risk of dying on the highway in an accident or from ST while participating in civil society, and the latter risks no longer exist. **D4.** Everything is as in D3, except that the villains target only those who are interested in participating in civil society and kill a few of them every month in their homes. The risk to each person of being killed is no greater than the risk of dying on the highway or from ST while participating in civil society, and the latter risks no longer exist.

It might be claimed that in these cases, too, we would each prefer a world in which we faced the risk of death and in which a few deaths occurred rather than have the villains cause all of us, by nonharmful means, to be afraid and so to give up civil society. This judgment is given as support for the claim that though the outcome in which the deaths come about by villainy is morally worse than when they do not, it is not as bad as no such deaths but instead fear leading to the absence of civil society.

(v) The issue we have been dealing with in (iii) and (iv) is whether smaller losses to each of many people (such as fear leading to nonparticipation in civil society), which will amount to elimination of civil society, is a worse state of affairs than a few killings in that group of people. Suppose, for argument's sake, that the answer is yes. (This would imply that we cannot rank the badness of states of affairs just by considering how badly off the worst-off people in them would be.) What would this imply about the wrongness of producing each state of affairs? Suppose a terrorist had a choice between pressing one button that would certainly cause a few deaths of certain people or another button that produced no deaths but caused terror leading to the collapse of (non-life-preserving elements of) civil society.[43] Would he commit a more serious moral wrong if he pressed the second button rather than the first? I do not think so. For it may be a more serious wrong to do something that would result in a better state of affairs rather than something that results in a worse state of affairs.

This is a common view among nonconsequentialists. Typical examples involve the impermissibility of harming a few people in order to save many others. In these cases, however, if one does not harm some, one will not have harmed others but only not saved them from some harm. If we were given a choice between killing one person and killing five, other things being equal, even a nonconsequentialist would say that it is a less serious wrong to kill one. Suppose that this is because we cause (rather than allow) the harm in both cases, and more harm is a worse state of affairs than less harm. Then if the destruction of civil society through terror is a worse state of affairs than a few people being killed, why does a terrorist not do a less serious wrong if he kills a few rather than causing terror and destroying civil society? For him it is a choice between causing one or the other.

It might be said that when the terrorist kills, he is completely responsible for the deaths, but in pressing the other button he at least shares responsibility with his victim for the collapse of civil society if there is N terror. For this reason, it might be said, he commits a less serious wrong in doing the latter. That is, he only brings about a state in which people make bad judgments based on fear that may itself be inappropriate. I think that we should put aside this issue of responsibility in trying to defend the view that it is a more serious wrong to kill the few. The issue we should focus on instead is the difference it makes to what we should cause when the worse state of affairs would have in it at least as many individuals who are as badly off as others will be in less bad states of affairs—for example, at least one person will be dead whether we kill five or one—in contrast to worse states of affairs in which this is not true. Consider a different example. Suppose that, given the choice between saving many people from total paralysis and saving a few from death, we should do the former because we thereby prevent a worse state of affairs. This need not imply that it is permissible to direct a threat where it will kill a few people instead of toward totally paralyzing many. This is so even though it would be permissible to direct a threat to where it will kill a few instead of to where it will kill many.[44]

Why may we not kill the few rather than produce (what we are assuming for the sake of argument is) the worse state of affairs, in which many people will each suffer a lesser loss? When it is permissible to do something to people, this reflects morality's endorsement of a certain status persons have as individuals, one by one. (When we let bad things happen to people, morality is not thereby endorsing the bad that is being done to them.) It shows greater disrespect to the high status of a person to kill him than to paralyze him or terrorize him, for it endorses the view that it is permissible to violate a person in a more serious way. Violating a few strong rights involves a greater wrong *to each* than violating the weaker rights of many because doing the latter need not imply that it is ever permissible to do something to someone that is as wrong as wrongfully killing him. Hence the act that produces the worse state of affairs can be more respectful of persons even if it insults more people and would make for a worse state of affairs.

I conclude two things here: (1) The wrong done to each person is greater when the few are killed than when each of many is terrorized and deprived of civil society; and (2) the seriousness of the wrong done when many are affected should be ranked by the worst one wrongfully does to any given person and only after that by the numbers affected.[45] Hence it is open for us to say that the ST agent does his greatest wrong against a populace in killing a few rather than in only causing terror to a greater number of people that shuts down non-life-preserving aspects of civil society, even if the latter were the worse state of affairs.[46]

2. Harm

We have already said that the harm involved in ST is severe since it is often death. This is the much more serious part of ST than the terror per se, I believe, at least because it involves doing a greater wrong to a person. One of the oddities of the term "terrorism" is that a nondistinctive part of ST (i.e., a part that occurs in non-terror killing) has a greater role in making terrorism wrong than the distinctive part of it that gives it its name. Even if ST were unsuccessful in causing any deaths, increasing the probability of death for insufficient reason can also make the terrorist agent's act seriously wrong. And even if the deaths from ST are less frequent and less numerous than those from car accidents, it is not irrational to be more concerned with crimes than with accidents. It is consistent with being less afraid of being attacked by a criminal than of getting a deadly disease to insist that wrongfull acts be extirpated first before health care is provided. So it is not necessarily irrational to spend more money on stopping ST than on stopping accidents.

Of course, generating terror alone as an end in itself, as a necessary productive means, or even as a side effect can sometimes be rights-violating conduct that one can appropriately resist. Nothing I have said in comparing terror per se with severe harm per se implies that causing the terror cannot add a wrong-making feature to an act and contribute to the prima facie wrongness of ST or that it is not often impermissible to do what causes people terror independent of any harm. But if the terrorized response is not entirely rational and is also subject to inner control by persons, this bad effect—unlike grave harm—might sometimes be avoided in some less costly way than stamping out or even defending against the people who try to produce it.

G. THE TERROR-FROM-HARM/HARM-FOR-TERROR/TERROR-FOR-GOAL DISTINCTIONS

Now consider the possible contribution to the prima facie wrongness of ST of the interaction of harm and terror. (This is in contrast to the mere addition of the factors.) We should consider the interaction of terror and harm because it is always possible that a factor like terror, considered on its own, has less weight than a factor like harm, considered on its own, but when terror is placed in a particular context with harm, its importance might become greater.[47]

1. Terror from Harm

Is terror a worse or a greater contribution to prima facie wrongness when it is caused by actual harm that has already occurred than when it is caused by bombing trees, as in the Trees Case? Earlier, in section IIIF1(a), I said that when impermissible harm is the cause of terror, those terrorized may complain, as they should not have been terrorized given the way the terror was brought about. In addition, along with the misery and trauma of loss, sympathy for those actually harmed accompanies terror when terror comes from known grave harm that has already occurred. The terror may even interfere with proper mourning for those already lost. This makes the event (if not the terror itself) worse than terror in the Trees Case and can contribute to the wrongness of ST. (Of course, in the Trees Case, people might not merely fear future harm; they might incorrectly believe that others had been harmed. The misery and trauma relating to others would then also occur even if they are not truly justified. But there could be no interference with proper mourning.) But are these factors plus terror worse than death?

No. To test this claim, imagine that we could either engage in psychological counseling to stop NCs from suffering terror, misery, and trauma caused by the known deaths of NCs in group A or stop the deaths of NCs in group B. Presumably, we should do the latter. This supports the conclusion that the deaths are worse.

2. Harm for Terror

Is causing death worse and/or a greater contribution to the wrongness of an act because it is used to create terror rather than for other purposes? For example, is it a greater moral wrong if one is killed as a means to starting terror rather than as human tinder in the Human Tinder Case? What if the terror is created to be a mere mechanical response that will interfere with a military operation, as in the Stampede Case, in contrast to being created in order to change the judgment and will of people in politics? It seems morally worse to have wrongful harm done to one for an effect that is intrinsically worse, and this could bear on the seriousness of the wrong. If creating terror in NCs is a greater wrong than setting aflame a military facility, then it will be morally worse to cause the death for terror. If will-undermining terror for political purposes is uglier for the victims, but producing mechanical terror in them is a greater wrong, then it will be morally worse to cause the death in order to produce mechanical terror. (This does not mean that it makes sense to fear the morally worse deaths more.)

    In this interaction between harm and terror, it is still the victim of harm who should be the focus of our concern with the badness and wrongness of ST rather than the victim of terror per se. Here, a distinctive part of terror killing (that is, the terror) may make the killing that is necessary, given one's act, to produce the terror morally worse and (sometimes) a greater wrong. However, the nondistinctive part of terror killing (that is, the killing) is still the part that is morally most significant and most to be feared (in virtue of death).

3. Terror for Goal

Some may think that it is morally bad that people's appropriate, terrified response to harm to others is used for the terrorists' further aims. This focuses on a further wrong done to the people who are responding to the harm. It introduces the further distinction between using terror for a goal and using harm for terror. However, I think that the concern about misusing the person terrorized should pale in comparison to the concern for the person gravely harmed, especially if he is harmed to bring about terror. It is consideration of the Trees Case that leads me to this conclusion. For in these cases there is no harm created, only people's terror as a necessary means, given one's act, to some goal, and a less serious moral wrong occurs.

H. SUMMARY

On the basis of our discussion in section III, I believe we can conclude the following: (a) The fact that a nonlegitimate state acts sometimes helps make ST or NST prima facie wrong. (b) Harm and terror to NCs, alone or together, help make

ST or NST prima facie wrong. (c) That the harm or terror is causally necessary, given one's act, to produce one's end, helps make ST or NST prima facie wrong. (d) That harm or terror play a role in undermining people's judgment, will, and involvement in civil society helps make ST or NST prima facie wrong. (e) That undermined judgment and will are causally necessary, given one's act, to produce one's end helps make ST or NST prima facie wrong. These factors will not make an act wrong (or, possibly even make it ST) if the act has other effects that need not be produced by harm and terror and that can justify the harm and terror.

Distinctive features of ST or NST are the intention to harm and terrorize NCs as an end or a means. But the distinctive intentions in themselves do not account for the prima facie wrongness of ST. Nevertheless, the intentions can be wrong and be appropriately resented even if they do not make the act impermissible. The distinctive element of terror in ST also does not play as large a role in accounting for the prima-facie wrongness of ST as does the harm it causes, which is an element it shares with nonterror killings.

IV. Determining When Standard Terrorism Might Be Permissible

Despite all of the factors that make for the prima-facie wrongness of ST, we cannot conclude that a terrorist act is wrong until we consider other things. We have already seen that on a "meaning" conceptual analysis of "terrorism," it is terrorism when Baby Killer Nation bombs militarily useful Nazi targets in a manner that is no different from how the Resistance would do this, though it does so with the intention of terrorizing NCs. If the meaning theory were correct, then some acts of terrorism would be permissible. But now I wish to abstract from such cases, in which the act that harms and terrorizes is permissible because it also has other effects that are useful in a conflict and that could justify deaths and terror as side effects. Could even acts whose effects can produce a good only via harm and terror sometimes be permissible? To decide, I think we must consider the following points.

We must consider both the importance and kind of good effect that will occur because of the terrorism and whether terrorism is the only way to produce that effect. (These are analogous to the proportionality of good to evil and the necessity conditions of standard just war theory, except that the latter are put in terms of good goals sought rather than good effects.) These factors must be considered if one is a "threshold deontologist" rather than an absolutist about the wrongness of certain means. A threshold deontologist holds that means that are most often impermissible even if they are necessary to produce overall good or to avoid overall evil can become permissible if the evil to be avoided or the good to be produced is great enough and of the right type and there is no other way to achieve it.

To imagine a case where such terrorism is permissible, suppose that a Resistance movement was fighting an immensely powerful Nazi nation and that it would lose the fight without a small amount of terrorism and win it with this terrorism. I assume that it is objectively true and reasonable to believe that such a nation is a very bad threat. (What if someone thinks that the United States is an infidel nation and as such a major threat to souls and he bombs the WTC for that reason? What if someone thinks that France is a major threat in virtue of its worldwide distribution of alcoholic beverages and therefore bombs the Eiffel Tower? Believing that some group is a tremendous source of evil is not enough to make what one believes true or reasonable and not enough to make one's terrorist act permissible.)

In cases where terrorism is not the only means available, we must consider the means and their effects that would or could be used instead of terror killing. For example, suppose that near a park that contains no military operations there is a military facility. Suppose that if that facility is struck (for militarily sound reasons), then ten thousand people would be killed and more terrorized as a side effect. Instead, three hundred people in the park could be directly killed in order to terrorize other people. Furthermore, suppose that an agent would achieve his aims equally well with either strategy. There are two major variants of this Park and Military Facility Case.

1. First Variant of the Park and Military Facility Case

A small subsection of the *very same people* who would have been killed if the military facility had been hit would die if the park is hit instead for terrorist purposes. Suppose it would have been wrong to bomb the park if it were all one could have done. I suggest that it would be morally better to bomb the park instead of bombing the military facility. This is so though it involves using the harm to people in the park as necessary means and though we assume that this involves a type of causal role for people that can sometimes make an act impermissible when other acts with the same deaths as a side effect would be permissible. In this case, such substitution of one act is right because the very same people who would die anyway are killed, and other people are thereby not killed. This is an example of an act which on its own would be impermissible becoming the thing to do secondarily as a substitute for some other act.

(a). Some cases involving such substitution of acts involve in the substituted act being permissible or even the only permissible harmful act (as we shall see in [b]). But we can extend substitution reasoning to cases where an act that would be impermissible on its own should be substituted for another *impermissible* act, resulting in the substituted act still being a wrong act, just a less seriously wrong act. Imagine that the Park and Military Facility Case involves Al Qaeda attacking the United States, when the United States is perfectly just and it is only reasonable to recognize this. Al Qaeda has no goal that justifies causing great collateral damage by bombing the military facility. Its bombing the park instead of alternatively bombing the military facility—which is the correct choice of the two—would be a true case of doing the lesser evil, as the act would still be an evil and would not be a permissible act at all. We can call it a *substitute wrong*, by which I mean an act that it would have been wrong to perform if it were the only act possible to achieve a goal yet that should be substituted for another wrong act (bombing the military

facility), all the while retaining its status as a wrong act.[48] At least part of the justification for the substitution of one act for the other is that the number of lives lost will be very greatly reduced, and all those who die as mere means would have been dead as a side effect in any case. Hence no one is worse off than he would have been and some are better off (which creates a Pareto-optimal outcome). In addition, an underlying idea is that the stronger moral constraint against doing an act that requires harm and terror as a means to producing an outcome is not as strong when the same harm and terror will not be avoided by abiding by the constraint.[49]

(b). Now imagine a case in which it would have been permissible to bomb the military facility despite collateral death and terror. For example, imagine that the United States is controlled by Nazis, and the Resistance would do this action. If a much smaller subsection of the very same people who would die if the Resistance bombed the military facility would die if it bombed the park instead, then I believe that bombing the park would no longer be a substitute wrong. It would be permissible—even becoming the only permissible harmful act—and not merely a less seriously wrong act. This is so even if bombing the park would have been wrong (in virtue of how the victims were used as mere means to producing a goal) if it were the only act the Resistance could have performed. As a substitute for a permissible act that would have caused the deaths of the same people who will die in the park plus many more, what would be impermissible on its own becomes permissible (and even the only permissible harmful act) as a substitute. It is secondarily permissible. (This is an instance of what I call the Principle of Secondary Permissibility.)[50]

When people speak about doing the lesser evil, they sometimes speak as though they have in mind a choice between two acts that remain wrong whichever one is done, but this model of a substitute wrong is present only in our case in 1(a) involving Al Qaeda. By contrast, when we do an act (that would otherwise be wrong) because it involves less harm instead of a more harmful permissible act, the second act seems not to be a lesser moral evil; rather it is permissible and even becomes the only permissible harmful act. This reminds us that the act that gets supplanted was originally permissible even though it would cause more harm than an originally impermissible act. Hence, the supplanted act was worse in that sense (if not a greater moral evil). It is because of this that, in some cases, what was originally a greater moral evil (bombing the park) can become permissible secondarily when it involves less harm overall and no more harm to the same people who otherwise would have been harmed.

(c). In the cases in 1(a) and (b), we moved away from the typical case of ST, which involves killing people who would not soon die anyway. But we can reintroduce this factor. For suppose that everything is as in 1(b) except that those who can permissibly bomb the military facility would not actually do so because they cannot bring themselves to harm so many innocent NCs as a side effect. Then they find out that they can achieve their aims by directly killing a small subset of those NCs that they still can (are able to) but will not permissibly kill as side effects. These are people who would not die shortly anyway, but they would be alive only

because the Resistance refrains from doing what it still can permissibly do. Due to this, I think it becomes permissible for the Resistance to do to the smaller subset of people whatever I argued in 1(b) that it could permissibly do if it would alternatively have actually permissibly killed the same people plus others as a side effect.[51]

2. Second Variant of the Park and Military Facility Case

Let us now assume that the few people in the park who will be killed and terrorized as a means to victory are entirely different from any of the large number who would have been killed as side effects in bombing the military facility.

(a). Suppose bombing the military facility would have been impermissible and bombing the park would also have been impermissible were it the only thing that could have been done. Then this might still make bombing the park the less serious wrong (despite its use of the morally less-favored role for people in producing a goal). This is a further instance of the idea of a substitute wrong. However, because different people would be killed, here it is just the great difference in the number who would die that might move us above a threshold on the deontological constraint that rules out harm to people having a necessary causal role in producing an outcome.

(b). What if bombing the military facility would have been permissible (in the imaginary Nazi United States Case) considered on its own, but bombing the park would have been impermissible even if only it could have been done? When entirely different people will be affected in the park from those in the military-facility bombing, and they will be in the disfavored necessary-means role, it is quite likely that it will remain wrong to bomb the park rather than the military facility. For we cannot, in general, do equal or lesser harms to fewer people in an impermissible way in order to avoid doing equal or greater harm to a greater number of entirely different people in a permissible way. (This assumes that the additional number killed do not constitute enough of an evil that preventing it moves us above the threshold for not killing the smaller number of people as a mere means to producing a goal.)

Hence, in addition to what was said in section IIIC(2), we cannot say whether terrorist acts should not be done, at least until we know the number who will be harmed if another act is done, who those affected will be, and whether the alternative act is permissible or impermissible. This is in addition to having to know whether a threshold on abiding by constraints on treating people in certain ways is reached. This examination of terrorism reveals that no easy answers are to be had on the general topic of the moral permissibility and impermissibility of terrorist acts, though in specific cases the answers can be clear.

Notes

1. The bulk of this chapter was published as an article of the same name in *Legal Theory* 12 (2006), 19–69. That article began as an invited presentation at a conference on terrorism organized by Prof. Joseph Raz at Columbia Law School. This chapter also incorporates parts of my

"Types of Terror Bombing and Shifting Responsibility," in *Action, Ethics, and Responsibility*, eds. J. K. Campbell, M. O'Rourke, and H. Silverstein (Cambridge, MA: MIT Press, 2010), pp. 281–294. I benefited from comments on earlier versions of those articles by L. Alexander, E. Harman, J. Heale, J. McMahan, D. Parfit, L. Temkin, S. Kagan, R. Chang, J. Raz, S. Scheffler, an anonymous reviewer for *Legal Theory*, and members of seminars, conferences, and colloquia at Columbia Law School, the University of California at Berkeley Law School, Massachusetts Institute of Technology, the London School of Economics, the Cambridge University Moral Sciences Club, and the 2006 Inland Northwest Philosophy Conference. "Terrorism and Several Moral Distinctions" was the predecessor of "Terrorism and Intending Evil," *Philosophy & Public Affairs* 36 (2008): 157–186, a revised version of which is chap. 2 in my *Ethics for Enemies: Terror, Torture, and War* (Oxford: Clarendon, 2011). Some of the conclusions reached in "Terrorism and Several Moral Distinctions" were modified and superseded in "Terrorism and Intending Evil," and endnotes 19, 20, and 23 in this chapter present some of those changes.

2. Punishing opponents might be end in itself. What if agents deliberately, with the intention of terrorizing people, damage only property? For example, agents who dislike modern architecture might bomb certain modern buildings. People would then fear that if they build modern architecture, their buildings will be destroyed. These agents would then be engaged in NST. Suppose that people are killed as a mere side effect of these attacks and that people come to fear death rather than fear having their new buildings destroyed, though this would not have been the intention of these terrorists. It seems that the agents are terrorists in virtue of aiming to terrorize people into not building modern architecture, but the fear of death they actually create does not account for why they are terrorists.

3. Luc Bovens reminded me of this point.

4. If God is considered a state agent, this action would be NST.

5. Jeff McMahan believes that this is so. Henceforth, I shall use "prima facie" to also cover "pro tanto".

6. I have argued elsewhere that a person can bring about the means to his end without necessarily intending (and even refusing to intend) these means. This is one reason to discuss these distinctions separately. See F. M. Kamm, "The Doctrine of Triple Effect and Why a Rational Agent Need Not Intend the Means to His End," supplement, *Proceedings of the Aristotelian Society* 74(1) (July 2000): 21–39, and F. M. Kamm, *Intricate Ethics* (Oxford University Press, 2007). For example, suppose that destroying a munitions plant cannot help one's cause unless people are also harmed and terrified so that they do not rebuild the plant. If an agent bombs the munitions plant only because he foresees that the side effects of harm and terror are unavoidable, this need not mean, I believe, that he intends to bring about the harm and terror.

7. There are many well-known problems with relying on intending harm and terror as grounds for the impermissibility of acts that I shall ignore here. For a description of some of them, see F. M. Kamm, "Nonconsequentialism," in *Blackwell's Guide to Ethical Theory*, ed. H. LaFolette (Oxford: Blackwell, 2000), 205–226.

8. I actually think that such justifications for collateral damage are incomplete and faulty. For more on this, see F. M. Kamm, "Failures of Just War Theory," *Ethics* 114 (2003): 650–692.

9. Intentions are often important because people who have them will act differently in changed circumstances from those without the intentions even when they act in the same way in some circumstances. I am supposing throughout this discussion that there is no opportunity for different intentions to show up in different behavior and different effects. All behavior and effects are the same; only the intentions differ.

10. These points were raised by Jeff McMahan and Shelly Kagan.

11. I owe this Gricean point to Matthew Boyle.

12. This point was also suggested by Matthew Boyle.

13. This is like a case that Judith Thomson imagines in her "Self-Defense," *Philosophy & Public Affairs* 20 (1991), 282–310, where she argues against intentions determining permissibility. She, however, does not use the case to investigate how we should nonmorally categorize an act.

14. Immanuel Kant, *Groundwork of the Metaphysics of Morals*, trans. H. J. Paton (1958). (New York: Harper & Row, 1964).

15. See Thomas Scanlon, "Permissibility and Intention," *Proceedings of the Aristotelian Society* (2000), Suppl. 74, 301–317.

16. That one act is a more serious wrong than another need not mean that it is more wrong. Some hold that all wrong acts are equally wrong. However, murdering someone is a more serious wrong than breaking someone's arm, other things being equal.

17. We could also use a Bad Man Trolley case as an analogue, but I will omit this for brevity's sake.

18. I take it that the fact that an agent has two intentions in acting is not the same as his act being overdetermined. I reserve the latter term to refer to cases where either intention without the other would suffice to lead to the act. But it is possible that only one or none of several intentions is sufficient on its own to lead to an act.

19. It is important to note that in a subsequent article, "Terrorism and Intending Evil," I added the following remarks:

> However, this conclusion may be a mistake . . . suppose that although Al Qaeda would have bombed the military WTC at t1 when this would have only destroyed the building, it would also have put off bombing from t1 to t2 if it could also kill and terrorize Civilians at t2 . . . Then the facts that Al Qaeda would have destroyed the military facility on its own, if that were all it could do, and that it acts on its intention to kill and terrorize Civilians conditional on destroying the military WTC, do not show that there is no Terrorism. This is because Al Qaeda, in this imaginary case, could have achieved its (impermissible) military goal at t1 without killing anyone but it chose not to. So Al Qaeda does not do only what someone who lacked the intention to harm and terrorize but was interested in military victory would have done, namely, bomb the military WTC at t1 instead of t2.
>
> However, suppose that it was not possible to select a time to hit the military WTC when no Civilians nearby would be harmed. Then the fact that Al Qaeda would do even an impermissible act of bombing a military facility in a just United States with the intention to harm and terrorize Civilians need not imply that its act is Terrorism. This is so if it also intends the impermissible act of destroying a military facility, that intention would have been sufficient for its act, and it is a condition of pursuing its other intention to harm and terrorize. (172–173)

20. But I think it is important to note that in "Terrorism and Intending Evil" I altered the conclusion:

> [I]n order to determine if the wrong act is in the category of Terrorism, we have to consider (a) whether Al Qaeda would have bombed the nonmilitary WTC in order, for example, to show how vulnerable its enemy was, even if no deaths or terror would have occurred, and (b) how it picked the time of its attack. If it chose to bomb when it did

only because both destruction of the WTC and harm and terror to Civilians would occur, rather than at another time when only destruction of the WTC would occur, its wrong act was Terrorism rather than impermissibility [sic] bombing with impermissible collateral damage. (p. 174)

In addition, I went on to discuss other aspects of the actual 9/11 case that I thought I had missed in the article that constitutes the bulk of this chapter; see note 1.

21. These cases have their roots in my discussion elsewhere of various trolley cases and Munitions Grief cases. See F. M. Kamm, *Morality, Mortality*, vol. 2 (New York: Oxford University Press, 1996).

22. On this, see the article and book cited in note 6 in this chapter. I argue there that the Counterfactual Test for intending fails to distinguish acting "because of" and "in order to."

23. The discussion in section D (which I have revised for clarity's sake from the article in which it first appeared) draws on distinctions that are discussed in much greater detail in the book cited in note 21; Kamm, "Towards the Essence of Nonconsequentialist Constraints," in *Fact and Value: Essays for Judith Thomson*, eds. A. Byrne et al. (Cambridge, MA: MIT, 2001), 155–182; and F. M. Kamm, *Intricate Ethics* (New York: Oxford University Press, 2007). I subsequently revised this description of the sort of role for harm and terror that might make their production prima facie impermissible and also tried to deal with cases where no effect of one's act could justify the harm and terror but the act, while impermissible, was not terrorism. See also *Ethics for Enemies*, 95–97, and "Terrorism and Intending Evil."

24. It might be said that we could isolate the acts that require harm and terror in order to produce goals by also looking for the acts that it is only reasonable to think someone must intend in virtue of their causing harm and terror. By contrast, acts in which someone actually intends harm and terror but that can produce a goal in some other way are ones in which a reasonable agent could have a different intention (making reference to the other route to his goal). Why not then say that acts that could be done (by a reasonable agent) only with a bad intention are impermissible? One response is that in the Cow Case the act is impermissible, though a reasonable agent in that case does not require a bad intention to do the act, given that he believes there are cows below. (Perhaps the condition could be amended to say that a reasonable, fully informed agent could do the act only with a bad intention.) More important, we will decide that only an agent with a bad intention could do the act by looking at the properties of the act and its consequences (including, I believe, how it causally relates to its consequences). If these properties could not be the object of someone with only good intentions, then the act will be declared impermissible. Hence it is really the properties of the act and its consequences, not the possible intentions of agents, that determine the act's permissibility.

25. I would now—subsequent to the publication of the article on which this chapter is based—accept that something more complicated could be involved in torture. See on this David Sussman, "What's Wrong with Torture?" *Philosophy & Public Affairs* 33 (Winter 2004): 1–33; and my *Ethics for Enemies*, chap. 1.

26. Jeremy Waldron draws a similar distinction. What he refers to as "Arendtian" fear corresponds to what I call "mechanical," and what he refers to as "Jack Benny" fear corresponds to what I called "nonmechanical." In Arendtian fear, one is in an unreasoning panic; in Jack Benny fear, a threat leads one to weigh the costs and benefits of giving in. However, Waldron does not discuss the uses of either type of fear in the pursuit of achieving a purely military goal. See his "Terrorism and the Uses of Terror," *Journal of Ethics* 8 (2004): 5–35.

27. Waldron also emphasizes the latter possibility.

28. This section is drawn from "Types of Terror Bombing and Shifting Responsibility".

29. Unfortunately, I am so far unable to completely reference this program.

30. Prof. John Lewis, Ashland University (in conversation, Bowling Green University, November 2007).

31. It was Professor Lewis's view that military operations also were meant to undermine the will to fight, but that was not their sole function.

32. This is different from creating pressure on the government itself by killing and terrorizing its citizens, thus making the government incapable of fulfilling its duty to protect its citizens. Here the fate of the citizens would be used to alter the judgment and will of the government. And the government might be giving in not from fear but from a sense of duty to care for its citizens.

33. There appears to be a problem of explaining why terror of grave harm is generated by infrequent ST such as we have known, for the actual chance of being killed seems to be much smaller than that of dying in a traffic accident. Indeed, if one alters one's behavior to avoid being terror-killed to the extent one can by, say, not going out to public venues as much in one's car, then one may actually reduce one's chances of dying from what they were *ex ante* ST. (In the case of bioterrorism, however, even if the probability of its occurring were low, the enormous number of people who would be severely harmed would make the expected disutility to each person very high. But even here, it seems to me to be an open question whether it is rational to fear in accordance with expected disutility or instead to give more weight to the low-probability element.)

Why is there terror of future attacks such as we have experienced already but no terror of going out in one's car? Some suggest that this is because there is a fear of lack of control; an individual can do nothing much to avoid ST, but one can drive safely to avoid the car accident. (Judith Thomson suggested this in conversation.) But why should this be important if, despite greater control, there is in fact a higher death rate on the highway than there would be from terror killing?

Perhaps, it may be said, fear is also appropriate when there is an increased chance of death (even if small) because one is not accustomed to that. But this suggests that while fear may reasonably occur after an attack, the fear should diminish over time as one becomes used to living with a small increase in the probability of great harm. Furthermore, a greater increase in the chance of death to which one is not accustomed may occur when the speed limit is raised moderately than when there is a chance of ST, yet there is no terror in going on the highway immediately after the speed limit is raised. What if road accidents occurred not one at a time but less frequently and involved large numbers of victims at once? Might the prospect of dying in such a mass death justify terror of driving? Why would it, if the probability of dying does not change? (Fear of flying is sometimes attributed to lack of personal control—though one puts oneself in the hands of an expert—and the prospect of mass death.)

All of this suggests that long-term terror in response to ST and perhaps even terror in the short term by those not actually in the vicinity of a repeatable ST attack would not be rational. (An alternative conclusion is that one should be much more frightened of going out on the road in a car than one is.)

34. Elizabeth Harman and Joseph Raz suggested this.

35. I owe this argument to Julian Lamont.

36. I owe this point to Jane Heale.

37. This was pointed out to me by Alex Voorhoeve and Michael Otsuka.

38. Some think that there is a human right not to be tortured. I do not think this is true if we understand by a human right one that *is had* by anyone just so long as he or she is a human being. (The following points derive from my discussion in Kamm, *Intricate Ethics*. I discuss torture further in *Ethics for Enemies*, chap. 1.) For consider the following case: A is about to kill B unjustifiably. It is permissible for us to kill A if this is necessary to stop the fatal attack on B. We are about to do this when we realize that we could stop A's attack by torturing him (physically and/or mentally) for a few hours (with a long-distance radar device). It would be better for him to be temporarily tortured than to be dead. It is not always morally appropriate to do something to a person because it would be better for him than something else we could do. (I discuss a case like this later on.) Nevertheless, I believe, it would be permissible to torture him against his will in the way described rather than kill him aganst his will in order to stop his attack. Furthermore, suppose it would be permissible to kill B to stop his attack, but we lacked the means to do this. Should we not be permitted to do what is less bad for him in order to stop his attack, and this includes torture in the manner described? It may be that there is a human right not be tortured in the sense that being a human being is enough to *give rise* to a right not to be tortured. (Indeed, this may be the correct way to understand any human right.) But this does not mean that this right cannot be defeated or forfeited on occasion, for example, in virtue of acts that the person performs. So some human beings may lack the right not to be tortured in certain ways in certain circumstances. It also may be true that someone's right not to be tortured is *not* defeated or forfeited merely because it would be useful to torture him when he is not doing or has not done acts that threaten others and whose bad effects could be stopped by torturing.

39. As noted earlier, I now believe this is an overly simple conception of torture. Rather than undermining a will, it may give someone a reason to do something but not just by pointing to a bad future prospect. Instead, it does something bad to him at the time. See also note 25.

40. If one actually had WMD, then spreading word of this fact could also involve NST. However, suppose others spread word of the fact that someone has WMD in order to produce terror that will help mobilize and hence protect potential victims. This would not be terrorism because the aim would be to serve the prudential interests of those who are terrorized. Another case of NST without harm to NCs involves terrorizing NCs in wartime by killing a combatant. For example, suppose that combatants are attacking you. You can stop them only by killing one of the combatants at the rear, near the NC population. Doing this will terrorize the NCs, who believe that you are trying to hit them, and they will then help stop the attack on you. In all of the cases I have described, terror is not produced by creating a false belief that NCs have already been harmed (e.g., by showing a three-dimensional video image of NCs being killed when in fact no NCs are being killed). However, doing this would also involve creating terror without harming any NCs.

41. Could we also say that it is wrong to kill an NC, A, not only because he has a right not to be killed but also because another NC, B, has a right that A not be killed as a means of terrorizing B? It seems odd to say this. Suppose that A is a condemned criminal who has no right not to be killed by the state executioner, but the killing of A will be carried out only in order to cause terror in ordinary citizen B. I do not think the fact that the killing is done to terrorize B makes killing A impermissible if the killing would be permissible even though terror is an unavoidable side effect. But perhaps it is correct to say that when terror comes about by means that are wrong quite independently of being a wrong way to terrorize B (e.g., it is a wrongful killing of NCs as an end or a means), then B can complain not only

about the wrongful killing and the terror caused but also about the fact that an act that should not have been done leads to terror. And the fact that an act that should not have been done also leads to terror can become an additional ground for condemning the wrong act.

42. A possibility that I did not consider in the article one which this chapter is based is that the Paradox of Risk is a sort of Prisoners' Dilemma: for each person it is not a great loss to give up civil society in order to eliminate a small chance of his dying. However, when everyone does this, what results is a state of affairs (no civil society at all) that is worse than a few deaths. However, ordinarily each person takes a small risk of dying in traffic accidents so as not to suffer the purely personal loss of not participating in civil society. This suggests that for each person it is a great loss to give up civil society in order to eliminate a small chance of his dying.

43. I would now add that this might be morally different from imposing a small risk on many that will lead to some certainly dying, as discussed earlier. However, suppose that the terrorist had a choice between (a) pressing a button that will cause the death of certain (though not necessarily identifiable) people at tn or (b) another button that will impose on each of many people a small risk that will eventuate in the same number of deaths at tn. Would it make a moral difference which he did?

44. I discussed this case in Kamm, *Morality, Mortality*, vol. 1.

45. It might be said that there are also arguments based on citizen responsibility and effectiveness in changing policy that can account for the wrongness of killing a few rather than only terrorizing many. First, if many citizens are thought to be responsible for a government's policy, then it is more just to impose smaller losses on each of the many than to impose a disproportionate greater loss on a few. But suppose that the citizens are not responsible for the government's current policy. They might still be in a position to change it in the future by voting the government out. Then from the point of view of effectiveness, it is again better to do what terrorizes many voters rather than killing a few (on the assumption that there is an exclusive choice between doing one or the other). I owe these points to Daniel Elstein.

46. It may also be true that sometimes, when a few deaths would occur because we fail to save lives (rather than because we cause deaths), it is wrong to fail to save the lives and instead save many more from lesser harms.

47. I refer to the general phenomenon that might be at play here as the principle of contextual interaction. See Kamm, *Morality, Mortality*, vol. 2, for more on this.

48. This is in contrast to speaking of "doing the lesser evil" as doing an act that is usually wrong but which can sometimes be justified so that it actually is permissible in some circumstances.

49. For more on this, see Kamm, *Morality, Mortality*, vol. 2; Kamm, "Failures of Just War Theory."

50. For more on this see Kamm, *Morality, Mortality*, vol. 2; Kamm, "Failures of Just War Theory."

51. For more on this, see Kamm, "Failures of Just War Theory." This analysis does not, I think, also apply to a variant of 1(a), where the act from which Al Qaeda would refrain is impermissible.

9

Self-Defense, Resistance, and Suicide: The Taliban Women

1. Harming and Injustices

Suppose it is asked "How should we address the greatest evils and injustices of our time?"

The first thing that might occur to one in response is how to determine whether some injustice or evil is greater than another. One approach is to consider how many people are going to be affected and to what degree they will be badly affected. One considers how badly off each individual will be and how many individuals will be so affected. But part of our question is to consider whether injustices and evils make a difference to how we should react in contrast to how we would react to a natural disaster in which as many people are each harmed as badly. An example bearing on this issue comes from Thomas Scanlon. Suppose you see an individual in one pool who is drowning, and you know he was wrongfully pushed into the water by a person trying to murder him. In another pool, farther away, there is another person who just fell in because a lightning bolt struck him. Should you decide whom to save based on the fact that in one case the person would die as the result of an injustice and in the other the person would die as a result of a natural disaster? Scanlon said no, that difference is irrelevant. You should decide on the basis of the probabilities of saving the individuals, assuming other factors are equal.[1] His aim was to show that the answer to why it is wrong to kill another person is *not* that it is a worse outcome when someone dies of unjust killing rather than from a natural disaster, for if it were (much) worse, you should save the victim of injustice, and this Scanlon thinks, is intuitively implausible.

I think I agree with Scanlon about whom to save in this case, but I do not think it shows that a victim's dying of injustice never contributes to our choice of whom to save. Certainly, if one has oneself pushed the person into the pool, one should take care of one's own victim before taking care of the other person. However, this will be true whether the other person is the victim of a natural disaster or of *someone else's* injustice. Consider another case: In one place, five people are being threatened with death by a group of terrorists. Elsewhere, there are five people being threatened with death by a volcano. I think the fact that we would stop an injustice in the process of happening if we went to the first place could matter to what we should do. (Notice that, in Scanlon's case, the act of the villain is over, and we can prevent only the unjust harm due to it.) Indeed, I think it could be reasonable to prevent indignity or unjust acts to one set of people rather than prevent even greater material harm, but due to natural causes, to another set of people. (We do this on a mass scale, e.g., if we invest more money in a police force rather than in health care.[2]) We could reasonably be concerned with preventing unjust acts and indignity and not only harm.

2. Permissible Responses to Injustice

With this as background, I want to discuss some other questions about only those people who are victims of injustice and moral evil (and not of natural disasters). If the rights of innocent persons are being seriously violated, we might first ask what it would be permissible for the victim himself to do and then what it might be permissible for others to do on his behalf. I shall be concerned with the outer limits of permissible action, that is, the most one could permissibly do. It certainly may not be permissible to do everything that is physically necessary and sufficient in order to stop injustices, as doing so may actually produce more injustice by being an unproportionate response. On the other hand, for reasons of prudence we may often choose not to do what is at the limit of what is permissible. However, knowing what the outer limits of permissibility are can help us see just how serious an injustice or moral evil is and why doing less than the most that is permissible would also be justified.

What is it permissible for a potential victim to do to a perpetrator? One factor we should recognize in answering this question may help us to distinguish between morally evil and unjust acts. I shall here consider such an evil act to be an unjust act that is done by a perpetrator whose *final goal* is to cause bad things such as pain, suffering, death, or humiliation to others.[3] Those who cause such things merely as means to another goal or those who cause such things as side effects need not do evil acts in this sense. Nevertheless, they may still act unjustly because, prima facie, we owe it to people not to treat them in these ways even though we do not seek the bad effects per se.

An unjust agent who does not do evil acts may be acting under false beliefs. Suppose he thinks that, when he causes his victims harm, he is carrying out the plans of God and this makes his act just. If this is actually a false belief, then his treatment of his victims is a violation of his victims' rights, and his act is unjust. Suppose an agent is in fact acting unjustly, though he himself does not recognize this. I think he can be liable to his victims' acts of self-defense just as if the agent's final goal were to cause pain, suffering, death, or humiliation. By saying such an agent is liable, I mean at least that, in virtue of what he has done, he has no complaints and is not wronged by his victims' response if it is necessary to stop the harm to them.[4] So I do not think that an evil act—as I have identified it—or knowledge by an agent of his injustice is necessary in order to respond in self-defense to an unjust act in the most forceful way possible, at least if this stops the act or harm from it. Perpetrators of unjust acts, evil or not, can be liable to certain harmful acts being done to them in order to stop their unjust acts.

Sometimes, however, the victim's resistance would not succeed as self-defense; that is, it would not stop the wrong act or the harm from it, and in some cases a victim can know this. (I shall call this "mere resistance.") Even in these cases, resistance that harms a perpetrator, though it does not help the victim, might be permissible, I think. Mere resistance might be justified only as an appropriate response to what the perpetrator is doing independently of its further useful consequences.[5] I shall return to this issue later.

Furthermore, I think that a victim may sometimes impose greater harm on a perpetrator than the latter would impose on his potential victim. Consider a hypothetical case called Locked in the House: Somebody will keep you (an innocent person) locked up in a house permanently. (He thinks God commands this as the appropriate way to treat you.) He is not going to kill you or physically harm you so long as you stay in the house, and you know that this is so. In one variant of this case, if you leave, he will attack you and even kill you. It seems to me that if the *only* way you could escape is by killing the perpetrator, it would be permissible to kill him. This is so even if we assume that what you do to him would be worse than what he would do to you if you did not try to escape. He is committing a serious injustice in keeping you in the house against your will, whether or not under threat of death if you leave, and that is going to count in determining what response is permissible.

Now suppose a gang of perpetrators, rather than one, will keep you locked up. They each act unjustly, and *they are all* liable to attack. Hence, you may kill *many* perpetrators so that you escape unjust confinement that itself will not cause your death.

In most places in the world, locking an innocent person in a house, as in the Locked in the House Case, is prohibited by law even if one treats the person well. Hence, in these places, the perpetrator would commit a *legal* injustice, acting contrary to law. However, suppose there were no law barring innocent people from being permanently locked up against their will in a house, sometimes under threat of death if they leave. Would this imply that it was morally wrong of the victim to kill the perpetrator in order to prevent or end his being locked up? I do not think so, for being locked up in this way when it is not a legal injustice is still a serious moral injustice, and it *should* be legally prohibited even if it is not. What if there is a law that actually makes it permissible or required to permanently lock up innocent people against their will in a house? Such a state-sponsored moral injustice seems to be grounds for morally justified rebellion if this is necessary to stop the injustice. It is not always morally wrong to disobey morally unjust laws. (It was not morally wrong of slaves to escape slavery in pre–Civil War America. If slaveholders tried to prevent this, a slave who resisted in self-defense in a manner proportionate to avoiding slavery would have done no moral wrong.)

Nevertheless, I think that victims ought to try to defend themselves with as little harm to those who are perpetrators as possible, as long as reducing the harm to the perpetrator is not likely to impose great costs on the victim. Subsequent punishment of perpetrators may impose additional harm on them when this is no longer needed to resist their injustice. But self-defensive harm is not punishment; it is needed both to resist a perpetrator and to help a victim. However, a victim's causing harm to a perpetrator while resisting him seems to be permissible even if it is not reasonable to expect that it will improve the victim's condition and it will, in fact, not improve his condition. Such mere resistance to unjust action as an appropriate response to it when it is occurring is also different from punishment. The latter could occur if acting during an unjust act is intended to produce harm to the perpetrator only after his act and its bad effects are over. Mere resistance, however, can raise special moral problems because there is no obvious goal whose attainment signals the end of permissible harm to a perpetrator the way a successful escape signals the end of permissible self-defensive harm. For this reason, mere resistance can be more harmful to a perpetrator than successful self-defense. It should not be engaged in when successful self-defense is possible, in part because escaping harm to oneself is a way of resisting the *effects* of a wrongful act while showing appropriate concern for the good whose importance helps account for the wrongfulness of the perpetrator's act. (This is so even if an unsuccessful wrongful attempt to harm the victim were to continue).

Finally, I think that, in the cases that I have described, it would be permissible for third parties to act on behalf of the victim, doing what the victim himself could permissibly do in self-defense and even in "mere resistance," at least if (but not only if) the victim approved of such intervention. Of course, third parties might choose not to act because of the cost to themselves, and I think that is also a permissible response if the cost is great enough.

(In these remarks, I have spoken only of action against a perpetrator. I shall here not deal with the problem of innocent bystanders who might be hurt in the course of a victim's self-defense or resistance or in the course of acts by others. This is a very complicated issue, though I think that innocent bystanders might sometimes permissibly be endangered in this way, though they, unlike perpetrators, would have their rights infringed and might be owed compensation.)

3. Taliban Women

A. SELF-DEFENSE AND MERE RESISTANCE.

In order to consider possible implications of what I have said for an actual injustice in our time, I shall take the example of the treatment of Taliban women prior to 2001 (Taliban Women Case). Suppose the Taliban women were kept essentially under "house arrest," as described in my previous hypothetical case. Suppose that they would be physically attacked, raped, or killed only if they left the houses on their own.[6] And suppose they were sequestered because the Taliban truly believed that the word of God required this control of women. Furthermore, we can assume that those who do this to the women represent the views of the group that controls the state, so their actions are not contrary to state law and may actually enforce it. Does what I have said in part 2, using the Locked in the House Case, imply that nothing about the perpetrators would stand in the way of these women being morally justi-fied in killing the perpetrators if this were necessary in order to free themselves?

It might be said that there is a morally important difference between the two cases. In Locked in the House, we might have been imagining that if you escaped the perpetrator's house and his physical attacks upon you once you left, you would rejoin a society in which you would be safe from attack and further attempts to restrict your liberty. That is, your self-defense would have improved your condition not just with respect to the perpetrator's control over you but overall as well. In the Taliban Women Case, a woman who escaped from the house and her perpetrator's power would enter into perhaps a more hostile environment populated with other potential perpetrators. (This might not be true if her escape were part of a group uprising strong enough to ward off further threats, but I shall assume this will not occur.) If a woman who successfully defends herself against one perpetrator realizes that she gains little, if anything, for herself in terms of overall improved conditions or even makes her fate worse, does this imply that it is morally wrong of her to attack and even kill those who keep her in the house and may physically harm her if she leaves? I do not think it does.

If someone commits the serious moral injustice we are considering, it seems to me that he is liable to being attacked if this is necessary to stop the wrong he does even though others will step in to take his place and commit the same or even more serious wrongs to the same victim. The perpetrator is not wronged, and he has no complaint if this is done to him rather than allowing him and not others to harm the victim. It is for the victim to choose whether she will act contrary to prudence (i.e., making herself worse off) in order to react against an injustice to her. After all, would we say that those who rose up in the Warsaw Ghetto during World War II had no right to kill some Nazis who were oppressing them when they knew their fate would not improve and might worsen because other Nazis would take the place of those they successfully killed in self-defense?[7]

What if only a severe nonlethal attack by the Taliban woman on the present perpetrator is possible but she knows it is not sufficient to free her from that perpetrator? This is a case of mere resistance to an injustice, which cannot stop any part of the injustice but only harm the perpetrator. It seems to me that the perpetrator is liable to being harmed by his victim simply as an appropriate response to the wrongful act he is doing even if it is known that this will not be effective in stopping or reducing the bad effect of what he is doing. Analogously, suppose a victim knows that a perpetrator will certainly succeed in raping her. The rapist is not immune to being attacked by the victim during the course of the rapist's successful act. The victim may even resist (if it is an appropriate nonpunitive response to what is being done to her) by doing what she foresees will lead to the death of the rapist following his successful rape.

I conclude that it would be morally permissible, even if not wise, for Taliban women to sometimes even kill God-fearing perpetrators who would not kill the women if they remained in the house. The women would also be justified in mere resistance to the perpetrators as it is an appropriate response to wrongdoing independent of good consequences. What I have said also implies that third parties could appropriately respond to wrongdoing with mere resistance, in addition to being permitted to do on behalf of the women what the women would be permitted to do in self-defense.[8]

I emphasize that there may be prudential reasons why neither third parties nor the women should do these things because the consequences would be worse for the women or the third parties. In addition, side-effect harm to innocent bystanders, including harsher treatment of other women, could be a moral reason for not killing perpetrators. The important point is that if it were unwise or morally impermissible for anyone to react in the extreme way I have described, when killing would be necessary in order to free certain women or even merely to resist unjust acts against them, it would not be because the perpetrators have a right not to be harmed to this extent.

Of course, an additional important question is whether killing perpetrators would really be necessary in order for the women to escape (or even to appropriately resist) being kept in the house. If not, then in these circumstances, *out of concern for the rights of perpetrators*, killing might become impermissible.[9] For example, suppose several women in a household could overpower those guarding them or a woman could use nonlethal means to escape. Suppose communication was possible between women in different households so that nonviolent group resistance would be effective. Then killing might be impermissible. (However, if such nonviolent resistance would be put down violently, killing might again become necessary as a means of self-defense or mere resistance.) If alternative means besides killing were possible, but the cost of using them were too high—for example, alternatives made it more likely that women would be recaptured—then violence might again be permissible. This is not to deny that supererogatory continuation of nonviolent resistance by particular women might be more effective in ultimately altering the status of all women in the country.

B. CAUSE FOR WAR?

Jeff McMahan and Thomas Hurka have said that war by an outside nation merely in order to free Taliban women would not have been justified.[10] McMahan gave as his justification that third parties would be permitted to kill in defense of others *only* if those others would be permitted to kill in their own defense. However, victims who lack equal legal rights to employment and political participation are not justified in killing those who denied them legal equality in order to achieve legal equality.

Neither McMahan nor Hurka dealt with whether being sequestered at home, with or without threat of death if one left, was a sufficient reason for killing those who kept one sequestered. Suppose it was a sufficient reason at least sometimes and only those perpetrators would be killed in a self-defensive action. Then McMahan might agree that third parties could permissibly kill the perpetrators, at least if the women consented to this. But would this be sufficient to show that a nation-state could permissibly declare war (or even engage in "targeted assassinations") to free the Taliban women from "house arrest"? If not, then there must be some reason other than that the women themselves and third-party individuals may not kill the Taliban perpetrators that stands in the way of a just war by a nation-state. It may be issues of state sovereignty that impede intervention. (Currently, exceptions are made only in cases of genocide.) Also, war may involve out-of-proportion amounts of side-effect killing of innocent bystanders or greater side-effect harm to the women themselves than they choose to risk. Suppose the women would be permitted to kill their perpetrators in self-defense or mere resistance, but they choose not to in order to avoid greater harm to themselves. Then if they would be harmed to the same degree in a war (or by the acts of any third parties), then it seems impermissible for others to attack perpetrators whom it is permissible for the women to attack. For various reasons, a victim's being permitted to kill a perpetrator may not be a sufficient condition to permit a state (or even individual third parties) to kill the perpetrator even if it is a necessary condition.

In addition, it is also not clear that it *is* a necessary condition (i.e., it is not clear that *only if* it is permissible for the women to kill is it permissible for others to do so on their behalf). There might be factors other than the relation between perpetrator and victim that affect whether a victim herself is permitted to kill the perpetrator. For example, suppose the women had duties to family members that would make it wrong for them to engage in resistance that would otherwise be justified. They might then lack permission to kill perpetrators on grounds that would not undermine the permission of third parties to kill the perpetrators on their behalf.[11]

4. Suicide Bombers

Now consider a further possible implication of what has been said. Reports by Amnesty International and the Red Cross say that many women ruled by the Taliban prior to 2001 killed themselves instead of killing the perpetrators of injustice to them. They committed suicide by swallowing acids that burned the esophagus (a slow and painful death) in order to avoid the type of life they were living.[12] Suicide seems to have been a needed escape for these women. It may have given them the sense that they, not others, controlled their lives and it may have been used to psychologically punish or create guilt in their oppressors. Nevertheless, it also suggests that the women had no hope of reprieve and, perhaps, that they were deeply depressed by their circumstances. Such depression would have made it unlikely that these women, at least, could have used other violent or nonviolent means of escape and resistance, even had this been physically possible. But let us now consider the issue of the permissibility of such alternatives to suicide, not the physical or mental possibility of their use.

Suicide is not a means of escape from house arrest that is a morally required alternative to harming the perpetrator of house arrest. It involves a cost to the victim that is too great just to avoid harming the perpetrator for the sake of escape. Might this imply that even those who felt the need to escape by suicide could *also*, were they capable of it, permissibly have killed the perpetrators? In other words, instead of killing *only* herself, could a woman committed to killing *herself also* have permissibly killed the perpetrators?

At least two grounds might be suggested to justify a suicidal Taliban woman's also killing a perpetrator. The first justification is defense of others. That is, given that the person committed to suicide need not kill a perpetrator in order to escape injustice to herself, she might still permissibly kill a perpetrator if this were necessary and useful to help other victims. (Here, a victim takes on the role of a third party toward other victims.) The second justification is related to the permissibility of attacking someone while he oppresses as mere resistance even if this does nothing to stop the injustice. In this case, a victim plans suicide as the means to escape her oppression, and killing the perpetrator is merely a response to his unjust action. The second justification implies that if one must escape a grave injustice by suicide, it is permissible to take the perpetrator along in an act of mere resistance. One might even think of this as a form of "suicide bombing," very different from the form with which we are acquainted.

These two justifications for killing a perpetrator when the victim's suicide will otherwise occur anyway may seem inadequate. First, how could a woman permissibly kill perpetrators even if this would help other women, given that she runs no risk of costly consequences to herself in using nonlethal means of helping others, as she will shortly commit suicide anyway? This objection, however, would not apply when killing the perpetrator is truly necessary to help other victims or when using alternative means to help others would interfere with her suicide. A second objection is to attacking a perpetrator as mere resistance. If one will successfully avoid oppressive acts by suicide, it seems there is no personal oppression left to resist by killing a perpetrator. And it does not seem that the fact that someone is driven to use self-harming means of escape licenses her to *punish* the perpetrator with death.[13]

However, suicide (which involves intending one's death) is not the only response to no longer caring to live if one is required to live in a certain way. A woman who no longer cares that she will die in escaping from the perpetrator could also engage in mere resistance to the perpetrator, perhaps foreseeing with certainty but not intending that she will die. For example, she may foresee that others will kill her for her resistance. If she wishes not to fall under the control of those who might recapture her, however, she may secondarily have tools ready with which to commit suicide. Such a two-step course of action seems both permissible and better than leaving perpetrators unresisted by choosing suicide as a first step. People ideally should become stronger and more resolute in their resistance once they are willing to forego the life that acquiescence to oppression would bring.

5. Actual Third-Party Approaches

In conclusion, I want to analyze two actual approaches that were taken by nonstate agents in dealing with the crisis of the Taliban women prior to 2001. One approach was to combine condemning the Taliban with isolating them. Oxfam, for example, stopped operations on an important project redirecting water to a certain area in Afghanistan because, it said, "We concluded that our core principles are not negotiable. Oxfam will work with women in Kabul, or not at all."[14] Oxfam was not allowed to work with women because that would have involved the women's being in public. The nature of this statement—Oxfam will work with women in the area or not at all— might suggest that Oxfam thought it would itself be engaging in invidiously discriminatory behavior if it worked in the area in accord with Taliban rules. For example, it would have had to abide by the policies of the regime and employ only men in the area.

Perhaps this may be a misleading description of what would have been involved in Oxfam's continuing to redirect the water. After all, redirecting water would not require Oxfam actually to discriminate against women if it did not employ any Afghanis to do the job or if women would not have applied for work on the project even had they been free. And the women would also have benefited by redirection of the water. Hence, it is possible that the underlying principle of the Oxfam action is better described as noninvolvement with others who are perpetrators of injustice. After all, given what they are doing to the women, the perpetrators may lose a right to have Oxfam assistance to redirect water. Even at the cost of not providing water to innocent bystanders and victims of the Taliban, Oxfam's first aim could have been noninvolvement with perpetrators of the injustice. Oxfam might also be interpreted as putting concern with the dignity of the Taliban's victims ahead of the victims' short-term material interests in water. I think that this is a morally permissible approach to the problem.

Ultimately, however, Oxfam may have thought that threatening noninvolvement was a means of winning concessions for women's legal rights. This approach was explicitly taken by the UN World Food Program.[15] During a food crisis in Afghanistan, that organization had the opportunity to distribute wheat through the efforts of Afghanis. It insisted that it would work with Afghani people in distributing the wheat only if Afghani women were allowed to work in the distribution process. At first, the government refused, as it believed women were supposed to stay at home, but, apparently, they eventually let the women work on the project. This suggests that the rulers were willing to sacrifice their own religious principles for the sake of their interests. Whether one thinks that laudable or not, that is what they appear to have done.

The underlying principle suggested by these approaches to dealing with injustice is that, without involving oneself in a discriminatory policy, one may offer a benefit to perpetrators of injustice who no longer have a right to the benefit given their unjust conduct, in exchange for some improvement in the de facto status—not just the short-term material interests—of the victims of injustice. I think this approach to dealing with injustice is morally acceptable even though women in the society who are not involved in the immediate project will continue to be required to stay at home.

But it is important that such policies be used with an eye to the status and fate of all the victims, not just of the small group who may immediately and directly benefit.

Notes

This chapter is a revised version of a short (fifteen-minute) unpublished talk given at the Princeton University Center for Human Values as part of a panel on the topic "How Should We Address the Greatest Evils and Injustices of Our Time?" April 27–28, 2000. In revising it, I have tried to retain its character as a talk given to nonphilosophers. The topic has renewed relevance in the light of events in Afghanistan in 2010. The chapter was also given as a Popper Seminar paper at the London School of Economics in March 2011. I am grateful to the audience and to Prof. Alex Voorhoeve for their comments on that occasion and to Gerald Lang for additional comments.

1. See the reference to Scanlon's example in Samuel Scheffler, *The Rejection of Conse-quentialism* (New York: Oxford University Press, 1994).

2. I discuss this issue a bit in chap. 9, "Conflicts of Rights," of my *Intricate Ethics* (New York: Oxford University Press, 2007).

3. In other work, including other chapters in this volume, I have not restricted the use of "evils" to moral evils; it has included mere harms.

4. I here follow Jeff McMahan's use of the term in his *Killing in War* (New York: Oxford University Press, 2009). A deluded child who aims a loaded gun or someone who mistak-enly attacks an innocent person can be permissibly forcibly stopped.

5. Barbara Herman might be interpreted as saying something similar in her "Murder and Mayhem," reprinted in her collection, *The Practice of Moral Judgment* (Cambridge, MA: Harvard University Press), 113–131: "I must not assent to be the victim of aggression. This gives more than permission for an act of self-defense when that is necessary to resist the aggression; it imposes a requirement that aggression be resisted. Though I may not be able to prevent the aggressor's success, I may not be passive in the face of aggression. Passivity is here like complicity" (p. 129). However, I do not argue for a requirement and I do not think nonresistance constitutes complicity. A possible alternate account of mere resistance (which I do not accept) sees it as carrying out a deterrent threat that has failed to deter.

6. Apparently, there is an expression voiced by some Afghani, whether Taliban or not, that translates as "a wife should be in the home—or in the grave" (quoted by Nicholas Kristof, in the *New York Times* [Oct. 25, 2010]). However, the supposition (for the sake of argument) that women will not be harmed if they stay at home is unlikely to be true. A 2010 *New York Times* article describes the beatings and abuse within marriage of Afghan women, who subsequently burned themselves to death. These are not described as specifically Tal-iban marriages. See Alissa J. Rubin, "For Afghan Wives, a Desperate, Fiery Way Out," *New York Times* (Nov. 7, 2010). Derek Parfit has suggested that if the women were treated well in captivity this would make a difference to the permissibility of killing their captors. I disagree.

7. I first discussed the case of the Warsaw Ghetto in my "Harming Some to Save Others from the Nazis," in *Moral Philosophy and the Holocaust*, ed. E. Garrad and G. Scarre (Lon-don: Ashgate, 2003). It is reprinted as Chapter 5 this volume. Even if Nazi plans had not been

extermination but only confinement in "model" camps, a doomed uprising would have been permissible, I believe. In this regard, it is interesting to consider cases where an agent is liable to being killed to stop his attack even though what he does is not unjust. In these cases, it does seem impermissible for a victim to resist such an agent when this would do the victim no good. For example, a pilot may be justified in attacking a military facility despite collateral harm to civilians. Nevertheless, he may be liable to being killed by those civilians if this is necessary and sufficient to stop the collateral harm to themselves. (Jeff McMahan discusses this issue in *Killing in War*.) However, suppose his being killed is not sufficient to save the civilians from collateral harm because they will certainly soon be harmed to the same extent by another pilot. Then it does seem that the first pilot's being justified in his act implies that the civilians would be morally wrong to kill him as resistance to his act.

8. Acting on behalf of the women—rather than just in resistance to wrongdoing—may have to assume their consent to this. Suppose that no individual suffers an injustice great enough to be permitted to kill in self-defense, but each of *many* individuals is oppressed in the same way. Is it also possible that so many people being treated improperly is a sufficient condition for *any individual* to kill to stop the oppression of these many women? This possibility seems to raise the problem of aggregation, that is, whether for moral purposes, it is correct to add up small losses wrongfully imposed on separate individuals in order to create a large loss, albeit only in aggregate. Is there something about many people, not just one, being treated unjustly that allows us to add up the small losses even if in the absence of injustice it would be wrong to aggregate smaller losses? This is a topic that deserves discussion it will not get here.

9. This issue was especially important in 2010, when the Afghani government was not controlled by the Taliban and had some commitment to the rights of women. There was a responsibility on the part of victims to take advantage of alternative legal means provided to protect themselves.

10. Comments in response to questions at the Conference on War, University of Calgary, October 2006.

11. Of course, women may be mistaken in thinking that they have duties to care for others (such as children) that override their right to act for their legitimate self-interest and to oppose wrongdoing.

12. See Jan Goodwin, "Buried Alive: Afghan Women under the Taliban," *OTI Online* (Feb. 27, 1998), http://www.freerepublic.com/focus/f-news/524499/posts. In 2010, there were reports of Afghani women (not necessarily under the Taliban) setting themselves afire. See note 6.

13. Killing a perpetrator to rescue some other victims may still not be permissible if using it will make the situation worse overall for yet other victims. By contrast, even if the situation will become worse for other women if one woman commits suicide—greater controls are introduced on them—I do not think this is sufficient reason to rule out her escape by suicide. A victim need not stay in a very bad situation, sacrificing herself personally in an important way, just because perpetrators will respond to her escape by maltreating others. However, if she decides to act to help others (by killing a perpetrator), it seems reasonable for her to consider the interests of all others and not just some others (with the possible exception of loved ones).

14. See Goodwin, "Buried Alive."

15. See UN Economic and Social Council, "Discrimination against Women and Girls in Afghanistan," *Report of the Secretary-General*, Jan. 28, 2002, p. 6.

10

Nuclear Deterrence and Reliance on Harm

Introduction

It has been said that keeping nuclear weapons deters war. The threat of harm to civilians that would result even merely collaterally from strikes on military targets deters nations from using the weapons. Fear of escalation to nuclear war also deters the starting of conventional war. Suppose this is so. Then we seem to be relying on the *possibility* of harm to civilians as a part of our justification for keeping weapons that allow us to avoid actually harming soldiers and civilians in any wars while protecting political sovereignty and freedom. The question is whether such reliance on the *possibility* of collateral civilian harm is morally wrong even if it leads to great goods. A related question is whether it is morally wrong to rely on a prospect of civilian harm that will unavoidably occur in the future or on civilian harm that has already occurred. I shall be dealing with aspects of this question.

My discussion revisits issues discussed during the Cold War by war theorists Michael Walzer and Paul Ramsey but from the perspective of some new proposals about nonconsequentialist ethical theory.[1]

For those who support a moral theory known as consequentialism, there is no problem with relying on bad events or the possibility of them in order to produce great goods when the overall outcome is positive. Nonconsequentialists, however, deny that only consequences determine whether an act is permissible; they claim that some acts or policies can be morally wrong even if they lead to the best consequences. Some nonconsequentialists, like Walzer and Ramsey, accept the Doctrine of Double Effect (DDE) as a guide to morally permissible conduct. The DDE claims that it is impermissible to intentionally bring about (by act or omission) evil (such as harm to civilians) as an end or even as a means to a greater good. However, when it is foreseen (even with certainty) that an evil is an unavoidable side effect of means necessary to achieve good, the evil (commonly called "collateral damage") does not make action impermissible if it is proportional to (e.g., less than) the good sought. (Presumably, this proportional evil may be a side effect of the good itself, not just the means to it.) However, unintended evil side effects that are out of proportion to the good sought can make action impermissible.[2]

Here are some specific examples to help clarify the doctrine. Suppose bombing a military facility is *necessary* to win a just war but it will cause both the deaths of five civilians and fear in many others as a foreseen side effect. The deaths and fear are not intended. The mission would have been as fully successful, and we would have proceeded with it if the deaths and fear had not occurred, when everything else remained constant. It might be that this amount of death and fear is proportional to the good to be achieved (e.g., winning the war). However, if a million civilians would be killed as a unintended side effect of hitting the military facility, this could be an unproportional side effect relative to the good to be achieved, and it would make the mission morally impermissible. Now suppose that to win the war it would instead be *necessary* to deliberately kill five innocent civilians either as a way to destroy a military facility or because the killing will create fear in others, leading an opponent to surrender. The amount of death and fear and all other effects are assumed to be the same as in our first case. Hence, the size of bad effects per se is not out of proportion to the good to be achieved. Still, the DDE rules out causing the lesser evil because it would be intended as a means to the greater good. This is how the DDE supposedly justifies the distinction between collateral damage, some of which need not make a military mission impermissible, and terror bombing, which the doctrine implies is impermissible.

Walzer and Ramsey are concerned with whether the DDE rules out or permits reliance on the prospect of collateral harm to civilians when this prospect produces the good of deterrence. In particular, they are concerned with whether the DDE's conditions of proportionality and not intending evil are satisfied in such cases. In discussing Ramsey's and Walzer's views in this chapter, I shall, for the most part, avoid raising fundamental objections to the DDE, given that their disagreement exists even though they do not fundamentally object to the DDE.[3] However, later in the discussion, dealing with a fundamental objection will be unavoidable.

I. Discussion of Ramsey's Position

A. RAMSEY'S THESES

Consider first, in rough form, what I believe are two of Ramsey's theses. (We shall examine them in more detail later.) Thesis 1 may be put as follows: "Suppose that a military action is permissible despite an unavoidable, foreseen, but unintended bad side effect because the bad side effect is not out of proportion to the good to be achieved by the military action, which is itself necessary to produce the good. Then it could be permissible to *intend* to make good use of the foreseen bad side effect even if it is impermissible to intend to bring the bad effect into existence as a means to the greater good." For short, we could say that Thesis 1 concerns intending the further use of an unintended proportional side effect.

Ramsey gives the following example, which illustrates Thesis 1: Suppose a limited nuclear strike on military targets would inevitably cause some unintended harm to civilians as a side effect, but it would be permissible to engage in the military action nevertheless for the sake of a nation defending its political sovereignty because the side-effect harm is not unproportional to the good. Then we could intentionally arrange for the dissemination of information about those possible side effects before they exist if awareness of them could deter military action by providing an incentive to settle problems by peaceful means. In this illustration of Ramsey's Thesis 1, the intended use of unavoidable, proportional side effects of military action involves making use only of the *possibility* of future side effects. It may seem, however, to involve intentionally causing fear in people as a means to deterrence and thus be suspect due to the intention to bring about the evil of emotional fear. However, Ramsey's case could involve merely broadcasting the truth about possible side effects, foreseeing that emotional fear will be caused rather than intending the fear. Or the "fear" might be only an unemotional and merely rational, prudential reflection prompted by awareness of the possibility of harm. To intentionally cause such prudential reflection is not to cause an evil. Further, the prospect of collateral harm might be broadcast only to leaders responsible for the welfare of civilians, not to civilians.

Ramsey might also agree that use of the proportional side effects, *once* they actually come about, is permissible. An example of the latter would be planning to broadcast the fact of actual proportional side-effect deaths so as to (or merely foreseeing that it will) deter future battles. In both "Prospective Possible" and "Actual" side effect cases (as I shall refer to them), the military action and its proportional side effects would be justifiable, independently of whether the side effects (are used to) cause a further good of deterrence.

Ramsey's Thesis 2 may be put as follows: "Suppose that a military action would be impermissible because its inevitable unintended side effect would be harm out of proportion to the good to be achieved by the military action. Suppose also that a further, much greater good could be achieved by the prospect (in the sense of known possibility) of this side effect occurring. Then the prospect (of this side effect) might itself be an effect that *is* proportional to achieving this much greater good even if the actual harmful side effect would not be proportional to the military action." Ramsey thinks he captures this thought succinctly in saying, "A threat of something disproportionate is not necessarily a disproportionate threat."[4] By "threat," Ramsey here means only the possibility of unproportional harm occurring. His use of "threat" does not imply that anyone actually *deliberately* threatens anyone else with unproportional harm. Indeed, it will be important to remember that Ramsey assumes it would be wrong to deliberately threaten to do what causes an unproportionally harmful side effect even if this threat would deter the actual occurrence of any harm.

Ramsey gives the following example that illustrates Thesis 2: A nuclear strike on military targets would be impermissible if there were massive civilian casualties even though these were unintended side effects. Possibly, we can never completely convince others that we would not engage in such impermissible behavior so long as we keep nuclear weapons capable of being used impermissibly as well as permissibly. Hence, even if we do not intentionally threaten actions that would have such massive, bad side effects, the threat (in the sense of possible occurrence) of such effects exists. Then the prospect (understood as known possibility) of such massive civilian damage coming to pass could deter any use of nuclear weapons because each side fears that the other side will do the impermissible in response. The existence of weapons whose very nature carries with it the *unintended* threat of unproportional civilian deaths is an evil. However, Ramsey says, it could be an evil that is proportional both to the good of deterring any use of nuclear weapons without yielding political sovereignty and to the good of settling disputes by peaceful means. This is so even if the massive deaths would not be proportional to any actual military action.

II. Walzer's Objections

A. THREE OBJECTIONS

Now consider some objections to Ramsey's theses that Walzer raises. First, what I shall call the No Proportionality Objection claims (roughly) that Ramsey's Thesis 2 does away with the DDE's distinction between the permissibility of causing proportional bad side effects and the impermissibility of causing unproportional bad side effects. Walzer says that if this objection is correct, Ramsey's entire argument in Thesis 2 must rest merely on the fact that we would not intend the unproportional, harmful side effects. Second, what I shall call the Reliance Objection claims (roughly) that the fact that in both theses Ramsey would have us rely on bad side effects or their prospect (which we do not intend), for their further usefulness makes them no longer be mere side effects as discussed by the DDE. This is so even if we do not intend the possibility or actuality of the bad effects. Third, what I shall call the Intended Threat Objection claims that if the only reason we keep nuclear weapons is precisely their deterrent effect (based on the prospect of possible harm), then we *will* be *intending to* produce at least the possibility and the prospect of their harmful effect. This is to deliberately threaten harm, contrary to what Ramsey claims is permissible.

Walzer raises the third objection, I believe, because he presupposes that the deterrent use of nuclear weapons cannot depend on the prospect of side-effect harm that would be *proportional* to the good done by a nuclear attack on a military facility. He thinks that if harm is justified (because it is proportional to a necessary attack), the prospect of the harm could not deter use of the nuclear arms that would lead to the harm. Hence, he thinks, Ramsey's argument that the prospect of side-effect harm can deter must involve side effects that are *un*proportional to the good to which the military action would lead.

This presupposition of Walzer's is incorrect, I believe, and it is not shared by Ramsey. That it is justified for country A to attack a military facility, causing country B's civilians proportional harm, does not mean that B might not fear the harm to its civilians even if it recognizes that the harm is proportional to a good. This fear could lead to its being deterred from doing what would lead A to its permissible military response.[5]

Suppose Walzer is wrong to think that Ramsey cannot believe that the prospect of justified proportional collateral damage will deter military action. This implies that when Walzer raises the Reliance Objection, he must be prepared to accept its implications for cases that involve only proportional side-effect harm as well as those that involve unproportional side-effect harm. So let us now consider the implications of the Reliance Objection for cases in which the only harm to civilians would be proportional to and, according to the DDE, justified by the military action that would cause it.

B. RELIANCE, NO INTENTION TO HARM, AND INTENTION NOT TO HARM

The Reliance Objection says that if one relies (or intends to rely) on some effect of one's act, then that effect is not a mere foreseen "side effect" in the sense permitted by the DDE. But suppose that we must bomb a military facility, and this causes unintended proportional civilian harm. Subsequent to the bombing, we decide to arrange for news of this damage to be broadcast to civilians and/or leaders, when it would otherwise have been overlooked, in order to create an incentive to avoid further fighting (Broadcast Case I). (Suppose the incentive will be created through rational reflection rather than by creating the evil of emotional fear.) Such reliance on a bad effect that already exists and was justified by the military mission in order to bring about a good effect seems permissible. The reliance does not mean that the harm was not a mere foreseen side effect of our military action. One sufficient (but perhaps not necessary) reason for this is that the use we can make of the harm was not in any way necessary in order for us to have undertaken the military action. We acted when we did not know we would broadcast and would have acted even if we thought we would not be able to broadcast the news. The same could be true if, knowing that we will engage in a necessary military operation that will unavoidably cause proportional civilian harm, we arrange *in advance* of the military attack to broadcast news of the harm in order to deter further fighting (Broadcast Case II). It is consistent with planning a broadcast that we would have acted even if we thought we could not have broadcast. Nor need broadcasting be an additional, though nonnecessary, goal that we have in deciding to bomb. This could be shown by the fact that if we could have found a way to bomb without causing any harm to broadcast, everything else being constant, we would have done that.

However, I hypothesize that Walzer might want to distinguish morally between the two Broadcast Cases because he believes that the DDE does not demand enough of us. That is, he says it is not enough to *not intend* to harm civilians; one must also *intend not to* harm civilians (without, however, giving up all justified military action).[6] In Broadcast Case II, when one contemplates a use for the collateral damage *before* it occurs, one may forget to look for means to carry out the military mission that do not cause the collateral damage. Failing to look for alternative means need not signify that one intends civilian harm. It may just mean that one neglects to do things that follow from the intention *not to harm* civilians when one is arranging for a broadcast to secure further benefits from the expected harm. (Of course, if there were alternatives, the harmful means would also fail the part of the DDE that requires that means having harmful side effects be *necessary* to reach a greater good. So, this part of Walzer's distinction seems to already be taken account of by the DDE. However, the DDE does not seem to require that we seek a different, somewhat less good goal in order not to harm as many civilians, and Walzer's distinction may imply that we should also do this.)

Walzer says that Ramsey's view is that "[c]ollateral damage is simply a fortunate feature of nuclear warfare; it serves no military purpose, and we would avoid it if we could, though it is clearly a good thing that we cannot,"[7] for its deterrent properties result in an overall better state of affairs in which we need not use our weapons at all. If an overall better state can come about only if there is a deterrent effect from the prospect of (even proportional) collateral harm from a military strike, then (as noted earlier) we may neglect to do what an *intention not to harm* civilians would lead to. The latter intention could lead us to develop military weapons that would accomplish a military strike without collateral damage at all and so without the deterrent effect of the prospect of harm, leading to more actual military conflict.[8]

But Ramsey, of course, is not a consequentialist, so he need not refuse to intend *not* to harm civilians just so that a better state of affairs (no military conflict at all) comes about.[9] I conclude (on the basis of cases like Broadcast I and II) that reliance on civilian harm after it occurs or reliance on its prospect (whether to achieve the good of no further civilian harm or of no civilian harm at all) need not be contrary to the DDE merely because we plan to make use of bad side effects. Such forms of reliance need not involve intending the harm or its possibility to civilians. Nor need they involve depending on the prospect or the occurrence of the harm and its good effect to provide a justification for the military capacity or action that would cause the harm, at least in cases where collateral damage would be proportional to the original, intended good of the military capacity or action. In such cases, military capacity or action would be justified even if the prospect or occurrence of harm did not have further good effects of deterrence. One certainly need not abandon military capacities that, if used, would cause collateral damage proportional to an intended greater good simply because other good effects come from the harm or the possibility of it, including not having to use the weapons at all. However, Ramsey might have gone further, agreeing with Walzer that one should also intend not to cause civilian harm even if this means producing a second-best state of the world in which military weapons that could not cause collateral harm would be developed *and* actually used.

C. THE INTENDED THREAT OBJECTION

1. Deterrent Effects Only from Unproportional Harm

Walzer's third objection claims that if the only reason we keep nuclear weapons is that they have a deterrent effect, then we will be intending a possibility of civilian harm. This may be contrary both to what the DDE allows if risk of harm is an evil and to what Ramsey claims is permissible. (Notice that this objection can be raised even when keeping and using weapons could be justified without considering their deterrent effect; for example, a particular country might not keep such weapons for the sake of the properties that could justify keeping and using them independently of deterrence. This country would refuse to ever use nuclear weapons on military targets even in self-defense and where side-effect harm would be proportional but would hide this refusal. It would intend only the weapon's deterrent properties and so intend the possibility of civilian harm that leads to deterrence. As supporters of the DDE, Walzer and Ramsey cannot endorse this country's keeping the weapons. This is so even though a second country with different intentions could permissibly keep the same weapons even if it might cause greater harm than the first country because it could wind up permissibly using its weapons and so cause the actual harm as a *side effect*. The first country would be *intending* a lesser evil, that is, the possibility of harm that is necessary to produce deterrence, and according to the DDE, intending the lesser evil would be wrong even if acting with mere foresight to the greater (proportional) evil (of actual harm) would be permissible.)

One response to the Intended Threat Objection involves rejecting the DDE, understood as focusing on the actual intentions of agents, as a standard of permissibility. It involves denying that intending harm or risk of it is what makes acts impermissible.[10] Contrary to Walzer and Ramsey, I believe that one need not abandon military defenses that could cause only harm proportional to the good their actual use would do even if one's only intention in setting up the military defenses is that deterrence occur due to the possibility and prospect of collateral damage. That is, suppose a military operation would be justified despite its unavoidable side-effect harm and it would be good overall to defend oneself rather than to have domination occur. Then I think it does not affect the permissibility of setting up such military defenses that one intends only its deterrent effect.[11]

There is another response to Walzer's Intended Threat Objection that does not involve such a fundamental objection to the DDE. It depends on Ramsey's denying that he is considering cases in which a country keeps weapons it would never be willing to actually use even if such use would be morally permissible according to the DDE. Then the Intended Threat Objection would have to be revised to focus on keeping weapons that could cause civilian harm *only* out of proportion to the good produced by any military use. Given that Walzer thinks deterrence arises only from the threat of such unproportional harm (as noted earlier), this is probably how he meant the Intended Threat Objection to begin with. If we invest in such weapons but are committed to not using them, it must be because we *intend* that the possibility of our changing our mind and *impermissibly* using them will give rise to a concern of massive civilian harm, thus deterring aggression from fear of escalation. Having this intention is directly inconsistent with trying to alter the weapons so that they could not have unproportional effects.

To this narrowed objection, Ramsey could only respond, I think, that he is concerned with keeping weapons that *might* lead to unproportional side-effect harm but need not do so when properly used; that is, the weapons could also be useful in cases where they give rise to only proportional harm. (This is just to deny that the weapons cause only unproportional harm.) One cannot show that one keeps the weapons only from an intention to have the capacity to produce unproportional harm if there is another justification for having them *even if we assume that only the unproportional* harm could have the deterrent effects. (Being a supporter of the DDE, Ramsey may have to focus on cases in which an agent actually has an interest in the justifiable use of the weapons.) If such an agent is not required to give up weapons that have a justifiable use just because of concern about unproportional effects, then the fact that this concern *alone* will have a useful deterrent effect will not imply that this agent must give up the weapons. Table 1 lays out the possibilities discussed.

Table 1

		Defend	Deter
		Potential Effect of Weapons	
		Defend	Deter
Potential Side-Effect Harms of Weapons	Proportional	Yes	a. Yes b. No
	Unproportional	No	Yes

The following discussion may further clarify how to deal with cases where the deterrent effect depends only on the possibility of *un*proportional harm. I shall assume, until further notice, that the agent would be interested in justifiable use of the weapons when they produce proportional harm but that the possibility of proportional harm cannot have a deterrent effect.

Military Capacity May Lead to Military Action and Other Side Effects

Side Effect 1
  1(a) actual proportional civilian harm (PCH) of military action
  1(b) probability of PCH × amount of PCH (expected amount of PCH)
  1(c) prospective concern about PCH from military capacity

Side Effect 2
  2(a) actual unproportional civilian harm (UCH)
  2(b) probability of UCH × amount of UCH (expected amount of UCH)
  2(c) prospective concern about UCH from military capacity

FIGURE 10.1   **Military Capacity May Lead to Military Action and Other Side Effects**

If a military action would be justified despite actual side-effect harm, as in 1(a) in figure 10.1, then it is likely that maintaining the military capacity that can lead to that military action will be justified despite both the possibility of PCH occurring and concern about PCH—side effects 1(b) and (c). It is agreed (by hypothesis) that the military action would not be justified if it would actually produce UCH—side effect 2(a). But a military capacity that is needed to make possible a military action with PCH can be justified even if its establishment has as a side effect the *possibility* and the prospect of UCH. Then 2(b) and 2(c) could be caused by and be *proportional* to the goods that can come from having a military capacity that makes possible an appropriate military action. Notice that in this argument, side effects 2(b) and (c), like side effects 1(a), (b), and (c), *are proportional* to the goods that can come from military action (and the capacity to carry it out) that need only cause actual PCH, not actual UCH. Hence, these side effects are justified if they are unavoidable. This means that we need not refer to the additional great benefit of deterrence that can result only from the possibility and concern of UCH to justify the possibility and concern of UCH and the military capacity that gives rise to them. And even acting with an intention to make use of such already justified foreseen side effects, 2(b) and 2(c), for deterrence purposes need not involve *intending* actual UCH or the possibility of it.

2. Making Unproportional Evils Proportional

What we have just said shows that we can understand cases where a deterrent effect is due only to the possibility of UCH, without introducing Ramsey's idea that a threat of a side effect whose actual occurrence would be unproportional can be a proportionate threat *relative to the great good of deterring war that the threat causes.* Ramsey's idea here was to expand the good against which we measure whether the evil of the possibility and concern of UCH is or is not proportionate. He expanded the good from successful defensive military action to include the much greater good of deterring war. However, I think it should have been Ramsey's point that the unintended possibility and concern of UCH produced by having any nuclear weapons may be proportional *to the good that could be permissibly produced by weapons whose use could have PCH.* This is the ordinary way the DDE licenses bad effects as proportional. By contrast, Ramsey says the possibility and concern of UCH is proportional to the deterrence of war that they cause. This is a mistake, I think. That is, it is a mistake for Ramsey to say that the possibility of and concern about UCH are proportional *not* to the good that can come from the permissible use of military capacity (or action) but to the great good of deterring war, which the concern of unproportional harm causes.

His saying this is a mistake for two reasons. First, speaking of the proportionality of threats relative to deterring war is not an accurate description of cases where the use of nuclear weapons could lead to both PCH and UCH. It is actual UCH that is out of proportion to the goods achieved by such military actions or capacity, not necessarily the possibility of UCH and the prospective concern of it. Ramsey's statement that "the threat of an unproportional effect might not be an unproportional threat" *can* apply to the proportionality relation between the possibility and concern of UCH and the good producible by a military capacity that may lead only to actual PCH. That is why Walzer's first objection to Ramsey—"No Proportionality"—is wrong. Ramsey does not do away with the moral distinction between proportional and unproportional side effects. He just distinguishes between two different side effects: (a) actual unproportional deaths and (b) the possibility and prospective concern of unproportional deaths. The latter need not be unproportional to the good coming from the military capacity whose proper actual use need produce only PCH.

Here is a second reason for thinking it is wrong for Ramsey to introduce deterrence from war as the good that justifies the possibility and prospect of UCH. These side effects are imagined to be necessary to cause the great good of deterring war. Suppose they were bad effects that were *not* proportional to and so not already justified as side effects of the military capacity that could produce a good with only actual PCH. Then the bad effects would be as yet unjustified and supposedly justified by the completely new good of deterrence that they are necessary to produce. I believe that such a required productive route via evil to greater good violates a nonconsequentialist side constraint of causal purity in the production of greater good. That is, on a nonconsequentialist view greater goods cannot generally justify bad effects that are necessary to produce them. This is so even if the bad effects are less than the good and are not *intended* as means to the greater good and so do not violate the parts of the DDE that focus on proportionality and not intending evil.[12]

Contrast this necessary causal role for bad effects in producing greater good with the following scenario (called Two Side Effects): A military capacity necessary to produce a military action with PCH has two types of side effects. One is the possibility of UCH and the concern about it. The second is a sense of security from attack and domination that awakens a spirit of cooperation that eliminates war without surrendering political independence. In this case, the great good of no war plus political independence is caused by the military capacity independently of its threat of UCH. (This is consistent with the threat of PCH itself not being capable of causing deterrence.) Suppose, for the sake of argument, that the first bad side effect (possibility and concern about UCH) was not proportional to the good that can be achieved by a military capacity whose appropriate use need cause only PCH. However, the second good side effect (the set of security, confidence, no war) is good to a greater degree than the bad side effect is bad even to all the people who are subject to both. I suggest that here the good of no war might counterbalance the bad side effect of possible UCH and concern about it even if this bad side effect is unproportional to the good made possible by the proper use of military capacity in itself. This would create a set of side effects that are overall proportional to the military capacity. And the bad side effect would not be required to produce the great good of deterrence.

The Two Side Effects Case also raises the possibility of another objection to the DDE. The DDE seems to emphasize not only that it is wrong to intend evils as ends or means but also that a bad side effect can be proportional to and justified by an *intended greater good*. I suggest, however, that the *unintended greater good* of no war in our case could play the same role in justifying the lesser evil as the intended good of deterrence (if we intended this effect of the military capacity).[13]

Though Ramsey is a supporter of the DDE, he too seems to rely on unintended goods to justify lesser evils. Indeed, when Ramsey says that side effects 2(b) and (c) are proportional to deterrence, he may have had in mind that an *unintended* good of deterrence could help to justify bads. That is, the good effect of deterrence, even if not intended, could outweigh 2(b) and (c). The problem is that, in some cases Ramsey imagines, deterrence is *not* a side effect of the military capacity needed for appropriate military action independent of the possibility of UCH (as the good of no war is in Two Side Effects). Rather, he imagines that the threat of UCH, which is a side effect of that military capacity, causes deterrence. If this bad side effect were not justified by the good made possible by that military capacity appropriately used, then an as yet *un*justified bad would be necessary to produce the greater good of deterrence in Ramsey's case. I have suggested above that such a *necessary* causal route to producing deterrence would be morally problematic even if the bad were not intended.[14]

It is also important to emphasize the distinction between a necessary causal route and a merely actual causal route. To see this suppose everything is as described in Two Side Effects with the following exception: Although security arising from military preparedness could in fact lead to confidence and deterrence, before it has a chance to do so the same effect is produced by concern about UCH. Here the *actual* causal route to producing peace is via the possibility and concern about UCH that (we are supposing) is not justified by any good made possible by the military capacity that causes the possibility of UCH. But this is not a *required* causal route; if the possibility of UCH were not an unavoidable side effect of the military capacity (or not known to be such), the sense of security would have actually caused peace without relying on any bad effect that is not justified independently of the deterrence it produces. It seems to me that in this case (call it Two Side Effects Modified), it is as permissible to maintain the military capacity as it was in the original Two Side Effects Case. If so, this helps show that it is the *required* productive role rather than an actual one that is morally significant.[15]

If a required productive route to a greater good through a bad that cannot otherwise be justified is problematic even if no one intends the bad, focusing on the DDE will have misled Ramsey. For not needing to intend a bad side effect is consistent with its being morally problematic for the side effect to have a necessary causal role in producing a greater good if the bad side effect is not justified by (and proportional to) the good that can be produced by the proper use of the military capacity that produces the bad effect. In this sense, I agree with Walzer that Ramsey relies too much on whether or not we intend the bad effects that lead to greater good, though not for the exact reason Walzer gives.

III. Further beyond Walzer and Ramsey

I have compared my views on purity in a required productive route with the DDE on which Walzer and Ramsey rely. I shall now further contrast my own views with those of Ramsey and Walzer on the issue of reliance on and intentionally creating threats.

A. DOING AN ACT BECAUSE OF A BAD EFFECT PRODUCED BY THE ACT

As we have seen, part of what Ramsey tries to do is justify the intention to rely on the use of already justified bad side effects. Walzer responds in his Reliance Objection that reliance on bad effects makes them no longer be unintended effects in the sense employed in the DDE. I have argued that Walzer is wrong about this. However, Ramsey also believes that harm to civilians should not play any role in military strategy per se. I take this to mean that a reason for doing an act should not be that it will cause harm to civilians even if the act's having that effect is a reason for doing another act (such as broadcasting). He also believes, I think, that it should not be a reason for doing an act (or having a capacity) that it will create a *threat* of harm to civilians. By contrast, I believe that it is sometimes a reason to engage in a military action that *it* will cause harm or a threat of harm to civilians. "A reason" is here used in a broad sense, such as "a consideration in favor of," where this need not imply that the harm or threat of harm is an intended effect or a goal of an act.[16] Hence, sometimes harm or threat of harm to civilians could permissibly play such a role in military strategy.

My suggestion is that engaging in a military strategy that produces the bad side effect could be morally justified *only because* it produces the bad effect, and so the fact that one's act would cause harm or a threat of harm to civilians could be a reason to do that act. Yet this need not involve intending the bad effect or a bad effect being justified by something good it is necessary to *produce*. This is so, I believe, when the bad side effect of a strategy is necessary in order to *sustain* what we have achieved in carrying out that military strategy. If what we achieved were not sustained, there would be no point in carrying out the strategy because the harmful side effect it causes would be unproportional to a mere short-lived military achievement. In these cases, a harmful effect of what we have already achieved can be justified by the further good it causes because this good involves *sustaining* what we have already achieved by the military action itself.

For an example of what I have in mind when the bad effect is actual deaths, consider Nuclear Munitions Grief (a version of a case I call Munitions Grief): If we use nuclear weapons to destroy military targets and the response is that they are immediately rebuilt, it will be pointless to use the nuclear weapons. Furthermore, unavoidable side-effect civilian deaths that would be proportional and justified if the targets were not rebuilt would not be proportional or justified if they were rebuilt. However, we know that if and only if there are civilian deaths will other citizens be consumed by grief and unable to rebuild the targets. Hence, it would be reasonable to use the nuclear weapons only *because* (we know that) we will unavoidably cause civilians to die.[17]

In this case, we foresee both that the civilians will be killed and that their deaths will have further sad effects on others. These factors are needed to make it permissible to destroy the military target. In this case, we do not merely rely on an unavoidable bad side effect that is already justified by a good produced by our military action itself; the bad side effect is *not* justified by the results of the military action independently of the further causal effects of the bad side effect itself. In this case, we should not do the military action unless we produced the bad side effect, unlike the cases in which we should act even if the bad side effect did not occur or could not subsequently be used for good. Yet, I believe, it is still true in this case that we need not intend the civilian deaths, though we act only because we will produce them and would not act if we did not. The dependence of action on its expected effect may be a necessary condition for the presence of intending the effects, but it is not a sufficient condition. This is suggested by the fact that it is consistent with destroying the military target because civilian deaths are unavoidable to (a) refuse to do anything extra—no matter how easy or morally innocuous in itself—in order to make sure bombing would cause the deaths when it need not, and to (b) try to save the civilians from dying if, unexpectedly, this becomes possible after the mission begins even if their not dying ruins the mission. Doing something extra (vs. [a]) and refusing easy rescue (vs. [b]) would be indications of intending the deaths. But taking advantage of an unavoidable connection between bombing and deaths and the expected impossibility of rescue to decide to bomb in this case is consistent with refusing either to intentionally bring about that connection or to not interfere with it. This is an indication that we do not intend the deaths.[18] Hence, this case differs from terror bombing civilians even though, as in terror bombing, an agent would not bomb if he did not kill civilians and he bombs because he does. Terror bombing can be impermissible even if bombing in Nuclear Munitions Grief is permissible.

This sort of case contrasts also with ones we considered in discussing Ramsey, in which a bad effect that is thought not to be justified by a good properly achievable by a military capacity or action is necessary to cause a *different* good, such as deterrence from war. I claimed that, from a nonconsequentialist point of view, bad effects cannot, in general, be justified by the new greater good effect that they *produce*. In Nuclear Munitions Grief, I am claiming that the bad effect could be justified by the good it is necessary to cause because the bad effect *sustains* rather than produces the good effect (destruction of the munitions) that produced the bad effect.[19]

Cases like Nuclear Munitions Grief led me to develop what I call the Doctrine of Triple Effect. This doctrine distinguishes between effects that are intended, those that are merely foreseen, and those on whose existence we rely in order to help justify doing the very act that produces them.[20] Walzer had objected to using the term "side effects," as employed in the DDE, to apply to *already* justified effects on which we rely for further action. I agree with Ramsey that calling such effects "side effects," as employed by the DDE, is not problematic. My reason is that they are *not relied on to justify the very act that produces them*. It is when we rely on bad effects to justify the act that produces them that I think we should at least take note of the fact that we act "because of" the effects. Doing acts because of their effects involving actual or threatened harm occurring to civilians seems to be something that Ramsey and Walzer both want to rule out. I have argued that it should not be ruled out and that it need not involve an agent *intending* to *produce* the bad effect.

B. THE PRINCIPLE OF SECONDARY PERMISSIBILITY AND ITS EXTENSION

My next point is that while neither Walzer nor Ramsey thinks it is morally permissible to intentionally threaten either PCH or UCH per se as a means of deterrence, I think that what I have called the Principle of Secondary Permissibility at least seems to sometimes give us reason to doubt that they are right. I shall first try to make clearer what this principle claims in nonnuclear cases and then apply it to nuclear cases.

(1) Suppose an out-of-control trolley is headed on track A toward killing five people. A bystander can save them by redirecting the trolley onto track B. However, one person on track B will be killed by the trolley. Many nonconsequentialists think it is permissible to redirect the trolley. Another way to stop it is to push someone standing on track C, to which we cannot redirect the trolley, so that he falls in front of the trolley on track A, thereby stopping it. This, however, will kill him. Many of those who think we may redirect the trolley believe we may not push the one person on C into the trolley's path. Indeed, I believe that even if it were permissible to redirect the trolley, thereby killing the person on track B, it would not be permissible to instead stop the trolley by pushing the person on track C into the path of the trolley when this will only *paralyze his legs*. But now suppose that just before we are about to permissibly redirect the trolley onto track B, we discover that there is one alternative: Pushing the person on track B into the path of the trolley on track A will also stop it and only paralyze his legs. My view is that because pushing him is the only alternative better *for him* than the more harmful initially permissible act we would otherwise do to him against his will, what would ordinarily be impermissible becomes permissible and may even make the initial permissible act impermissible. This includes *intending* to put him in harm's way and doing this as a *required* means to producing a greater good. This is an example of what I call the Principle of Secondary Permissibility (PSP): A type of act that would be impermissible were it the only way of treating someone can be at least permissible secondary to—as a substitute for—doing what was initially permissible, namely doing something even worse to him against his will. The PSP can supersede concerns about intending harm as a means or requiring as yet unjustified evils to produce new goods.

Consider another case. Suppose we cannot bring ourselves to do what we are physically capable of permissibly doing, namely redirecting the trolley and thereby killing the person on track B. Then we discover that there is an alternative: If we push that person into the path of the trolley on track A, this, too, will stop it and only paralyze him. In this case, it *is not* true that pushing him is better for him than what we *would* otherwise permissibly do to him against his will since we will not otherwise kill him. Still, he will not be killed only because we supererogatorily refrain from doing what we are physically able to permissibly do (were it the only option available). This may make it permissible to push him, only paralyzing him, in order to stop the trolley, especially given that we *would* permissibly turn the trolley if this only paralyzed him. It seems wrong that our being more thoughtful of his interests than we have to be should stand in the way of our doing what it would be permissible to do (according to PSP) were we less thoughtful. (By contrast, it remains impermissible to push the person on track C because there is nothing worse than paralyzing him that we initially have the capacity to permissibly do to him against his will.) As this is an extension of the Principle of Secondary Permissibility, I call it the Extended Principle of Secondary Permissibility (EPSP). It seems more contentious than the PSP.

(2) Now consider how the PSP might bear on intentionally creating threats of civilian harm in order to deter war. In general, it seems to me that using a threat of harm to some civilians to avoid permissibly causing actual harm to the same civilians could conform to the PSP.

(a) Suppose a country keeps a nuclear capacity that it *will* permissibly and successfully use to defend itself against aggression, thereby creating only PCH. It will shortly engage in military action that will cause actual collateral harm to a certain group of civilians who do not know this collateral harm will occur. Before launching its missile it discovers that it can also ward off aggression in another way. Intentionally threatening civilians with the harm that would occur to them, thus terrorizing them, will deter the aggression. It seems to be permissible to deliberately threaten the civilians in this way rather than do what actually kills them against their will. It could be permissible to do this even if it were impermissible to threaten civilians in the same way to deter aggression when harm to them would not otherwise result from permissible attacks on military facilities.

In this case, we create terror by sincerely threatening people with the proportional side-effect harm of a permissible military attack in order to avoid actually attacking. We can imagine another case in which, in order to avoid using nuclear weapons with proportional collateral harm to civilians, the only thing to do (consistent with not surrendering to aggression) is to tell the civilians that we will cause them harm that is *not* merely collateral to and justified by a military mission. For example, we must tell them we will use weapons that cause UCH, killing the same civilians who would be harmed proportionately plus many others, even though using such weapons is impermissible and we have no intention of doing so. Does the PSP imply that it is permissible to engage in such a threatening lie if it will allow us to avoid *actually* doing the grave harm that it is permissible for us to do? More people would be subject to terror than would have actually been killed if we broadcast to a population so large that actual harm to them would be UCH. Those who would not have been killed by way of proportional harm are thus made worse off than we would have permissibly made them, as a means to helping prevent worse harm to others. The PSP alone does not imply that this is permissible.[21] However, suppose we broadcast the lying intention to cause UCH only to people who *would* have actually been victims of only proportional harm. We do this believing that their altruistic concern for others will contribute to their surrendering. This could be justified by the PSP, for the very same people who would otherwise have been permissibly harmed against their will will be much less badly affected by the lying threat.

Suppose the PSP did justify some intentional lying threats of UCH. If deliberate lying threats about intentional or collateral UCH are ordinarily impermissible as ways to deter aggression, they will remain so for those who are not capable of doing initially permissible worse things to civilians, such as those who lack weapons that cause PCH.

All these cases differ from ones in which we deliberately threaten civilians or deliberately create weapons that cause massive collateral civilian harm in order to deter wars that would harm only combatants. My cases involving the PSP do not show that it is permissible to have weapons that could harm civilians when we could have weapons that do not do this even if more combatants would die were there no threat to civilians. The PSP can only justify lesser harm against the will of those we would otherwise permissibly harm against their will. Creating weapons that harm civilians collaterally rather than ones that do not could be justified by the PSP only if they reduced the harm that we would permissibly otherwise do to those very civilians against their will in some other way.

(3) How could the EPSP be applied to nuclear cases? A country that has the capacity to permissibly use nuclear weapons that cause only PCH may nevertheless refuse to do such harm rather than suffer unjust aggression and/or domination. Then it discovers that the only other way to save itself from aggression and/or domination is to deliberately threaten opponents with the prospect of the collateral harm that would come to them if its weapons were used. Alternatively, it might discover that the only other way to save itself is to direct a threat to cause UCH only to those who would have been victims of PCH were it willing to use its weapons. It relies on their altruistic concern for many others to prompt their surrender. The EPSP implies this is permissible even if it involves misleading or lying about the willingness to use weapons that cause PCH or UCH. In this case, the country's threat is not a less harmful substitute for harm it would have permissibly done, as it would not have caused any harm.

Suppose a country does not yet have nuclear weapons that can cause PCH and UCH. Suppose it would be permissible to acquire such weapons and use them with PCH. However, the country refuses to do what it is capable of permissibly doing. Instead it decides to acquire weapons only because this will give rise to concern in others that it would use them, and this will deter aggression. It does not intend to ever use the weapons. Instead of doing what it is capable of permissibly doing (i.e., acquire weapons for actual use that would cause PCH), it decides to do something else that would cause less harm to the same civilians, namely, build weapons to pose something like a lying threat to only those who could be permissibly harmed. Suppose such a lying threat would be impermissible where there was no possibility of the country's actually acquiring the capacity to permissibly cause harm. The EPSP seems to imply that it would be permissible to acquire the weapons because doing what merely threatens people is better for them than what one can permissibly do to them against their will (namely acquire the weapons that will produce the same exact threat but also be willing to actually use the weapons with PCH).[22]

Others have raised completely general objections to the view that it is impermissible to deliberately threaten to do something it would be impermissible to actually do (e.g., create UCH). The PSP makes a narrower claim: At least as a substitute for causing actual permissible harm (PCH) against people's will, it may be permissible to deliberately threaten the same people with doing something impermissible (UCH). The EPSP aims to show that one does not lose this permission to deliberately threaten to do something otherwise impermissible merely because one would decline to permissibly exercise a capacity to actually harm people against their will.

C. A ROLE FOR INTRICATE MORAL DISTINCTIONS

Walzer thinks that the distinctions he draws between intending and merely foreseeing harm and also between not intending to harm and intending not to harm set the outer "border" of the use of the intention in just war theory. He thinks that Ramsey's further distinctions are overly subtle and consist in producing epicycles that do not ring a true moral bell.[23] Being a believer that the truth in ethics can be "intricate," I would diagnose the matter differently.

Walzer's stated aim is to provide a deontological (or nonconsequentialist) rather than a consequentialist account of when acts in war are permissible or impermissible. I have argued that some of Walzer's specific objections to Ramsey are incorrect. There is no deontological objection to making use of already justified bad effects. Doing so does not require intending the bad effects and is consistent with intending not to produce the bad effects. Sometimes even relying on bad effects that are not already justified by one's act and its goal itself but whose justification depends on either an independent further side effect of one's act (as in Two Side Effects) or a further effect of the bad side effect itself (as in Nuclear Munitions Grief) can be permissible. None of this need violate the proportionality or nonintention of evil conditions of the DDE. Furthermore, acting in these ways may often be permissible from a deontological point of view even if the DDE is not the correct guide to deontological permissibility.

I suggest, therefore, that some of Walzer's objections may really be consequentialist in nature. As noted earlier, he may be concerned with our relying on a bad effect that we prospectively foresee (rather than one we know about after our act). This is because we may be tempted not to break the connection between our act and the bad effect when we could do so, and so we will fail to do things that reduce harm to civilians when we could. These problems do not necessarily follow from relying on a foreseen bad effect, but such reliance might raise the probability of these problems occurring. This seems to be a concern with the consequences of permitting what is not necessarily wrong in itself.[24]

For those concerned with deontological (or nonconsequentialist) accounts, it is important to realize, I believe, that the correctness of more intricate or subtle distinctions than those to which one already consciously adheres cannot be ruled out a priori independently of specific criticisms. There is no a priori reason to believe that only more easily drawn distinctions, not subtle ones, are involved in differentiating right from wrong. There is also no such reason to believe that we do not or cannot respond to and constrain our conduct on the basis of subtle distinctions even if we have trouble consciously formulating the distinctions to which we respond.[25]

Notes

This chapter is based on an unpublished article originally written in 2008. It was presented as one of my Comte Lectures at the London School of Economics in 2011 and to a graduate seminar at the University of Toronto. I am grateful for comments I received on those occasions from members of the audiences and from Alex Voorhoeve, Michael Otsuka, and Thomas Hurka. I am also grateful for comments from Ruth Chang, Shelly Kagan, Jeff McMahan, and Larry Temkin.

   1. These new proposals are discussed in my *Intricate Ethics* (New York: Oxford University Press, 2007) among other places. I focus on Ramsey's discussions in chaps. 13 and 14 of his *The Just War: Force and Political Responsibility* (New York: Scribner's, 1968). All references to Ramsey in this text are to that book. I focus on Walzer's discussion in his *Just and Unjust Wars* (New York: Basic Books, 1978), chap. 17. All references to Walzer in this text are to that book.

   2. However, not all foreseen unproportional bad effects may count against an action. In particular, ones that involve an act of an intervening agent may often not count. For example, suppose I deflect a lethal bomb sent to me back to the wrongdoer who sent it, foreseeing that he will certainly deflect it away from himself and toward many innocent bystanders. The unproportional side-effect deaths may be counted against the wrongdoer's act, not mine. It might seem that the DDE is incomplete in not requiring that the greater good sought itself be necessary. That is, suppose a somewhat less good outcome would suffice and it could be brought about with no bad side effects. Is it permissible to produce the greater good even with side-effect harm that *is* proportional to it? It would seem not. I shall ignore this possible problem with the DDE here. Jeff McMahan discusses it in his "Proportionality" (unpublished), as does Thomas Hurka in his "Proportionality in the Morality of War," *Philosophy & Public Affairs* 33 (2005): 34–66.

   3. I have noted one concern about the DDE in endnote 2. Elsewhere, I have raised other fundamental objections to the DDE. See, for example, *Intricate Ethics* (New York: Oxford University Press, 2007), chaps. 3–5. See also Thomas Scanlon's *Moral Dimensions: Permissibility, Meaning, Blame* (Cambridge, MA: Harvard University Press, 2008), as some of the objections I raise originate with him and with Judith Thomson, whose work he cites.

   4. Ramsey, 303.

   5. Further, Ramsey clearly believes that even the very agent who would be justified in doing an act that causes proportional side-effect harm could be directly deterred from the act by the prospect of the harm it would cause. Evidence for this is his belief (326–327) that the following case—call it the Uterus Case—is the closest analogy to the deterrent effect of collateral damage in war: A woman is told that she has a damaged uterus that cannot sustain another pregnancy without her being at risk of grave harm. However, before she is told this, she has already become pregnant. Ramsey believes that it would be permissible for her to have the uterus that threatens her health removed even though this will result in the death of the fetus. This is because, he thinks, the fetal death is not intended and is a proportional, merely foreseen side effect of preventing grave harm by removing the damaged uterus. Nevertheless, he says, the woman could be deterred from having her uterus removed

by the prospect of the death of the fetus. Furthermore, Ramsey believes that while the woman certainly does not intend that the removal of the uterus be accompanied by death of the fetus, she could reasonably intend that the prospect of harm to the fetus will deter her from removing her womb. This is not because she believes the removal would be impermissible but simply because she could prefer to avoid doing what is good for her when it harms the fetus. Hence, she could keep on reminding herself of the fetal harm that would occur if she removed her womb. This seems like she is deliberately threatening herself with an unwelcome prospect. (Later I shall argue that the Uterus Case is not, in fact, a close analogy to the deterrent effect of collateral damage. Notice also that the Uterus Case is *un*like the one in which the woman has a cancerous uterus that is a threat to her independently of the presence of the fetus. In the latter case, Catholic moral theologians think it is permissible to remove the womb despite the side-effect death of the fetus. However, in Ramsey's case, the uterus threatens the woman only if a fetus is in it. It is less clear, therefore, that there is a reason for removing the uterus independently of removing the fetus. Hence, it is not clear that, given his other views, Ramsey should think removing the uterus is permissible. I shall ignore this issue, henceforth.)

6. He does not make this point when discussing Ramsey but does so earlier in *Just and Unjust Wars* when discussing collateral damage in *jus in bello* (155). I am suggesting that this point may explain his attitude to some of Ramsey's views.

7. Walzer, 280.

8. It might be said that an intention not to harm civilians could lead to *not* divorcing military action from collateral damage if the prospect of the damage would certainly deter all action leading to any civilian harm. But then we would be omitting to do something that divorces military action from collateral damage from an intention to maintain (or create) a link between the use of weapons and civilian harm. We would do this for the sake of creating a prospect that deters all harm. However, Ramsey says that he is opposed to using means to deterrence that involve such an intention to create a possibility of harm to innocent civilians (an evil).

9. Still, Ramsey's discussion *does* only emphasize restricting the pursuit of good consequences by the requirement not to intend harm rather than by the requirement to intend not to harm. Furthermore, his view that the Uterus Case (discussed in endnote 5) is "the closest analogy" to the nuclear-deterrence case suggests that he fails to appreciate the role of good consequences being caused by the prospect of collateral damage. Let me explain. Suppose it were possible to remove the uterus without killing the fetus in the Uterus Case. Then an even better state of affairs would occur if the woman had her uterus removed than would occur if she were deterred from having her uterus removed because of the prospect of the fetus's death. That is, removal of the uterus with a fetus in it, independently of the fetus's death, is a good thing in this case. Avoiding such removal does not in itself help contribute to a better state of affairs. It is only good not to remove it if it helps prevent the fetus's death (assuming the fetus's death is bad). Hence, if one wants to produce the overall best state of affairs in this case, one would not neglect to find a way to separate the removal of the uterus with a fetus in it from the death of the fetus (e.g., by creating a mechanical gestation device in which the fetus could be placed). By contrast, having to use one's military weapons to avoid domination, independently of the death of civilians, is a bad thing; not having to use them at all, consistent with nondomination, is a good thing even apart from not causing civilian harm. So (1) having a good outcome (of not using nuclear weapons at all) and (2) intending not to harm civilians (by separating the use of nuclear weapons from

collateral damage) can pull in opposite directions. This contrasts with what is true in the Uterus Case.

10. This denial is defended in recent discussions by Judith Thomson and Thomas Scanlon.

11. For criticism of the DDE leading to this conclusion, see Scanlon's *Moral Dimensions* (where he also discusses Judith Thomson's objections) and my *Ethics for Enemies: Terror, Torture, and War* (New York: Oxford University Press, 2011), chaps. 2 and 3. The emphasis on the justified military operation being a good overall is added in order to eliminate the following possibility: Suppose military action despite harm is justified only because we seek to give people something they care about, namely, their right to defend themselves against aggression. Suppose some people did not care about defending themselves by military means. Then giving them what they care about would not justify permission for them to set up the military system just for deterrence purposes. But suppose the permission to self-defend depends just on the good of repelling an unjust attack independently of whether this gives people what they care about. Then this factor justifying a military system will be in place even if an agent does not care about it but only intends deterrence.

12. On causal purity in the production of good (what I call productive purity), see *Intricate Ethics*, chap. 5, though I shall briefly describe it later.

13. For more on the role of unintended greater good, see *Intricate Ethics*, chap. 4.

14. Here is another case illustrating a wrong productive route through an unintended bad effect that is not already justified by what causes it. If a trolley is about to hit and kill five people, it would be good to turn it away from them, but this would not be permissible if we foresee that it will then kill six other people instead. This is still true even if the death of the six is not intended and the loud noise from their screams is the only way for *twenty* other people to be saved (by, for example, startling someone who was about to kill them). It would not be permissible to do what kills the six just because it will save the twenty when saving the five (or anything else) has not already justified killing the six. So, there is no justification for killing the six.

15. I emphasize the difference between actual and required causal role for determining permissibility in *Intricate Ethics*, chap. 5, among other places. I say that modal notions such as possibility (not required) and necessity (required) are needed in principles of permissibility. Two Side Effects Modified is in some ways similar to the case presented by Judith Thomson in which bombing a military target that could help end a war by reducing enemy munitions also causes unavoidable side-effect harm and terror to civilians. In her case, it is the latter that actually leads the enemy to surrender before the reduced munitions has this effect. In Thomson's case, however, the side-effect harm and terror are proportional to the military bombing. (See her "Self-Defense," *Philosophy & Public Affairs* [Fall 1991]: 283–310.) By contrast, in Two Side Effects Modified, the threat of UCH that actually causes peace is imagined to be justified only because peace could otherwise come about by way of military preparedness and the confidence it builds.

16. This is the sense of "a reason" that is used by Thomas Scanlon in *What We Owe Each Other* (Cambridge, MA: Harvard University Press, 1998). Others, such as Jonathan Dancy, do not consider a factor that operates in this nongoal sense to be a reason. So long as we know what I am referring to, it does not matter whether everyone would agree to this use of "a reason."

17. I discuss the Munitions Grief Case and the following Two Plants Case in my *Morality, Mortality,* vol. 2 (New York: Oxford University Press, 1996), and in *Intricate Ethics.*

18. Can it also be consistent with *intending not* to cause deaths without, however, giving up one's mission? But suppose one could create weapons that cause no side-effect civilian harm. Assume one should develop such weapons. This implies one should be willing to do what leads missions like the one in Munitions Grief to be impossible. Why then should one not be willing to cancel the mission even when the useful side effect will occur, as this is just another way to avoid collateral harm even at the cost of giving up missions? Perhaps refusing to develop weapons that cannot harm civilians would involve intending to harm them whereas using weapons that cannot but cause certain side-effect harm still does not involve intending the harm?

19. Nuclear Munitions Grief can be contrasted with the following Two Plants Case. In this case, the threat to the usefulness of our bombing mission is not a response to it (i.e., to rebuild) but the continuing functioning of another munitions plant. The deaths we would unavoidably cause in bombing one plant would lead to grief that alone could interfere with running the other plant. Here, the bad side effect we produce does not merely sustain what we have achieved by defeating the rebuilding of the plant we destroyed. It plays a necessary causal role in bringing about another good (closing the second plant), without which what we have done in our bombing would not be sufficient to justify the side-effect deaths. Two Plants has a causal structure in some ways similar to the one Ramsey seems to think is present when a supposedly unjustified bad effect (i.e., possibility of and concern about UCH) causes the great good of deterrence. Two Plants may be morally problematic in the way in which, I have argued, justifying foreseen UCH by its deterrent effect would be problematic. The one difference is that in Two Plants *part* of a good (destroying one plant) causes the bad effect that leads to the other part of the good in Two Plants. By contrast, the bad effect that leads to deterrence is not caused by a part of a good but by a mere means (military capacity) to some good. This may be a morally significant difference between the cases, making Two Plants less problematic. I discuss the difference between bad effects resulting from mere means and those resulting from parts of a greater good most recently in *Intricate Ethics.*

20. See chap. 4, *Intricate Ethics.*

21. I owe this point to Alex Voorhoeve.

22. Earlier (p. 234) we reached the same conclusion by arguing that intending a threat did not make an act impermissible if it would not otherwise be impermissible. It should be noted that presenting the threat of PCH or UCH is different, in at least one way, from doing less rather than more physical harm to people to get them to surrender: From their perspective, the people who feel threatened give in due to the prospect of the *greater harm* that is threatened (e.g., UCH), not due to the effectiveness of actual lesser harm. This is part of what makes a lying threat different from other lesser harms (e.g., broken legs) that could be effective in causing surrender.

23. Walzer's view is like that of Thomas Nagel. When Nagel discusses his views about a principle of permissible harm (based on the DDE), he says, "I won't try to draw the exact boundaries of the principle. Though I say it with trepidation, I believe that for my purposes, they don't matter too much, and I suspect they can't be drawn more than roughly: my deontological intuitions, at least, begin to fail above a certain level of complexity" (*The View from Nowhere* [New York: Oxford University Press, 1986], 179–180).

24. Further support that Walzer takes a more consequentialist perspective is provided by his response (in discussion) to the observation that refusing to intentionally harm civilians does not necessarily reduce the number of civilians harmed. (That is, more civilians may die as side effects of military bombing than in carefully focused terror bombing.) He said that he was not sure he would emphasize not intending civilian deaths if he did not believe it reduced the number of such deaths overall (response at Columbia Legal Theory Colloquium, 2003). This is a consequentialist justification for ruling out terror bombing.

25. Psychologists have shown that people implicitly learn to respond according to complex principles that they do not consciously recognize. See Timothy Wilson, *Strangers to Ourselves* (Cambridge, MA: Harvard University Press, 2005), 28.

INDEX